SUSTAINABLE ASIA

Supporting the Transition to Sustainable Consumption and Production in Asian Developing Countries

SUSTAINABLE ASIA

Supporting the Transition to Sustainable Consumption and Production in Asian Developing Countries

Edited by

Patrick Schroeder
Kartika Anggraeni
Silvia Sartori
Uwe Weber

SWITCH-Asia Network Facility &
Collaborating Centre on Sustainable Consumption
and Production (CSCP)

funded by switchasia PROGRAMME

World Scientific

Published by

World Scientific Publishing Co. Pte. Ltd.

5 Toh Tuck Link, Singapore 596224

USA office: 27 Warren Street, Suite 401-402, Hackensack, NJ 07601

UK office: 57 Shelton Street, Covent Garden, London WC2H 9HE

Library of Congress Cataloging-in-Publication Data
Names: Schroeder, Patrick, 1976– editor.
Title: Sustainable Asia : supporting the transition to sustainable
consumption and production in Asian developing countries /
Patrick Schroeder, Kartika Anggraeni, Silvia Sartori, Uwe Weber, [editors].
Description: New Jersey : World Scientific, [2016]
Identifiers: LCCN 2016024729 | ISBN 9789814730907 (hc : alk. paper)
Subjects: LCSH: Sustainable development--Asia. | Conservation of natural
resources--Asia. | Industrial ecology--Asia.
Classification: LCC HC415.E5 S863 2016 | DDC 338.95/07--dc23
LC record available at https://lccn.loc.gov/2016024729

British Library Cataloguing-in-Publication Data
A catalogue record for this book is available from the British Library.

Disclaimer
This publication has been produced with the assistance of the European Union. The contents of this publication are the sole responsibility of GFA Consulting Group GmbH and can in no way be taken to reflect the views of the European Union.
network.facility@scp-centre.org

Desk Editors: Suraj Kumar/Dong Lixi

Typeset by Stallion Press

Printed in Singapore

Contents

List of Contributors

Kartika Anggraeni has experience in Environmental science, Sustainable Consumption and Production, and sustainable management. She has been working with the SWITCH-Asia Network Facility and as Project Coordinator at the Collaborating Centre on Sustainable Consumption and Production (CSCP) since 2012. Prior to her university studies in Germany, she worked as a journalist at one of the most reputable newspapers in Indonesia, *Kompas Daily*, and as an editor at the Kompas Gramedia Group. She holds a degree in Biology, majoring in environmental microbiology and ecology, from the University of Indonesia, and a master in International Management from the University of Nuertingen-Geislingen, Germany.

Lewis Akenji is Policy Fellow at the Institute of Global Environmental Strategies. As well as conducting policy research to support SCP goals, sub-themes, and targets in the Sustainable Development Goals (SGD) framework, he has advised multiple national delegations in the Open Working Groups and during negotiations for the SDGs framework. Akenji has led several international science-policy initiatives. Currently he coordinates the consortium on REDUCTIONS (Reducing Environmental Degradation & Unsustainable Consumption Trends & Impacts on Nature & Society), and is Guest Managing Editor of the Journal of Cleaner Production special volume on Absolute Reductions.

Magnus Bengtsson is working at the Institute for Global Environmental Strategies (IGES), based in Japan, where he is Principal Researcher in charge of institute-wide flagship initiatives. He has held positions as Director of the Sustainable Consumption and Production group (2010–2013) and Manager of the Waste Management and Resource Efficiency project (2008–2010). Before joining IGES in 2007, he was a Post-Doctoral Fellow at the University of Tokyo where his research focused on water demand scenario analysis and global water futures assessment. Magnus received his PhD in Environmental Systems Analysis at Chalmers University of Technology in Göteborg, Sweden, where he worked on Life-Cycle Assessment (LCA), stakeholder consultation processes and sustainability controversies. Magnus has conducted and led research on a wide range of topics, in recent years mainly focusing on policy approaches towards Sustainable Consumption and Production and Sustainable Materials Management, particularly in Asia.

Pham Thi Ngoc Bich's professional experience covers different aspects including socio-economic development combined with solid knowledge on urban development, housing and environment, institutionalisation and advocacy, business administration and participation of local communities. Working for UN-Habitat Vietnam, she is familiar with capacity building, training and networking, research, working with local authorities to conduct leadership and eco-community tourism courses, monitoring and evaluation, project management and budgeting. Bich is particularly interested in ecological innovation and sustainable production and consumption. She is also a teaching assistant on the subject of Public International Law for the Faculty of International Study at Hanoi University. She holds a Master Degree in Economics/Marketing from Solvay Brussels School of Economics and Management (ULB).

Raju Pandit Chhetri lives in Kathmandu, Nepal. He studied development as an undergraduate course and has a degree in sociology. Raju now passionately advocates sustainable development and climate change issues. He has over 10 years of professional experience in the field of climate change policy and sustainable envelopment. Raju has also attended and followed the climate change negotiations under the UNFCCC for several years. In the past, Raju has worked for United Mission to Nepal (UMN) and Climate Action Network International (CANI). Currently, he is Director of Prakriti Resources Centre (PRC), a NGO based in Kathmandu that promotes climate change policy and environment friendly development practices.

Catalin Curea is an environmental expert with over 20 years of experience. For the last 13 years, he has worked on various projects relating to waste management, EU waste directives, waste management statistics and conducting statistical surveys on waste generation and management including collection, recovery and treatment. He has cooperated with the European Union's DG Environment and DG REGIO, EIB, Eurostat, the Romanian Ministry of Waters and Environment and EU private environmental consulting companies. He holds a MSc on Urban Public Works' Optimisation awarded by the Civil Engineering University of Bucharest, Romania, Water Engineering Section in 1997.

Sangay Thinley Dorji has been working as a consultant in Bhutan in areas of programme monitoring, evaluation and assessment, and in the formulation of national policies through the political system. He has also served as the Vice President for Youth Affairs in Druk Phuensum Tshogpa, one of Bhutan's political parties, prior to which he was engaged as a programme consultant with the United Nations World Food Programme in Bhutan. Sangay has also taught business students at the Royal Thimphu College in Bhutan and is interested in areas of energy security, good governance and interdisciplinary approaches to problem solving. While working for the International Institute of Sustainable Development, he also co-authored a paper on green bonds published by IISD, Canada. He has Master of Environmental Management from Yale University and an MBA from Assumption University, Thailand.

Sara Castro-Hallgren is based in the United Nations Environmental Programme's (UNEP) Division of Technology, Industry, and Economics working on Sustainable Development Goal 12 — "Ensure Sustainable Consumption and Production Patterns." Through the EU-funded SWITCH-Asia Programme, her work aims to strengthen policies in Asian countries for more resource-efficient consumption and production. Sara focuses on research, capacity development, and policy advocacy on SCP, especially to achieve SCP measurably across government, business, and consumer purchasing decisions. Previously, Sara worked for the United Nations Institute for Training and Research (UNITAR) on capacity development and technical assistance projects for strengthening national to local governance and local economic development in Asia, Latin America, and Eastern Europe. She has also worked on financial inclusion and gender-based research in microfinance and local development. Sara's educational background is in economics and international development, with undergraduate and graduate degrees from the George Washington University and Erasmus University of Rotterdam's Institute of Social Studies (ISS). She is from the small town of Usulutan, El Salvador and is currently based in Paris, France.

Julie Godin is a programme officer at UNEP DTIE in Paris working on sustainable consumption with focus on eco-labelling and voluntary sustainability standards. She is in charge of the Programme on Consumer Information for Sustainable Production and Consumption under the 10YFP and also supporting national policy efforts in Asia and Latin America on sustainability information tools and strategies. Prior to joining UNEP, Julie Godin was working at the World Bank in Washington DC on climate finance and market-based instruments. Julie holds Masters Degrees in Public Administration from Harvard University and Chemical Engineering from École Polytechnique.

Le Thi Mai Huong's experience derives from both full-time professional and independent work as a consultant for international and Vietnamese development organisations, non-governmental organisations as well as inter-governmental organisations in Vietnam and in the Mekong Region. Huong is an experienced trainer/facilitator for various training in soft skills and technical skills, such as communication, leadership, strategic planning, negotiation, integrated water resource management, project cycle management, monitoring and evaluation, and outcome reporting. She holds a Masters Degree in Public Policy from Lee Kuan Yew School of Public Policy, National University of Singapore.

Romina de Jong holds a PhD in Educational Studies and has extensive experience in education as lecturer, trainer and researcher. As Country Director of PicoSol Cambodia, she ensures the delivery of high quality services such as training and education, workshops, consultancies, M&E studies, and awareness-raising activities in the field of renewable energy. In April 2014, she was appointed Secretary of the Board of Directors of the first Solar Energy Association of Cambodia. The SEAC worked together with development partners in the Solar Microfinance Programme to develop the first accreditation procedure and quality standard for solar companies and products in Cambodia, the Good Solar initiative.

Pem Lama is responsible for research and communication for the SWITCH-Asia project, Green Public Procurement in Bhutan, which is targeted towards building a strategic approach to scale-up public demand for environmentally and socially preferable goods, services and infrastructure in Bhutan. She has experience in the non-profit sector and in development research grounded in the principles of wellbeing and sustainability. She has a BA in Economics and International Relations from Tufts University in Massachusetts, USA, and an MBA in Sustainability from Aarhus School of Business in Denmark.

Kezang is the Project Director for the EuropeAid SWITCH-Asia Green Public Procurement in Bhutan Project being implemented by an international consortium of five organisations led by the International Institute for Sustainable Development (IISD). He is the Honorary Executive Director of the Evaluation Association of Bhutan and the Managing Partner of Thimphu-based InfoAge Consulting. He combines 19+ years of unique tri-sector (public–private–civil society) collaboration and management experience. He is a passionate holistic sustainability practitioner and "happiness in business" transformation explorer. Kezang holds a Bachelor of Electronics and Communication Engineering degree from the Indian Institute of Technology-Roorkee, India, and a Masters in Communications Management (with Distinction) from the University of Strathclyde in Glasgow, United Kingdom.

Karin Merle is passionate about driving green growth. In her career as project manager and technical advisor, she has worked for different donor agencies and private businesses in emerging economies across the world. She started working in Peru and Spain in 2004 on projects relating to organisational reengineering in the industry and services sectors (digital marketing, paper manufacturing industry). She lately has focused on economic growth, sustainability policy (SCP/eco-innovation) and the involvement of the private sector in development aid in South East Asia. In this context, she has conducted policy studies, performed institutional mapping and provided technical advice. She holds a Masters degree in Business and Cultural Sciences (University of Mannheim/Germany; University of Seville/Spain) and followed further studies on Governance & Policy Analysis (University of Maastricht/Netherlands), Food and Beverages Management (Bocconi University/Italy) and climate-related subjects (WBI, Climate Consortium).

Emi Kawai is a tourism consultant at Oriental Consultants Co., Ltd. in Japan and specialises in sustainable tourism and tourism policy development. She worked for enhancing eco-tourism in Japan, which made Emi realise the importance of a sustainability mind-set in the whole society, especially for the 2020 Tokyo Olympics. Emi also is member of the Global Sustainable Tourism Council. Emi specialises in tourism and hospitality, sustainable tourism indicators, project management and administration, and is experienced in the regions of Africa, Asia and Europe. She holds a post-graduate degree in tourism from Assumption University of Thailand.

N.M. Esa Abrar Khan completed his post-graduate studies at the City University of New York. Currently, he is serving as the director of an architectural consultancy firm, "d.zignscape Consultants Ltd" and working as visiting faculty at Department of Architecture, University of Asia Pacific, Dhaka, Bangladesh. Khan has been working as an architect since 2006 and developing his idea in the area of hybridisation of urban development, urban regeneration, urban environment and architecture. Along with his professional career as an architect and academic, he is also interested in promoting young researchers from South-Asia and to promote ideas that he developed. Along with his co-founders, he initiated a research group named "Avant-Grades" in 2013.

Do Hung Nguyen holds a Masters degree in fisheries & aquaculture economics and management from Trømso University, Norway. She is current a research assistant and lecturer for Nha Trang University, Vietnam. Mrs. Nguyen is interested in working on projects regarding to poverty alleviation, rural development, non-market evaluation and value chain management for agricultural products.

Thongphet Phonsavath is a Lao national who studied in East Germany at the University of Technology in Dresden from 1990 to 1997. After completion of his studies, he worked at the Lao-Indian Paper mill in Vientiane from 1997 to 1998, the sawmill factory of Burapha Agroforestry as head of the maintenance division from 2000 to 2003 and as assistant to the Managing Director from 2003 to 2005. He joined UNIDO in August 2005 as Deputy Coordinator of the cleaner production promotion project. Since 2013, he serves as the National Coordinator and the Director of Cleaner Production Centre Lao PDR. He is married and has two children.

Judith Pretty has over 25 years of professional experience, and specialises in editing and writing, and the provision of business development support. An experienced EU evaluator, she currently provides bid appraisal and development services to European companies and universities. She also has profound experience in the animation and co-ordination of human networks, and in marketing. She is a skilled management consultant and communicator, as well as have expertise in the transfer of experience across borders. A Chartered Marketer, her Master of Arts is from the University of Edinburgh, and she holds two post-graduate diplomas, in Marketing and in Sales Promotion.

Leonardo L. Sta. Romana is an independent Senior Economic Consultant based in Manila. He was formerly a full-time academic with the University of Hong Kong's Department of Economics. He has also been a Visiting Research Associate at Hitotsubashi University in Tokyo and the

University of the Philippines, as well as a Research Scholar at the Australian National University. A specialist in the economics of emerging and developing countries, with special reference to the Philippines and East/South East Asia, his previous research has dealt with the topics of development indicators, income inequality, and industrialisation-international trade linkages. Recently, he has focused on the issues of sustainable development and the economy-environment nexus. He is also the website publisher of EmergingFrontierMarkets.com.

Damitha Samarakoon is Senior Manager at Janathakshan (Gte) Ltd in Sri Lanka. He has 10 years of work experience in community-based renewable energy, implementing projects on biomass energy, biogas, hydro and solar PV technology. He conducted the first energy poverty study in Sri Lanka under Practical Action. Prior to joining Practical Action, Damitha worked in the field of agriculture and as an investment analyst. From 2010 to 2012, he worked as the coordinator of the Hydro Empowerment Network South/South Asia. Presently, he oversees the energy programme and SME development programme for Janathakshan, including the SWITCH-Asia Sri Lanka Biogas project. Damitha is a mechanical engineer and a certified chartered accountant.

Silvia Sartori has been working in the field of development and sustainability in Asia since 2005, in partnership with local and international NGOs, academia, institutions, media and the private sector. From 2009 to 2013, she led a European Commission SWITCH-Asia project promoting energy-efficient buildings among 2000 Chinese SMEs in the Greater Shanghai Region. Since September 2009, she works as Communication and Networking Expert with the SWITCH-Asia Network Facility. She majored in International Diplomatic Sciences (Trieste University, Italy) and holds a Master's Degree in SME Management & Development (IULM University, Italy) and a Master's Degree in Asian Studies (Lund University, Sweden).

Patrick Schroeder works as the Sustainable Consumption and Production Expert at the SWITCH-Asia Network Facility. He also serves as Research Associate of the Institute of Development Studies at the University of Sussex. Previously, from 2009 to 2013, he worked as International Advisor at the China Association for NGO Cooperation based in Beijing, supporting GIZ cooperation with China on climate change and low-carbon development. From 2005 to 2006, he gained experience in New Zealand in the field of biodiversity protection and invasive species control. He holds a MA in International Relations and a PhD in Environmental Studies from Victoria University of Wellington, New Zealand.

Gamini Senanayake has over 38 years of experience and has served in semi-governmental and private sector establishments in Sri Lanka and Singapore as well as in international development agencies. Presently he is working for the EU-funded SWITCH-Asia National Policy Support Component of Sri Lanka, and as a consultant to the World Bank and GEF/UNDP funded NAMA project on energy generation and energy use. He is a Fellow and a Corporate Member (Chartered Engineer) of the Sri Lanka Institute of Engineers, Corporate Member (Professional Chartered Engineer) of The Institute of Engineers Australia and a Corporate Member Sri Lanka Energy Managers' Association and is an Accredited Energy Auditor. He holds BSc (Hons) Engineering from the University of Moratuwa, Sri Lanka, and an MBA degree with Distinction in Industrial Policy & Corporate Strategy from Maastricht School of Management.

Nguyen Tien Thong holds a PhD degree in marketing research and also has a background in natural resource economics and management, and applied economics for public policy. Thong is a Vietnamese citizen and currently he works as an assistant professor for the Department of Environmental and Business Economics, University of Southern Denmark. Thong's research interests are demand forecast and production performance analysis, with a focus on food products. Sustainable consumption and production are also his focal topics.

Meryse Tissera has over a decade of experience in media and communications; she started her media career at Young Asia Television where she worked as a television producer for five years. Passionate about being a voice for the voiceless and wanting to work closely with communities affected by the protracted conflict in Sri Lanka, Meryse joined the INGO sector in 2008. During her tenure in the INGO sector, Meryse served as Communications Manager through Sri Lanka's transition from emergency relief to rehabilitation and recovery and reconstruction. Meryse has a degree in IT and enjoys photography, yoga, diving and is a self-confessed ocean addict.

Uwe Weber joined the SWITCH-Asia Programme's Network Facility as Team Leader in September 2013. He has more than 20 years of work experience in Asia and over 30 years of thematic work experience. Having lived and worked as project and programme manager in Beijing, Osaka and Singapore, his professional network covers nearly all South- and East Asian countries. His thematic expertise includes economy, training, product testing, standardisation, energy efficiency, renewable energy and a broad range of environmental themes. This breadth of experience enables him to effectively support and advance the crosscutting and multi-disciplinary Sustainable Consumption and Production agenda in Asia. He received his Doctorate for his studies on Urban Hydrology from the Aachen Technical University, Germany.

List of Acronyms and Abbreviations

3R	Reduce, Reuse, Recycle
10YFP	10 Year Framework Programme on SCP
AAGR	Annual Average Growth Rate
ABTO	Association of Bhutanese Tour Operators
ACIA	ASEAN Comprehensive Investment Agreement
ADB	Asian Development Bank
ADFIAP	Association in Development Financing Institutions in Asia and the Pacific
AEC	ASEAN Economic Community
AMAS	Automotive Manufacturing Automation System (Thailand)
AREC	Austrian Recycling
ASD	Action for Sustainable Development
ASEAN	Association of South East Asian Nations
ASSIST	Asia Society for Social Improvement and Sustainable Transformation
ATAG	Air Transport Action Group
BAT	Best Available Technique
BDT	Bangladeshi Taka
BEP	Best Environmental Practice
BMO	Business Membership Organisation

BOIC	Business Opportunity and Information Centre (Bhutan)
BSB	Bhutan Standards Bureau
BTN	Bhutanese Ngultrum
BTS	Bangkok Mass Transit System
CALABARZON	CAvite, LAguna, BAtangas, Rizal, and QueZON Provinces
CBT-I	Community-Based Tourism Institute
CF	Community Forest
CFO	Carbon Footprint for Organisations
CFP	Carbon Footprint for Products
CFR	Carbon Footprint Reduction
CFUG	Community Forest User Groups
CIA	Central Intelligence Agency
CINTRI	A private sanitation company in Phnom Penh Municipality, Vietnam
CLMV	Cambodia, Lao PDR, Myanmar, Vietnam
CO2e	Carbon Dioxide Equivalents
CP	Cleaner Production
CP4BP	Cleaner Production for Better Products
CPC-L	Cleaner Production Centre Lao PDR
CSI	Cottage and Small Industry
CSME	Cottage, Small and Medium-sized Enterprise
D4S	Design for Sustainability
DANIDA	Danish International Development Agency
DASTA	(Thai) Designated Areas for Sustainable Tourism Administration
DCSI	Department of Cottage and Small Industries (Bhutan)
DCSI	Department of Cottage and Small Industries (Nepal)
DENR	Department of Environment and Natural Resources (The Philippines)
DEQP	(Thai) Department of Environmental Quality Promotion
DG DEVCO	Directorate-General for International Cooperation and Development (European Union)

DHUP	Department of Housing and Urban Planning (Lao PDR)
DIW	(Thai) Department of Industrial Works
DOE	Department of Energy (The Philippines)
DoEPC	Department of Environmental Pollution Control (Cambodia)
DoF	Department of Forests (Nepal)
DoI	Department of Industry (Nepal)
DOSMEP	Department of SMEs Promotion (Lao PDR)
DOT	Department of Tourism (The Philippines)
DRE	Department of Renewable Energy (Bhutan)
DTI	Department of Trade and Industry (The Philippines)
Dzongkhag	District (Bhutan)
EC	European Commission
ECCP	European Chamber of Commerce of the Philippines
EDP	Economic Development Policy
EECP	Energy Efficiency and Cleaner Production (Vietnam)
EFA	Energie Effizienz-Agentur (or Energy Efficiency Agency, Germany)
EIA	Environmental Impact Assessment
EIS	Environmental Information System
ENPAP	Energy Efficiency Practitioners Association (The Philippines)
EPI	Environmental Performance Index
ETIS	European Tourism Indicator System
EU	European Union
EUR	Euro
FAME	Fashion Accessories Manufacturers and Exporters
FAO	Food and Agriculture Organization
FDI	Foreign Direct Investment
FMU	Forest Management Unit
FNCSI	Federation of Nepal Cottage and Small Industries
FSC	Forest Stewardship Council
FYP	Five-Year Plan
GAP	Good Agricultural Practice

GCTF	Green Credit Trust Fund
GDP	Gross Domestic Product
Gewog	Block/Sub-district (Bhutan)
GGGI	Global Green Growth Institute
GGKP	Green Growth Knowledge Platform
GHG	Greenhouse Gas(es)
GIM	Green Industry Mark
GIPO	Green Industry Promotion Office (Thailand)
GIZ	German International Cooperation
GJ	Giga Joule
GLF	Green Leaf Foundation
GMO	Genetically Modified Organisms
GMS	Greater Mekong Sub-region
GNH	Gross National Happiness
GNHC	Gross National Happiness Commission (Bhutan)
GOI	Government of India
GPIoS	Green Philippines Islands of Sustainability
GPP	Green Public Procurement
GrAT	Gruppe zu Förderung der Angepassten Technologie (Center for Appropriate Technology, Austria)
GRI	Global Reporting Initiative
GSO	General Statistics Office (Vietnam)
GSTC	Global Sustainable Tourism Council
GTH	Gifts, Toys and Housewares
HAN	Hotel Association Nepal
HDI	Human Development Index
HDR	Human Development Report
Hivos	Humanist Institute for Cooperation with Developing Countries (The Netherlands)
ICASEA	International Copper Association Southeast Asia
ICIMOD	International Centre for Integrated Mountain Development
ICS	Improved Cook Stove
ICT	Information and Communication Technologies
iDE	International Development Enterprises
IEE	Initial Environment Examination

IFC	International Finance Corporation
IGES	Institute for Global Environmental Strategies
IIEE	Institute of Integrated Electrical Engineers of the Philippines
ILO	International Labour Organization
IMF	International Monetary Fund
INGO	International Non-Governmental Organization
IPEN	International POPs (or Persistent Organic Pollutants) Elimination Network (Sweden)
ISC	Institute of Standards of Cambodia
ISO	International Standards Organisation
IUCN	International Union for the Conservation of Nature
IVAs	International Visitor Arrivals
JICA	Japan International Cooperation Agency
KHR	Cambodian Riel
Lao PDR	Lao People's Democratic Republic
LAK	Lao Kip
LC	Low Carbon
LCC	Low Cost Carriers
LCI	Life Cycle Inventory
LDC	Least Developed Country
LKR	Sri Lankan Rupee
LNCCI	Lao National Chamber of Commerce and Industry
M^3	Cubic Metre
MDG	Millennium Development Goal(s)
MFSC	Ministry of Forests and Soil Conservation (Nepal)
MICE	Meetings, Incentives, Conventions and Exhibitions
MIH	Ministry of Industry and Handicrafts (Cambodia)
MNRE	Ministry of Natural Resources and Environment (Thailand)
MOEA	Ministry of Economic Affairs (Bhutan)
MOF	Ministry of Finance (Bhutan)
MoF	Ministry of Finance (Nepal)
MoI	Ministry of Industry (Nepal)
MOI	Ministry of Industry (Thailand)
MOIC	Ministry of Industry and Commerce (Lao PDR)

MOIT	Ministry of Industry and Trade (Vietnam)
MONRE	Ministry of Natural Resources and Environment (Lao PDR)
MoNRE	Ministry of Natural Resources and Environment (Vietnam)
MoSTE	Ministry of Science, Technology and Environment (Nepal)
MOTS	Ministry of Tourism and Sports (Thailand)
MPAI	Master Plan for the Automotive Industry (Thailand)
MRT	Mass Rapid Transit
MSME	Micro, Small, and Medium-sized Enterprises
MSMEDC	Micro, Small, and Medium Enterprise Development Council
MSW	Municipal Solid Waste
MSWM	Municipal Solid Waste Management
MW	Mega Watt
NAFRI	National Agriculture and Forest Research Institute (Lao PDR)
NCAW	National Commission for Advancement of Women (Lao PDR)
NEA	Nepal Electricity Authority
NEAP	National Environmental Action Plan
NEC	National Environment Commission (Bhutan)
NECS	National Environment Commission Secretariat (Bhutan)
NEDA	National Economic and Development Authority (The Philippines)
NES	National Ecotourism Strategy and Action Plan
NESDB	National Economic and Social Development Board (Thailand)
NFPs	National Focal Points (Lao PDR)
NGO	Non-Governmental Organisation
NGPES	National Growth and Poverty Eradication Strategy (Lao PDR)
NIMBY	Not In My Back Yard
NPR	Nepali Rupee

NRREP	National Rural and Renewable Energy Programme (Nepal)
NSB	National Statistics Bureau (Bhutan)
NSDP	National Strategic Development Plan (Cambodia)
NSDS	National Sustainable Development Strategy (Lao PDR)
NSEDP	National Socio-Economic Development Plan (Lao PDR)
NTA	National Tourism Authority (Lao PDR)
NTB	Nepal Tourism Board
NTFP-EP	Non-Timber Forest Products — Exchange Programme (The Philippines)
NWFP	Non-Wood Forest Product
NZODA	New Zealand Overseas Development Agency
OECD	Organisation for Economic Co-operation and Development
ONEP	Office of Natural Resources and Environmental Policy and Planning (Thailand)
PATA	Pacific Asia Travel Association
PCCI	Philippine Chamber of Commerce and Industries
PCD	Pollution Control Department (Thailand)
PCSD	Palawan Council for Sustainable Development (The Philippines)
PDI	Power Distance Indicator
PEIS	Philippine Environmental Impact Statement
PHP	Philippine Peso
PM10	Particulate Matter of 10 micrometres or less
PPP	Public–Private Partnership
PREMA	Profitable Environmental Management
PRR	Procurement Rules & Regulations
PSA-CIEMAT	Plataforma Solar de Almeria-Centro de Investigaciones Energéticas, Medioambientales y Tecnologicas
PSCT	Policy Support Component — Thailand
R&D	Research and Development
RECP	Resource Efficient Cleaner Production

REDD+	Reducing Emissions from Deforestation and Forest Degradation
RESDALAO	Renewable Energy for Sustainable Development Association
RGC	Royal Government of Cambodia
RGOB	Royal Government of Bhutan
RHG	Rice Husk Gasification
SAARC	South Asian Association for Regional Cooperation
SCP	Sustainable Consumption and Production
SDG	Sustainable Development Goals
SEID	Sustainable & Efficient Industrial Development
SEP	Strategic Environmental Plan
SEP	Sufficiency Economy Philosophy
SMART Cebu	Small and Medium enterprises for environmental Accountability, Responsibility and Transparency in Cebu
SMEs	Small and Medium-sized Enterprises
SNV	Stichting Nederlandse Vrijwilligers (Foundation of Netherlands Volunteers)
SOEs	State-Owned Enterprises
SPIN	Sustainable Product Innovation
SSCM	Sustainable Supply Chain Management
SSFA	Small Scale Fund Agreement
TAT	Tourism Authority Thailand
TCB	Tourism Council of Bhutan
TCEB	Thailand Convention and Exhibition Bureau
TCOP	Thailand Carbon Offsetting Programme
TCVN	Vietnamese Standards
TERI	The Energy and Resources Institute (India)
THB	Thai Baht
TU	Technical University
UDAA	Urban Development and Administrative Agency (Lao PDR)
UN	United Nations
UNDP	United Nations Development Programme
UNEP	United Nations Environment Programme

UNEP-DTIE	UNEP-Division of Technology, Industry and Economics
UNESCAP	United Nations Economic and Social Commission for Asia and the Pacific
UNESCO	United Nations Organisation for Education, Science and Culture
UNFCCC	United Nations Framework Convention on Climate Change
UNWTO	World Tourism Organization
URENCO	Urban Environment Company (Vietnam)
USD	United States Dollar
VCEP	Vietnam Clean Energy Program
VFR	Visiting Friends and Relatives
VNCPC	Vietnam National Cleaner Production Center
VND	Vietnamese Dong
VNEEP	Vietnam National Energy Efficiency Program
WEC	World Ecotourism Conference
WEF	World Economic Forum
WEPA	Water Development Partnership in Asia
WFP	World Food Program
WHO	World Health Organisation
WREA	Water Resources and Environmental Administration
WtE	Waste to Energy
WTO	World Trade Organization
WTTC	World Travel and Tourism Council
WWF	World Wildlife Fund
ZCR	Zero Carbon Resorts

List of Figures

List of Tables

Chapter 1

Introduction

P. Schroeder, K. Anggraeni, S. Sartori and U. Weber

"Being a tiger is not important. The important thing is for us to have a sufficient economy. A sufficient economy means to have enough to support ourselves ... we have to take a careful step backward ... each village or district must have relative self-sufficiency."

"... The word for having enough is sufficient; sufficiency is moderation ... If all nations hold this concept — I don't mean sufficiency economy — this concept of moderation, without being extreme or insatiable in one's desires, the world will be a happier place ..."

His Majesty King Bhumibol Adulyadej of Thailand

1.1 Introduction

Sustainability is not a foreign idea to Asian countries. As the concept of "Sufficiency Economy" and the quotes of King Bhumibol Adulyadej of Thailand above demonstrate, Asian countries and cultures have a sophisticated understanding about the needs of their people, and heightened awareness about the environmental and social challenges brought about by modernisation and industrial development.

What is often foreign to Asia are the concepts, terminologies, and approaches which emerge out of academic discourses and international political processes related to sustainable development. One of these concepts is 'Sustainable Consumption and Production', (SCP), which has emerged over the last decade reflecting heightened awareness about deeply problematic ways in which unsustainable patterns of production and consumption have become entrenched. SCP has appeared as a new international agenda with promising solutions contributing to solving multiple global crises including environmental degradation, poverty, growing inequality, and resource scarcity.

As recently as September 2015, SCP was approved as the 12th of the Sustainable Development Goals (SDGs) and adopted by the United Nations. The adoption of SCP as one of the SDGs was preceded by a decade of work preparing the so-called 10-Year Framework of Programmes (10YFP) on SCP. With the recent inclusion of SCP as one of the SDGs, it can be expected that in the coming years, support for the inclusion of SCP across national development policies in areas of economy, environmental protection, industrialisation, trade, consumer protection, public health will increase notably. An overview of "SDG 12 — Ensure SCP Patterns" and the set of sub-targets is provided in Box 1.1.

Box 1.1 An overview of SDG 12 — *Ensure SCP Patterns*

12.1: Implement the 10YFP on SCP, all countries taking action, with developed countries taking the lead, taking into account the development and capabilities of developing countries.
12.2: By 2030, achieve the sustainable management and efficient use of natural resources.
12.3: By 2030, halve per capita global food waste at the retail and consumer levels and reduce food losses along production and supply chains, including post-harvest losses.
12.4: By 2020, achieve the environmentally sound management of chemicals and all wastes throughout their life cycle, in accordance with agreed

(*Continued*)

Box 1.1 (*Continued*)

international frameworks, and significantly reduce their release to air, water, and soil in order to minimise their adverse impacts on human health and the environment.

12.5: By 2030, substantially reduce waste generation through prevention, reduction, recycling, and reuse.

12.6: Encourage companies, especially large and transnational companies, to adopt sustainable practices and to integrate sustainability information into their reporting cycle.

12.7: Promote public procurement practices that are sustainable, in accordance with national policies and priorities.

12.8: By 2030, ensure that people everywhere have the relevant information and awareness for sustainable development and lifestyles in harmony with nature.

12.a: Support developing countries to strengthen their scientific and technological capacity to move towards more sustainable patterns of consumption and production.

12.b: Develop and implement tools to monitor sustainable development impacts for sustainable tourism that creates jobs and promotes local culture and products.

12.c: Rationalise inefficient fossil-fuel subsidies that encourage wasteful consumption by removing market distortions, in accordance with national circumstances, including by restructuring taxation, and phasing out those harmful subsidies, where they exist, to reflect their environmental impacts, taking fully into account the specific needs and conditions of developing countries and minimising the possible adverse impacts on their development in a manner that protects the poor and the affected communities.

Source: UN-DESA, 2015.

Environmental issues had been addressed by the development cooperation of the EU and other development agencies for a number of years. Examples are the Asia Pro Eco Programmes I and II which ran from 2003 to 2007, the predecessors of the SWITCH-Asia Programme, which was the first international development cooperation programme which has taken SCP as main topic to guide its strategies and activities. The main objective of the SWITCH-Asia Programme is not environmental protection, but to reduce poverty in Asia, and SCP is one approach of how this can be achieved.

Operating in 18 Asian developing countries, the SWITCH-Asia Programme, after eight years of implementation, involves a wide network of development practitioners, SCP researchers, cleaner production experts, industry associations, in particular those working with small- and medium-sized enterprises (SMEs), policymakers of national ministries, financial institutions, and the United Nations Environment Programme (UNEP). Starting in 2007 with a first call for proposals and 16 grant projects, the SWITCH-Asia Programme has evolved to a complex arrangement consisting of several components including 95 grant projects (as of January 2016), five National Policy Support Components (NPSCs), one Regional Policy Support Component coordinated by UNEP, and a Network Facility which serves as the knowledge hub of the Programme. Several chapter authors of this book have been involved in one or more projects and activities of the SWITCH-Asia Programme, while others have been external experts of the Programme, thereby providing a good balance of perspectives.

The SWITCH-Asia Programme works not independently of the larger trends and features common to Europe and Asia, two regions which are increasingly fused together through globalised value chains, socio-cultural exchanges and common political interests. On the one hand, Asia is home to a large number of SMEs which serve as suppliers for multinational companies and consumers in Europe and other industrialised countries. On the other hand, the proportional share of global consumption is increasingly located in Asia and the region's urbanisation and consumerism have become mega trends with global impact. At the same time, hundreds of millions of people are still trapped in poverty.

Asia and Europe are at a crossroads to either pursue business-as-usual development or to accelerate the transition to a sustainable future. The switch to SCP patterns is a common challenge for Asia and Europe as well for the rest of the world. A deeper understanding of how SCP can contribute to economic and human development in Asian developing countries is needed. The global SCP agenda is not in conflict with local strategies and approaches to development, such as the Thai Sufficiency

Economy quoted above, but it stands in contrast to the pursuit of fast and high economic growth, without consideration of the environmental and social costs associated with it. The various chapters in this book will provide deeper insights into this issue.

The aim of this book is to capture the experiences of SWITCH-Asia projects against the backdrop of socio-economic development and environmental protection in Asian developing countries. We hope that by sharing the experiences of the SWITCH-Asia Programme with other networks, platforms and experts dealing with similar challenges, we can contribute to finding solutions to the multi-dimensional threats of the present and coming decades. For readers looking for a comprehensive introduction to the topic of SCP together with a detailed analysis of the current developmental situation in various Asian developing countries and key sectors such as manufacturing, tourism, and agriculture, this book is an invaluable tool. Its chapters examine in detail the SCP approaches and innovative solutions demonstrated by the SWITCH-Asia supported projects in Asia and thus serves as a reference for practitioners, researchers, and policymakers alike.

The book further seeks to forge bridges between the concept and opportunities SCP approaches offer in principle, policy options available to decision makers, the situation in Asian developing countries, and the approaches and results of selected SWITCH-Asia projects. A second objective is to deepen the body of knowledge on SCP in Asia, to identify where the region stands, and what needs to be done. The book is not an exhaustive summary that covers every aspect relating to SCP in Asian developing countries. While many issues are not included, the book provides a comprehensive collection and analysis of country-specific background information on SCP and case studies from the SWITCH-Asia Programme.

We hope that this volume of "Sustainable Asia" provides a fruitful and informative perspective and may help policymakers in Asia and Europe, development professionals, researchers, progressive businesses and innovators to envision, and implement solutions that promote SCP not only in the Asian region, but also in other regions committed to the effective implementation of SDG 12 "Ensuring SCP Patterns."

1.2 Organisation of the Book

The chapters of this book are organised into three parts that cover different aspects of SCP in Asia. The first part is devoted to exploring the role of SCP in international development cooperation, looking at SCP as an alternative approach to mainstream sustainable development and specific examples how the EU-funded SWITCH-Asia Programme implements SCP practices and supports policy development. The main and second part of this book comprises of nine country studies which explore the current state of SCP implementation together with potentials and remaining barriers. The country case studies link the country-specific circumstances with SWITCH-Asia projects and demonstrate how projects have promoted sector-specific SCP practices. The final part includes two sectoral chapters looking at sustainable tourism and waste management issues in Asian developing countries.

Part I of this book begins with a conceptual overview by Lewis Akenji, Magnus Bengtsson, and Patrick Schroeder (Chapter 2) of the evolution of the SCP concept and approaches in the global environmental agenda, and its relevance for Asia's development. It underscores the need for SCP in the Asian context to expand the consumption opportunities of the poor while simultaneously trying to bring society's aggregate consumption within ecological boundaries. The authors argue that a one-sided emphasis on the latter, environmental, aspect of SCP is likely to be unproductive. This chapter also discusses how SCP is beginning to re-shape international development cooperation programmes and the authors make a strong point that SCP is a departure from conventional development-as-growth approaches and present an interpretation of SCP that differs from the mainstream. In practice, this approach would need to be reflected in the way issues such as poverty, local socio-economic development, and consumption patterns are addressed. Based on the proposed SCP approach, the chapter reviews various debates on international development cooperation and shows how the SCP approach is influenced by these discourses. In particular, the relevance of SCP for solving three major tensions in existing international development are discussed: First, the tension between industrialisation and environmental protection; second, the tension between consumerism and poverty, existing in parallel; and, finally, the tension between development-as-westernisation and pluralism and traditional livelihoods.

The chapter by Sara Castro-Hallgren (Chapter 3) explores the policy dimensions of SCP in Asia and finds that Asian countries today are already making innovative policy changes to shift towards SCP patterns, mainstreaming SCP into national development planning. The inclusion of SCP in development planning, in several cases facilitated by the SWITCH-Asia Regional and NPSCs, is increasingly focused on the demand-side of the equation, including policies for sustainable consumption, and supporting behavioural change. The region is also leading efforts for sub-regional cooperation on sustainable public procurement, and implementing a growing number of policy measures to enhance competitiveness in line with Green Growth priorities. Castro discusses how the 2030 Agenda for Sustainable Development and its SDGs includes SCP not only as a standalone goal, but also transversally as targets within 12 of the 16 other goals. With these newly adopted global goals, SCP will continue to be mainstreamed in public governance of Asian developing countries with greater focus needed on building national to local capacities and expertise to guide the achievement of all SCP-related goals and targets.

In their chapter, Kartika Anggraeni and Patrick Schroeder (Chapter 4) analyse and assess the intermediary outcomes achieved by the SWITCH-Asia Programme activities that were carried out during 2007–2014. Based on submitted impact sheets of 43 SWITCH-Asia grant projects, the main question the chapter tries to answer is to what extent and in which ways the SWITCH-Asia Programme has contributed to implementation and expansion of SCP patterns in Asia. Answering this question has not been a straightforward process, in fact it has been a challenging endeavour. The main reason is that SWITCH-Asia's complex objective of promoting sustainable growth, to contribute to the economic prosperity and poverty reduction in Asia, and to mitigate climate change through SCP practices is difficult to evaluate. The reasons for this difficulty are common limitations of impact evaluation, in particular, issues like data (un)availability, selection biases, lack of resources, and limits to being able to apply experimental approaches, are all relevant in varying degrees to the assessment of the SWITCH-Asia Programme. Despite these limitations to providing a robust impact assessment, Anggraeni and Schroeder are confident in stating that many positive changes towards SCP in various industry sectors and at the policy level in Asian countries can be attributed to the SWITCH-Asia Programme.

Part II of the book comprises nine Asian developing country chapters on SCP presented in alphabetical order. Esa Abrar Khan analyses the topic of sustainable consumption and SCP in Bangladesh (Chapter 5). It begins with an overview of the current state of Bangladesh's industrialisation, the role of SMEs and environmental policies. He then contrasts two important industry sectors, one of which is the highly polluting tannery industry, the other the traditional jute sector, a renewable resource that is seeing a revival. The leather industry sector is the fourth largest foreign exchange earner of the country, but contaminates water resources and produces significant amounts of toxic solid waste, which are polluting the environment. Jute is known as the golden fibre of Bangladesh and jute processing is one of the country's oldest traditional manufacturing sectors, earning a large share of foreign currency by exporting jute products. The chapter looks specifically at one of Bangladesh's largest tannery areas, which is situated in Hazaribagh, Dhaka, to assess the present situation arising from tannery activities and proposes several mitigation measures. In addition, this chapter introduces how the existing site could be converted into a liveable and workable city district. Finally, the chapter features two case studies from SWITCH-Asia projects, which have addressed the pollution from tanneries and are promoting a healthy development of the jute sector.

The chapter by Kezang, Pem Lama, and Sangay Thinley Dorji (Chapter 6) introduces SCP implementation in Bhutan, which is guided by the development philosophy of Gross National Happiness (GNH). Bhutan's 11th Five-Year Plan for 2013–2018 focuses on a range of issues closely related to SCP, namely inclusive social development, accelerated green economic development, and strategic infrastructure development. The chapter also provides an overview of Bhutan's industry structure, especially the cottage and small-sized enterprises, and the present government's objective of promoting private sector development and policies and legislations that advance SCP in Bhutan. In particular, the GNH Policy Screening Tool has been used to help align all development policies and activities in Bhutan to the GNH philosophy within which environment and social aspects are carefully considered. In terms of international cooperation, the National

Environment Commission (NEC) is working with UNEP on SCP initiatives in Bhutan, such as mainstreaming SCP, green hotels, sustainable public procurement, green products, and developing a SCP curriculum. The chapter further puts a spotlight on sustainable tourism in Bhutan, which has been promoted in the context of the SWITCH-Asia Programme. While there is no standalone national SCP policy or framework currently being pursued in Bhutan, recent developments show the interest and the will of the government to streamline and integrate the compartmentalised pursuits of sustainability across the Bhutanese economy. The start of activities under the UNEP's 10YFP and mainstreaming of SCP into national policies and programmes will allow for the integration of various sustainability initiatives that the Royal Government of Bhutan has been pursuing under the umbrella of sustainable development.

The chapter by Romina de Jong (Chapter 7) introduces the role of SCP, with a focus on renewable energy and energy efficiency, for current and future socio-economic development in the Kingdom of Cambodia. Increasing energy consumption has created a situation in which the country's energy demand outpaces supply. This has resulted in lack of power and power outages although only about 30% of Cambodia's population had access to electricity in 2012. The chapter discusses the challenges of private-sector involvement in renewable energy sources and Cambodia's transition towards more sustainable energy practices. The two case studies of SWITCH-Asia projects, the "MEET-BIS Cambodia" project and the "Waste-to-Energy" project, illustrate the potentials for SCP solutions to create a sustainable and efficient energy system in Cambodia. The success factors are the provision of technical support, education and awareness on SCP, and financing options for SMEs.

Thongphet Phonsavath discusses SCP in the context of the Lao People's Democratic Republic (Chapter 8). SCP has been recognised by the Lao government as an approach to balance economic and social development and to reduce the impact on the environment. The chapter provides information about Laos' population, economy, the situation of Lao industry, in particular SMEs and existing policies and strategies regarding sustainability. Many policies, strategies and action plans have been devised to increase the basic general knowledge on sustainability of the population and to contribute to poverty eradication. However, simultaneously to an economic development aiming at satisfying basic needs of Lao citizens, the country continues to exploit its natural resources. For instance, over the last seven decades, the natural forest has decreased almost by half from 70% forest cover in the 1940s to about 40% in 2010. An evolving framework to encourage SCP offers promising alternatives to this type of resource-intensive development. The chapter concludes with two case studies of projects supported by the SWITCH-Asia Programme in the areas of sustainable forestry and efficient cook stoves.

The country chapter on Nepal (Chapter 9) by Raju Pandit Chhetri identifies several opportunities and challenges for spreading SCP practices in the country. Since the country is in its early stages of economic development and is currently recovering from the damages inflicted by the 2015 earthquake disaster, there is ample opportunity to combine development, environment conservation and sustainable livelihoods. The chapter provides an overview of Nepalese industry and policies related to sustainable industrial development and environmental protection, and identifies opportunities for SCP in priority sectors such forestry, tourism, renewable energy, and agriculture. The realisation of SCP in Nepal will require significant international assistance and collaboration in terms of awareness raising, skills training, knowledge dissemination, access to finance for SMEs, and technology transfer.

The chapter by Leonardo L. Sta. Romana (Chapter 10) examines the current consumption and production patterns of the Philippines presenting the findings of the author's research on the topic of sustainable development in the Philippines. He analyses the impact of consumption and production patterns on the environment and climate, with a view to finding out whether or not they are environmentally sustainable. The chapter looks first at the national policy and legal framework relating to SCP. It then describes the contribution of the on-going SWITCH-Asia National Policy Support Component that provides technical assistance and support to the national government on SCP-related policy and implementation issues. Then it reviews indicators that attempt to assess the overall state of the environment in the country, together with those that take stock of the country's ecological footprint and greenhouse gas emission. The chapter also delves into indicators on air pollution and waste generation. Next, it discusses the state of micro-, small-, and medium-sized enterprises (MSMEs) in the country, and notes how policy and logistical support towards them is relevant to the issue of inclusive growth and poverty alleviation. It then examines two case studies of already completed SWITCH-Asia projects in the country, which are related to MSMEs. The chapter concludes by noting the "double dividend" that the Philippines stands to gain from any action to "switch" consumption and production to more sustainable patterns.

The Sri Lanka chapter (Chapter 11), authored by Meryse Tissera, Damitha Samarakoon, and Gamini Senanayake, first reviews existing environmental policies that relate to SCP, such as the Haritha (Green) Lanka Programme, and introduces the work of the SWITCH-Asia NPSC that aims to create a national SCP development plan. With a focus on the role of SMEs, the chapter looks at the challenges and achievements of three interlinked sectors of the Sri Lankan economy: renewable energy, agriculture, and tourism. Present in Sri Lanka since 2008, the SWITCH-Asia Programme has implemented five key projects in the country focusing on renewable energy, waste management, food labelling, and two related projects directed at the hospitality sector, which will be discussed in this chapter. The main findings and conclusions of the study indicate that more emphasis on sustainability is required in current development strategies to avoid unnecessary environmental degradation resulting from rapid economic growth. Timely inclusion of SCP in Sri Lanka's development strategies offers the opportunity to circumvent negative environmental and social impacts.

In her chapter on Thailand (Chapter 12), Karin Merle introduces the relationship of SCP with the concept and approach of "Sufficiency Economy". This specific Thai concept builds on values of self-reliance, perseverance, and wise living. The chapter also compiles national and regional level policies on SCP and its state of implementation in Thailand, with a focus on specific instruments that support SCP. It synthesises key factors and incentives including policy measures that stimulate the uptake and implementation of these instruments. Against this background, the author introduces several SWITCH-Asia projects and their contribution to the advancement of SCP practices in Thailand, highlighting factors that could support the consolidation of existing success stories and shape the ground to upscale potential positive impact. In conclusion, the chapter finds that Thailand, being among the most advanced economies in Asia when it comes to SCP policies and implementation, and given its strategic position as a production hub in Southeast Asia, has strong potential to shape domestic and international consumption of green(er) goods and services.

Nguyen Tien Thong, Do Hung Nguyen, Pham Thi Ngoc Bich, and Le Thi Mai Huong concluded the second part of the book with their country chapter on Vietnam (Chapter 13). This chapter provides an overview of the current state of green industry and SCP in Vietnam, starting with the brief introduction of Vietnam's natural resources, society and economic conditions. This is followed by insights in the situation of the main Vietnamese industries, in particular SMEs, and their contribution to the country's development as well as negative effects to the environment as they pursue their industrial development goals. The chapter finds that many of Vietnam's SMEs still operate with out-dated and inefficient technologies and equipment in many sectors with unnecessary high energy consumption. Vietnam's Green Growth Strategy was approved in 2012 and aims to achieve a low carbon economy, enrich natural capital, and direct sustainable economic development. The strategy focuses on the three priorities of climate change mitigation and adaptation, green production, and green lifestyle. In particular, the efforts of greening production and lifestyles are very closely related to SCP objectives. The chapter also provides a brief review of the status of international aid supporting sustainable production and consumption in Vietnam, and illustrates two SWITCH-Asia case studies of the "SPIN" and "GetGreen Vietnam" projects. The importance of international support to enable Vietnam's green industry and sustainable development to grow is highlighted at the end of the chapter.

Part III of the book begins with the chapter by Emi Kawai on sustainable tourism (Chapter 14), which discusses the role and opportunities of sustainable tourism for Asia's developing countries, in particular for Bhutan, the Philippines, Sri Lanka, and Thailand. First, the chapter discusses current unsustainable trends and challenges resulting from mass tourism in those four countries, in particular socio-economic issues such as the leakage of tourism revenues and its impact on local communities, and the relationship of carbon emissions and international visitor arrivals. Additionally, this study also explores existing sustainable tourism policies in the four countries and examines the approaches towards sustainable development pursued through tourism in each country. The chapter finds that the understanding and perception of sustainable tourism is still abstract and largely skewed towards "being green" or "eco-friendly," as opposed to recognising the balance of economically, socio-culturally, and environmentally sound tourism development practice. The four Asian countries, except Bhutan, focus on high revenue growth and increasing international visitor arrivals. A comparison of governance approaches (top-down/bottom-up) for sustainable tourism in the countries reveals that sustainability mainly remains a marketing slogan, compared to the required implementation of sustainable practices, despite government initiatives and NGO advancement of many grassroots pilot projects. The current unsustainable situation of the tourism industry in these countries highlights three key issues requiring attention: enacting a national sustainable tourism policy or plan, providing access to financial support for SMEs in the tourism sector, and the necessity for a standardised monitoring system for the further development of tourism projects. The chapter also reveals the opportunities for scaling-up SWITCH-Asia projects and approaches in the region, and provides an outlook on sustainable tourism for the coming years.

In the final chapter of this book, Catalin Curea analyses waste management in the three Southeast Asian countries Cambodia, Lao PDR, and Vietnam (Chapter 15). He finds that the countries have just started to move away from the traditional collect-and-dispose model to an integrated approach that maximises resource recovery and economic value from waste. The chapter outlines possible solutions for the different stages of waste management including generation, collection, transportation, treatment, and disposal, based on SCP principles, 3Rs (reduction, reuse, and recycling), and circular economy principles. Finally, it highlights the roles of policies, SMEs and consumer awareness raising campaigns, including a SWITCH-Asia project case study on the reduction of plastic bag usage, to create more effective municipal solid waste management (MSWM) systems and sustainable societies in cities of Cambodia, Lao PDR, and Vietnam.

Part I:

Sustainable Consumption and Production in International Development Cooperation

Chapter 2

Sustainable Consumption and Production in Asia — Aligning Human Development and Environmental Protection in International Development Cooperation

L. Akenji, M. Bengtsson and P. Schroeder

2.1 The Evolution of the Global SCP Agenda

The broader concept of sustainability can be viewed as a crisis management concept; it emerged out of the growing conflict between economic development and the ecological boundaries within which its activities and impacts must be contained. Sustainable consumption and production (SCP) then emerged as a practical approach to achieve human well-being, the supposed objective of development, within this crisis management concept of sustainability. An assessment of recent history of the co-evolution of the two concepts would show that SCP has rapidly evolved as an integrative framework for the various dimensions of sustainability, as well as the nuts and bolts of sustainable development (SD) [Akenji, 2014; Chappells and Trentman, 2015].

This chapter looks at the recent evolution of SCP as a concept, from the perspective of the global United Nations (UN) policy process, with examples of how this has been reflected in Asia [Akenji, 2012; UNEP, 2012a; Zhao and Schroeder, 2010]. The intention is not to provide a comprehensive history, but to situate SCP in Asia within the larger SD discourse and to highlight some features that could be built upon to facilitate institutionalisation of SCP patterns in the region.

Sweden's proposal from 1986 to the UN General Assembly to convene a conference on the human environment was a ground-breaking step. Although the specific term 'SCP' had not yet been coined, in the run-up to the first UN conference in 1972, effects of industrialisation on society and the environment were perceived in a very limited scope — such as air and water pollution, poor waste management, and the consequences on cities and communities. They were largely treated as isolated issues that were site-specific and, in most cases, left to be dealt with at the local level without any broad national legislation. The 1972 UN Conference on the Human Environment held in Stockholm was the first time discussions were convened in an action-oriented manner at the global level on the patterns and consequences of industrialisation. The conference produced a Declaration that contained an Action Plan with 109 recommendations, and a set of 26 "common principles to inspire and guide the peoples of the world in the preservation and enhancement of the human environment" [UN, 1972] (see Table 2.1).

The 1972 Stockholm Declaration expressed the good will of the signatories; the outcomes are still very relevant in today's context, over 40 years later. Even to the extent that the conference exposed interdependence among countries and the transboundary environmental impacts of one country's development on another, the issue was not yet as politicised as is currently experienced in global policy processes.

The 1980s saw the development of a cleaner production approach to policy making. This was as a strategy to increase efficiency of natural resource use and waste minimisation, and also a precautionary approach to reduce pollution impacts and health risks from production. Here the focus was on impacts of manufacturing activities on the environment. It largely involved the application of new technology for maintenance or improvement of production processes to achieve economic savings or

Table 2.1: A timeline of SCP-relevant UN summits

Year	1972	1992	2002	2012	2015
UN summit	Conference on the Human Environment	UN Conference on Environment and Development	World Summit on SD	UN Conference on SD (Rio+20)	SD Summit
Outcome document	Action Plan for the Human Environment	Agenda 21	Johannesburg Plan of Implementation	The Future We Want	The 2030 Agenda for SD
Relevance for SCP	26 environmental principles, including SCP	Chapter four specifically covers sustainable consumption	Call for 10-year global programme on SCP	Adopting 10YFP and calling for Sustainable Development Goals (SDGs)	SDG12: Ensure SCP patterns

increased efficiency. The publication "Global Outlook on SCP Policies: Taking Action Together" [UNEP, 2012b] shows that the historical practice of SCP shifted from an end-of-pipe approach of the 1970s to a cleaner production approach as follows:

- from reactive measures, a preventative approach to environmental damage (like pollution prevention) was applied,
- problems were more likely to be addressed through the source of impact,
- instead of single-pollutants, multi-impact pollutants were targeted,
- from optimising throughput in production chains, the more complex approach of addressing entire material cycles became more widely accepted,
- approaches to solutions went beyond improving single-company processes to improvements in the wider supply-chains.

The 1990s would see further shifts, even if somewhat limited, towards more systemic approaches. Production efficiency was upgraded and characterised as eco-efficiency. The United Nations Industrial Development Organisation (UNIDO) and United Nations Environment Programme (UNEP) jointly launched the Cleaner Production Programme in 1994 for the establishment of National Cleaner Production Centres or Programmes to support actual implementation of and capacity building within eco-efficiency approaches. A slowly increasing understanding of a life-cycle perspective to analysing impacts of products and services meant that beyond just producers and technical fixes, all stakeholders and all stages in the production–consumption systems needed to be involved in solutions. Although this was still primarily centred on products and production process modifications, it clearly established the notion of sustainable consumption as the other side of the coin, and a complement to cleaner production. This evolving conceptual understanding of the interaction between and the critical importance in addressing consumption and production in articulation of sustainability was endorsed and promoted by the 1992 UN Conference on Environment and Development in Rio de Janeiro (Rio Conference).

The Rio Conference is marked as the first time at a global agenda-setting level when world leaders acknowledged the widespread environmental degradation resulting from our production and consumption patterns. Principle 8 of the Rio Declaration on Environment and Development proclaims that "to achieve SD and a higher quality of life for all people, States should reduce and eliminate unsustainable patterns of production and consumption ..." Agenda 21, also adopted at the same conference as a blueprint for action, highlights two broad objectives towards achieving SCP:

(a) Promote patterns of consumption and production that reduce environmental stress and meet the basic needs of humanity.
(b) Develop a better understanding of the role of consumption and how to bring about more sustainable consumption patterns.

Critical to developing countries, Agenda 21 also acknowledged the imbalances in consumption between different income groups and among countries at different levels of development, noting, "Although consumption patterns are very high in certain parts of the world, the basic consumer needs of a large section of humanity are not being met. This results in excessive demands and unsustainable lifestyles among the richer segments, which place immense stress on the environment. The poorer segments, meanwhile, are unable to meet food, health care, shelter, and educational needs." The agenda recommended a "multi-pronged strategy" in pursuing SD at the international level, "focusing on demand, meeting the basic needs of the poor, and reducing wastage and the use of finite resources in the production process."

The momentum of the Rio Conference and the ambitious outcomes failed to see practical changes in the following decades; multiple studies showed more apparent impacts of increasingly unsustainable patterns of consumption and production. Observers noticed a number of contradictions. The so-called rebound effect became very apparent: Most of the sustainability gains made due to increases in efficiency of energy and material use had been lost because of the sheer increase in the total volume of consumption [Jackson, 2009]. Because products were getting more efficient and cheaper, people could afford to buy more units than they did before; an increasing population further compounded this trend coupled with many people having more disposable income.

Monitoring results of previous policy efforts and actions showed that there was an "implementation gap" — most of the work done ended up on paper and did not translate to action, with trends showing a decreasing level of activity. Another important gap observed by behavioural sciences was the knowledge–action gap [Barth *et al.*, 2012]: even when people were aware of the environmental problem and had the information about more sustainable options for products or services, for the most part, actual action did not reflect that awareness. Information is sometimes not enough — eventually the more sustainable options are prohibitively expensive without available green financing options, the lock-in effects of long-term unsustainable infrastructure and policies make it hard to choose the better option, etc. This poor articulation of the importance of individual, corporate or institutional consumers and both their individual and systemic limitations to take action would inform the outcomes of the next UN summit to demand a more strategic and integrative approach to addressing production-consumption systems.

The World Summit on SD in 2002 produced the Johannesburg Plan of Implementation [UN, 2002], and re-emphasised SCP in two main ways. The Johannesburg Declaration on SD placed aspirations for SCP at the very core of the SD process, highlighting that "poverty eradication, changing unsustainable patterns of production and consumption and protecting and managing the natural resource base of economic and social development are overarching objectives of, and essential requirements for, SD." To buttress this, and in order to accelerate the shift to SCP, the summit called for the development of a 10-Year Framework of Programmes (10YFP) in support of national and regional initiatives in the transition to SCP.

The mandate to develop a framework of programmes was taken up by UNEP under the multi-stakeholder Marrakech Process launched in 2003. National and regional consultations, support for development of policies, as well as pilot projects under thematic task forces would be carried out globally over the next decade in parallel to these intergovernmental processes. As a response, in Europe a number of SCP-related policies were developed and implemented to promote SCP within Europe. In 2008, the European Commission presented the *SCP and Sustainable Industrial Policy* (*SIP*) *Action Plan*. It included a series of proposals on SCP that aim to improving the environmental performance of products and increase the demand for more sustainable goods and production technologies. It also sought to encourage European industry to take advantage of opportunities to innovate.

Under the Marrakech Process, in 2009, Asia identified the following regional priorities: green public procurement, development of fiscal instruments, resource-efficient and cleaner production, and greening business and markets. The *Asia-Pacific chapter of the Global Outlook on SCP* [Akenji, 2012] provides a detailed analysis of the status of SCP in the region around this period. Several established platforms began to incorporate SCP into their key themes, although mainly still from an environmental perspective. In 2003, the Bali *Declaration of ASEAN Concord II* created a Socio-Economic Community as a third pillar of the association and under which ASEAN environmental issues were addressed through a working group. The Roadmap for an ASEAN Community 2009–2015 under the *ASEAN Socio-Cultural Community Blueprint* positions SCP as a cross-cutting theme, "promoting clean and green environment by protecting the natural resource base for economic and social development" under Section D, on Ensuring Environmental Sustainability. In 2005, the Tripartite Environment Ministers Meeting (TEMM) member countries Korea, China, and Japan formed a working group on common standards for environmental labels; the three countries agreed to develop common standards for water-based paints, stationery, personal computers, and plastics and to harmonise their eco-labels to facilitate green purchasing with each other.

In parallel with the intergovernmental UN agenda on SCP, the EU's development of the SCP/SIP Action Plan and accelerated economic development in Asia, SCP has also been placed strategically in international development cooperation programmes. The European Union revised its cooperation strategy with Asia already in 1997 and a multi-pronged approach was developed involving a number of areas including:

- building Asia's environmental management capacities: more efficient and rational use of natural resources, the introduction of a sustainable wealth-creation model and environmental institutions,
- adopting market-based environmental measures: Mobilising the private sector (providing the necessary incentives for foreign direct investment that is more effective than state aid),

- focusing cooperation on priority sectors: urban and industrial pollution, protecting natural resources, etc.,
- fostering environmental research and development networks between Europe and Asia.

Based on this strategy, subsequent programmes were launched, including the Asia Pro Eco Programme, which ran in two phases from 2003 to 2007 with a global budget of EUR 31.5 million. The Asia Pro Eco Programme introduced European best practices of sustainable economic development to Asian countries, mainly the ASEAN region and China. The projects funded under the programme benefited from networking, capacity building, and knowledge creation, and knowledge management. Although the programme also developed a significant number of policy recommendations for sustainable economic development, uptake of these recommendations was low [MacKellar *et al.*, 2009], leaving scope for future SCP policy work.

The Asia Pro Eco I + II set the scene for the future programmes actively promoting SCP approaches. The EU explicitly included the topic of SCP in its international aid cooperation programmes and launched the SWITCH-Asia Programme in 2007, targeting in particular the update of SCP practice by small- and medium-sized enterprises (SMEs). The SWITCH-Asia Programme was also designed in view of SCP policy development through regional and national policy support components. The Programme has subsequently been followed by the SWITCH-Med in the Mediterranean and SWITCH-Africa Programmes. How SCP has so far been promoted and implemented under the SWITCH-Asia Programme in practice, in bridging international cooperation on environment and development in Asian developing countries, is the topic of this book.

Japan has promoted SCP-related approaches primarily through the 3R concept — reduce, reuse, recycle — over a number of years through the country's development cooperation with Asian neighbours. JICA was merged with the country's bank for development cooperation (JBIC) in 2008 and created a strengthened framework to manage Japan's official development assistance (ODA). The focus on 3R included initiatives on municipal solid waste management and e-waste management.

From Asia, as well as changes at country level, many countries and actors are beginning to play more active roles at both regional and international levels. The Institute for Global Environmental Strategies (IGES) submitted a proposal to the chair of ASEAN for a forum on SCP to be placed at a senior level within the organisation to facilitate SCP transition among member states. Championed by Indonesia, the ASEAN Forum on SCP has now been formally adopted; UNEP was invited to facilitate its development and act as Secretariat. Internationally, Bhutan, India, Korea, China, Japan, etc., were very active in negotiations of the SDGs. Japan, Korea, Indonesia, and Bangladesh have been members of the first international board of the 10YFP on SCP patterns. Asia was also the first region to adopt a roadmap outlining how to implement the 10YFP.

2.2 SCP in International and Asian Development Discourse

A recent report by UNEP [2015a], *Sustainable Consumption Guide for Policymakers*: *Debunking Myths and Outlining Solutions* (*Asia Edition*), explores the relevance of SCP in Asia. It argues that SCP is often misconstrued as an environmental agenda which aims mainly to limit or reduce consumption levels in order to protect nature from human impact. This misunderstanding stems from the fact that SCP has its background in Europe and the United States where most of the available literature, including both academic and practice-oriented publications, focuses on environmental aspects and the need to reduce the high negative impact these societies exert on the planet. In addition, at the international policy level, the work on SCP is led primarily by UNEP, which has environmental protection as its main mandate, thus further reinforcing the impression that SCP is above all about environmental issues.

This misconception is unfortunate since it makes SCP seem unsuitable for developing countries. In these countries, large segments of the population currently lead lifestyles with comparatively low environmental impacts and increased levels of consumption can improve many people's lives significantly. Naturally, calls for "responsible consumption" and "voluntary simplicity," which are common in the Western-dominated SCP literature, do not resonate well in contexts where many people are undernourished and lack access to safe drinking water and other basic services. Frugality and moderation are important values in many ancient Asian philosophies, and also central in the ideologies of some more recent influential thought-leaders like Mahatma Gandhi, but these ideas do not apply to the desperately poor and were not based on environmental concerns, but rather on moral, social, and spiritual grounds.

Another common misconception is that SCP is primarily about adopting advanced technologies (often from abroad) and in general becoming more like western countries. This misunderstanding makes SCP hard to achieve in developing countries, since eco-efficient and cleaner technologies are often expensive — at least initially due to higher investment costs — and especially for SMEs. Furthermore, capacity for proper implementation and maintenance are also often insufficient. However, while technology and efficiency improvements play important roles in making production and consumption more sustainable, SCP is a much broader concept. In this chapter, we elaborate this point further and show the reader the broad range of issues that SCP seeks to address.

In developing Asia, environmental problems and social issues are often deeply intertwined and need to be addressed in an integrated manner. For example, development projects that degrade the environment, cause pollution, and deplete natural resources often harm local communities and undermine the prospects of future wellbeing and prosperity. Similarly, environmental conservation projects that risk depriving low-income communities of their livelihoods often become politically contested and need to be complemented with support measures for those affected. Such tensions are much more direct and felt more strongly in developing Asia than in wealthy countries where polluting and degrading extraction, processing and manufacturing can more easily be outsourced to far-away locations.

In order for SCP to be relevant to developing Asia, for it to be taken up actively by governments and various stakeholders in this region, it thus needs to be framed very differently from in high-income countries. SCP should be understood and pursued in a way that is sensitive to the close and complex interlinkages between environmental and social issues.

A particular challenge in Asia is also the enormous disparities in income and ways of living. While most countries in the region have sizable segments of their populations enjoying material standards equal to or higher than average Europeans, Asia is also home to the majority of the world's poor. The Indian expression "jet plane India, oxcart India" captures well this situation with drastically different life-worlds existing in parallel. SCP practitioners in Asia can and should draw from the experiences made in high-income countries, but there is always a need to assess the relevance of those experiences carefully and to adapt tools and policy approaches to the circumstances at hand. Doing that in practice is often more challenging than initially thought and there is usually a need for pilot projects and other kinds of experiments for testing, adaptation, and embedding solutions in local contexts.

The SCP approach is flexible; it acknowledges the need to work out tailored solutions in response to local circumstances and thus does not offer cook-book recipes. Rather than a template, SCP provides a lens through which to view the environment and development in an integrated manner. As such, it draws from two large bodies of scholarship and practice: one on how to overcome the environmental crises caused by modern civilisation (the environment discourse), and the other on how to improve living conditions of people in low-income countries and to enhance their opportunities to achieve individual and social wellbeing (the development discourse). The SCP approach emphasises the need to break away from conventional development models and to find viable alternatives. It seeks to enrich and broaden the mainstream discourse on development by interrogating basic assumptions underpinning development thinking and practice and opening up space for conversations about options.

SCP in the context of developing Asia is thus not primarily about putting a lid on consumption, at least not for the great numbers of people whose lives would greatly benefit from consuming more and consuming better. The SCP approach is not similarly about protecting the environment at the expense of human development. On the contrary, it is about achieving human and social wellbeing on a more long-lasting and equitable basis. SCP also addresses social aspects of production and consumption, trying to ensure decent jobs, secure livelihoods, and thriving local economies. Furthermore, SCP in an Asian context tries to build on, protect, and improve what already exists in terms of traditional practices that promote well-being, strengthen social bonds, use natural resources wisely, encourage religious beliefs, and social norms that promote sustainable behaviours — such as vegetarian diets — and policy concepts like Bhutan's Gross National Happiness (see Chapter 6).

In the following sections, we discuss *three tensions* that have resulted from the conventional development paradigm: environmental degradation brought about by industrialisation, inequality resulting in the coexistence of rampant private consumption and persistent poverty, and westernisation's undermining effect on traditional livelihoods and cultures. These tensions have been intensely debated among international development experts and practitioners for decades, but their significance has only increased over time. We explain how the SCP approach contrasts with conventional development thinking at a conceptual level and share some experiences from the SWITCH-Asia Programme on how this approach can help address the tensions in practice. SWITCH-Asia has a strong focus on SMEs, so a number of examples in this chapter draw mainly from the situation of Asian SMEs — but this is only one out of many possible entry-points for discussing SCP.

2.3 The SCP Approach versus Conventional Development Thinking

2.3.1 *Industrialisation versus environmental protection*

Industrialisation driven by market-oriented economic policies has, over the last decades, been the most important element of mainstream development strategies. Many Asian developing countries have followed this route and continue to experience strong economic growth and rising income levels. For instance, in the ASEAN region, gross domestic product (GDP) is expected to reach USD 10 trillion by 2030, up from USD 2.3 trillion in 2012 [Biswas, 2012]. This dramatic growth in economic activity is accompanied by increases in population and urbanisation. By 2030, ASEAN anticipates a population growth of around 18% and a significant migration shift to urban areas [Khandekar, 2013]. Already some 67 million households in ASEAN states are part of the "consuming class," and that number is predicted to double to 125 million households by 2025 [Vinayak, Thompson, and Tonby, 2014], making ASEAN a pivotal consumer market of the future. Recent resource consumption data from the Asia Pacific region show that industrialisation over the last two decades has resulted in significant rise of emissions and rapid increase in resource consumption: Asia-Pacific's material consumption grew about threefold in the two decades between 1990 and 2010, making the region's resource consumption larger than that of the rest of the world combined [UNEP, 2015a, 2015b].

The tension here stems from the process of industrialisation seen as representing societal development in a more general sense, and the detrimental impacts of this model on the environment and natural resources. Conventional development thinking holds that all countries will go through a phase with high levels of pollution and environmental degradation, but as they get richer, they will increasingly be able to overcome these challenges. This belief is reflected in the so-called environmental Kuznets curve, which shows a hypothesised inverted U-shape relationship between economic development and environmental quality [Shafik, 1994]. It is also reflected in the catchphrase "grow first, clean up later" [Rock and Angel, 2005].

In contrast, the SCP approach is based on empirical studies that reveal other patterns, leading to different conclusions [Stern, 2004]. Firstly, SCP does not see the historical pattern with a highly polluting phase as inevitable; in contrast, it emphasises the opportunities for developing countries to leapfrog to more sustainable modes of production and consumption without necessarily repeating mistakes of the past. The availability of better technology and know-how, in combination with improved scientific knowledge higher levels of public awareness, make such leaps more feasible than ever. Secondly, while high-income countries have addressed many local environmental problems reasonably well, they still have a much larger per-capita impact on the planet than low-income countries, to a large part due to their high levels of consumption. Even the richest countries have not managed to shrink their per-capita impact on the planet to sustainable levels — quite the contrary. Emulating the wealthy countries thus seems to be only a partial solution, at best. Finally, some of the environmental problems in high-income countries have been "solved" by outsourcing polluting and resource-intensive production to developing countries. Such outsourcing will not be a feasible strategy for the currently industrialising countries. So, to summarise, when looking at the global scale, just getting rich will not solve the environmental problems caused by mass consumption and industrial production — there is a need for structural changes and public policies that promote alternative development pathways, including strong promotion of leapfrog-style development that avoids repeating known mistakes of the past.

Following the increasing global trends to protect the environment, some of East Asia's large industries, in particular those which aim to build global brands, multinationals operating across various countries and state-owned enterprises which often monopolise national industry sectors, have taken a lead and begun greening their business operations through implementing environmental management practices and pollution control measures [Stalley, 2014]. However, these activities represent an effort to prolong an essential unsustainable development trajectory by reducing apparent contradictions in the short term. Much more needs to be done to realise a true shift towards SCP.

The task of implementing SCP does not rest only on the shoulders of corporations. A common argument is that SCP approaches, such as cleaner production, resource efficiency or environmental management systems, are only suitable for large companies with sufficient capital. However, Asia's economies are still very much in a transition phase where private sector development is almost synonymous with SME development. This reality cannot be ignored. It is unproductive to regret that available SCP tools and approaches are not well-suited to Asia's industrial structure. A more productive stance is to recognise both the many challenges associated with SMEs and the values they can bring to society. With that as a starting point, the SCP approach should seek pragmatic solutions. One of the great challenges that SCP is trying to address is how the environmental performance of SMEs can be drastically enhanced, while their social benefits can be preserved. SMEs play an important role in development for two main reasons: their contribution to employment and income from exports, and their significant role in local communities and local production and consumption systems. At the same time, SMEs often cause immediate local environmental pollution, directly impacting the quality of life of the surrounding communities through contamination of water resources, air, and soils. The need for cleaner production measures, environmental management and energy efficiency for SMEs in Asia, have been recognised for a long time [Visvanathan and Kumar, 1999], but actual practice has been lagging, including in high-polluting sectors such as textiles, automotive, electronics, and leather processing. Addressing these impacts effectively increases the value SMEs can bring to communities, while resource efficiency and energy efficiency measures often save money for SMEs, rendering their employment opportunities more resilient [SWITCH-Asia Network Facility, 2015].

SMEs face many well-known challenges when it comes to pollution control and environmental management, including lack of awareness, limited capacity to adopt new practices, fierce competition and lack of funds for equipment upgrades [Ho, 2008]. One approach to overcome some of these challenges, which has been tested in some of the projects run under the SWITCH-Asia Programme, is to promote the formation of SME associations or cooperatives. Through such entities, it becomes easier for governments and development actors to provide assistance and the individual SMEs can also pool capacity and provide self-help. Fundraising for investments in energy efficiency and environmental protection can also be easier when SMEs are grouped together in legally recognised entities. In many sectors that are currently dominated by informal SMEs, it may not be feasible, or even desirable, to promote a full-scale transformation into shareholder-owned enterprises; other forms of ownership, such as cooperatives, may be better-suited for balancing the economic, social, and environmental outcomes of these activities. This provides an illustration of how developing countries could leapfrog, not only in terms of what technologies are used, but also institutionally.

2.3.2 *Consumerism (and resulting overconsumption) versus poverty alleviation*

The second tension — inequality — manifests itself in rampant consumerism and persistent poverty existing side by side. One of the common misunderstandings about sustainable consumption is that it always implies reducing current consumption levels, or lowering the standard of living. It is therefore interpreted as conflicting with the need for poverty eradication and continued economic prosperity. However, a transition towards sustainable consumption patterns has to become an imperative if global efforts at poverty eradication are not to be seriously undermined [Ekins and Lemaire, 2012]. For SCP, addressing under-consumption and meeting the basic needs of the poor are seen as equally important to keeping the impacts of consumption within ecological boundaries.

The issue of consumption is not new in the international development discourse. Back in 1998, the Human Development Report, published annually by the United Nations Development Programme (UNDP), titled "*Consumption for Human Development*" [UNDP, 1998] and already noted, "for more than one billion people living at or near the margin, increased consumption is essential. For those at the top, increased consumption has become a way of life." Likewise, Dasgupta [2007] in his study of the world's poorest countries, which investigated whether these countries experienced SD during the period 1970–2000, concluded that "…the creation of better institutions to enable people in the world's poorest regions to both consume more and invest more (inclusively, of course!) is the first step toward achieving SD."

Yet, current development cooperation practice often tends to stimulate western-style consumerism in Asian countries. The most visible signs of this development are the ubiquitous shopping malls that drive out traditional marketplaces — the world's 10 largest shopping malls are located in Asia — prioritising investment in infrastructure that promotes private over public transport, or loan schemes for consumer credit which increase household debt. This approaches to development, and to poverty alleviation, is often based on neoliberal ideology and its assumption that low taxes and other financial incentives for private companies and wealthy individuals will lead to stronger economic growth, which, in turn, will eventually benefit also the poor. The idea that wealth will "trickle down" to everyone and that economic growth will work as a "rising tide that lifts all boats" have been quite influential in political and development cooperation circles for several decades [IMPACT, 2009]. Proponents of SCP view this approach to poverty as ineffective and obsolete, for social and environmental reasons, but also for strict economic reasons. There is growing evidence supporting this critical view. For example, a recent study published by the International Monetary Fund (IMF) concluded that there is no empirical support that trickle-down approaches actually work

[Dabla-Norris *et al.*, 2015]. On the contrary, increasing the income share for the wealthy was found to have a negative impact on economic growth, while government interventions that directly benefit low-income households appeared to have a positive economic effect.

Poverty alleviation based on hopes via trickle-down approaches not only slow the delivery of improvements for the poor, but are also likely to entail serious environmental consequences. A recent study of poverty trends over the last few decades found that if China is regarded as an exceptional case, unlikely to be replicated in other countries, achievements have been modest and uneven [Woodward, 2015]. The same study found that if the current trends continue, it would take over a century to eradicate extreme poverty globally, and achieving this goal would also require average global per capita GDP to exceed USD 100,000 — almost 15 times its 2010 value. It is more than questionable whether such a high level of economic activity would be compatible with the need to stabilise the global climate while also addressing a range of environmental and resource issues, including biodiversity loss, deforestation, and water stress. Escalating environmental degradation would have a disproportional impact on the world's poor, which would further compound or even undermine the fight against poverty.

Approaches to development that drive up inequality are also undesirable for other reasons. Unequal societies are often characterised by strong competition between individuals and a strong desire to signal social status by consuming status goods; inequality thus stimulates excess consumption, resulting in increased environmental impact [Jackson, 2009]. Highly unequal societies are also often plagued by high crime rates [e.g., Enamorado *et al.*, 2014].

The SCP approach thus needs to address both middle-class consumption, with its high impact on the environment, and under-consumption by the poor, aiming for a more equal distribution of consumption opportunities and expanded chances to achieve wellbeing. Common measures of poverty are based on income or consumption levels, which register important dimensions of deprivation but provide only a partial picture. The UNDP Human Development report [UNDP, 2014] shows one way to evaluate progress by tracking the growth in consumption for the poorest 40% of the population. By this measure, some countries have done well. In Asia, Cambodia's consumption growth for instance for the poorest 40% has been faster than that for the population as a whole, but in countries where inequality has been high or rising — as in China or Malaysia — growth in consumption for those at the poorest end of the distribution has been slower than for the population as a whole. However, both absolute and relative poverty have multiple dimensions; monetary income and the ability to purchase goods and services is only one factor that influences people's opportunities to achieve wellbeing. Multi-dimensional poverty indexes show that people can be deprived of many things beyond income, for instance, they may have poor health and nutrition, low education and skills, inadequate livelihoods and poor household conditions, and they may be socially excluded or discriminated against [UNDP, 2014].

The SCP approach recognises this complexity and stresses the need to look beyond people's capacity for private consumption. A range of other factors, such as social relations and community support, the availability and quality of public goods, and the fulfilment of spiritual needs, affect people's perceived quality of life and thereby also their desire for private consumption. Perspectives that emphasise the complex relationship between poverty, consumption, and wellbeing have a long history in the development discourse. A more critical strand of thinking views poverty as a product of the modernisation process itself. An example can be found in the writings of the former diplomat and Iranian Minister and ambassador to the UN, Majid Rahnema, who considered the disintegration of subsistence economies that were producing for the household and the community, and the monetisation of societies as major causes for the creation of poverty. According to Rahnema, in the current economic system, which is characterised by unsustainable consumption and production patterns, the poor are reduced to nothing more than an object or statistic, defined by a fixed income level often imposed on them by the very institutions that have dispossessed them from their means of subsistence in the first place. He coined the term *modernised poverty* to describe this form of poverty that was generated through the Industrial Revolution and which has been exacerbated through globalisation. This process stands in direct relationship to the profusion of unsustainable consumption and production patterns.

"In this totally new type of poverty, the "lacks" felt by the individual are systematically produced by an economy whose prosperity depends on a regular increase in the number of its addicted consumers, while that economy cannot, by definition, do anything for providing the newly addicted with the means necessary to meet their new consumption needs." [Rahnema, 2005]

SCP approaches to overconsumption and poverty alleviation also need to encourage rethinking of the so-called cake syndrome [Rahnema, 2005], i.e., that a *sine qua no* condition for meeting the growing needs of a growing population is, before anything else, to increase the size of the cake. Through a critical SCP perspective, it becomes clear that "the already fabulous size of the 'super cake' produced by the world economy has ultimately resulted in dispossessing the poor of the only ways and means they had in preparing the cakes and the bread of their own choice. [Rahnema, 2005]. In this perspective, it is thus not only the overall size of the 'cake', what it consists of, and how it is redistributed that matters; on a more fundamental level, it is about who has significant influence over the making of the cake in the first place. This line of thinking resonates with the development philosophy of Mahatma Gandhi who emphasised the need to consider not only how wealth is distributed (and redistributed) but also how the means of wealth generation are distributed. This deeper critique of the dominant development paradigm raises important questions relevant to the theory and practice of SCP. In the words of Rahnema, "What is necessary for whom and for what kind of a life? And who is qualified to define all that?" Such questions of perspectives and power need to lie at the heart of reflective SCP practice.

2.3.3. *Westernisation versus pluralism and traditional ways of being*

The third and final tension to be discussed here is the one between westernisation and cultural pluralism. The basic question has to do with whether a worldwide convergence towards western institutions, government policies, infrastructure systems, lifestyles, and solutions in a broad sense, is feasible and desirable. The western model has been enormously successful in creating economic competitiveness and growth, and in raising material standards of living, but it is also associated with unsustainable levels of natural resource consumption. Conventional development thinking tends to have strong similarities with Rostow's stages model, according to which low-income countries are expected to move up the development ladder through a number of consecutive steps before finally reaching the end goal of becoming mass-consumption societies [Rostow, 1960]. It is thus guided by a vision of convergence at the top and holds out the prospect that all countries can become wealthy. By adopting western institutions and policies, all countries are expected to modernise and thus be able to join the ranks of the rich.

However, more than half a century has passed since Rostow presented this model and there is a wealth of experience on how development (sometimes) happens. This experience shows, for example, that development pathways can be very diverse and seldom follow a neat stages model. Those countries that have been the most successful in climbing up the economic ladder, such as the Asian "Tiger Economies" and more recently China, did not follow the free-market policy recommendations provided by western economists and international organisations, but formulated their own approaches, often with the government playing a key and active role by nurturing and protecting selected industries. Even so, these countries have generally followed a conventional development pathway with strong emphasis on export-led industrialisation, urbanisation, and infrastructure construction, which has led to widespread environmental degradation and pollution as well as high consumption of natural resources, including fossil fuels. Just like the early industrialisers — in Europe, United States, and Japan — their economic success has come at a high ecological price, and none of these countries can be regarded as sustainable. They are now facing pressing ecological challenges and are struggling with reformulating their approaches to development, putting it on a more robust and long-lasting footing. Experience also shows that, despite several decades of development assistance, a number of least developed countries have made only marginal progress on poverty reduction and economic diversification while inequality has increased drastically in many countries. For example, a study by the Organisation for Economic Co-operation and Development (OECD) found that income inequality in South and Southeast Asia, measured as Gini, increased from

35 in 1980 to 48 in 2000 [van Zanden *et al.*, 2014]. The idea that all countries can eventually become mass-consumption societies seems less and less likely to work in practice, especially in consideration of the Earth's limited resources and the increasingly felt impacts of climate change. It remains a legacy of the 20th century that the desires and normative expectations of Asian developing countries for a better tomorrow are predominantly directed towards modernisation through development-as-growth, thereby imitating the pathway of industrialised countries. Most Asian countries and societies aspire for industrial modernity and countries like Singapore or Malaysia, and cities like Hong Kong and Kuala Lumpur have become hypermodern conglomerates, having surpassed many of the capitals in industrialised countries in various aspects. SCP does not challenge this aspiration for a better life, but underscores the need to ensure ecological sustainability. SCP is therefore also relevant for urban consumption trends in Asia's megacities. In its medium-term economic outlook, the OECD predicts that export-led economic growth in Asian emerging economies and developing countries will be replaced by domestic consumption [van Zanden *et al.*, 2014] and a rapid rise in regional demand is predicted.

The process of modernisation tends to replace traditional lifestyles and practices with western alternatives, which in many cases are associated with higher environmental impacts. SCP, in the context of developing Asia, needs to recognise that some traditional practices and lifestyles have high sustainability values and deserve recognition. Traditional ways of life can be especially valuable by maintaining social capital at the community level, while providing for human needs in ways that have low environmental impact. It is essential that people in developing Asia become aware of the sustainability values of their existing, often disappearing, ways of living; that they learn to appreciate and feel proud of such practices instead of regarding them as outdated and backward or something that only poor people do out of necessity. SCP needs to encourage reflection on what is at risk of being lost in the process of modernisation and seek ways to maintain or improve traditional solutions with sustainability values.

One challenging issue for SCP practitioners is the suspicion that industrialised countries promote SCP as a strategy to restrain development and growing resource use of developing countries, in order to be able to maintain their own high levels of consumption. The often-stated phrase by western SCP experts "Don't repeat the mistakes we have made" is thus sometimes perceived as an attempt to hold back Asia's development, rather than sincere advice on how to avoid future challenges and how to help solving common global problems. There is no patent solution to this challenge, but it stresses the need for SCP practitioners to reflect carefully on their practices, whose agenda and interests they are promoting, and to listen carefully to the people they try to assist.

2.4 The Potential of SCP as a New Post-Development Worldview

The sections above show that conventional development thinking tries to address the three tensions based on very simplistic theoretical models, which all basically generate the same policy recommendation: to maximise economic growth. This is expected to help in dealing with and overcoming environmental problems, to eradicate poverty, to create employment and secure livelihoods for all, and to make all countries reach the envisaged end-state of development: to become mass-consumption societies. However, the experience from decades of development assistance shows that these prescriptions usually do not work, or are very ineffective as solutions to the issues they seek to address, or have unintended effects that make them unsustainable. Although such conventional thinking is deeply rooted in many people's minds as well as in institutions, there is a growing realisation of its shortcomings. That is part of the background to the increasing interest in SCP and related approaches that try to formulate alternative responses to the pressing and interlinked environmental and social issues that many societies are facing.

The unfolding ecological crises make the promise of development — that all countries, with the adoption of western institutions, good policies (read: market- and trade-friendly policies), and some patience, can eventually become mass-consumption societies — sound increasingly hollow. The worsening ecological state of the planet is giving new urgency to the need to rethink the objectives and approaches of mainstream development practice. SCP is one attempt to address this nexus of challenges. Whilst unbridled economic growth and the primacy of the market economy as the key solution to poverty and environmental sustainability has lost credibility, in particular among many academic experts, development professionals, and civil society stakeholders. Yet, the belief in this form of 'development' has not yet been fully dismantled. "...a decolonisation of the imagination has not occurred. Quite the reverse: across the world hopes for the future are fixed on the rich man's patterns of production and consumption" [Sachs, 2010]. The full potential of 'strong' SCP is not yet being utilised to replace the conventional development-as-growth paradigm.

Another issue, which comes to light through the lens of SCP: developing countries are mostly characterised by what they lack — in most cases, industrial development, technological know-how and capabilities — but not in terms of what they have to build upon or offer others. SCP changes this perspective as many developing countries have much to offer, particularly in terms of sustainable lifestyle models based on traditional values and local customs. Some home-grown concepts in Asian countries show a close relationship to SCP, e.g., Bhutan's Gross National Happiness, which is discussed in detail in the Bhutan country chapter of this book (see Chapter 6). Another example is the Sufficiency Economy philosophy, which has been developed and promoted by Thailand's King Bhumibol Adulyadej over the past three decades. In principle, this philosophy is a guide to making political and economic decisions to generate outcomes that are beneficial to the development of the country. How the Sufficiency Economy is implemented in practice is discussed in the Thailand country chapter of this book (see Chapter 12).

The last two decades have solidified the understanding that fringe changes around production and consumption systems alone would do little to stem the increasing and complex issue of *de facto* unsustainability. What is needed is to address the entire paradigm around which humans organise themselves in society and depend upon the environment to provide the economic means to meet their needs. Technical fixes and a focus on technology-driven efficiency have proven grossly insufficient on their own; what is needed even more is a human-centred approach of sufficiency, and a reform of institutions that constrain or encourage particular patterns of consumption and production. This goes beyond national levels. Transgressions on some planetary boundaries, material flow analysis, and environmental implications of complex international trade have also exposed the imperative of a more global approach addressing consumption and production patterns. And finally, whether looking at actors in a supply chain or analysing national or international roles, the political economy around production and consumption systems is needed to inform design for effective actions. In the same vein as an ecologically literate consumer being constrained by lack of sustainable products, or a more sustainable supplier going out of business in a supply chain dominated by an unsustainable brand owner, or a country unable to implement more sustainable trade policies because of WTO rulings, the power structures and dynamics that drive interaction need to be reflected in a systemic approach to a transition towards SCP.

Early signs of the above are reflected in the Rio+20 outcomes document: The Future We Want. Despite the noted failures of the conference to advance the global sustainability agenda, it did manage to adopt the 10YFP on SCP, and to set in motion the establishment of the SD Goals, which include SCP as one of its 17 headline objectives (see also Chapter 3). SCP is thus now at the top of the global environmental policy agenda, with the potential to function as an integrative framework for sustainability [Akenji and Bengtsson, 2014]. A recent UN study [Le Blanc, 2015] of the SDGs found the SCP goal to be the goal with the largest number of linkages to other goals, making it a good candidate for an integrative framework for SDGs implementation overall. SCP has also been identified as one of the most relevant goals to be addressed by the industrialised countries in the post-2015 development agenda [Osborn *et al.*, 2015]. Here we see a clear departure from the previous paradigm of the MDGs where goals and targets where set only for developing countries by the so-called developed countries. Clearly, the success of the SDG framework will hinge to a large extent on the achievements of the evolving global SCP agenda.

References

Akenji, L. (2012). Global outlook on SCP policies: Asia-Pacific. In UNEP (ed.), *Global Outlook on SCP Policies: Taking Action Together*. Paris: United Nations Environment Programme.

Akenji, L. (2014). Consumer scapegoatism and limits to green consumerism. *Journal of Cleaner Production* 63, 13–23. Available on: http://doi.org/10.1016/j.jclepro.2013.05.022.

Akenji, L. and Bengtsson, M. (2014). Making sustainable consumption and production the core of sustainable development goals. *Sustainability* 6(2), 513–529, doi:10.3390/su6020513.

Barth, M., Fischer, D., Michelsen, G., Nemnich, C. and Rode, H. (2012). Tackling the knowledge: Action gap in sustainable consumption — insights from a participatory school programme. *Journal of Education for Sustainable Development* 6(2), 301–312.

Biswas, R. (2012). ASEAN's rise as the next economic superpower. *ASEAN Trade Union Council*. 10 Aug 2012.

Chappells, H. and Trentman, F. (2015). In Reisch, L. A. and Thogersen, J. (eds.), *Handbook of Research for Sustainable Consumption*. Edward Elgar, Cheltenham, pp. 51–69.

Dabla-Norris, E., Kochhar, K., Suphaphiphat, N., Ricka, F. and Tsounta, E. (2015). Causes and consequences of income inequality: A global perspective. *IMF Staff Discussion Note 15/13*.

Dasgupta, P. (2007). Measuring sustainable development: Theory and application. *Asian Development Review* 24(1), 1–10. Retrieved on May 22, 2015. Available on: http://zunia.org/sites/default/files/media/node-files/ad/163939_ADR-Vol24-1-Dasgupta2.pdf.

Ekins, P. and Lemaire, X. (2012). *Sustainable consumption and production for poverty eradication*. United Nations Environment Programme, Paris.

Enamorado, T., López-Calva, L.-F., Rodríguez-Castelán, C. and Winkler, H. (2014). Income inequality and violent crime: Evidence from Mexico's drug war. *World Bank Policy Research Working Paper* No. 6935.

Ho, P. (2008). *Leapfrogging Development in Emerging Asia: Caught Between Greening and Pollution*. Nova Publishers, New York.

IMPACT (2009). Trickle-down economics revisited. *Harvard Kennedy School* 2(1). Available on: http://www.hks.harvard.edu/news-events/publications/impact-newsletter/archives/autumn-2009/trickle-down-economics-revisited.

Jackson, T. (2009). *Prosperity Without Growth: Economics for a Finite Planet*. Earthscan, US, Vol. 14. Available on: http://doi.org/10.1111/j.1530-9290.2009.00213.x.

Khandekar, G. (2013). ASEAN-EU: Time for a strategic partnership. EurActiv 14/05/2013. Retrieved on May 22, 2015. Available on: http://www.euractiv.com/global-europe/asean-eu-time-strategic-partners-analysis-519684.

Le Blanc, D. (2015). Towards integration at last? The sustainable development goals as a network of targets. *DESA Working Paper* No. 141. Available on: http://www.un.org/esa/desa/papers/2015/wp141_2015.pdf.

MacKellar, L., Dosch, J., Ney, S., Anthony, M. C., Madrid, R., Veit, C. and Goeke, M. (2009). Evaluation of European commission's cooperation with ASEAN, Regional level evaluation, Final report, June 2009.

Osborn, D., Cutter, A. and Ullah, F. (2015). Universal sustainable development goals. *Understanding the Transformational Challenge for Developed Countries*. Report of a study by Stakeholder Forum. Available on: http://www.stakeholderforum.org/sf/images/stories/SF_-_SDG_Universality_Report_-_May_2015.pdf.

Rahnema, M. (2005). *Eradicating Poverty or the Poor?* Redrafted 25 August 2005. Retrieved on May 17, 2015. Available on: http://www.sbilanciamoci.org/forum2005/relazioni/Rahnema.pdf.

Rock, M. T. and Angel, D. P. (2005). Industrial transformation in the developing world. *Oxford Geographical and Environmental Studies Series*. University Press, Oxford.

Rostow, W. W. (1960). *The Stages of Economic Growth: A Non-Communist Manifesto*. Cambridge University Press, Cambridge.

Sachs, W. (2010). *The Development Dictionary: A Guide to Knowledge as Power*. 2nd ed., Zed Books, London.

Shafik, N. (1994). Economic development and environmental quality: An econometric analysis. *Oxford Economic Papers New Series, Vol. 46, Special Issue on Environmental Economics (Oct. 1994)*, pp. 757–773.

Stalley, P. (2014). Corporations and the environment in East Asia: Responsibilities and responses of businesses. In Harris, P.G. and Lang, G. (eds.), *Routledge Handbook of Environment and Society in Asia*. Routledge, London and New York.

Stern, D. I. (2004). The rise and fall of the environmental Kuznets curve. *World Development* 32(8), 1419–1439.

SWITCH-Asia Network Facility (2015). Asian SMEs adopting sustainable consumption and production. *SWITCH-Asia Programme*. November 2015.

UN (1972). Declaration of the United Nations conference on the human environment, Stockholm 1972. *United Nations Environment Programme, UN Doc., A*, 77.

UN (2002). Plan of Implementation of the World Summit on Sustainable Development. United Nations. Retrieved on June 17, 2015. Available on: http://www.un.org/esa/sustdev/documents/WSSD_POI_PD/English/WSSD_PlanImpl.pdf.

UNEP (2012a). Capacity building and policy needs assessment for sustainable consumption and production. *A technical report to the SWITCH-Asia Regional Policy Support Component*.

UNEP (2012b). Global outlook on sustainable consumption and production policies: Taking action together. *UNEP*.

UNEP (2015a). Sustainable consumption guide for policymakers: Debunking myths and outlining solutions (Asia edition). *Bangkok: United Nations Environment Programme*. Retrieved on July 17, 2015. Available on: http://www.switch-asia.eu/fileadmin/user_upload/RPSC/News/16June15SC/SC-Guide-For-Policymakers.pdf.

UNEP (2015b). Indicators for a resource efficient and green Asia and the Pacific. Measuring progress of sustainable consumption and production, green economy and resource efficiency policies in the Asia-Pacific region. Authored by Schandl, H., West, J., Baynes, T., Hosking, K., Reinhardt, W., Geschke, A., Lenzen, M.

van Zanden, J. L., Baten, J., Mira d'Ercole, M., Rijpma, A., Smith, C. and Timmer, M. (Eds.) (2014). *How Was Life?: Global Well-being since 1820*. Organisation for Economic Co-operation and Development Paris.

Vinayak, H. V., Thompson, F. and Tonby, O. (2014). Understanding ASEAN: Seven Things You Need to Know. McKinsey Insights. Retrieved on 4 August, 2016. Available on: http://www.mckinsey.com/industries/public-sector/our-insights/understanding-asean-seven-things-you-need-to-know.

Visvanathan, C. and Kumar, S. (1999). Issues for better implementation of cleaner production in Asian small and medium industries. *Journal of Cleaner Production* 7, 127–134.

Woodward, D. (2015). Incrementum ad absurdum: Global growth, inequality and poverty eradication in a carbon-constrained world. *World Economic Review* 4, 43–62.

Zhao, W. and Schroeder, P. (2010). Sustainable consumption and production: Trends, challenges and options for the Asia-Pacific region. *Natural Resources Forum* 34(1), 4–15. Available on: http://doi.org/10.1111/j.1477-8947.2010.01275.x.

Chapter 3

Regional Policy Trends for Strengthening the Inclusion of Sustainable Consumption and Production (SCP) in Public Governance

S. Castro-Hallgren*

3.1 SWITCHing towards Sustainable Consumption and Production (SCP) — An Overview of Changing Policy Agendas in the Asia Pacific Region

SCP is a transversal issue in national and regional governance, and an objective that needs to be embedded in regulatory policy on resource extraction, manufacturing, health, consumer information, fiscal policies, and much more. SCP is about influencing both the supply and demand essentials of an economy from macro to micro levels, as well as understanding and in some cases influencing human behaviour. Policymaking in this context of complexity requires a crosscutting approach. It is in this vein that SCP is

---

* Supported by contributions from Julie Godin, UNEP.

included as a transversal and central element of the new 2030 Agenda for Sustainable Development (SD) and the Sustainable Development Goals (SDGs). This transversality of SCP will ultimately need to be reflected in the associated national policies of countries. Recognising the importance of this transversal approach to policymaking for SCP, the United Nations Environment Programme (UNEP), under the framework of the EU-funded SWITCH-Asia Programme, provides SCP policy support across regional, sub-regional and national policy agenda for the Asian region. In this context, the objective of SCP policymaking is to create resource efficient production systems for sustainable goods and services (*supply*), coupled with shifts in consumption patterns and consumer behaviour (*demand*) for SD, economic growth, and societal well-being.

Global policy agendas are changing to increasingly give central consideration to the environment and natural resources constraints, embedding these within national growth and development planning. In parallel, a number of developing countries have begun to pursue SD strategies which leapfrog the "grow now, clean up later" approach associated with the traditional industrialisation model. Asian countries have mainstreamed environmental considerations into national development planning, with strong national ownership. South Korea exemplifies this with the early launch of its Presidential Council on Green Growth to guide Green Growth[1] as a strategic vision that would cut across national to local governance, influencing even foreign relations and development cooperation policies. This national strategy was announced in 2008 with 'Low Carbon, Green Growth,' the formal vision for mid- to long-term development from 2009 to 2050, including a voluntary target of 30% reduction of greenhouse gas (GHG) emissions by 2020 [OECD, 2014]. The case of South Korea's rapid mainstreaming of its own approach to SD into national planning and governance showcases the importance of leadership and political will from the highest levels to guide this switch. One can also suggest that the country's overarching promotion of its green growth strategy, which

[1] "The concept of "**green growth**" has its origins in the Asia and Pacific Region. At the Fifth Ministerial Conference on Environment and Development (MCED) held in March 2005 in Seoul, 52 Governments and other stakeholders from Asia and the Pacific agreed to move beyond the SD rhetoric and pursue a path of "green growth."

also included development cooperation, set a trend for other countries to embark on similar policy reforms.

Since 2010, the specific inclusion of SCP in governance and policy agenda in Asia has greatly advanced. However, this progress in the policy arena has not yet reversed regional trends on rapidly escalating natural resource use. While many Asian countries can be touted as models of rapid economic growth, this has come at a tremendous cost to the environment. With recently acquired data (see Box 3.1), the resource efficiency of the region can be more clearly assessed in terms of its implications for the environment, economic growth, and human well-being.

Today, the region consumes more than half of the world's materials (e.g., fossil fuels, metals, and minerals) with an annual growth rate in materials consumption of 5% [UNEP, 2015a]. The high growth rate of material consumption equally matches the region's high Gross Domestic Product (GDP) growth rates. This correlation highlights the close link between

Box 3.1 Asian trends in resource efficiency [UNEP, 2015a]

- On average, Asia and the Pacific need 3 kg of materials to produce one dollar of GDP and this lags far behind of the rest of the world where on average only 1 kg is needed per dollar.
- Developing countries in the Asia-Pacific region use five times as many natural resources per dollar of GDP (5 kg/USD) as the rest of the world and 10 times more than industrialised countries (0.4 kg/USD) in the Asia-Pacific region, signalling the need for increased resource efficient technologies and production processes.
- The regional averages mask wide ranges from a high of 17 kg/USD in Mongolia and 12 kg/USD in Lao PDR, down to 0.3 kg/USD in Japan, with lower income countries most dependent on natural resources often having very low resource efficiency.
- Regionally, demand for electricity, gas, and transport fuel has increased more than fourfold between 1970 and 2010, influenced by the growing needs of a rapidly urbanising China, which accounts for 52% of Asian energy consumption.
- On average, material efficiency has been improving in developing countries in Asia and the Pacific at a steady rate of 1.5% per year.

materials consumption and GDP growth in Asia, as well as the need for "decoupling" this link through more resource efficient production systems and policies.

The clear drivers for these trends, signalling that regional development is not yet decoupled from environmental degradation, are urbanisation, increasing regional consumer demand, and the fact that the region has become the manufacturing hub for the world. Much of the global market relies on Asia's manufacturing, thus centralising resource use intensity in the region for the production of goods exported into global markets and increasingly also for intra-regional consumption [UNIDO, 2014]. Ensuring that national and intra-regional trade policies and supply chains are aligned with SCP could greatly assist in achieving increased competitiveness of green goods and services in the region, including for export of these into global markets [Bucher *et al.*, 2014].[2]

Demographic trends are also increasing resource use in Asia. It is increasingly apparent that with 4.2 billion or over 60% of the world population already in Asia and this proportion set to grow, resource consumption challenges in the region are likely to continue (see Figure 3.1).

By 2030, Asia's consumers are expected to represent the world's largest consumer group, with consumer spending predicted to reach USD 32 trillion [ADB, 2010]. As the region's middle-class swells in size, increased consumption of natural resources will likely occur to fuel growing consumer demand. Forecasting future resource pressures in the region and modelling the carrying capacity of regional ecosystems will be necessary. These forecasts and models can assist policymakers in mapping critical thresholds of natural ecosystems as a result of "unsustainable" consumption, to better inform policy decisions and national planning. In addition, integrating SCP considerations into national planning will be essential to ensure that the availability of quality natural resources for generations to come is prioritised in policymaking today.

[2] The global market for environmental goods and services was estimated to have reached US$ 866 billion in 2011 and is expected to rise to US$ 1.9 trillion by 2020. (Quoted from the publication by ITC, page 1.)

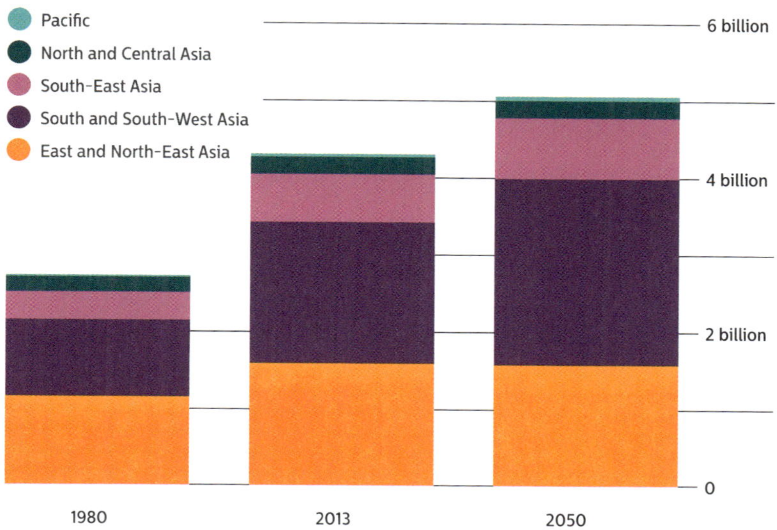

Figure 3.1: Projected population size by Asia-Pacific sub-regions [UNESCAP, 2013]

3.2 A Framework for National Environmental Governance on SCP

Based on the SWITCH-Asia Programme experience on SCP policymaking, this chapter introduces how a transition toward SCP can be promoted through a mixed strategy at three levels addressing both supply and demand (see Figure 3.2). This following section examines regional trends on SCP in public governance systems across Asia focusing on the institutional framework for SCP.

The "Institutional Lever" includes policies such as preferential trade agreements on certified sustainable products or green technologies, and for government to act as the main overarching actor driving SCP. The "Technological Lever" ensures a supply-side focus for the flow of goods and services into the market with a lower environmental and resource footprint. This lever also includes informing key actors in the market, especially the private sector, to increase resource efficiency in production, using approaches such as eco-innovations or cleaner production into business practice. Lastly, the "Cultural Lever" focuses on the consumer

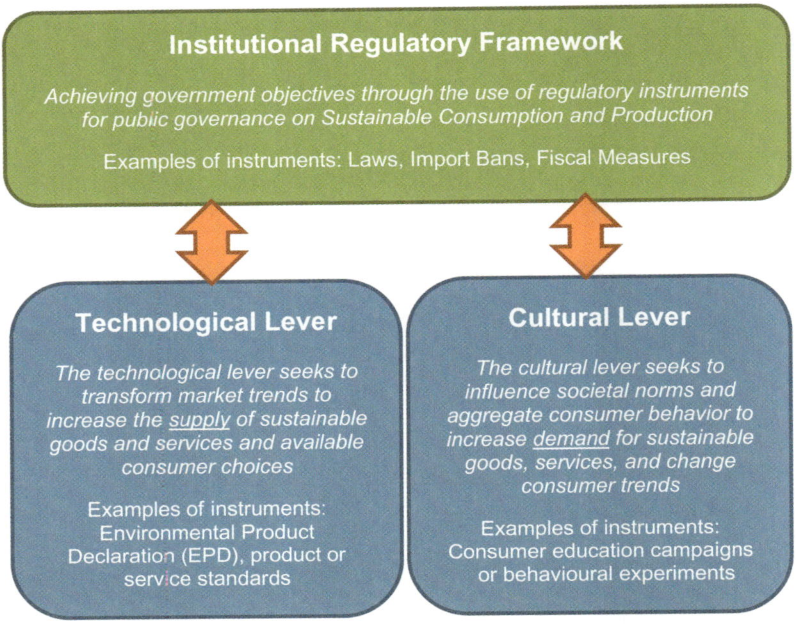

Figure 3.2: Institutional roles in national governance for SCP [UNEP, 2015b]

demand side of the market, shaping aggregate consumer behaviour, social norms, and sustainable lifestyles. This lever targets key institutions and actors involved in shaping social norms and consumer behaviour, such as media, education, and more.

In national public governance, an SCP policy framework encompasses strategies, policies, and instruments to consider and minimise the negative environmental impacts from all life cycle stages of consumption and production processes while promoting quality of life for all. SCP offers a holistic perspective to align society and the economy with the goals of sustainability, as well as concrete operational approaches targeting different sectors, stages of life cycle and various market players that make consumption and production choices. SCP also encompasses policies to support technological and social innovation, and there are a variety of policy instruments and tools that can be analysed in the context of national policymaking for industrialisation and especially in the context of national SD strategies [Bentley, 2008].

Table 3.1: Selected SCP policy instruments [United Nations, 2015, p. 98]

Policy Instrument	Description
Regulatory instruments	These include elements such as product and substance bans, emissions limits, production process standards, minimum product standards, and building codes aimed at determining which products, services, substances, and production methods are allowed.
Economic instruments	These include instruments such as fees and charges, taxes and subsidies, cap and trade schemes, tradable permits, feed-in tariffs, deposit-refund systems, etc. Examples include energy taxes, water user fees, subsidies for clean technology adoption, and feed-in tariffs for renewable energy installations.
Information-based instruments	These include instruments such as eco-labelling, consumer guidelines, corporate sustainability reporting, consumer campaigns, education on SCP, and training seminars for authorities and/or the private sector, all aimed at raising awareness. Most of these instruments influence the demand side and thus play an important role in stimulating the market for more sustainable solutions to which the supply side can respond.
Behavioural instruments	A behaviourally informed instrument represents a non-regulatory means to influence human behaviour towards more sustainable choices. Essentially a demand-side instrument and a recent policy innovation in and of itself, contain elements from cognitive psychology, behavioural economics, and cultural studies. Behavioural instruments aim to understand fundamental drivers for behaviour and use those to encourage consumers to change consumption behaviours in their choices and use of resources — such as through increasing water efficiency or energy efficiency behaviours at the household level.

On the production side, to increase competitiveness of sustainable goods and services, there are policy instruments that can strengthen the supply of goods, services, technologies, and the overall infrastructure required. *On the consumption side*, there are equally a variety of policies to change consumption purchasing trends among government, businesses, and consumer households. These sets of policy instruments are broadly classified as follows in the table below [UNEP, 2013a, 2013b].

These policy instruments should be embedded within a comprehensive national strategy for shifting towards SCP patterns in a national economy.

Certain countries are including SCP priorities in national development plans or five-year plans, as the crosscutting nature of SCP in public governance is more widely recognised [UNEP, 2013a, 2013b].

3.3 Global and Regional Progress on SCP Policy Agenda

SCP has been present on global development agenda since the United Nations (UN) Conference on Environment and Development in Rio de Janeiro in 1992. In 2012, recognising the importance of shifting to more sustainable patterns of and policies for consumption and production, at Rio+20, Heads of State strengthened their commitment to accelerate the shift towards SCP with the adoption of the 10-Year Framework of Programmes on SCP (10YFP), in paragraph 226 of the Rio+20 Outcome Document "The Future we Want".

UNEP, which hosts the 10YFP Secretariat, also offers regional policy support on resource efficiency and SCP through the European Union's SWITCH-Asia Programme. In this vein, UNEP is tasked with the development of the Asia-Pacific Regional Roadmap for the 10YFP. From November 7–8, 2013, representatives from more than 50 countries met in Bangkok to craft a regional roadmap for a priority action agenda on consumption and production. This "First Asia Pacific Meeting of the 10YFP on SCP" brought together government officials, regional and international organisations, civil society, and business representatives. Asian countries highlighted that the region is leading the way on advancing greener growth and SCP policies. The regional message was clear — countries recognise their challenges and priorities, and are strengthening focus towards the implementation of practical solutions for SCP. The following were the identified priorities for policy support and capacity building on SCP [UNEP, 2014]:

1. National and regional indicators on SCP.
2. Assessment of gaps in knowledge and practice.
3. Sustainability reporting benchmarking schemes for industry.
4. Eco-labels, sustainable public procurement, and sustainable consumption in general.
5. Coordinated awareness-raising campaigns.
6. Financing SCP, including financing for small- and medium-sized enterprises (SMEs).

7. Eco-innovation and adaptation of new technologies for cleaner production, and
8. On a sector level, energy, buildings, food, mobility, and tourism are sectors of interest as expressed by most of the countries in the region with sustainable cities, water management and waste being also cross-sectoral issues.

As a direct result of the UN commitment and the SWITCH-Asia Programme's efforts to advance concepts of SCP and greener growth for SD, policymakers in the region now have a clear mechanism to guide the 10YFP's implementation in the region. The current roadmap's activities have been implemented almost fully, especially with the financial support of the EU SWITCH-Asia Programme. This Roadmap will continue to be developed and implemented through the 10YFP as a multi-stakeholder process guiding regional action on SCP. The 2016–2017 Regional Roadmap is, at the time of writing, under development with more impetus, as SCP has become a key part of the 2030 Agenda for Sustainable Development (SD).

3.4 SCP's Central Role in the 2030 Agenda for Sustainable Development (SD) and the SDGs

In September 2015, the UN Member States adopted the 2030 Agenda for Sustainable Development (SD). This agenda comprises of 17 SDGs and 169 targets. SCP is not only featured as a standalone SDG (12) to "Ensure SCP Patterns", but has also been recognised as a "nexus" for the network of SDGs and their respective targets, along with the topic of inequality [LeBlanc, 2015]. SCP is linked to multiple targets across 13 of the 17 goals, showcasing the interlinkages and interdependence of the SDGs themselves.[3] For example, target 12.1 focuses on implementation of the 10YFP; while SDG 8 on economic growth and employment also explicitly mentions the

[3] "SCP is reflected as a crosscutting enabler (in the form of both targets and means of implementation) for the achievement of many of the SDGs as well as in a stand-alone goal 12 on ensuring sustainable consumption and production patterns" [UNEP/10YFP Secretariat, 2015]. SCP Indicators for the Future SDGs Discussion paper — March 2015. Online at: http://www.scpclearinghouse.org/d/the-clearinghouse/94-scp-indicators-for-the-future-sdgs-discussion-paper.html.

10YFP and SCP. Specifically, SDG 8's Target 8.4 states: "*Improve progressively, through 2030, global resource efficiency in consumption and production and endeavour to decouple economic growth from environmental degradation, **in accordance with the 10YFP on SCP**, with developed countries taking the lead*" [United Nations, 2015]. With the transversal inclusion of SCP in the SDGs, it is expected that support for SCP's inclusion across national governance in areas of economic, industrialisation, trade, and consumer health policies will increase.

The Asia-Pacific region has actively contributed to achieving global support for SCP in the SDGs. The regional voice has been integrated into the 2030 Agenda as per the process and outcomes of the UNESCAP Asia-Pacific Forum on Sustainable Development (SD), along with the First Forum of Ministers and Environment Authorities of the Asia-Pacific in 2015 [UNESCAP, 2015]. These regional discussions have highlighted the importance of achieving SD and growth "in line with Planetary Boundaries." In addition, the discussions highlighted the policy progress countries have made in the region on national models for SD. Some of the national models and strategies highlighted in this process included the sufficiency economy of Thailand (see Chapter 12); the "3R" (reduce, reuse, recycle) model of Japan; China's circular economy; the Gross National Happiness model of Bhutan (see Chapter 6), the Vietnam Green Growth Strategy (see Chapter 13), and Cambodia's Green Growth Roadmap (see Chapter 7), among others. The region's input into the global process to develop the 2030 Agenda echoed priorities of other regions in terms of national ownership, addressing inequality and social justice measures, including the private sector and civil society in policy development. In addition, Asia's position called for ensuring that the SDGs are integrated into centralised and comprehensive national development strategies to reduce any duplication and to strengthen governance. This latter point is especially significant, as currently countries often face policy recommendations that seem to suggest separate national policy documents responding to climate change, green growth, SCP, circular economy, SD, and similar concepts. In Asia, countries have especially taken national ownership and exerted their policy space to integrate global development concepts, such as SCP, into existing national plans and strategies, in a nationally determined manner.

3.5 Framing Asia's Progress on SCP — A Focus on ASEAN and South Asia

As regional trends have highlighted in the previous section, Asia is rapidly developing to become a region not just characterised by rapid economic growth rates, but also by the observed negative effects of unchecked consumption. By 2030, Asia is projected to account for two-thirds of the 4.9 billion global middle-class consumers, which will equal larger disposable incomes to drive a trend of consumption-led growth patterns in the region [ADB, 2010]. However, these trends towards rapid development come with dramatic challenges to well-being. As a result of unsustainable production and consumption trends and increasing industrialisation, consumer health challenges are on the rise with decreasing water quality, air quality, and more. Obesity, a "lifestyle disease" of over-consumption is also rapidly rising among Asian citizens, increasingly affecting children and youth in urban centres. Studies indicate that these lifestyles diseases, technically termed "non-communicable diseases", are a growing health threat as Asia develops [WHO, 2013]. Addressing consumption through this comprehensive lens on consumer well-being, including health, is central to ensuring sustainable consumption. This comprehensive or systematic outlook on consumer well-being is now part of the newly updated UN Guidelines on Consumer Protection. These updated UN Guidelines include a comprehensive section on Sustainable Consumption, including specific policy recommendations for Member States on areas of health and more [UNCTAD, 2015]. Consumer protection policies in Asia have been hard pressed to keep up with fast-evolving consumption trends and risks. In the region, consumer protection policies have most notably made reforms to include e-commerce protection measures, but rarely consumer health and well-being concerns. With the region's rapid development, debt-fuelled consumption is also on the rise in Asia, financing a rising demand for products and the natural resources required to make them. Rising household consumption in the region depends on increased disposable incomes, consumer spending and potentially higher debt. In Thailand, consumer household debt has risen to nearly 80% of GDP, among the highest in Asia, whereas a decade ago it was only 45% [Sriring, 2013]. This signals a dramatic increase of Asian consumer household reliance on credit to fuel spending on goods and services. National consumption rates are a fundamental part of economic growth and productivity in countries. GDP is often positively correlated to consumption expenditure. One can see that many countries in the region are today shifting from investment-led growth models towards consumption-led growth for a continuously increasing GDP rate [Mayer, 2013]. In some Asian economies, rising consumer debt is fuelling GDP growth in economies such as the Philippines, China and others shift to further reliance on consumption-led growth. The Philippines Development Plan (2011–2016) recognises the impact of the country's "*consumption-driven nature of the growth*" calling for "*a re-balancing of the economy towards greater investments*" or savings [NEDA, 2014, p. 3]. This is a central challenge to be addressed in reconciling SCP with national growth policies in the region. On the one hand, consumption is a central part of GDP and national accounts, with many national policies promoting more household consumption. On the other hand, greater consumption trends are often coupled with negative environmental impacts. It is suggested that with increased resource efficiency and SCP policies, this trend can potentially be controlled, but the Jevons Paradox suggests otherwise [see Polimeni *et al.*, 2008]. With rising populations, rising incomes, and rising consumer demand, the region's investments in resource efficiency may be cancelled out — continuing current trends of unsustainable environmental degradation. Exploring the effects of the Jevons Paradox will require greater country analysis at the national level as resource efficiency and SCP patterns evolve in the coming years. Equally, the dynamics and correlations between sustainable consumption and economic growth will require greater applied research in the Asia-Pacific region.

3.6 ASEAN Progress on SCP Policies

The Association of Southeast Asian Nations (ASEAN) has prioritised SD. The ASEAN Vision 2020 (adopted in 1997) aims for "a clean and green ASEAN with fully established mechanisms for SD to ensure the protection of the region's environment, the sustainability of natural resources and the high quality of life of its peoples" [ASEAN, 1997]. Tackling SCP policymaking through the ASEAN group of countries is of particular importance given the region's growing integration in 2015 into the

ASEAN Economic Community. In 2015, the EU SWITCH-Asia Programme completed four years of policy research and advocacy in Asia to strengthen regional policy frameworks and policymaker awareness of the benefits of sustainability in consumption and production. Southeast Asia or ASEAN has been a priority region for SCP policy support over these five years. In September 2013, as a result of the UNEP's policy advocacy efforts through SWITCH-Asia's Regional Policy Support Component and the strengthening of regional commitment to SCP, ASEAN Ministers issued a "Joint Statement on the Implementation of SCP in ASEAN by the ASEAN Ministers Responsible for Environment" [ASEAN Secretariat, 2013]. This statement noted the commitment to strengthen "cooperation within ASEAN and with ASEAN Dialogue Partners, relevant UN Agencies and other international partners on the implementation of SCP" setting the basis for advancing SCP in the region, and establishing an annual ASEAN SCP Forum. The ASEAN Forum on SCP was hosted in April 2014 and served to strengthen ASEAN's growing commitment to SCP in priority areas, such as green public procurement and eco-labelling, and will continue to serve as a voluntary policy mechanism. This provides an umbrella forum for policy dialogue on the range of SCP policy priorities in ASEAN, however there are still topic-specific activities. For example, in 2013, the ASEAN+3 countries also came together to create the ASEAN+3 Green Public Procurement and Eco-labelling network formally entitled "Strengthening the capacities and improving the knowledge on green public procurement and eco-labelling in the ASEAN+3 region." The objectives of the network are to (i) Strengthen sustainable public procurement and eco-labelling in ASEAN, (ii) Enhance South–South collaboration on these topics, and (iii) Ensure a broad and effective participation of ASEAN+3 countries in activities of the 10YFP. Since the establishment of the ASEAN Forum on SCP, there has been progress on implementing the priority activities and topics outlined by this forum on capacity development for SCP and green public procurement for example. There has also been progress on policy change in the area of energy efficiency or sustainable consumption of energy resources, through harmonising Minimum Energy Performance Standards (MEPS) in ASEAN (see Box 3.2).

Ensuring energy efficiency is of particular importance to increase the competitiveness of the SME sector in ASEAN countries as well as saving

Box 3.2 Harmonisation of ASEAN standards to drive SCP of energy efficient products

In 2015, the integration of the ASEAN Economic Community into a single market presents a remarkable opportunity to foster intraregional trade and uptake of high-quality lighting products to speed up the transition to energy efficient products, such as in lighting technology. At the 19th annual meeting of the Energy Efficiency & Conservation Sub-Sector Network (EE&C-SSN), ASEAN countries agreed that high efficiency lighting solutions, such as light emitting diode (LED) technology and controls offer immense potential to significantly reduce energy consumption in the region. The harmonisation of lighting standards in ASEAN could result in an annual savings of over USD 3.5 billion in electricity bills for consumers and a reduction of 35 TWh in electricity consumption, as well as an associated decrease in CO_2 emissions of more than 20 million tonnes. At the July 2015 SWITCH-Asia regional networking event on Advancing Energy Efficiency in Asia through SCP and Green Finance [SWITCH-Asia Network Facility, 2015], UNEP launched a policy guide on Developing Minimum Energy Performance Standards for Lighting Products [Scholand, 2015] with the ASEAN Centre for Energy (ACE). The harmonisation of standards approach through MEPS has been applied to air conditioners as well in the case of the SWITCH-Asia ASEAN "SHINE/Efficient Air Conditioners" project. The project successfully delivered MEPS for air conditioners for the ASEAN market. In 2016, the approach will also be upscaled into other product sectors to achieve greater resource efficiency of energy consumption in ASEAN.

households financial resources in countries where the cost of energy is high. By harmonising energy standards in ASEAN, governments can ensure that inefficient appliances and technologies, such as low performance lighting products, are phased out of the market. Improving energy standards means that consumers have access to more energy efficient products, while relying on harmonised standards to make informed purchasing decisions. In 2015 and beyond as the ASEAN Economic Community's integration strengthens, the creation and harmonisation of standards, labels and other policies to drive SCP, resource efficiency will become more feasible across ASEAN.

3.6.1 *SCP and Resource efficiency policy advancements in South Asia*

The South Asia Co-operative Environment Programme (SACEP) is an environmental policy body established in 1982 to guide the sub-regional policy agenda on the environment in the eight South Asian Countries.[4] Following the November 2013 UNEP meeting on the Asia-Pacific Roadmap of the 10YFP on SCP, SACEP's Governing Council issued a special decision on SCP which was formally adopted by South Asian states with the objective of promoting SCP within policymaking mechanisms of the South Asian countries. As a follow-up to implement the decision, in February 2015, UNEP and SACEP organised a "Preparatory Meeting for the Establishment of the South Asia Forum on SCP." UNEP contributed to the meeting in its role as host of the 10YFP Secretariat and implementing organisation of the SWITCH-Asia Regional Policy Support Component. The aim was to establish an annual policy platform, replicating the ASEAN policy platform for SCP. In addition, the platform aims to build knowledge and networks for South Asian policy makers and stakeholders on how SCP policies can support SD in South Asia and its expanding consumer and producer base.

South Asian cooperation bodies like SACEP are taking steps to increase resource efficiency and SCP in member countries. In line with its December 2013 governing council decision, SACEP and the South Asia Association for Regional Cooperation (SAARC), proposed the establishment of a South Asia Forum on SCP to serve as a regional policy platform convening annually. The South Asia Forum on SCP was formally approved by South Asian countries in February 2015 with the following objectives [SWITCH-Asia Programme, 2015]:

1. In the context of the Post-2015 Development Agenda, to provide a venue for policy dialogue and collaboration on SCP national, sub-regional, and regional strategies, planning, and implementation, increasing the profile of SCP in national development planning, and policymaking.

[4]SACEP's member countries include: Afghanistan, the Maldives, Bangladesh, Nepal, Bhutan, Pakistan, India, and Sri Lanka.

2. To meet annually to assess progress towards SCP and resource efficiency in South Asia, and to propose policy priorities to address under the specific working groups of the forum in line with an annual prioritisation exercise.
3. To provide a venue for discussion on research and innovation for SCP that can support tailored, effective policy design and actions to effectively embed SCP in national and sub-regional governance.
4. To develop a South Asian resource pool and explore technical support services for governments and other stakeholders at national and regional levels in a transition to SCP patterns, and
5. To encourage discussion on emerging issues on SCP, including the development of links with SAARC and other regional bodies, to develop a South Asian community of practice on SCP in policymaking.
6. The Forum was launched by South Asian countries at the next SACEP Governing Council meeting in early 2016. Policy support has already started through sub-regional technical cooperation activities. In addition, national policy support activities on resource efficiency and SCP are underway in countries which have expressed key interest, such as in Sri Lanka, Bhutan, Nepal, and most recently India.

3.7 Integrating SCP Transversally into Public Governance in Asia

Today, in an increasing number of Asian countries, one can see the inclusion of SCP concepts in national planning documents. However, one key challenge for the success of SCP policies in countries is local level enforcement to implement national SCP policy commitments. Starting the process of integrating SCP in a transversal way into national planning documents is the first step forward. Countries in the region are making concerted strides to achieve this and to prioritise SCP. This will only increase with the priority the SDGs have placed on SCP as a standalone goal together with its transversal links. The following sections present snapshots of the concerted progress specific countries are making in the region on mainstreaming SCP in national governance.

3.7.1 *Indonesia — a national 10YFP for SCP in national public policies*

The Republic of Indonesia is one of the most active countries in the Asian region regarding SCP policy development. Following the adoption of the 10YFP at Rio+20, the Indonesian government decided to develop a national 10YFP on SCP, the development of which was supported by the SWITCH-Asia Programme's National Policy Support Component (NPSC) for Indonesia which was implemented from 02/2012 to 01/2015. The SWITCH-Asia Programme's NPSC for Indonesia equally focused on demand and supply-side interventions for SCP, on public procurement and labelling. The SWITCH-Asia NPSC in Indonesia also delved deeper into tackling the aforementioned challenge of sub-national implementation of these policies in cities like Surabaya [SWITCH-Asia NPSC Indonesia, 2014].

The national SCP framework was adopted by the Ministry of Environment and Forestry and the Ministry of National Development Planning (BAPPENAS) on 5 June 2013. Since then, the uptake of SCP in the national development policy has advanced further; the national 10YFP is now reflected in the Presidential Decree Number 43 of 2014 as one of the seven cross-cutting priorities in national planning. As of 2015, SCP was formally adopted into the National Development Plan Document 2015–2019 [Ministry of Environment and Forestry of Indonesia, 2015]. Joint planning and implementation are being undertaken by the government, the business and industry sector, and civil society to implement specific national commitments for climate change and SD through targeted policy action. The national framework puts forward a vision where quality of life is improved towards SD and builds upon three main goals: (1) the inclusion of SCP into national development planning; (2) asset management and service to stakeholders for SCP implementation: "SCP Resource Pool Indonesia"; and (3) "Quick Win" policies with thematic public programmes on: "Ecolabel & Green Public Procurement", "Green Industry", "Green Building", "Green Tourism", and "Waste Management." One of the sectors where the government is particularly active is sustainable buildings and construction, due to increasing urbanisation trends in the country. The government is applying sustainable public procurement practices in the buildings and construction sector. It relies on a life-cycle approach that takes into account not only the construction but also the usage phase of the building. The country is also actively engaged in consumer information, as one of the co-leads of the 10YFP Consumer Information Programme through its Ministry of Environment and Forestry. In addition, SCP indicators for eco-tourism, as well as a Green Hotel Award programme, have been put in place as part of a national Green Tourism programme. These policies and initiatives cover almost all of the six programme areas of the 10YFP and show early progress in Indonesia's implementation of SDG 12.1 on implementation of the 10YFP. To encourage financing for green SMEs and green business models, the government also launched a model policy in 2014 to "certify" green SMEs, and signal their creditworthiness to the finance sector. This also included the adoption of national standards and certification to define the green SMEs in the country's policy context. In addition, the certification of green SMEs by the government was seen as a way to provide a creditworthiness signal to stimulate demand for these SMEs in specific bids, supporting matching demand for green products from green public procurement policy changes. In 2009, the country also enacted a new Type I ISO 14024 environmental ecolabel called "Ekolabel Ramah Lingkungan," supported by Act No. 32/2009. This label is equally designed for specific green products, certifying these to simultaneously strengthen consumer information in the country. Overall, the Indonesian economy already shows signs of improvement in natural resource management, with the material intensity of the economy decreasing sharply in the last decades from around 11 kg of material per USD of GDP in 1970 to 5 kg/USD in 2008 [UNEP, 2015c].

3.7.2 *The Case of Malaysia — Embedding SCP centrally into planning and policy*

In the case of Malaysia, the government has centrally embedded SCP into the new 11th Malaysia Plan — the country's Five-Year Plan for 2016–2020 (see Figure 3.3). The Plan has 'six strategic thrusts' — and the fourth strategic thrust focuses on "Pursuing Green Growth for

Figure 3.3: Extract of the 11th Malaysia plan's SCP policies and targets [Subramaniam, 2015]

Sustainability and Resilience" with an explicit focus on SCP and key SCP concepts such as "green government procurement."

The SWITCH-Asia Programme's NPSC for Malaysia supported exactly these types of policy mainstreaming activities for SCP. It started in 2012 and continued until January 2016, largely achieving all its original goals for policy mainstreaming, thanks especially to the country's political will and support for SCP policy. The SWITCH-Asia NPSC Malaysia was embedded within the Prime Minister's Economic Planning Unit (EPU). This strategic location for the NPSC into the central planning body of the national government demonstrates not only the importance of high-level political will, but also the potential policy successes available if SCP is prioritised in central planning bodies in a country. In line with this SCP policy support at central levels, the EPU has also led policy change in areas such as Green Government Procurement (Malaysia's term for Sustainable Public Procurement). The current 11th Malaysia Plan includes a target for at least 20% of government procurement to be "green" by 2020. This is complemented by a specific strategy focusing on green procurement according to feasible and impactful products as designated by the government, and policies to support businesses to satisfy this new demand. To guide further mainstreaming of SCP in national policies in line with the new SDGs, with the support of SWITCH-Asia, the EPU is also leading the development of a "National SCP Blueprint." This action plan will guide national activities on SCP until 2030, also the target year for the SDGs. It focuses on all priority government sectors for SCP, such as goods and services, housing, low-carbon transport, tourism, and other specific sectors.

Malaysia has also made of advances with applying or integrating SCP within the education sector, which is of crucial importance in SCP to achieve necessary changes in behaviour, lifestyle, and eventually the necessary social norms. Formal education can be a large and effective determinant to shape individual, household, community, and even national behaviour. In Malaysia, the government has embedded the topic of SCP and Sustainable Lifestyles into the national curricula to foment behavioural change in young generations through applied learning [National SCP Portal of Malaysia, 2015]. The SCP portal for Malaysia notes that:

> *"The Government has formulated an education system that integrates the concept of Sustainable Consumption and Production (SCP) and Education for Sustainable Development (ESD) across the school's curricula. Currently, all of the 27 teacher training institutes are contributing towards SCP and ESD by offering environmental education to*

teacher trainees. Once the teachers-to-be understand the concept of SCP, they'll be able to convey their knowledge to their students that are the gem of our nation."

In addition, Malaysia has implemented special learning initiatives through a partnership between the World Wide Fund for Nature (WWF) and the Malaysian Ministry of Education to bring students outside the classroom for SCP learning and to "build an effective environmental education model to bring about positive behavioural change among students" [National SCP Portal of Malaysia, 2015]. This programme is implemented in selected schools at primary and secondary levels. Among many activities, the programme develops in-school herb gardens, vegetable patches, and aquaculture ponds, where these serve as "learning stations." Through these learning stations, students develop practical "hands-on" knowledge and skills to complement what they learn in textbooks through the integration of the environment and SCP in the formal curriculum.

3.7.3 *Overview of SCP in Asian national development plans*

In summary, there are many countries in Asia advancing SCP policy commitments, especially in national development plans. As Table 3.2 shows, what has especially been embedded into national planning documents is a focus on changing consumption behaviour — with national plans reflecting goals of changing "behavioural patterns," developing an environmentally-friendly "consumption culture" and similar goals. For countries to achieve these national goals, effective national to local implementation and enforcement of polices that can effectively change behaviour and social norms will be key in order to advance. Equally important is how to measure progress of national changes in behaviour and purchasing patterns in line with the SDG indicators proposed for Goal 12 on SCP. Countries will need to focus on increasing investments to change the consumption or demand-side of the equation, through education programmes, as in the example of Malaysia above, and more behaviourally-informed policies.

Table 3.2: Selected countries in the region mainstreaming SCP in national development plans

Country	Key National Plan's Inclusion of SCP
Mongolia	**Mongolia's Comprehensive National Development Strategy up to 2021** includes environmental commitments. The UNEP is also engaged with Mongolia to provide Green Economy and SCP technical policy support on SCP topics such as Sustainable Public Procurement and eco-labelling. Currently, the public procurement legislation is being reviewed with SPP to be enacted in 2016.
India	**The 12th Five-Year Plan (2012–2017)** denotes that "the issue of environmental sustainability cannot be ignored. We need a growth process that is consistent with protecting our environment" and it lays out specific financial instruments recommendations to ensure SCP — "*economic instruments can help achieve SD through their influence on behavioural patterns leading to SCP in the economy.*" It also mentions other central concepts in SCP and resource efficiency, such as energy efficiency, cleaner production, greening procurement, and more.
Sri Lanka	**National Action Plan for the Haritha (Green) Lanka Programme (2009–2016)** was developed through a high-level participatory process and was intended to ensure that sustainability would not just remain a concept but would translate into practical reality. The Mission 10 area of the plan entitled "Knowledge for Right Choices" focuses explicitly on SCP by key strategies and actions for behavioural change among youth, women, etc. The plan also details specific Key Performance Indicators, baselines and details responsible government institutions for each strategy, and action area. For example, key strategies focus on: "6. Promote behavioural changes amongst youth towards sustainable production and consumption," "7. Promote women to become change agents towards sustainable production and consumption practice," and "8. Promote sustainable production and consumption practice amongst the general public."

(Continued)

Table 3.2: (*Continued*)

Country	Key National Plan's Inclusion of SCP
Vietnam	**Vietnam's Sustainable Development (SD) Strategy from 2011 to 2020** specifically focuses on SCP. It aims "*to develop a civilised, harmonious, and environmentally-friendly consumption culture. Gradually implement eco-label and green shopping. Develop an eco-product market and community-based initiatives for sustainable production and consumption. Apply policies to correct unreasonable consumption behaviour.*" It also focuses on efficient energy and water consumption. The **National Strategy on Green Growth** (promulgated in 2012), also has strategic tasks focused on "greening production," "greening lifestyle" and "promoting sustainable consumption." In addition, the **National Action Plan for Green Growth (2014–2020)** specifically mentions sustainable consumption and cleaner production, complementing other plans for SCP (e.g., the 2009 National Strategy on Cleaner Production in the Industry Sector).
Thailand	**The 11th National Economic and Social Development Plan (2012–2016):** the plan consists of eight development strategies and their respective implementation plans. SCP is clearly mentioned throughout the Plan. Chapter 8 details focus areas such as "3.2 A lifestyle that follows the Philosophy of Economic Sufficiency, the Thai way of life, and awareness of the benefits and values of natural resources and the environment" with clear objectives and targets for SCP and resource efficiency to be achieved such as in sub-chapter 4.1.2 *to promote production and consumption that is environmentally sound in order to redirect the country toward a low carbon emission society.*
Cambodia	**National Policy and Strategic Plan for Green Growth (2013–2030):** the policy and plan were developed with the aim to establish the economy with consideration for environment and natural resources sustainability. The national policy targets a balance between economic development and environmental protection, culture preservation, social stability, and sustainable consumption of natural resources to improve people's living conditions and welfare. Meanwhile, the plan aims at developing a green economy by the effective use of natural resources, environmental sustainability, green jobs, green technologies, green finance, green credit, and green investment.

3.8 Conclusions and Lessons Learned in Strengthening SCP's Inclusion in Public Governance

In national governance, an SCP policy framework encompasses strategies, policies, and instruments to increase consumer well-being and minimise the negative environmental impacts from all life-cycle stages of consumption and production processes. From experience gained since 2012 in implementing policy support on SCP in the region, there are a series of lessons learned by the SWITCH-Asia Programme that can aid in strengthening national planning and governance for SCP.

Enhancing policy coherence: in public governance, there are coordination challenges between ministerial mandates and policies. One ministry may implement policies that directly contrast the efforts of another. SCP is a transversal topic that requires policy coherence and coordination across national ministries to eliminate these challenges. Mainstreaming SCP across government policies can best be achieved through either a central planning agency taking the lead on this process or through embedding SCP as a priority in national development plans. In the case of Malaysia, both of these methods have been applied to ensure more coherent SCP policies in national governance. It should be noted in this regard that enhancing policy coherence is also Target 17.14 of the SDGs.

Contextualisation of policy support in accordance with national planning processes and levels of decentralisation: in many Asian countries, national planning is done through five-year cycles. Aligning policy support for SCP with these Five-Year Plan cycles is key to its success. In addition, countries have differing levels of decentralisation, which may centralise planning and policymaking or devolve this to state and local levels. Indonesia, for example, engages in a decentralised planning process from local to national levels — the Musrenbang (Musyawarah Rencana Pembangunan) — highlighting its higher level of decentralisation. Neighbouring countries, such as Malaysia or Singapore, engage in more centralised planning and policymaking. Ensuring that SCP policy support accounts for a country's decentralisation would allow for more effective interventions tailored to national governance. In a country with greater decentralisation, more emphasis should be placed on minimising national to local SCP capacity gaps and including state and local governments in policy support.

Nationally-determined and owned strategies for SCP implementation: in line with SDG target 17.15, technical cooperation for SCP should "respect each country's policy space and leadership to establish and implement policies for poverty reduction and SD." In Asia, national ownership of SCP and the overlapping concept of green growth have developed side by side. It is likely the same will follow for the implementation of the SDGs and relevant SCP targets. While some countries may not explicitly develop National Action Plans on SCP, they may integrate SCP systematically into national planning documents or key sector-based policies. Ensuring that the focus areas under SCP policy support for each country are based on nationally-determined priorities through inter-ministerial consultations, as well as existing strategies or plans, will assist in this regard.

Specialised focus on Least Developed Countries (LDCs), Land-locked Developing States (LLDCs), and Small-Island Developing States (SIDS): while Asia has large diversity in the stages of development of its countries, the region also has the largest group of LDCs after Africa, also SIDS and LLDCs. These country groups require specialised attention and should be especially prioritised in SCP policy support, with this being delivered as part of a tailor-made and cohesive package of technical cooperation for attaining the SDGs. LDCs in Asia for example with the lowest resource intensity, such as Bangladesh, Myanmar, Cambodia, Lao PDR, and others, are poised to integrate SCP equally as governance is strengthened in their current development paths.

Partnerships for collective impact: SCP is now a central part of a global agenda for SD. SCP policy support to countries to implement this new agenda can be strengthened by delivering through a "one UN approach" and coordinated multi-partner activities in each country. The SDGs Fund has already launched with this objective of "delivering as one" UN in each country, under the inclusive leadership of each country's UN resident coordinator. This allows for coordination with not only UN organisations operating in each country, but equally includes all development actors in a country, such as non-government organisations to achieve the SDGs collectively.

Increasing national policy champions and SCP experts: to assist countries in achieving measurable progress on all SCP relevant goals and targets, countries will need national pools of SCP expertise. In Asia, policymakers in SWITCH-Asia countries have developed strong knowledge and skills on SCP, resulting in a network of experts that can act as SCP policy champions in their respective countries. However, other countries in the region and globally could benefit from increased national capacity and policy expertise, to ensure greater national ownership of SCP activities and guide these towards scalable achievements.

Communicating the value-added of SCP for a resource efficient private sector: SCP must always be presented in terms of the value added it can create. SCP can drive innovation, eco-innovation in business, and resource efficient production can increase business profitability for large national companies and SMEs. It can assist developing countries to avoid the "lock-ins" observed in developed nations, ensuring that they avoid inefficient modes of production, urbanisation, and lifestyles. SCP's potential value-added must be communicated in an understandable way to all key stakeholders in the production and consumption process. This requires greater engagement and customisation of the academic or scientific language that can at times underpin resource efficiency and promotion of relevant "proof of concept" examples to all. Many SWITCH-Asia grant projects, which work directly with SMEs, have achieved successful results proving the business case for SCP in practical contexts.

Ensuring SCP policy effectiveness through behavioural insights: to truly change current resource intensive consumption patterns, policies must affect behavioural change and bridge the all too commonly observed gap between consumer intentions and actions [Umpfenbach *et al.*, 2014]. This includes both (i) the supply-side (through policies for ensuring more resource efficient global value chains, which promote life-cycle thinking and eco-innovation), as well as (ii) the demand-side (policies for changing consumers' demand). Using insights from psychology and economics, behavioural economics addresses the complexity involved in consumer decision-making by exploring how people (consumers) make choices. Policies attempting to influence consumer decision-making could benefit from these types of behavioural insights. Multiple countries emphasise the need for behavioural change in ensuring SCP (see Table 3.1), but in Asia few to no countries have begun to include behavioural analysis and insights in policy interventions and government programmes. The approach is typically applied by identifying a behavioural "problem" or challenge, researching the potential causes or contributing behaviours, proposing corrective actions, and a randomised control trial in the field. Aiming for scalable results and scientific rigour in changing the behaviour, the approach is being mainstreamed to address many different challenges. By including this component into policy design, countries can ensure greater policy effectiveness at lower costs to address consumption challenges of water efficiency, energy efficiency or food waste among households.

Specialised policy focus on achieving SCP in MSMEs: improved policy attention should be paid to increasing resource efficiency in the production and consumption happening within micro-, small-, and medium-sized enterprises (MSMEs). As engines of growth for rural as well as urban areas, SMEs generate income and economic empowerment for producers and consumers everywhere — from developed to developing countries. As diverse as this business group is for many countries, it provides direct access to the Bottom of the Pyramid (BoP) to ensure SCP contributes to poverty alleviation, job creation, and income-growth for the majority of households. SMEs are the backbone of Asian economies and their development is essential for SD and economic growth. Given their central role to ensure SD in the region, SMEs are a key catalyst for the switch to really make sustainable patterns of production and consumption happen in communities everywhere. As the switch to more green production and consumption practices takes place, supported by enabling policy structures, finance and opportunities for scaling-up, SMEs can lead the way for green growth in Asia's economies.

Linking SCP with health and trade policy arenas: lastly, SCP policies must be more connected to two essential areas, which have not been extensively linked as of yet, despite being pivotal for sustainable consumption's global success. This first area is human health policies. SCP is greatly connected to areas of air quality, water quality, cleaner production, and reduced toxicity hazards, the rise of "lifestyle diseases", and more. SCP policy support at national level should be more integrated with national health policies, through greater inter-ministerial coordination and policy coherence for the systematic well-being of consumers. The second essential area yet to be systematically linked to SCP policymaking is trade. Given the growing global amount of "sustainable" goods being traded, SCP objectives could be greatly complemented by greater links with national or global trade policy. SCP and trade are centrally linked in policy areas of eco-labelling, sustainable public procurement, standards harmonisation, and more.

3.9 Conclusions

This chapter has shown that in recent years, in particular since the implementation of the SWITCH-Asia Regional and NPSC, SCP has become increasingly integrated into Asia's public governance frameworks, such as overarching national development plans and strategies. In addition, countries in the region are prioritising a shift in the social norms and behaviours that lead to unsustainable consumption, promoting traditional concepts of sufficiency, and adopting newer concepts of green growth. On the production side, the region will continue to make advancements in resource efficient technologies and practices. Overall, it is clear that the region will require greater nationally-focused research, capacity development, and overall policy support to ensure SCP's implementation, especially at the local level. While national policy commitments on SCP increase, ensuring that policy support is customised to national contexts and to the challenges of local policy enforcement will guarantee that measurable progress can be made in achieving the SDGs on the ground. In addition, developing the regional knowledge base to advance SCP in line with national growth strategies will require greater attention, including the forecasting of future resource pressures as a result of national trends in consumption and production. Developing this knowledge base, especially at the national level, can equip policymakers with greater tools to guide resource use in line with policy priorities and development planning. The region will continue to be a primary driver for global economic growth, including in the production — and now more so in the consumption — of goods and services. Prioritising SCP policy implementation, from the highest national level to local level policies, will contribute to Asia's SD, improving the overall well-being for the Earth's inhabitants — for those today and for those yet to come.

References

ADB (2010). *The Rise of Asia's Middle-Class.* Asian Development Bank, Manila.

ASEAN (1997). ASEAN vision 2020. *Association of Southeast Asian Nations.* Retrieved on March 15, 2016. Available on: http://www.asean.org/?static_post=asean-vision-2020.

ASEAN Secretariat (2013). Joint statement on the implementation of sustainable consumption and production in ASEAN by the ASEAN Ministers responsible for environment. Retrieved on March 15, 2016. Available on: http://environment.asean.org/joint-statement-on-the-implementation-of-sustainable-consumption-and-production-in-asean-by-the-asean-ministers-responsible-for-environment/.

Bentley, M. (2008). *Planning for Change: Guidelines for National Programmes on Sustainable Consumption and Production.* UNEP DTIE, Paris.

Bucher, H., Drake-Brockman, J., Kasterine, A., and M. Sugathan (2014). Trade in Environmental Goods and Services: Opportunities and Challenges. International Trade Centre Technical Paper, Geneva. The International Trade Centre (ITC) is the joint agency of the World Trade Organization and the United Nations. Available on: http://www.intracen.org/uploadedFiles/intracenorg/Content/Publications/AssetPDF/EGS%20Ecosystems%20Brief%20040914%20-%20low%20res.pdf

LeBlanc, D. (2015). Towards integration at last? The SDGs as a network of targets. *UNDESA, 2015.* Retrieved on March 15, 2016. Available on: http://www.un.org/esa/desa/papers/2015/wp141_2015.pdf.

Mayer, J. (2013). Towards more balanced growth strategies in developing countries: Issues related to market size, trade balances and purchasing power. *UNCTAD Discussion Paper* No. 214. Geneva.

Ministry of Environment and Forestry of Indonesia (2015). Powerpoint Presentation during SWITCH-Asia proceedings in New Delhi, November 6, 2015. Further information available on: http://bappenas.go.id/files/8814/1101/2887/INDONESIAS_GREEN_GROWTH_EFFORTS_18_september_2014.pdf.

National SCP Portal of Malaysia (2015). "Whatever you say, Teacher." and "bringing the education of SCP out of the classroom and beyond". SCP Malaysia. *Economic Planning Unit, Prime Minister's office*. Retrieved on March 15, 2016. Available on: http://www.scpmalaysia.gov.my/en/node/28.

NEDA (National Economic and Development Authority) (2014). The Philippines development plan (2011–2016). Retrieved on March 15, 2016. Available on: http://www.neda.gov.ph/wp-content/uploads/2014/08/NEDA-PDP-2011-2016-Midterm-Update+Errata2.pdf.

OECD (2014). Green growth in action: Korea. *Organisation for Economic Co-operation and Development, Paris*. Retrieved on March 15, 2016. Available on: http://www.oecd.org/korea/greengrowthinactionkorea.htm.

Polimeni, M., Kozo, M., Giampietro, M. and Alcott, B. (2008). *The Myth of Resource Efficiency — The Jevons Paradox*. Earthscan, London and Sterling, VA.

Scholand, M. (2015). Developing minimum energy performance standards for lighting products. *Guidance Note for Policymakers*. UNEP DTIE and UNEP-GEF en.lighten initiative. June 2015.

Sriring, O. (2013). Rising Thai household debt spurs rate tussle as economy slows. *Reuters Analysis*. August 6, 2013, Bangkok. Retrieved on March 15, 2016. Available on: http://www.reuters.com/article/us-thailand-economy-idUSBRE97513Z20130806.

Subramaniam, J. S. (2015). Mainstreaming SCP into national planning and priorities and how this relates to SDGs. *Presentation during 8th ASEAN-Plus-Three Leadership Programme on Sustainable Production and Consumption*. Kuala Lumpur, 20–23 October 2015.

SWITCH-Asia Programme (2015). Summary report of the — Preparatory meeting for the establishment of the South Asia forum on sustainable consumption and production (SCP), March 2015. Available on: http://www.switch-asia.eu/fileadmin/user_upload/RPSC/policy-dialogue/2015-South-Asia/Report_UNEP-SACEP_South_Asia_Forum_SCP_24Mar2015_Final.pdf.

SWITCH-Asia NPSC Indonesia (2014). Presentation on highlights from Indonesia PSC, 2014. More information available on: http://www.switch-asia.eu/fileadmin/user_upload/RPSC/policy-dialogue/switch-asia-psc-and-tac/6._Highlights_from_Indonesia_PSC__Edzard_.pdf.

Umpfenbach, K. *et al*. (2014). Influences on consumer behavior: Policy implications beyond nudging. Final Report, 8 April 2014. *European Commission & Ecologic Institute*.

UNCTAD (2015). Draft resolution on consumer protection for consideration by the general assembly. *United Nations*, 2015. Retrieved on March 15, 2016. Available on: http://unctad.org/Sections/ditc_ccpb/docs/UNGCP_Draft Resolution2015_en.pdf.

UNEP (2013a). *Sustainable Public Procurement: A Global Review*. United Nations Environment Programme, Paris.

UNEP (2013b). *Sustainable Consumption and Production — A Handbook for Policy Makers*. SWITCH-Asia Regional Policy Support Component, Nairobi.

UNEP (2014). Roadmap for the 10YFP implementation in Asia and the Pacific 2014–2015. *UNEP, Paris*. Retrieved on March 15, 2016. Available on: http://www.unep.org/10yfp/Portals/50150/downloads/Asia_Pacific_10YFP_Roadmap_2014_2015_FINAL.pdf.

UNEP (2015a). Indicators for a resource efficient and green Asia and the Pacific. *SWITCH-Asia Regional Policy Support Component*. Retrieved to March 15, 2016. Available on: http://greeninfo.asia/Publications/Indicator-for-a-RE (Low-resolution).pdf.

UNEP (2015b). *International Experiences on SCP — CCICED Sustainable Consumption Task Force*. Retrieved on March 15, 2016. Available on: http://www.switch-asia.eu/fileadmin/user_upload/PSCs/draft_study.pdf.

UNEP (2015c). *Case Study: The SCP Uptake in Indonesia*. Retrieved on February 15, 2016. Available on: http://www.unep.org/10yfp/Portals/50150/SCP%20case%20study%20in%20Indonesia.pdf.

UNESCAP (2013). Population trends in Asia and the Pacific. Retrieved on March 15, 2016. Available on: http://www.unescap.org/sites/default/files/SPPS-Factsheet-Population-Trends-v3.pdf.

UNESCAP (2015). Report of the Asia-Pacific forum on sustainable development on its second session. Retrieved on March 15, 2016. Available on: http://www.un.org/ga/search/view_doc.asp?symbol=E/ESCAP/FSD(2)/3.

UNIDO (2014). *World Manufacturing Report 2014 QII*. Retrieved on March 18, 2016. Available on: http://www.unido.org//fileadmin/user_media/Publications/Research_and_statistics/Branch_publications/Research_and_Policy/Files/Reports/World_Manufacturing_Production_Reports/STA_Report_on_Quarterly_production_2015Q2.pdf.

United Nations (2015). Global Sustainable Development Report, 2015.

United Nations (2015). *Transforming our world: The 2030 Agenda for Sustainable Development.* Retrieved on February 15, 2016. Available on: https://sustainabledevelopment.un.org/post2015/transformingourworld.

World Health Organisation (2013). *Health in Asia and the Pacific, Chapter 8.* Retrieved on March 15, 2016. Available on: http://www.wpro.who.int/health_research/documents/dhs_hr_health_in_asia_and_the_pacific_13_chapter_8_priority_noncommunicable_diseases_and_disorders.pdf.

Chapter 4

SWITCH-Asia Programme Impacts: Taking Stock and Looking Ahead

K. Anggraeni and P. Schroeder

4.1 Introduction

The SWITCH-Asia Programme is the flagship programme of the European Union promoting sustainable consumption and production (SCP) in Asia through the mechanisms of international development cooperation. It is an example of a development programme with increasingly ambitious and multi-faceted dimensions and objectives. The main objective of alleviating poverty in Asia is pursued by reducing environmental impacts of industrial activities, enhancing competitiveness of local small- and medium-sized enterprises (SMEs), changing consumption patterns, and providing policy recommendations for national development agenda. SCP practices, focusing on quality growth, through environmentally sound and socially inclusive strategies, are deemed a skilful approach to achieve these goals. Achieving the final objective of poverty reduction via the intermediate goal of promotion of SCP requires the active involvement of multiple non-traditional actors of development programmes. The programmes primarily focus on SMEs, business associations, consumer associations, non-governmental organisations, technical consultants, and national ministries. This multitude of actors poses new and additional challenges to a meaningful impact analysis.

This chapter discusses the approaches and challenges to understand the impact of the SWITCH-Asia Programme as a whole and its various components. This chapter does not present a rigorous impact evaluation, which would require a different kind of data collection; rather it is an experimental approach to assess the impact. It can be conceived as a measurement of intermediate outcomes [see Ravallion, 2008], which aims to assess the SWITCH-Asia Programme's midway impact based on selected indicators. As this assessment cannot be comprehensive, the boundary for this assessment is, therefore, the reported information about SWITCH-Asia grant project results, which are taken into account to establish an impact estimation of the Programme. Furthermore, this assessment draws on the experience, insights and information collected by the experts of the SWITCH-Asia Network Facility over the course of 2009–2015. The main question this chapter tries to answer in the following sections is how and by how much the multiple interventions of the SWITCH-Asia Programme are contributing to changing the current consumption and production trends in Asia towards becoming more sustainable.

4.2 Measuring Impact in Development Cooperation

Impact measurement and evaluations in development cooperation continues to be an intensely debated topic among practitioners, academics, aid recipients, and donors. There are methodological debates, controversies about the definition of impact evaluation and questions about the hierarchy of methods [see White, 2010]. Substantial resources are usually applied to designing a cooperation programme, monitoring its implementation, and measuring its outputs and results, but comparatively little effort is reserved for evaluating and measuring a programme's impact. Impact evaluation is also not mandatory for many programmes. This can on the one hand mean that good programmes are not expanded as widely or as rapidly as they should be. On the other hand, funds often continue to be spent on approaches that are failing [Savedoff *et al.*, 2006].

In the post-2015 development agenda and in conjunction with the Sustainable Development Goals (SDGs), the so-called "data revolution" [IEAG, 2014] is becoming increasingly relevant for sustainable development. This data revolution includes the explosion in the volume of data, a growing demand for data from all parts of society and the need to use these data to produce high-quality information that is more detailed, timely and relevant for users, in particular to foster and monitor sustainable development. Although the world is increasingly awash with data, there is a distinct lack of high-quality data [IEAG, 2014]. Household data are considered particularly important for monitoring progress in the post-2015 development agenda in particular for poverty, health, and human development [Alkire and Sammam, 2014]. This is particularly relevant for SCP as one of the transversal and cross-cutting SDGs. The SWITCH-Asia Programme has generated a large amount of data on SCP in Asia over the period from 2007 to date, in particular about the outcomes of project activities and stakeholders involved in the projects. Most of this data still awaits screening and thorough analysis, especially data collected in the form of baseline studies from SMEs. To establish the impact of the individual programme components and the whole SWITCH-Asia Programme, not only project data, but also baseline data on specific industry sectors and control groups will be required, which currently has not been budgeted.

Another important attribute of the SWITCH-Asia Programme is its layered structure of components, which renders an impact evaluation difficult. Individual grant projects and programme components are designed within a broader programme framework, sometimes resulting in parallel work, but in addition in hierarchical relationships to each other (see Figure 4.1). These components are, in turn, situated within the global SCP strategy, initially the Marrakech Process, from 2012 the 10 Year Framework Plan on SCP, and now the SDGs. The challenge for evaluation is to capture the impacts of the individual grant projects, identify the interrelationships between the different scales of impacts and attribute the aggregated impact of the whole programme beyond the scope of single projects or components.

The concept of interrelationships is a familiar concept in impact evaluation [Williams, 2015], with its focus on causal attribution. SWITCH-Asia grant projects extensively use the methods of results chains and log frames to map the interrelationships between activities, outputs, results and impact both in the design of project activities and reporting to the European Commission (EC). Furthermore, the implementation of each project depends on evolving interrelationships between European and Asian partners and the engagement of various stakeholders at national and local levels. This information is valuable to understand how things and partners become connected and with what consequence. In particular, the insights

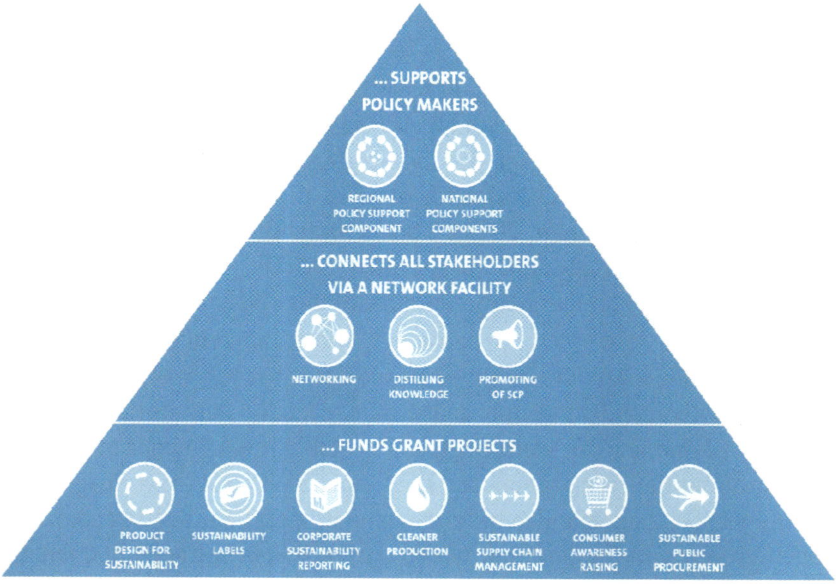

Figure 4.1: SWITCH-Asia programme structure [SWITCH-Asia Network Facility, 2014]

about project dynamics, how the interrelationships affect the behaviour patterns within a project over a period, and how interrelationships with project external stakeholders develop, are of value.

Important clues to understanding impacts can often be found in the geographic differences in impacts and how this relates to the characteristics of locations and specific interventions [Ravallion, 2008]. This aspect is also relevant for SWITCH-Asia as a multi-country programme operating in 18 Asian countries. An in-depth impact evaluation can reveal which SCP approaches are more successful than in others in specific country contexts.

4.3 SWITCH-Asia Project Impact Sheets

The SWITCH-Asia Network Facility publishes impact sheets of individual grant projects in an attempt to capture the variety of results the projects have achieved. The projects have submitted impact sheets and data based on self-reporting on the outcomes, results and impacts that they have achieved. The way projects collect data related to their impacts includes a range of mixed-method approaches, such as baseline studies among SMEs,

Box 4.1 A formal approach to SWITCH-Asia Programme impact

A simple formal approach to the impact of the SWITCH-Asia Programme can be described as follows. This approach can help to identify some of the information and data, which are currently not available for analysis:

$$\text{Impact (SWITCH-Asia Programme)} = Y_1 - Y_0.$$

Impact here is defined as the difference in the indicator of interest (Y), an observable outcome indicator, with the intervention (Y_1) and without the intervention (Y_0). Data for the statements below were collected through interviews, project site visits and document reviews.

In the case of *Y = Uptake of SCP practices by SMEs involved in project activities*, to have positive impact requires $Y_1 > Y_0$. It is almost certain (close to 100%) that $Y_1 > Y_0$. However, it is not yet possible to determine the exact difference between Y_1 and Y_0, as it would require data of control groups of SMEs that are not involved in project activities.

If *Y = Pollution caused by SMEs (involved in the SWITCH-Asia project activities)*, $Y_1 < Y_0$ will indicate a pollution reduction impact. It is almost certain (close to 100%) that $Y_1 < Y_0$. However, again it is not possible to determine the exact difference between Y_1 and Y_0. The main reason is inadequate data about the reduction or increase of emissions and pollution caused by SMEs.

In case of *Y = Domestic material consumption of the Asia-Pacific region*, it is almost 100% certain that $Y_1 < Y_0$, but the difference between Y_1 and Y_0 is very small (less than 1%). The SWITCH-Asia Programme has contributed to slowing down the increase of resource consumption in Asia-Pacific, but not (yet) achieved changing the trend of growing resource consumption.

factory audits, consumer surveys and expert interviews. It is assumed that projects (see Table 4.1) have reported according to the indicators defined in their logical frameworks, which have been developed in the project design phase, with possible adjustments during the implementation phase.

Since September 2013, the SWITCH-Asia Network Facility has collected detailed information from grant projects, covering additional impact areas, using the existing format of project impact sheets (see Table 4.2). Previously, the project impact sheet covered only five impact areas, i.e., economic, social, and environmental impacts, along with target group

Table 4.1: List of 43 SWITCH-Asia projects included in this study

Project Short Titles	Project Official Titles
Train the Trainers	"Train the Trainers": a proposal to train Chinese construction sector SMEs in energy-saving techniques & technologies
MEET-BIS	Mainstreaming energy efficiency through business innovation support Vietnam (MEET-BIS Vietnam)
SUS TEX	Sustainable textiles for sustainable development
Eco-Jute	Jute: an eco-friendly alternative for a sustainable future
AEMAS	Establishment of the ASEAN energy manager accreditation scheme
Zero Carbon Resorts (ZCR)	ZCR — Building energy autonomous resorts creating appropriate technology solutions
SMART Cebu	SMART CEBU: SMEs for environmental accountability, responsibility and transparency
WEEE Recycle	Establishing e-waste channels to enhance environment friendly recycling
Industrial Symbiosis	Implementing industrial symbiosis and environmental management systems in Tianjin Binhai New Area
Eco-friendly bamboo	Sustainable revival of livelihoods in post-disaster Sichuan: Enhancing eco-friendly pro-poor bamboo production supply chains to support the reconstruction effort
SUS BIRD	Sustainable building interior renovation and decoration initiative in China
Greening Sri Lankan Hotels	Greening Sri Lanka hotels
Biomass-SP	Sustainable production (SP) of the biomass industries in Malaysia: Optimising economic potential and moving towards higher value chains
China Motor Challenge	Electric motor systems energy-saving challenge — Improving the operating efficiency of Chinese electric motor systems
Sustainable Rattan	Establishing a SP system for rattan products in Cambodia, Laos, and Vietnam
CSR Vietnam	Helping Vietnamese SMEs adapt & adopt CSR for improved linkages with global supply chains in SP

(*Continued*)

Table 4.1: *(Continued)*

Project Short Titles	Project Official Titles
ESEEC	Improving environmental and safety performance in the electrical and electronics industry in China
Re-Tie	Re-Tie Bangladesh: Reduction of environmental threats and increase of exportability of Bangladeshi leather products
SCI-Pak	Sustainable and cleaner production in the manufacturing industries of Pakistan
Wood	Sustainable and responsible trade promoted to wood processing SMEs through forest and trade networks in China, India, and Vietnam
Food & Beverages	SP in the food & beverages industry in Sri Lanka
SUPP URB	Sustainable public procurement in urban administrations in China (SuPP-Urb China)
Higher Efficiency of Transformers	China higher efficiency power and distribution transformers promotion project
GPIOS	Creating green Philippine islands of sustainability
Clean Batik Initiative	Encouraging and implementing SP and consumption of eco-friendly batik in Indonesia and Malaysia
PRO SUSTAIN	Promoting fair trade and sustainable consumption in India
SPIN VCL	Sustainable product innovation in Vietnam, Cambodia, and Laos
VA3	Improving energy-efficiency and environmental performance of Chinese SMEs and large companies facilitated by voluntary public–private partnerships
Low energy housing (LEH)	LEH in Sichuan and Shenzhen, China — Enable and enforce energy efficient building construction
SC in urban China	Implementing sustainable consumption in civil society of urban China
REWIN	Improving resource efficiency for the production and recycling of electronic products by adoption of waste tracking system
EMAS Global China	Premium environmental management for companies in China
Greener Construction Project	Supporting a greener and more energy efficient construction industry in Mongolia

(Continued)

Table 4.1: (*Continued*)

Project Short Titles	Project Official Titles
ACIDLOOP	SP through market penetration of closed loop technologies in the metal finishing industry
Micro-, Small-, and Medium-sized enterprise (MSME) Clusters	Scaling up sustainable development of MSME clusters in India
Tourism in Bhutan	Sustainable tourism in Bhutan: An integrated approach to production, consumption, and livelihood development
SEID	Sustainable & efficient industrial development (SEID) — Bhutan and Nepal
SPRING/Cotton production	Sustainable cotton production in Pakistan's cotton ginning SMEs
Lead Elimination Project	Lead paint elimination project
Waste to Energy in Rice Milling Sector	Waste to energy for the rice milling sector in Cambodia
Automotive SCCM (Thai Automotive)	Greening supply chains in the Thai auto and automotive parts industries
Get Green Vietnam	Get Green Vietnam — Sustainable living and working in Vietnam
Soybean processing	Scaling SCP in the soybean processing industry in Indonesia

engagement and policy development. Newly added impact areas are green finance, climate benefits, and Europe–Asia cooperation. The additional impact areas reflect a deeper focus in promoting project sustainability beyond the project's lifetime, climate change mitigation fully embedded in project activities, and new partnerships and relationships between European and Asian stakeholders that are facilitated by the SWITCH-Asia projects. However, these new themes only came in the second phase of the SWITCH-Asia Programme. Understandably, it is a challenge to collect information from projects that have already been completed. The following sections are thus based on the information made available by the grant projects.

In the following sections, these eight areas of impacts will be discussed in more detail, based on the information provided by 43 SWITCH-Asia

Table 4.2: Summary of type of impacts and results achieved based on SWITCH-Asia impact sheet categories

Type of Impact	Results Achieved
Economic impacts	The projects facilitated the creation of monetary value via various measures, e.g., sales of cleaner technology, new potential money saving at the SME level. SCP has provided new ways of doing business and options for sales/income generation, which in turn contribute to market development. New, or more sustainable, products and services not only help developing the market, but also provide alternatives for consumers. The projects contributed to new business linkages between SMEs and retailers/buyers. Reportedly, some projects have contributed to job creation, improved productivity, and increased income for the workers in SMEs.
Environmental impacts	The projects helped improve resource efficiency in SMEs' production processes and reduced pollution by introducing and implementing cleaner production, waste management, and the use of environment-friendly materials. Project-introduced labels, standards and certifications also contribute to reduced environmental pollution.
Social impacts	The projects contributed to better working conditions for workers in SMEs, improved livelihoods for communities, and increased awareness of SCP among target groups and beneficiaries, which support future behavioural shifts towards sustainable lifestyles.
Climate benefits	Through the introduction of SCP practices, SMEs now have both the knowledge and capacity to reduce their carbon footprint and to increase energy efficiency in their production.
Access to green finance	New financing schemes for SMEs were identified and facilitated by the projects. However, frequently SMEs still struggle to obtain financing for SCP-related investment since they lack bankable collateral. SME access to green finance still requires more attention.
Policy impacts	Despite the fact that most projects engaged with policy makers/ governments, there is still limited evidence of governments taking up policy recommendations prepared by the projects. Engagement with policy makers could still be improved. SCP policy implementation is largely beyond the scope of individual grant projects.

(*Continued*)

Table 4.2: (*Continued*)

Type of Impact	Results Achieved
Target group engagement	Most projects worked extensively with SMEs, business associations, financial institutions, and consumer organisations, as well as with universities and research institutes, bringing awareness of SCP to thousands of individuals. Some 29,000 SMEs have been reached so far by the projects.
Europe–Asia partnerships	Several projects successfully facilitated the signing of partnerships between European and Asian companies. Most projects reported co-organising events involving European and Asian experts/participants.

projects. It is important to keep in mind that the information reported by the projects emanated from different project stages. At the time of writing, most of the projects have been completed, while some were still being implemented or close to completion. The projects were resulted from the first, second and third SWITCH-Asia call for proposals between 2008 and 2011.

4.3.1 *Economic impacts*

In the following paragraph, we present a summary of the economic impacts achieved by 43 SWITCH-Asia projects. The information was collected from the impact sheets submitted by the projects to the SWITCH-Asia Network Facility during or after completion of their project activities. The SWITCH-Asia projects reported various economic impacts made during the project life, which can be grouped into eight categories as follows:

1. Monetary value created through the project.
2. Monetary savings, cost reductions due to resource efficiency measures, increased revenue, and increased competitiveness.
3. Increased sales.
4. New or more sustainable products or designs introduced to the market.
5. New business opportunities, market development.
6. Business linkages that improve the supply chain, e.g., trade fairs, new contracts signed.
7. New job creation, increased worker income.
8. Others, e.g., increased capacity of SMEs to expand businesses, reduced worker turnover.

The first two impacts might appear to overlap, but the SWITCH-Asia projects understood and achieved it differently. This partly indicates that the sector, industry, SMEs or even the projects were at different stages of development. A continuation of monitoring beyond the grant period could shed more light into the effectiveness of approaches or methodologies employed by the projects. Frequently project results are still in early stages of manifestation by the time the project contract ends. It is also important to note that one project can have more than one impact as listed above. Several projects provided figures reflecting the monetary value they have facilitated, while other projects reported money savings achieved by SMEs after implementing particular SCP measures. The *monetary value created* reflects increased sales of sustainable products, thus giving the SMEs more capital to enable their businesses to grow. With a slight difference, *monetary saving potential* comes from lowered costs of production as SMEs adopt, for example, more efficient technologies. Some projects further reported that the monetary saving potential has helped them increase the revenue and this, in turn, increased their competitiveness. Projects developing new or more sustainable products and designs reported increased sales by SMEs. Though not all green products and designs led to higher sales, SMEs were provided with new business opportunities. Due to the development of such products and designs, SME capacity was built where, in some cases, it enabled SMEs to enter new markets or introduced SMEs to better business practices that ultimately led to market development.

Due to the activities of SWITCH-Asia projects, i.e., building the technical and managerial capacity of SMEs, some projects eventually supported SMEs to reach out to local, regional or international buyers, creating new markets for the new products and designs. This was done by bringing SMEs and their products to (inter)national trade fairs, exhibitions or by facilitating new partnerships via memoranda of understanding (MoU) with bulk buyers and through newly-signed business contracts. Not only addressing company buyers, SWITCH-Asia projects also reached out to individual consumers via public awareness campaigns. In the end, all these efforts help to streamline the supply chain, e.g., from farmers, producers, suppliers, retailers up to consumers, making it more efficient and transparent.

The projects reportedly have facilitated the creation of new (green) jobs and increased workers' income. Since SMEs now have higher capabilities to enable their businesses to grow, it provides them with capacity to create new jobs for local communities, even to increase the welfare of their existing workers (increased income). Finally, we are confident to state that SWITCH-Asia projects have employed various SCP measures that help improve SMEs' profitability, for example by reducing staff turnover. This was mainly achieved by introducing and implementing international standards, such as occupational health and safety (OHS), environmental management and quality management in the SMEs' production floors.

Reported Economic Impacts in Numbers

Quantification of economic impacts is not straightforward as many of the savings, new value creation, and enhanced competitiveness only manifest themselves over time on the balance sheets of SMEs. In many cases, the reported monetary savings are calculations based on the estimates of SMEs or technical consultants, rather than the actual balance of expenditure and revenue of companies. The following figure provides an overview of how many projects reported specific economic results of their project activities (Figure 4.2).

More than half of the SWITCH-Asia projects have facilitated *monetary savings* resulting from an increased capacity of SMEs to produce more efficiently. However, only eight projects have provided detailed figures. The combined monetary savings of these projects reached about EUR 225 million. Four projects reported of *money created through project*

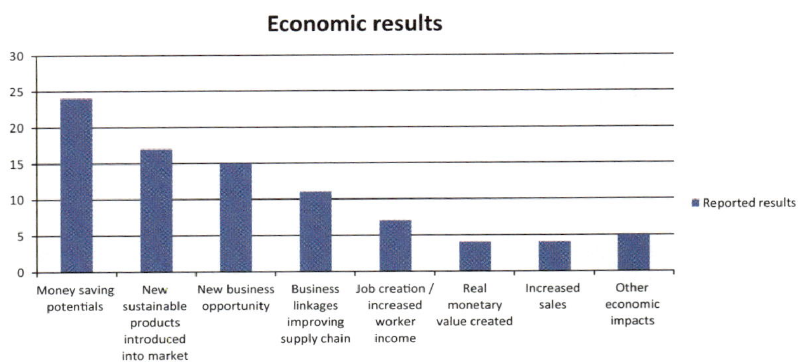

Figure 4.2: Economic results reported by 43 SWITCH-Asia projects [SWITCH-Asia Network Facility, 2015]

activities, totalling approximately EUR 15 million. An example is the "*MEET-Bis project*" in Vietnam. The technology suppliers involved in the project benefitted, with the total value of green products sold being EUR 2.43 million.

About two fifth of the projects reported *new/more sustainable products* as well as *new business opportunity* as economic impacts they have created, thus contributing to market development. The "*Eco-Jute*" project in West Bengal (India) and Bangladesh introduced eco-friendly jute, providing consumers with a better product alternative, and through this helped SMEs create sales of EUR 136,000 from selling eco-jute products. The "*ZCR*" project in the Philippines helped develop new markets for hotels and tourism operators by embracing more sustainable hospitality business practice.

Eleven projects reported *new business linkages* between producers and suppliers, or SMEs and buyers/retailers as an impact that makes the whole supply chain more lean and efficient. The "*Biomass-SP*" project in Malaysia established an improved biomass supply chain creating additional value of about EUR 0.22–0.66 million from the commercialisation of projects implemented by SMEs. The project also supported the creation of 11 new green biomass businesses and increased collaboration in bio charcoal production. It is no surprise that the project continues beyond its funding period. During a SWITCH-Asia conference in Jakarta on energy efficiency in July 2015, the "*Biomass-SP*" project manager reported that they continue to be actively involved in establishing the biomass industry in Malaysia and expect further growth, now with the support of the Malaysian government.

The "*SMART Cebu*" project in the Philippines and the "*LEH*" project in China addressed the upstream and downstream sides of the supply chain. Both projects linked supplier SMEs to retailers and large companies, and facilitated new business contracts to introduce sustainable products to the market. They also addressed consumers by engaging consumer organisations in their public awareness campaigns. Seven projects reported *new (green) job creation* as an achieved impact. This is followed by four projects reporting *increased sales* and five projects achieving *other impacts*, such as a reduced worker turnover and SME's increased capacity to expand businesses. Through the "*SUS TEX*" project in India, for example, textile SMEs developed more eco-friendly products and saw their sales increase by 40%.

4.3.2 *Environmental impacts*

In general, five environmental impacts can be identified from the 43 project impact sheets:

1. Improved resource efficiency (energy, water, raw materials).
2. Reduced pollution via waste management (e.g., reduced toxic materials).
3. Introduction of cleaner or more efficient technology.
4. Developed, applied or acquired environmental label, standards, or certification.
5. Use of eco-friendly materials (e.g., natural dyes) or introduction of eco-friendly products.

In line with the objective of the SWITCH-Asia Programme, the grant projects worked to bring about SP among SMEs. When there was no new technology involved, the projects provided capacity building to introduce *resource efficiency* measures in production processes. This is generally the first impact indicator cited by the projects. *Reducing pollution* is the second impact category often reported by SWITCH-Asia projects. This has been achieved by reducing the use of harmful materials in the production process that eventually reduces harmful discharge into water resources or reduces solid waste. Cleaner production measures and appropriate waste management helped SMEs to reduce material input, avoid waste, and also to recycle and reuse their generated waste.

Since many SWITCH-Asia projects worked to contribute to SP, resource efficiency was also achieved by introducing *cleaner or more efficient technologies*. Appropriate technology makes use of skills and technology that are available locally, an approach employed by "*ZCR*" project in the Philippines. Furthermore, in some cases, where the cost of technology acquisition was high, the projects worked with banks and financial institutions (FIs) to identify new potential financing schemes for SMEs. Introduction of international environmental *labels, standards, or certification* has been reported as a project impact. Some projects worked to help SMEs enter international markets where certain standards are required by customers, for example the Eco-Tex or Blue Angel labels. Other projects worked to develop customised standards that could be met as an intermediary step by SMEs with limited resources to comply with international label or standard requirements. Customisation was effected, for example, by adapting international standards to local contexts, such as ISO 26000 on Social Responsibility. The fifth most frequently cited environmental impact reported by the projects is the introduction of *eco-friendly materials* into SME production processes. This impact also covers projects that facilitated the introduction of new or more sustainable products to the market.

More than 60% of the projects reported *improved resource efficiency*, making it the most important reported impact from the projects. Several examples are as follows:

1. The "*SUS TEX*" project in India helped textile SMEs improve their resource efficiency by introducing water recycling and reuse. This approach now accounts for 85% of water use at the SMEs with fresh water consists only 15% of total usage.
2. The "*Eco-friendly Bamboo*" project in China reportedly had helped SMEs in Sichuan to increase their resource efficiency by reducing waste by 10–15%.
3. The "*Greening Sri Lankan Hotels*" project promoted the use of solar water heaters, key card switches, power factor correction, and LED lighting at the hotels to improve efficiency and to cut costs.
4. The "*AEMAS*" project, which was implemented in eight ASEAN countries, and "*China Motor Challenge*" project in China are two examples of how SMEs were supported in acquiring new technology to increase their production efficiency. In such cases, the projects also worked with banks and FIs to identify new potential financing schemes for SMEs. However, details of how successful these financing schemes are and how they work, are often not available.

Further, more than 50% of the projects reported *pollution reduction* as the next important impact. This was mainly achieved via implementing

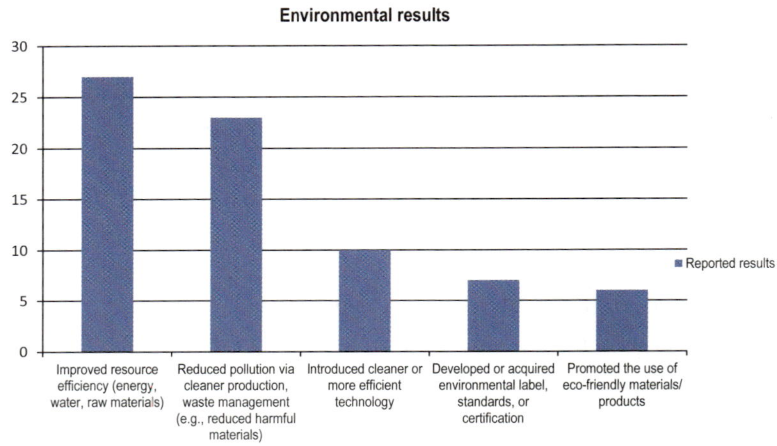

Figure 4.3: Environmental results reported by 43 SWITCH-Asia projects [SWITCH-Asia Network Facility, 2015]

cleaner production and waste management measures. Out of 27 projects reporting an *increased resource efficiency*, 17 projects reported that they achieved it by employing cleaner production or waste management, thus achieved *pollution reduction* (see Figure 4.3). Several examples are presented below to explain the cases.

The "*Sustainable Rattan*" project that was implemented in Cambodia, Laos, and Vietnam introduced cleaner production approach to SMEs, which included reducing diesel by 50%, chemicals by 20%, solid waste by 5–25%, and electricity by 5–10%. The "*GPIOS*" project in the Philippines worked to minimise the environmental impacts of SMEs in Metro Manila and the CALABARZON region. They engaged 95 companies, and then provided assessment and recommendations to improve the companies' environmental performance. The companies reportedly achieved hazardous chemical avoidance of up to 63% and solid waste avoidance of up to 76%, from the average baseline data of participating companies.

Further, 10 projects introduced, and in some cases helped to develop, new technologies contributing to cleaner production. The "*ACIDLOOP*" project in India worked to reduce resource consumption in the Indian metal finishing industries. Reported results include up to 90–95% fresh water use reduction by introducing appropriate rinsing technology and 95% drag-out reduction by appropriate technology use, such as changing surface tension of the solution, velocity of product withdrawal, and capture of lost plating solution/return to the bath.

The "*SEID*" project in Bhutan and Nepal worked with tourism and agri-business sectors, which are dominated by MSMEs. They trained local consultants to be SCP trainers that eventually provided each registered MSME with series of consulting programmes, including initial audits, technical investigation and recommendations through reports, in-house training, marketing of green products, and monitoring. Interventions for resource and energy saving, efficiency improvement, water and waste management, installation of better technical solutions, and higher standards of OHS resulted in cost savings, improved quality of services, and a cleaner and safer working environment.

Seven projects worked to reduce the environmental impacts of SMEs by "introducing or developing environmental labels, standards or certifications." As an example, the "*Tourism in Bhutan*" project sought to contribute to economic prosperity, poverty reduction, and climate change mitigation by promoting sustainable tourism development. To achieve the objectives, the project worked to adopt ISO 14046 (Environmental management — Water footprint — Principles, requirements, and guidelines) standards. Entities fulfilling the criteria will be certified, for example as a "Low Carbon Hotel" with the associated promotional benefits and brand creation, which results in premium returns. The *Lead Elimination* project implemented in Bangladesh, India, Indonesia, Philippines, Nepal, Sri Lanka, and Thailand, developed a local label and certification scheme for lead-free paints leading to reduction of hazardous waste and reduced lead contamination of users, in particular children.

Reportedly, six projects "used eco-friendly materials or introduced eco-friendly products to the market." The "*Clean Batik Initiative*" project in Indonesia and Malaysia is one of the examples. The project supported the *batik* producers (SMEs) to switch from chemical dyes to natural ones. While lowering the amount of chemical pollutants discharged into the environment, the SMEs were supported to use natural dyes, and in so doing produce more eco-friendly *batik* products. The "*SPIN VCL*" project implemented in Cambodia, Laos, and Vietnam built the capacities of

SMEs in the three countries to design innovative products that were environmentally friendly. About 570 new product lines had reportedly been developed while anticipating about 1,000 new or re-designed products. The project reported 10% material reduction per product and 5–10% packaging material reduction.

4.3.3 *Social impacts*

Despite not being the main focus, communities and marginalised groups are an integral part of many SWITCH-Asia projects. These projects' activities contribute to community development, gender equality, and worker protection. Depending on the type of project, SWITCH-Asia projects also work with consumer groups. Therefore, social impacts that are reported by the project can be grouped into three categories:

1. Improved working conditions via e.g., OHS implementation.
2. Improved communities' livelihood via, for example, lower electricity bills, formalising 'informal' workers, CSR, higher quality of life due to reduced pollution.
3. Increased awareness supporting behaviour change/increased capacity to implement SCP.

Even more than economic or environmental impacts, it is challenging to quantify social impact. This fact is evident from all project impact sheets. This difficulty results from the projects' relative short time period to measure social impacts that were just developing, as well as due to the SWITCH-Asia focus on SCP, i.e., producers and consumers and not primarily communities. From Figure 4.4, it can be derived that about half of the SWITCH-Asia projects report positive impacts for society.

Out of 43 impact sheets studied, about half reported that the projects have contributed to *improve working conditions* among the targeted SMEs. This was mainly achieved by introducing the concept of OHS via workshops and training. About one third of the projects reported, respectively, *improved livelihood* and *increased awareness that support a behaviour change* as other impacts created.

However, as convenient as this categorisation can be, it might not reflect the depth of impacts that SWITCH-Asia projects have made. Each

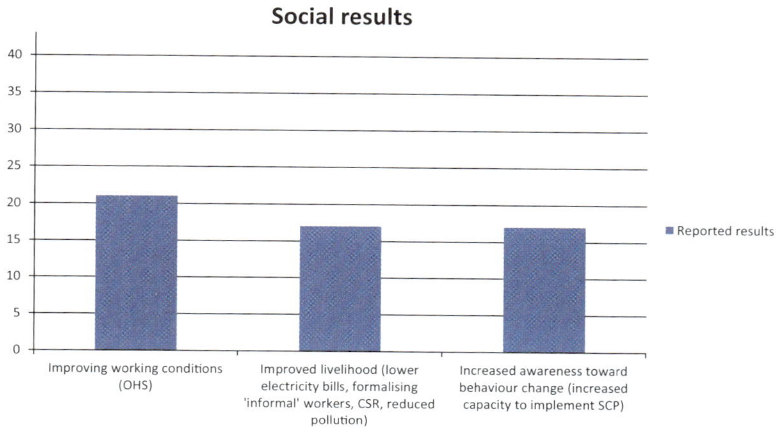

Figure 4.4: Social results reported by 43 SWITCH-Asia projects [SWITCH-Asia Network Facility, 2015]

of the projects is working with different community groups and active in different social contexts. The above categorisation is helpful to understand the bigger picture. It is advisable to approach the projects one by one to identify the social issues they have encountered and addressed.

The *WEEE-Recycle* project in India can be an example. The project has helped about 7,000 e-waste pickers to become formal, i.e., authorised by the government. This helped the marginalised populations and minorities working in e-waste sector. The *GetGreen Vietnam* project worked to bring about behaviour change in the country. To achieve this, they have worked with consumer organisations and companies in four cities, and created a pool of 1,000 change agents who will continue to spread the word and become examples of how sustainable living and working might benefit their peers.

4.3.4 *Climate benefits*

Since SCP aims to decouple economic growth from environmental degradation, climate change mitigation became increasingly relevant to SWITCH-Asia projects. This new impact "indicator" has been introduced in the second phase of SWITCH-Asia Programme in 2013 in order to consider specifically project activities contributing to climate benefits. Several already-completed projects did not report on climate benefits. Out

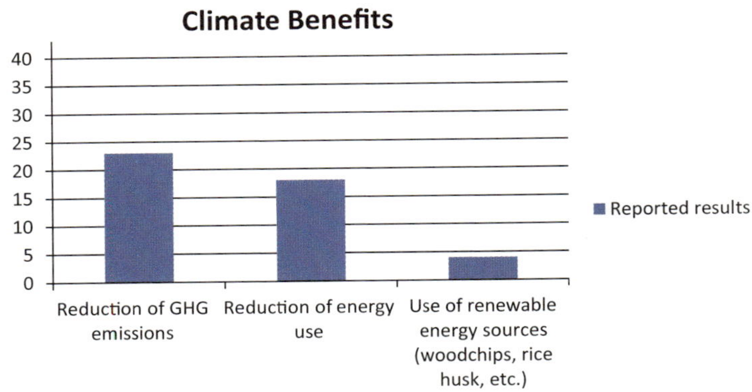

Figure 4.5: Climate benefits reported by 43 SWITCH-Asia projects [SWITCH-Asia Network Facility, 2015]

of 43 project impact sheets, 13 projects have not yet included climate benefits, leaving 30 projects to study in more detail.

Figure 4.5 indicates that about three-quarters of these 30 projects achieved greenhouse gas (GHG) emission reduction, directly as well as indirectly, through SCP measures they implemented in various sectors. Out of 23 projects reporting on GHG emission reduction, 18 projects provided a quantified data with six implementing two measures simultaneously, which are *GHG emission reduction* and *reduction of energy use*, showing a relation between both measures. Out of 30 projects, 16 projects reported *reduction of energy use* and four projects *use of renewable energy*.

Out of the 18 projects, 11 projects provided specific data on total CO_2 reduction achieved during the project's life, which is about 20.1 million tonnes CO_2 equivalent (CO_2e). Six projects reported CO_2 reduction per year, indicating larger potentials for reduction in the coming years. For one year, together those projects can achieve a reduction of approx. 5 million tonnes CO_2e. Two projects reported the potential of GHG emission reductions by individual SMEs per year. It is worth mentioning that one project could report of two or three quantified data simultaneously. For instance, the "*SMART Cebu*" project in the Philippines reported that one SME reached out to now can reduce its emissions by 7,900 kg/a. The "*Biomass-SP*" project in Malaysia has developed an exemplary model, where one SME has switched to woodchips as a substitute for fuel oil, consuming 2,100 tonnes of woodchips per month that reduces carbon emission of 16,000 tonnes CO_2e per year. All this is reflecting different measurement and reporting approaches used by the projects.

As mentioned previously, 16 projects reported *reduction of energy use* as a contribution made to mitigate climate change. However, only seven projects provided estimated figures, which together amounts to approx. 40 TWh. These data also show that sectors not directly related to energy or energy-intensive manufacturing can achieve emissions reductions. The "*Soybean Processing* (*SCOPE*)" project in Indonesia worked with tofu and tempeh cooperatives to promote energy-efficient technologies among small tofu and tempeh producers. Due to the high upfront cost of investment, the project created linkages with government programmes and FIs offering loans. Upon the completion of the project, it reported a GHG emission reduction of 83,200 tonnes per year as SMEs shifted from using firewood to more efficient combustion technologies using liquid petroleum gas (LPG). Using the new and cleaner technology, now SMEs can achieve about 27% energy efficiency that will lower their production costs.

4.3.5 *Green finance*

Similar to climate benefits reporting, the theme of 'green finance' was only introduced into SWITCH-Asia projects' impact sheets since 2013, to gain an overview of SME financing schemes employed. This is essential for the sustainability of SCP practice beyond a project's lifetime. It can be expected that projects under the fourth and fifth SWITCH-Asia call for proposals, those starting in 2013 and 2014, will address this aspect more specifically as it was integrated in their project design. It is known that 28 out of 43 projects have not yet included green finance in their reporting of impact sheets. Three projects were still being implemented until December 2015 at the time of the writing.

Ten projects reported their contribution to increasing access to finance, which was done by linking SMEs with FIs such as banks and leasing companies, and by identifying financing schemes under governmental programmes, e.g., national Five-Year Plan (FYP). Out of the 10 projects, three have facilitated SMEs to obtain loans from FIs, with seven projects identifying new financing schemes where SMEs can apply. The *SUSTEX* in India and LEH in China reported on SMEs acquiring government subsidies, with

SUSTEX leveraging about EUR 3.4 million. *LEH* leveraged a total of EUR 1 billion. The *Biomass-SP* project in Malaysia reportedly contributed to two SMEs obtaining soft loans from commercial banks, two SMES obtaining government grants, and assisting one SME to listing on the Kuala Lumpur Stock Exchange. *MSME Clusters* in India linked two foundry SMEs with the SIDBI Bank with financing agreements still to be made.

4.3.6 *Target group engagement*

SWITCH-Asia projects exclusively worked with micro, small and medium-sized enterprises in various sectors. Reportedly, about 29,000 SMEs had been engaged by the SWITCH-Asia projects during different stages of project implementation. Most of the SMEs were engaged via workshops or reached through their business associations or cooperatives that worked actively with the projects. Such workshops or training sessions were held to bring SCP into SMEs' awareness.

However, the core SMEs that were closely cooperating with the projects, are a much smaller number, ensuring the efficiency of support extended through project-contracted experts. However, there are a few projects whose activities were not directed at SMEs, such as "*AEMAS*", "*SuPP-Urb*", "*EMAS Global China*", and "*GetGreen Vietnam*". The "*AEMAS*" project, implemented in eight ASEAN countries, targeted energy managers rather than specific SMEs. "*SuPP-Urb*" in China targeted public procurement centres, while "*EMAS Global China*" targeted environmental consultants at companies. "*GetGreen Vietnam*" worked directly with consumers, bringing awareness of sustainable working and living directly to them (see also Chapter 13 for the project case study).

Depending on the industry and level of engagement, SWITCH-Asia projects generally have worked with:

1. business membership organisations (BMOs), providing access to SME-members,
2. policy makers and governments (various ministries) to obtain policy support,
3. FIs (banks, leasing companies), to identify potential financing schemes for SMEs,

4. academic institutions (universities), to support the projects with research and data,
5. retailers and consumer organisations, to create a demand for new or more sustainable products.

4.3.7 *Project contributions to SCP policy development*

The main objectives of the SWITCH-Asia projects have been the promotion of SCP practice among SMEs, practices that were to some extent new to the industries. In many cases, this required support from the governments. Frequently, conductive policy frameworks were lacking and, therefore, many projects engaged with policy makers and government agencies relevant to their industry sectors providing them with policy recommendations. Out of 43 projects, 36 projects reportedly have engaged local governments via workshops or policy dialogues. From these, eight projects succeeded in having their recommendations taken up by government departments to issue new policies, amend the existing ones or to be integrated into government's FYPs. Through this, the projects contributed their systematic knowledge of specific industry sectors and problem analyses, which were often not available to policy-makers without the SWITCH-Asia project, to evidence-based policy processes.

Several examples of new policy development facilitated by SWITCH-Asia project can be identified. The "*SUSTEX*" project in India submitted policy recommendations on OHS and Social Security of Artisans and Craft Workers that were adopted in India's 12 FYP for the handloom and handicraft sector. In the ASEAN region, the "*AEMAS*" project contributed in the amendments of existing Energy Efficiency and Conservation Laws in ASEAN countries. In the Philippines, the "*ZCR*" project contributed to policy changes with mandatory participation in the ZCR project for new resorts, hotels or any tourism-related establishment required to obtain strategic environmental plan (SEP) clearance in Palawan. The "*WEEE-Recycle*" project in India contributed to the e-waste management rules issued by the Ministry of Environment and Forest (MoEF).

These project approaches to policies have been complementary to the work undertaken by the Regional Policy Support Component (RPSC) and the National Policy Support Components (NPSC), which operate(d) in Malaysia, Indonesia, the Philippines, Thailand, and Sri Lanka.

4.3.8 *Evolving interrelationships in Europe–Asia cooperation*

In the SWITCH-Asia impact sheets, projects have been asked to describe how the cooperation models and relationships between the European and Asian partners have developed during the course of the project implementation and beyond. Several projects have reported ongoing cooperation with their former project partners after the SWITCH-Asia cooperation project completed. Furthermore, through SWITCH-Asia projects, organisations have become involved in cooperation activities with partners. However, these evolving and dynamic relations between the SWITCH-Asia stakeholders and external stakeholders have not yet been systematically analysed.

The SWITCH-Asia Programme, through its grant projects, has furthered cooperation between European and Asian policymakers, experts, businesses, and NGOs. Several projects reportedly have organised events involving experts and policy makers from both continents. However, information is still to be collected in the coming years of how this cooperation takes place, in what way and how it contributes to SCP take up in Asia.

Among the 13 projects that updated and submitted their impact sheets during 2014–2015, three projects showcased how they have furthered such policy maker cooperation. Reportedly, "*ZCR*" in the Philippines has facilitated the signing of five MoU between European and the Philippine organisations. The "*Biomass-SP*" project in Malaysia, not only facilitating the signing of three MoUs, in addition reported creating a potential EU-Asia project valued at EUR 440 million in Vietnam, and facilitated a partnership between a Malaysian company and the Danish Technology Institute (DTI). "*LEH*" in China reportedly has initiated 14 new partnerships between public and private stakeholders.

4.4 Lessons learnt and way forward for SWITCH-Asia impact

This intermediate impact evaluation of the SWITCH-Asia Programme and its grant projects is to be seen as work in progress. There are still several gaps and barriers some of which have been summarised in this chapter. Aggregating the grant projects' impacts into a programme impact is difficult as projects defined impacts in different ways and, therefore, use various methods to measure them. Much of the available evidence is anecdotal, but not systematic. Impact evaluation generally suffers from underinvestment of evaluation work and, to some degrees, this is also true for the SWITCH-Asia Programme. Evaluation of SWITCH-Asia projects and the programme as a whole, with all available data being made accessible is still underinvested. Furthermore, assessing impacts relating to sustainable consumption and lifestyle initiatives are not yet tailored in the project design, probably due to their complexity and the relative short period of time to identify and measure behavioural shifts. However, this should not hinder any attempt to look more systematically into these issues. The projects under the SWITCH-Asia Programme can, for example, cooperate with SMEs and access their sales data, reflecting a degree of sustainable consumption and change. However, SMEs often lack solid business records and do not have the resources for the establishment and provision of additional data. In the context of the SDGs, improved data from SMEs will be very important to measure progress towards achieving a number of goals, including clean water and sanitation (Goal 6), decent work and economic growth (Goal 8), SCP (Goal 12), and climate change (Goal 13).

The impact of SWITCH-Asia is being greater than the sum of its parts, which means the overall impact of the SWITCH-Asia Programme has more significance than the adding up the achievements of individual SWITCH-Asia projects. There are elements, which are almost impossible to quantify such as the spread of SCP knowledge among producers, and consumers that have been reached by projects via various events and media channels. Most importantly, SWITCH-Asia has contributed significantly to promoting awareness and understanding about the topic of SCP in Asian developing countries. Even stakeholders who have not been involved actively in the SWITCH-Asia Programme have benefitted, among others, from new product and service offers that came into existence via the projects.

Returning to the question we posed at the beginning of the chapter, whether the SWITCH-Asia Programme has achieved the goal of making consumption and production patterns more sustainable, the answer would definitely be yes. What the SWITCH-Asia Programme has not achieved is changing the current trend towards increased resource consumption in Asian countries. This means consumption and production patterns are still developing and unsustainable, resource consumption has not yet been decoupled from economic growth, and environmental impacts are worsening. However, the collaborative efforts of the four elements of the SWITCH-Asia Programme, i.e., grant projects, Network Facility, NPSC, and RPSC/UNEP, have created significant momentum for SCP in Asia. In addition to the measurable impacts reported by projects, the SWITCH-Asia Programme communication, advocacy, and outreach has been major factor in promoting SCP in Asia. As the SWITCH-Asia Programme continues in the second phase until 2020, this impact can be expected to increase.

References

Alkire, S. and Samman, E. (2014). Mobilising the household data required to progress toward the SDGs. Oxford Poverty & Human Development Initiative (OPHI). *OPHI WORKING PAPER* NO. 72.

IEAG (2014). A world that counts: Mobilising the data revolution for sustainable development. Independent Expert Advisory Group on a Data Revolution for Sustainable Development. November 2014.

Ravallion, M. (2008). Evaluating anti-poverty programs. In T. P. Schultz and J. Strauss (eds.), *Handbook of Development Economics*. North-Holland, Amsterdam, Vol. 4, pp. 3787–3845.

Savedoff, W. D., Levine, R. and Birdsall, N. (2006). When will we ever learn? Improving lives through impact evaluation. *Report of the Evaluation Gap Working Group*. Center for Global Development Washington, D.C.

SWITCH-Asia Network Facility (2008–2015). Project impact sheets. Available on: www.switch-asia.eu.

White, H. (2010). A contribution to current debates in impact evaluation. *Evaluation* 16(2), 153–164.

Williams, B. (2015). Prosaic or profound? The adoption of systems ideas by impact evaluation. *IDS Bulletin* 46(1), 7–16.

Part II:

Country Case Studies on Sustainable Consumption and Production in Asia

Chapter 5

SCP in Bangladesh: The Brown Hope of Hazaribagh and the Golden Fibre of Bangladesh

N. M. Esa Abrar Khan

5.1 Introduction

Bangladesh is a low-lying, riverine country located in south Asia with a largely marshy jungle coastline of 580 km on the northern littoral of the Bay of Bengal, formed by a delta plain at the confluence of the Ganges and Brahmaputra rivers and their tributaries. The total land area of 147,570 km^2 consists mostly of floodplains (almost 80%) leaving the major part of the country, with the exception of the North-western highlands, prone to flooding during the rainy season [Denissen, 2012]. Bangladesh's alluvial soil is highly fertile, but vulnerable to flood and drought. Hills rise above the plain only in the Chittagong region in the far Southeast and the Sylhet division in the Northeast. Straddling the Tropic of Cancer, Bangladesh has a tropical monsoon climate characterised by heavy seasonal rainfall, high temperatures, and high humidity.

Bangladeshi geography is varied and is characterised by two distinctive features: a broad deltaic plain subject to frequent flooding, and a small hilly region crossed by swiftly flowing rivers. Bangladesh is bordered on the West, North, and East by a 4,095 km land frontier with India and, in the Southeast, by a short land and water frontier (193 km) with Myanmar. On the South is a highly irregular deltaic coastline of about 580 km, fissured by many rivers and streams flowing into the Bay of Bengal. The territorial waters of Bangladesh extend 22 km, and the exclusive economic zone of the country is 370 km. As a low-lying country, it is vulnerable to flooding and cyclones and stands to be very badly affected by any rises in sea levels, storm surges, and salinity intrusion resulting from climate change [Mahmood, 2012].

Urbanisation in Bangladesh is proceeding rapidly. Cities in Bangladesh are already faced with the challenges of rapid population increase characterised by crises such as lack of economic dynamism, governance failures, severe infrastructure and service deficiencies, inadequate land administration, massive slums, and social breakdown [Hussain, 2013]. The areas around Dhaka and Comilla are the most densely settled. About 9% of the Bangladeshi population lives in the Dhaka metropolitan area, which contributes to 36% of the country's Gross Domestic Product (GDP). An additional 11% of the Bangladeshi GDP is generated by Chittagong, the second-largest city and home to 3% of the population [Hussain, 2013].

5.2 Industrial Pollution, Environmental Policies and SCP

The main thrust of industrialisation of Bangladesh began in 1971 following the country's independence, when a number of industrial plants were established in different areas of the country. Environmental issues were not considered seriously at that time, resulting in the present environmental condition of severe degradation [Hoque and Clark, 2013]. Urban centres like Dhaka City and Chittagong are major industrial hubs suffering from serious environmental pollution, which is creating major challenges to the city administrations. Environmental problems occur mainly due to population growth, urbanisation, industrialisation, rapid rise in transportation, inadequate and improper traffic management, poor sanitation systems, and inefficient solid waste management (SWM). Severe air, water, and noise pollution are threatening human health, ecosystems, and economic growth. Environmental degradation is also caused by poverty, overpopulation, and lack of awareness on the subject. It is manifested by deforestation, destruction of wetlands, soil erosion, and natural calamities.

The main industrial areas of Bangladesh are in Dhaka, Chittagong, Khulna, and Bogra districts and the most contributing industries for water pollution are pulp and paper, pharmaceuticals, metal processing, food industry, fertiliser, pesticides, dyeing and painting, textiles, and tannery. More than 200 rivers directly or indirectly receive a large quantity of untreated industrial waste and effluent. The Department of Environment (DOE) has listed 1,176 factories that cause pollution throughout the country, many of them tanneries located in Dhaka [Alam, 2009]. Furthermore, the indiscriminate discharge of solid waste and domestic and hospital sewage is the major source of water pollution. This solid waste is associated with problems of littering on roads, spilling around bins, clogging of drains, and indiscriminate dumping on vacant plots and causes serious environmental pollution impacting public health.

In order to promote environmental consciousness and halt further ecological degradation, the National Environment Policy was issued in 1992 as a guide to long-term sustainable and environment friendly development and outlined the following objectives:

1. Preservation and improvement of the ecological balance;
2. Identifying and controlling all environment polluting and degrading activities;
3. Minimising the impact of natural disasters on the environment;
4. Ensuring environment friendly development in all sectors;
5. Ensuring long-term sustainable/environmentally sound utilisation of natural resources; and
6. Active promotion and participation in all international initiatives for the improvement of the global/regional environment [The Fourth Five Year Plan, 1990–1995].

In 1995, the National Environment Management Action Plan (NEMAP) was issued, focusing on additional environmental issues in Bangladesh. The NEMAP proposes actions to align with the international sustainable development agenda that resulted from the Rio Summit in

1992, created by the Ministry of Environment and Forest (MOEF). NEMAP puts particular emphasis on the participation of people in its implementation and monitoring. The objectives were to identify the key environmental issues of Bangladesh, and the actions required to halt or reduce the rate of environmental degradation. The increase in industrial activities, such as textiles and tanneries, and the establishment of new industries, such as electronic component manufacture, are regarded as key issues [Ministry of Environment and Forest, 1995].

Furthermore, the Bangladesh Environmental Conservation Act (BECA) was passed in 1995, and with the accompanying 1997 Rules, are arguably the most important legislative documents for industrial water pollution. The Act is dedicated to the "conservation, improvement of quality standards, and control through mitigation of pollution of the environment" [Bangladesh Environmental Conservation Act, 1995]. The 1997 Environment Conservation Rules, made in accordance with the 1995 Act, provide additional guidance for specific components of the Act.

Industrial pollution has since worsened and become a major area of public policy concern in Bangladesh. Despite the NEMAP and the Environmental Conservation Act, controlling the quantity of industrial effluents and waste discharges that have adverse environmental impacts, especially regarding water pollution has proved difficult. According to Aminuzzaman [2010], Bangladesh's environmental policy can still be considered to be a good foundation to bring about necessary changes to address and mitigate the major challenges of pollution. What is required is a broad-based consensus among various stakeholders as well as the political will to implement the existing policies. Furthermore, modifications to existing frameworks are necessary, not only to reflect the latest international developments resulting from the Sustainable Development Goals (SDGs), but also to take a new and more sustainable path instead of pursuing business as usual. Embracing sustainable consumption and production (SCP) as a guiding principle could significantly contribute to a more environmentally friendly and healthy society and contribute to the country's economic growth and development.

It is therefore imperative to switch to SCP, to make the necessary changes to social, economic, and environmental systems and approaches in order to overcome the crises that Bangladesh now faces, which are mounting. To achieve this, a collective conscious decision to develop a sustainability transition approach is crucial. An example of such collective action is the *Blueprint for European SCP* [EEB, 2009], which was produced through collaboration between environmental and social non-governmental organisations (NGOs) and the research community. In sustainable production, Bangladesh needs to identify priority areas and objectives, beyond climate change and energy, while at the same time it needs to prioritise sustainable consumption for the country's development. This is not an easy task, but essential. For European companies and consumers, the transition to SCP patterns must mean more than just enabling consumers to buy products that are a little bit greener, but to take more active responsibility for the way products are produced in Bangladesh and other developing countries.

5.3 The Role of SMEs in Bangladesh's Economy

Bangladesh, as a growing exporter of primary goods, has been included as one of the "Next Eleven" of developing countries with the potential for serious foreign-investment-led growth [Eghbal, 2008]. Between 2004 and 2014, Bangladesh averaged a GDP growth rate of 6% and, according to a recent poll, Bangladesh has the second most pro-capitalist population in the developing world with 80% of the population supporting free market development [Dhaka Tribune, 2014]. The economy is increasingly led by export-oriented industrialisation.

For the Bangladeshi economy, the textile industry plays a vital role, being the second largest in the world. Other key sectors include pharmaceuticals, shipbuilding, ceramics, leather goods, and electronics. Being located in one of the most fertile regions on Earth, agriculture plays a crucial role, with the principal cash crops including rice, jute, tea, wheat, cotton, and sugar cane. The Bangladeshi telecoms industry has witnessed rapid growth over the years and is dominated by foreign investors. The government has emphasised the development of software services and hi-tech industries under the Digital Bangladesh scheme.

Bangladesh has substantial reserves of natural gas and coal; many international oil companies are involved in production and exploration activities in the Bay of Bengal. Regional neighbours are keen to use

Bangladeshi ports and railways for trans-shipment. Located at the crossroads of SAARC, the ASEAN+3, BIMSTEC, and the Indian Ocean, Bangladesh has the potential to emerge as a regional economic and logistics hub [Chowdhury, 2013; Rahmatullah, 2013].

In 2015, Bangladesh's per-capita annual income stood at EUR 1,185 [The Daily Star, 2015]. Accelerating growth and reducing poverty, and reducing income inequality and regional disparity continue to be the overarching goals of the current development paradigm in Bangladesh. The main strategy for achieving these goals include the creation of productive employment in the manufacturing and organised service sector, and the withdrawal of the labour force from the low-skilled and low-return agricultural sector and informal activities. The development of small- and medium-sized enterprises (SMEs) is envisaged as a key element in this development strategy [Bakht and Bashar, 2015]. According to Abdin [2012], there are about 6 million SMEs in the country constituting about 90% of all industrial units, which generate about 25% of the national GDP. SMEs employ about 31 million people and provide 75% of household income. Various categories of SMEs together contribute between 80 and 85% of industrial employment and 23% of total civilian employment in Bangladesh. The most promising SME industries and sectors are electronics, light engineering, plastic goods, leather goods and footwear, agro-processing, fashion design, knitwear and ready-made garments, pharmaceuticals, jute and jute goods, handicrafts, frozen fish, ceramics, and furniture. For the first time in 2010, the country's National Industrial Policy defined SMEs uniformly with numbers of employment and replacement cost indicators (see Table 5.1).

Table 5.1: Bangladesh SME definition [Abdin, 2012]

Category	**Small**	**Medium**	**Indicators**
Manufacturing	50–100 million	100–300 million	Replacement cost (in BDT)
	25–99	100–250	No. of workers
Service	5–10 million	10–150 million	Replacement cost
	10–25	50–100	No. of workers

According to the survey of manufacturing industries carried out by the Bangladesh Bureau of Statistics [cf. Bakht and Bashar, 2015], the manufacturing sector of Bangladesh with 10 or more workers had the following size distribution in 2010–2011 (see Table 5.2).

The survey results show that SMEs are an important element of economic growth and, considering the population of Bangladesh, SMEs offer large-scale employment and income-earning opportunities at relatively low costs, especially in the rural areas. Prime Minister Sheikh Hasina, who took pragmatic measures to boost SME development, has recognised the significance of the SMEs as source of new business creation and employment generation. The government's three-pronged programme has supported SMEs' technological innovation, provided banking support and market coordination, and thereby created new opportunities for SMEs to grow [Afzal, 2011] .

The EU-funded SWITCH-Asia Programme also recognises the roles of SMEs especially in establishing SCP patterns in Bangladesh. By equipping SMEs with new skills through capacity building, the SWITCH-Asia projects not only support them to grow economically, but also sustainably (see Table 5.3 for a list of SWITCH-Asia projects implemented in Bangladesh).

5.4 Bangladesh's Leather and Tanning Industry

The tanning industry is an old manufacturing sub-sector in Bangladesh with a long heritage of over six decades. There are at present about 240 tanneries operating in the country, 200 of them are concentrated in Dhaka. From the very beginning of industrialisation in Bangladesh, tanning industries have been playing a significant role in the country's economy. In international markets, its leather products have been earning Bangladesh significant amounts of foreign currency. Also domestically, it is lucrative business and the leather industry has a significant contribution on the economy and GDP. Due to the relatively inexpensive cost of labour and materials, over half the world's tanning activity now occurs in low and middle-income countries (MICS) including Bangladesh. Between 1970 and 1995, the percentage of low to MICS contributing to the global production of light leather increased from 35 to 56% and from 26 to 56%

Table 5.2: Size distribution of manufacturing establishments with 10 or more workers, 2010–2011

Description	**Micro (10–24 Workers)**	**Small (25–99 Workers)**	**Medium (100–249 Workers)**	**Large (250 or More Workers)**	**Total**
No. of establishments	17,384 (40.6)	15,666 (36.6)	6,105 (14.3)	3,639 (8.5)	42,792 (100)
Total persons engaged	271,644 (5.4)	738,801 (14.7)	1,041,220 (20.8)	2,964,272 (59.1)	5,015,936 (100)
Gross value added (million BDT)	92,092 (5.9)	369,974 (23.7)	363,646 (23.3)	737,235 (47.2)	1,562,947 (100)
Value added per worker (thousand BDT)	339	501	349	249	312

Source: Bangladesh Bureau of Statistics [cf. Bakht and Bashar, 2015].

Table 5.3: List of SWITCH-Asia projects implemented in Bangladesh

Name of Project	Period	Main Implementing Organisation	Places of Implementation	SCP Practice	Brief Description of Objectives or Impact
Re-Tie Bangladesh	2009–2012	sequa GmbH, Germany	Bangladesh	Cleaner production	To support leather SMEs to work more economically and ecologically and to be more sutainable with the use of aligned technologies and practices
Eco-Jute	2010–2014	Traidcraft Exchange, UK	Bangladesh, India	Sustainable value chain	To promote economic prosperity and reduce poverty in Bangladesh and India by encouraging a switch to more environmentally sustainable practices in the jute industry; and promote SCP of eco-friendly jute diversified products (JDPs) in Bangladesh and West Bengal, India
Jute diversified products	2013–2016	CARE, France	Bangladesh	Sustainable value chain	To contribute to pro-poor economic growth through social business promotion with an emphasis on sustainable agriculture sector growth and poverty reduction in Bangladesh; and to strengthen the export competitiveness of Bangladesh through promotion of environment friendly jute diversified products

(Continued)

Table 5.3: (*Continued*)

Name of Project	Period	Main Implementing Organisation	Places of Implementation	SCP Practice	Brief Description of Objectives or Impact
ECOLEBAN	2014–2018	Fundación Tecnalia Research and Innovation, Spain	Bangladesh	Resource efficiency, eco-labelling	To promote resource efficiency and sustainability of the leather sector in Bangladesh throughout the whole value chain of the leather related products such as footwear and other leather goods
Tomato and mango value chain (TMVC)	2016–2019	SNV the Netherlands	Bangladesh	Sustainable consumption, inclusive business	To contribute to greater consumer confidence in domestically produced processed horticultural products, reduced food safety incidences in the domestically processed horticultural products, inclusive business development in the fruit and vegetable processing industry
METABUILD	2016–2020	The Energy and Resources Institute (TERI), India	Bangladesh, Nepal, Sri Lanka	Resource efficiency and cleaner production (RECP)	To implement sustainable production processes and practices in 400 SMEs and to create a conducive environment for further adoption of sustainable production processes in the metal products supply chain for the building and construction sector
Bangladesh Sustainable Building	2016–2020	Oxfam, UK	Bangladesh	Sustainable building	To contribute to a reduction in GHG emissions, deforestation and land degradation in Bangladesh; and promote sustainable and eco-friendly building materials and practices within an enabling policy environment

for the production of heavy leather materials [Jenkins, Barton, and Hesselberg, 2004].

The Government of Bangladesh has identified the leather sector as one with considerable growth and investment potential, ranking fifth in the export sector. Currently, Bangladesh produces and exports quality bovine and ovine, caprine (buffalo and cow, sheep and goat) leathers that have a good international reputation for fine textured skins. Tanneries in Bangladesh produce more than 16 million m^2 of hides and skins per year. In addition, there are about 30 modern shoe manufacturing plants engaged in the production of high-quality footwear, with over 2,500 smaller footwear manufacturers. The sector employs approximately 558,000 people directly.

Bangladesh's leather sector is deemed competitive because of its low labour cost differentiation, local availability of hides and a favourable business environment. This is complemented by the existence of organisations and institutional arrangements like the Export Processing Zone (EPZ) and duty free access to major international markets. Leather manufactured from these places is shipped to the US, Europe, and other parts of the world for further processing. According to the footwear sub-sector of Bangladesh in 2010–2011 earned revenues in excess of USD 250 million. The European Union (EU) is the biggest destination for footwear exports with a 60% share, followed by Japan with 30%, and the rest of the world accounting for 10%. The BECA of 1995, and the accompanying 1997 Rules, contain specifications of waste discharge quality standards for all industrial units [Clemett, 2004], including the leather and tannery sector (see Table 5.4).

Among all industrial wastes, tannery effluents are ranked among the pollutants with the highest toxicity and impact on environment and human health [Shen, 1999]. According to a study conducted by Blacksmith Institute [2010], roughly 75% of chromium-polluted sites are located in South Asia and of these, nearly a third are associated with tannery operations, with mining, and metallurgy sites also contributing significantly. The high concentration of chromium sites in South Asia is primarily due to the abundance of tanneries in the region, including in Bangladesh. As many of the tanneries have very poor environmental controls and very few factories provide treatment facilities [Blacksmith Institute, 2010], the tanning industry is known to cause horrendous environmental pollution.

Table 5.4: Emission standards for tanneries according to the BECA and Rules [Clemett, 2004]

Parameter	Limit
Total suspended solids	150 mg/L
BOD5 20°C	100 mg/L
Sulphide as S molecule	1 mg/L
Total chromium as Cr molecule	2 mg/L
Oil and grease	10 mg/L
Total soluble solids	2,100 mg/L
Wastewater flow	30 m^3/tonne processed leather
pH	6.5 to 9

The high environmental impact of tannery effluents makes its treatment an essential fact, mainly due to its volume, nature, and the concentration of pollutants such as tanning agents (chromium and tannin), colour, organic matter, and others. It has been reported by UNIDO that only about 20% of the large number of chemicals used in the tanning process is absorbed by leather, the rest is released as waste [UNIDO, 2005]. Furthermore, discharged chemicals from the larger factories are often being re-used by the small factories, a practice unsafe for both the environment and tannery workers. Furthermore, tanneries produce other waste and by-products. To make value added products, a by-product manufacturing unit (chrome and protein recovery), and energy generation could be useful options. The industry in Bangladesh as a whole faces considerable concerns with regard to end-of-life, recycling, and reuse of leather and leather products.

Around 40 heavy metals and acids are used for processing raw hides [UNIDO, 2005] including chromium, a heavy metal that can exist in air, water, soil, and food. Common exposure pathways of chromium include ingestion, inhalation, and dermal contact. The primary health impacts from chromium, which is known to be carcinogenic, are damaging to the gastrointestinal, respiratory, and immunological systems, as well as reproductive and developmental problems. In addition, the chromium-laced solid waste from tanneries is often converted into poultry feed as is the case in areas of Bangladesh, which can further impact livestock and humans [Hossain, 2007]. Very few export-oriented factories use safety equipment to protect their workers, where others do not pay attention to their worker's health and safety. Jaundice, nausea, and headaches are workers' common sickness. According to the World Health Organisation (WHO), over 8,000 workers in tanneries have gastrointestinal, dermatological, and other diseases, and 90% of this population will die before the age of 50 [Maurice, 2001]. With the current trend of more focus towards ethical manufacturing processes, many countries and consumers are concerned about the way in which their products are being manufactured. The European Commission has considered an import ban on leather or leather goods to European countries from Bangladesh for several years, in particular concerning tanneries in the area of Hazaribagh, due to its unsafe manufacturing processes [Tremblay, 2009]. Therefore, there is strong pressure on the industry to lower the pollution level to protect the environment and natural resources. This will require SCP practices and improvements in the tanneries' daily operations. A case study from the EU-funded SWITCH-Asia project, introducing sustainable production to the leather industry in Bangladesh, is described in Box 5.1.

Box 5.1 SWITCH-Asia case study: Reduction of environmental threats and increase the exportability of Bangladeshi leather products (Re-Tie)

The SWITCH-Asia "Re-Tie Bangladesh" project worked with SME tanneries in Bangladesh, including Hazaribagh, to address the issues of water pollution and threats to environment and human health. The project was implemented from February 2009 until November 2012, by a consortium consisting of sequa (Germany), the United Nations Industrial Development Organisation (UNIDO), the Training and Development Centers of the Bavarian Employers' Associations (bfz) (Germany), the Dhaka Chamber of Commerce and Industry, and the Bangladesh Finished Leather, Leather goods, and Footwear Exporter's Association.

The approach of the project was to provide incentives for SMEs to adopt cleaner production practices, which are tantamount to increased exportability of products, due not only to cost reductions but eventually as a consequence of institutionalised sustainable production and compliance with international

(Continued)

Box 5.1 (*Continued*)

environmental standards. The activities of the project included more than 30 training sessions, workshops, and conferences, attended by more than 1,000 participants, on the efficient use of resources and significant reduction of pollution/waste. Furthermore, exportability through improved occupational health and safety (OHS), corporate social responsibility (CSR), and other international standards were part of the training. In addition, 15 national experts on cleaner production in the areas of water, energy, chemicals, and OHS were trained to continue with further training after the project completion.

Twelve pilot tanneries participated directly and more than 50 were frequently involved. With project intervention in the participating companies, the level of chemical and biological oxygen demand (COD/BOD) could be reduced by 30%, water consumption by 30–50%, and chrome content by 60%. Application of cleaner production practices were facilitated by the trained local experts and supervised by international experts. The specific measures implemented included: hair-saving unhairing processes, solar water heating, full-scale chrome management, strict water management systems, float recycling, segregation of streams, segregation of solid waste, avoidance and monitoring of banned/hazardous substances, desalting of wet salted hides and skins, non-ammonium salt deliming, low-energy drying, and water-based finishing. Technical assistance was provided to influence the cleaner production-relevant physical infrastructure of the new industrial site for the leather industry in Savar.

Business membership organisations (BMOs) in the Bangladesh leather sector have proven capable to promote SCP matters at both the policy and membership levels. These BMOs played a key role in disseminating information and in consolidating the political dialogue between the private sector and public stakeholders. This approach helped to identify and define the specific needs of the companies and solutions to implement cleaner production practices. The project also involved national and local policy-makers as much as possible and worked directly with government departments relevant to the sector. Its recommendations concerning the physical infrastructure of the new tannery development at Savar, North of Dakar, were acknowledged by the Government of Bangladesh. The Ministry of Industries requested more detailed project recommendations, for example regarding SWM.

More information about the project is available from: http://www.switch-asia.eu/projects/re-tie-bangladesh/.

5.5 Case Study: Hazaribagh Tannery Area — The Brownfield

The tanneries of Hazaribagh started their journey from 1960, first introduced by Punjabi traders from what was then Pakistan. The industries expanded and after the independence of Bangladesh in 1971, when the government took over the tanneries abandoned by the departing non-Bengali entrepreneurs, eventually becoming a 'cash cow' to earn foreign currencies. Hazaribagh is the largest tannery region in Bangladesh, consisting of more than 200 tanneries which dump 22,000 cubic litres of toxic waste each day into Dhaka's main river, including the cancer-causing toxin hexavalent chromium [Walsh, 2013].

The direct discharge of this waste has contaminated the ground and surface water with dangerously high concentrations of chromium, as well as cadmium, arsenic, and lead. The contamination of rivers also allows these pollutants to accumulate in common fish and shellfish species, which are used as local food sources. The dumping of untreated liquid tannery waste from tannery industries at Hazaribagh is the major source of pollution of the Buriganga River for the last 45 years. Statistics available from the DOE reveal that 95% of tannery industries have been built in an unplanned way during the last 50 years without environmental impact assessments in congested areas of Hazaribagh. In addition, the area is inhabited by low and middle income settlers without adequate urban facilities. As a solution to the problem, a tannery estate has been set up in Savar and Keraniganj on 199.40 acres of land to shift the Hazaribagh tanneries. The shift has been planned since 2003, but has been delayed many years due to petitions by industry associations. At the time of writing, a new deadline has been set for June 2016. According to Industries Minister Amir Hossain Amu, the government will shut down the tanneries at Hazaribagh in Dhaka if they are not shifted to the Savar Tannery Estate in time [The Daily Star, 2015].

5.5.1 *The challenge: Redevelopment of Hazaribagh into a livable community*

In 1992, the Environmental Protection Agency (EPA) of United States coined the term "brownfield" to describe an idle or abandoned area which was previously used for industrial or commercial activities that cause environmental pollution. The Hazaribagh area, near Dhanmondi in the heart of Dhaka, experiences a similar situation and can be categorised as brownfield, property where expansion, redevelopment, or reuse will be complicated due to the presence of potentially harmful substances causing pollution. Covering an area of 25 ha, the Hazaribagh tannery area harbours one of the most toxic tannery industries amid residential quarters in the south region of Dhaka towards Nilambar Shaha Road. Furthermore, the urbanisation pattern in Hazaribagh has evolved organically rather than being imposed, if one compares its growth with adjacent areas (Figure 5.1).

The area comprised of Hazaribagh tanneries and adjacent residential areas totals 3.94 km^2. This parcel of land is connected to other parts of Dhaka through some major arterial roads, and to the west where it is bounded by an embankment built in the late 1980s for flood protection. Dhaka and the area beyond this embankment is a flood plain of the Buriganga River. More than 0.2 million people live adjacent to the tannery complex and 20,000 people have been directly exposed to the tannery-related hazards. Effluents from all factories contain significant amounts of heavy metals, especially chromium (374.19 ppm on average) [Asaduzzaman *et al.*, 2014], which poses a health hazard to workers and residents. The residential part of Dhaka consists predominantly of medium-rise buildings with narrow setback spaces in between used for pedestrian movement. The industrial area has covered large chunks of plots where the majority of buildings are temporary structures with very few permanent. Within a mixed use and commercial development, schools, mosques, small and medium trades like fruit shops, barber and tailoring shops, tea stalls on the side of the streets, and *kacha* bazaars are prominent (see Figure 5.2).

The Hazaribagh area has a scarcity of green and open spaces. Most of the open spaces are covered with industrial facilities or have been used as waste dumping grounds. Therefore, most of the open and green spaces will need to undergo site remediation when the relocation or closure of Hazaribagh tanneries is completed. The condition of water bodies (lagoons, ponds, and lakes) in Hazaribagh is critical due to waste streams from tanneries. The North–South canal, which runs parallel to the flood

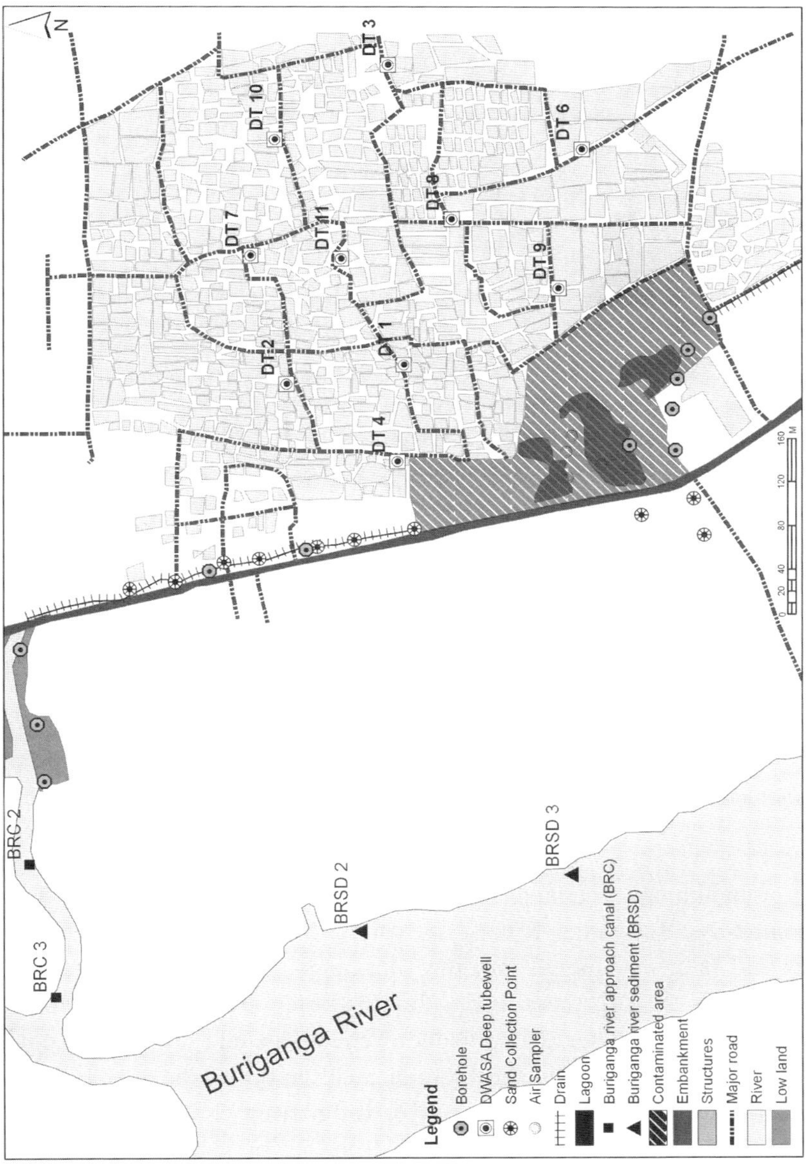

Figure 5.1: The Hazaribagh tannery area

Source: Author's own work using Google Maps.

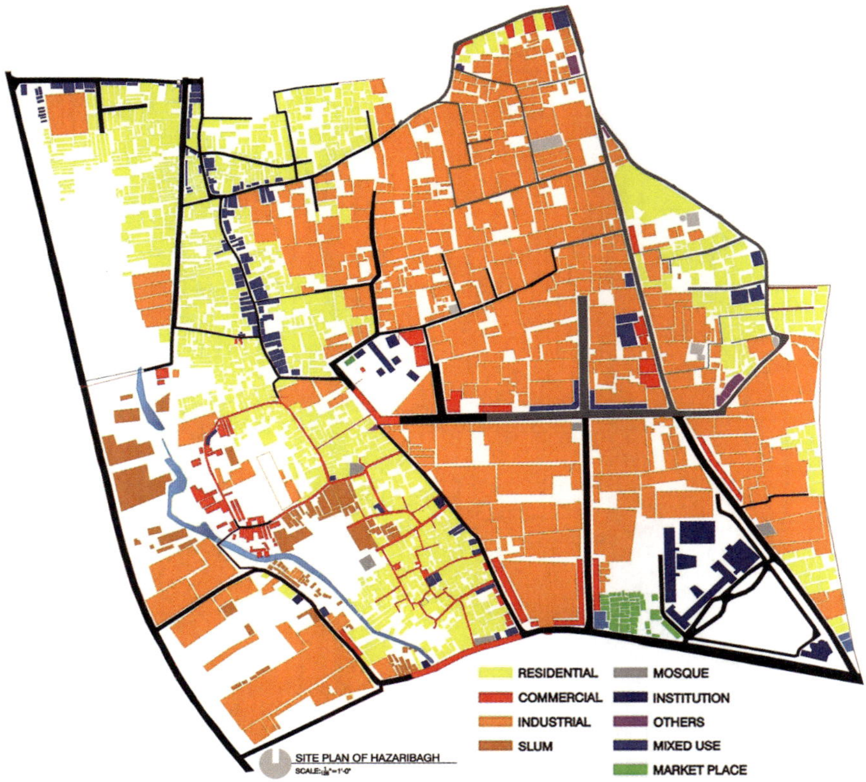

Figure 5.2: Existing land use pattern of the Hazaribagh area
Source: The Capital Development Authority of Bangladesh (RAJUK).

control embankment, is connected to the tannery runoff for ultimate discharge into the Buriganga River. The effluent is temporarily stored in lagoons and later discharged into the Buriganga River via a sluice gate [Bhuiyan *et al.*, 2010]. According to Bangladesh's DOE, toxins are also leaching into groundwater. The poisonous chemicals end up forming coloured ponds and lakes in the residential areas harming the people who work and live in the district. Most people suffer from chronic respiratory problems, skin diseases, and even destruction of the nasal septum [Lanteigne, 2010].

Despite the contamination and polluted sites, the Hazaribagh neighbourhoods are characterised by social homogeneity and tightly knit patterns of primary relationships. Thus, the linear *mahalla* (neighbourhood) represents a strong sense of neighbourly relations due to the same occupation, ethnicity, and caste and creates social cohesiveness within the members. It is projected that the total density of the area will increase up to 420 persons per acre in 2015, from 310 persons per acre in 2007. At a glance, the settlement pattern of Hazaribagh may look chaotic and lack order, but behind the chaos exist community structures and a contextual basis of Hazaribagh settlements of old heritage buildings, which characterise a neighbourhood and the social life it contains. Once the tanneries have completely relocated, a new chapter for Hazaribagh can begin.

5.6 Bangladesh's Jute Manufacturing Sector

In contrast to the polluting tannery sector, Bangladesh's jute manufacturing sector is one of the oldest traditional and sustainable manufacturing sectors of the country. The sector has witnessed and experienced fluctuating fortunes. In the 1960s and 1970s, the jute sector was considered the mainstay of the manufacturing industry, because of its significant contribution to the national income, export earnings, and industrial employment. Today, it is a major cash crop for over three million small farm households, the largest industry, producing about one-third of manufacturing output, and the largest agricultural national export commodity. The livelihood of some 25 million people is dependent on jute-related activities in agriculture, domestic marketing, jute production, retting, drying and marketing, manufacturing, and trade [Ullah, 2015].

Jute and allied fibres are the second most important natural fibres next to cotton. The increasing worldwide awareness of sustainability issues has created new opportunities for jute as a renewable resource, due to its environment-friendly characteristics. Jute is a natural fibre that can be used in many different areas, supplementing or replacing synthetics. It is used not only for traditional items, but also for other value-added products, such as pulp and paper, geo-textiles, composites, and home textiles. Jute is also an annually renewable energy source with a high biomass production per unit land area. It is biodegradable and its products can be easily disposed without causing environmental hazards. Jute plants also play a vital role in increasing the soil fertility.

Bangladesh produces 5.5–6.0 million bales of raw jute every year of which some 3.2 million bales are used in the existing 148 jute mills. The country exports 2.4 million bales of jute and some 1,600,000 employees of the country are directly employed in the jute mills. The total demand for jute goods in the international market is 0.75 million tonnes. Bangladesh exports 0.46 million tonnes of jute goods while India enjoys a share of 0.285 million tonnes in the international market. The capital Dhaka controls about 60% share of the total jute goods market of the world and earns BDT 20.125 billion [Uddin, Hossain, and Hoque, 2014]. From 2003 to 2013, production of jute products including yarn, hessian, sacking, and carpet backing has increased constantly and reached a total of more than 977,000 tonnes in 2013 (see Table 5.5).

Table 5.5: Production of Jute products by type in Bangladesh in 1,000 tonnes

Year	Yarn	Hessian	Sacking	Carpet Backing	Others	Total
2012–2013	618.58	57.59	275.82	10.81	14.51	977.32
2011–2012	537.37	51.07	269.02	16.33	11.47	885.26
2010–2011	451.41	45.24	196.21	16.79	19.43	729.07
2009–2010	425.56	40.86	202.53	15.99	10.22	695.17
2008–2009	330.84	37.83	198.02	13.39	8.76	588.85
2007–2008	372.22	50.80	188.61	21.22	18.20	651.05
2006–2007	341.03	39.58	171.10	18.83	13.08	583.61
2005–2006	298.61	52.84	177.00	23.75	11.23	563.46
2004–2005	201.47	120.24	175.57	18.93	—	521.77
2003–2004	187.8	49.4	145	19.8	—	404.7

Source: International Jute Study Group [2014].

Despite the strong jute production, manufacturing, and export position of Bangladesh, the industry currently faces some serious problems in both public and private sectors, which have converted this industry into an industry with heavy losses and relying heavily on governmental subsidies. Some of these problems include the rise in cost of production, increase in share of unused looms, managerial challenges, lack of effective operating policies, mismanagement in procurement of raw jute, shortage of varied orders received from buyers and obsolete and worn out equipment. The poor financial performance of jute mills also is a major concern. Today the Bangladesh Jute Mills Corporation is the second largest loss maker among public sector manufacturing enterprises, with annual losses of BDT 2.3 billion (about EUR 2.6 million), accounting for over 50% of total manufacturing state-owned enterprise (SOE) losses in financial year (FY) 2006 [Uddin, Hossain, and Hoque, 2014].

An example how the government has dealt with public jute mills running at losses is the closure of the Adamjee Jute Mill, back then the largest jute mill globally, which resulted in the loss of 25,000 permanent jobs and 5,000 temporary jobs [Muhammad, 2002]. It was officially closed down in 2002 despite protests from local policy makers and political opponents, in a move to privatise the jute sector. Closure of public jute mills resulted in the growth of private mills, particularly in northern Bangladesh, a jute growing area, where industrialisation was much needed. Five small mills have been set up in the Greater Rangpur area, but mostly using old machinery from the closed public mills. Investment in these five mills was around BDT 1 billion (EUR 12.7 million) and they provided employment for around 3,000 workers, producing about 40 tonnes of jute bags and fibre daily. Three new mills will be established in the northern districts, which will provide employment for an additional 5,000 people. However, privatisation has not proved to be the solution to alleviate the situation. According to Uddin, Hossain, and Hoque [2014], what is needed to re-establish the jute industry is effort from both employees and the Government to cooperate in the formulation of an effective and well-balanced jute policy, which will bring out operational efficiency.

A case study and lessons learned from the SWITCH-Asia project "Eco-jute" is presented in Box 5.2.

Box 5.2 SWITCH-Asia project case study: Supporting the jute industry in Bangladesh

Under the SWITCH-Asia Programme, two projects were designed and implemented to support the jute sector of Bangladesh and India. The first of the two projects was "Jute: an eco-friendly alternative for a sustainable future." It started its activities in Bangladesh and India's West Bengal area in 2010 and was completed in 2014. It aimed to ensure that there was a positive environmental and economic impact of the jute sector on its workers, producers, farmers, and consumers by encouraging a switch to more environmentally sustainable practice in the jute industry. The project encouraged sustainable production and consumption of eco-friendly JDPs in Bangladesh and India, and focused on increasing awareness of SCP practice. Thirty Bangladeshi and 10 Indian SMEs developed 193 new ranges of JDPs for local consumers, and later 21 Bangladeshi SMEs further developed 51 ranges for institutional buyers. The project thereby improved the capacity of businesses to produce more market-driven products, ensured that service providers had the right set of skills to work with SMEs, established a match making service through Business Facilitation Units to support sustainable service provision, and campaigned for increasing demand for eco-friendly products. The main project activities included building capacity of local service providers, training JDP SMEs to produce market-driven products, while working with consumers to get them to buy more eco-friendly products. The project worked with 181 JDP SMEs and 148 service providers, working both on the supply and demand side. This project benefited at least 500 SMEs, their 25,000 workers and their family members.

The project also encouraged the government to develop relevant jute sector support policies and advocated change on six key issues:

- Ensuring availability of quality jute seeds;
- Expansion of JDPs by ensuring availability of raw materials;
- Ensuring a fair price for jute;
- Commercialisation of innovative products of the Bangladesh Jute Re-search Institute;
- Balancing, modernisation, rehabilitation, and expansion of conventional jute mills; and
- Re-excavation of canals to solve the water crisis for ensuring the quality of jute.

(*Continued*)

Box 5.2 (*Continued*)

More information available at: http://www.switch-asia.eu/projects/jute-an-eco-friendly-alternative-for-a-sustainable-future/.

The second jute project, coordinated by CARE France, is the SWITCH-Asia project "Promoting SCP of Jute Diversified Products." It started in March 2013 with the objective to contribute to pro-poor economic growth through social business promotion, emphasising sustainable agriculture sector growth, and poverty reduction in Bangladesh. The project directly links 16,000 jute producers, 60 organic fertiliser producers, 2,000 jute sector workers, 20 SMEs, three jute mills, and other national associations and public agencies active in the national jute sector. In 2013, the project mobilised 10,000 farmers resulting in 400 producer groups. The following year, another 6,000 farmers joined the cause and formed 240 new groups. Based on this initial success, a database of 16,000 jute producers was compiled covering their livelihoods and other socio-economic aspects. Training on environment friendly jute cultivation, retting, and harvesting techniques were provided. The project has already achieved some significant results. Firstly, it increased the jute cultivation area in the target area: in 2013, producers cultivated jute over 2,034.21 ha of land, while in 2014, 2,111.5 ha, an increase of 77.29 ha. Secondly, it provided farmers with better cultivation practice: for the first time, in 2014, 860 farmers practised line sowing. This new practice reduces seed costs and yields more fibres and jute sticks. Thirdly, the project helped increase productivity: in 2014, the farmers produced 4,000 tonnes of fibres, which is about 797 tonnes more than previous year's production (3,203 tonnes). Fourthly, the project helped reduce agriculture-related CO_2 emissions: in 2014, 2,111.5 ha were used for jute cultivation, which is 77.29 ha more than the previous year. In 2013, 30,513.15 tonnes of CO_2 were absorbed by cultivating jute over 2,034.21 ha of land. In 2014, 31,672.5 tonnes of CO_2 were absorbed, an increase of 1,159.35 tonnes [Ullah, 2015].

More information available at: http://www.switch-asia.eu/projects/jute-diversified-products/.

5.7 Conclusion

The Bangladeshi economy is expanding with 5–6% annual growth during the last decade. The contribution of agriculture to GDP is decreasing, whereas that of industry has been increasing over the last two decades.

Recent statistics show that contribution of agriculture to GDP is much lower at 20% than that of the industry at 30%. The current government has envisioned that the contribution of industry to GDP shall be increased to 40% by 2021. It is clear that the Bangladeshi economy is being transformed from and agriculture to an industry-driven one. Between this amalgamation of agriculture and industry-based economies, both jute and tannery sectors are playing a vital role, while they both are still plagued with various problems and backlogs. In this process, SCP can offer a framework to guide industrial development in a sustainable direction and avoid the past mistakes of the leather and tannery sector. Hazaribagh, Dhaka's notorious tannery area, holds an immense potential in terms of its strategically well-connected location, geographical context and a diversified socio-economic, and cultural context. To be sustainable, the government needs to run the tannery industry properly and needs to act determinedly to facilitate the shift of tanneries towards the newly established designated areas in Savar. At the same time, preparing the Hazaribagh brownfield sites with the knowledge of productive reuse, requires integration of many elements such as financial issues, community involvement, liability considerations, environmental assessment, and clean up and regulatory requirements, as well as coordination among many groups of stakeholders. The SWITCH-Asia project "Reduction of environmental threats and increase of exportability of Bangladeshi leather products (Re-Tie)" has contributed to enhancing the ability of SMEs to implement cleaner production, thereby reducing pollution, and reducing health hazards to workers.

In contrast to the polluting tannery sector, jute has played a key role in the economy of Bangladesh, especially due to a recent renewed global interest in the golden fibres, for instance as replacement of plastic bags. The latest demand for jute creates a strong motivation to support the growth of the jute industry, which will benefit many nations. Whilst the sector suffers from a number of difficulties, the revival of jute sector offers a promising outlook for Bangladesh's sustainable development. Re-establishing the jute industry and enhancing productivity will require a sincere effort from the government as well as the private sector. The framework of SCP might enable us to achieve sustainable growth of the jute industry. Based on the experiences of the SWITCH-Asia projects operating in Bangladesh's jute sector, the country should attempt to expand its share in the global market by supplying more quality goods, including diversified jute products, which should be further developed, and familiarisation of producers and consumers is required. The application areas of jute need to be enlarged, i.e., jute should be used in new areas like agro-textiles, geo-textiles, technical textiles, as well as home textiles. Furthermore, the "Jute Policy" needs to be reviewed and revised, and in this context, the government's initiative to design a new jute policy is well-timed. The idea of an independent "Jute Board" may be considered in this regard, within which there will be representation of major stakeholders. The government and industry can thus advance and take the necessary steps in this direction, for example highlighting its eco-friendly and biodegradable characteristics. This can achieve the final goal of successful marketing and promotion of jute as a sustainable product for national and global markets.

References

Abdin, J. (2012). The Development Imperatives of SMEs in Bangladesh. Planning, Monitoring & Evaluation, SME Foundation, National Agency for SME Development, 17 October, 2012, Bangladesh.

Afzal, T. (2011). SME: a driver growth. *The Daily Star*. 21 December 2011. Retrieved on January 7, 2016. Available on: http://archive.thedailystar.net/newDesign/news-details.php?nid=214950.

Alam, J. G. M. (2009). Environmental pollution of Bangladesh — its effect and control. *Proceedings of the International Conference on Mechanical Engineering 2009 (ICME2009) 26–28 December 2009*, Dhaka, Bangladesh.

Aminuzzaman, S. M. (2010). Environment policy of Bangladesh: A case study of an ambitious policy with implementation snag. Paper presented to South Asia Climate Change Forum, organised by Monash Sustainability Institute, Monash University, Australia, 5–9 July, 2010.

Asaduzzaman, M., Hasan, I., Rajia, S., Khan, N., Kabir, K. (2014). Impact of tannery effluents on the aquatic environment of the Buriganga River in Dhaka, Bangladesh. *Toxicology and Industrial Health*.

Bangladesh Environmental Conservation Act (1995). Legal office, food and agriculture organisation of the United Nations. Bangladesh government. Retrieved on January 8, 2016. English translation available on: http://faolex.fao.org/docs/pdf/bgd42272.pdf.

Bakht, Z. and Bashar, A. (2015). *Strategy for Development of the SME Sector in Bangladesh*. Bangladesh Institute of Development Studies, Dhaka.

Bhuiyan M.A., Suruvi N.I., Dampare S.B., Islam M.A., Quraishi S.B. Ganyaglo S. and Suzuki S. (2010). Investigation of the possible sources of heavy metal contamination in lagoon and canal water in the tannery industrial area in Dhaka, Bangladesh. *Environmental Monitoring and Assessment* 175(1–4), 633–649.

Blacksmith Institute (2010). World's Worst Pollution Problems Report 2010. Top Six Toxic Threats: Six pollutants that jeopardize the health of tens of millions of people, pp. 39.

Clemett, A. (2004). *A Review of Environmental Policy and Legislation in Bangladesh, BEEL.* University of Leeds, UK.

Chowdhury, K. R. (2013). "Mongla seaport to get railway link in 4 years". *Dhaka Tribune*. May 19, 2013.

Denissen, A.-K. (2012). Climate Change & its Impacts on Bangladesh. *NCDO.* Available on: http://www.ncdo.nl/artikel/climate-change-its-impacts-bangladesh.

Dhaka Tribune (2014). Bangladesh world's 2nd most pro-free market country. *Dhaka Tribune*. November 1, 2014. Retrieved on January 7, 2016. Available on: http://www.dhakatribune.com/bangladesh/2014/nov/01/bangladesh-world%E2%80%99s-2nd-most-pro-free-market-country.

EEP (2009). Available on: www.eeb.org/.

Eghbal, M. (2008). The next 11 emerging economies. *Euromonitor International blog*. February 4, 2008. Retrieved on January 10, 2016. Available on: http://blog.euromonitor.com/2008/02/the-next-11-emerging-economies.html.

Hoque, A. and Clarke, A. (2013). Greening of industries in Bangladesh: pollution prevention practices. *Journal of Cleaner Production* 51, 47–56.

Hossain, A. M. (2007). Heavy metal concentration in tannery solid wastes used as poultry feed and the ecotoxicological consequences. *Bangladesh Journal of Scientific and Industrial Research* 42(2), 397–416.

Hussain, Z. (2013). In Bangladesh, the alternative to urbanization is urbanization. *World Bank blog*. May 13, 2013. Retrieved on January 11, 2016. Available on: http://blogs.worldbank.org/endpovertyinsouthasia/bangladesh-alternative-urbanization-urbanization.

International Jute Study Group (2014). Production of Jute Products by type in Bangladesh. Retrieved on January 12, 2016. Available on: http://www.jute.org/statistics_03.htm.

Jenkins, R., Barton, J. and Hesselberg, J. (2004). The global tanning industry: A commodity chain approach. *Environmental Regulation in the New Global Economy: The Impact on Industry and Competitiveness*. Edward Elgar Publishing, Cheltenham, pp. 157–172.

Lanteigne, D. (2010). Colours of water: Bangladesh's leather tanneries. *United Nations University*. Available on: http://ourworld.unu.edu/en/colours-of-water-bangladeshsleather-tanneries.

Mahmood, S. A. I. (2012). Impact of climate change in Bangladesh: The role of public administration and government's integrity. *Journal of Ecology and the Natural Environment* 4(8), 223–240.

Ministry of Environment and Forests (1995). National Environment Management Plan (NEMAP). Volume II, Main Report.

Muhammad, A. (2002). Closure of Adamjee jute mills: Ominous sign. *Economic and Political Weekly* 37(38), (September 21–27, 2002), 3895–3897.

Maurice, J. (2001). Tannery pollution threatens health of half-million Bangladesh residents. *Bulletin of the World Health Organization 2001* 79(1), 78–79.

Rahmatullah, M. (2013). Regional transport connectivity: Its current state. *The Daily Star*, March 20, 2013.

Shen, T. (1999). *Industrial Pollution Prevention*. 2nd ed., Springer, Berlin.

The Daily Star (2015). Hazaribagh tanneries to be shut if not shifted to Savar: Amu. February 17, 2015. Retrieved on January 3, 2016. Available on: http://www.thedailystar.net/hazaribagh-tanneries-to-be-shut-if-not-shifted-to-savar-amu-65306.

The Fourth Five Year Plan (1990–1995). Planning Commission, Ministry of Planning, Govt. People's Republic of Bangladesh, June 1995, Chapter IX, pp. 1–4.

Tremblay, J.-F. (2009). Leather From Another Era. Chemical and Engineering News. February 2, 2009. Volume 87, Number 5, pp. 18–21. Retrieved on January 12, 2016. Available on: https://pubs.acs.org/cen/business/87/8705bus1.html.

Uddin, M. J., Hossain, J and Hoque, M. A. (2014). Present condition of Jute sector in Bangladesh. *Banglavision*, 14(1), June 2014.

Ullah, M. M. (2015). Realising green growth using jute diversified products. In *SWITCH-Asia Magazine*, Issue 2, Summer 2015.

United Nations Industrial Development Organisation (UNIDO) (2005). *Cost of Tanned Waste Treatment, 15th Session of the Leather and Leather Products Industry Panel*. Leon, Mexico.

Walsh, B. (2013). Urban wastelands: The world's 10 most polluted places. *Time Magazine*. November 4, 2013. Retrieved on January 3, 2016. Available on: http://science.time.com/2013/11/04/urban-wastelands-the-worlds-10-most-polluted-places/slide/hazaribagh-bangladesh/.

Chapter 6

Gross National Happiness and SCP in Bhutan

Kezang, P. Lama and S. T. Dorji

6.1 Introduction

Bhutan is a small and landlocked country, situated between the Tibet Autonomous Region of China and India. It has an area of 38,394 km^2 with an estimated population of 745,153 in 2014 [NSB, 2014b]. It is located in the Eastern Himalayas and is mostly mountainous and heavily forested. Bhutan's economy is one of the fastest growing in the world and was ranked fifth in the world in 2013 in terms of the speed of growth [IMF, 2014]. Growing at an average of 8% since 2000, per capita GDP has more than tripled from USD 780 in 2000 to USD 2,460 in 2013. Bhutan's Human Development Index (HDI) value for 2013 is 0.584, which is in the medium human development category, positioning the country at 136 out of 187 countries and territories. Between 2010 and 2013, Bhutan's HDI value increased from 0.569 to 0.584, an increase of 2.7% or an average annual increase of about 0.88% [UNDP, 2014].

According to the Bhutan Poverty Assessment 2014, the country's poverty reduction has been rapid, broad-based, and inclusive. The report suggests three necessary interventions in order to sustain the trend in poverty reduction: (i) mitigating risks from persistent shocks facing the agricultural sector, (ii) increasing private sector led development, and (iii) building formal social protection for clearly identified vulnerable population groups. The overall Gini coefficient for 2012 was 38.75%, indicating a medium level of inequality by global standards. While Bhutan has done well in reducing poverty in the recent years, the risk of downward mobility is greater than average for rural residents, male-headed households, people in informal jobs (casual and self-employed), those with low education levels, and particularly high for those living in poorer *Dzongkhags* (districts) such as Pema Gatshel, Dagana, Samtse, Trashigang, and Tsirang [NSB, 2014a]. Thus, in its path to sustainable and equitable development, some challenges still exist for Bhutan.

Bhutan has gained worldwide attention for its unique development philosophy of Gross National Happiness (GNH), which encompasses the four pillars of sustainable and equitable socio-economic development, preservation and promotion of culture, conservation and sustainable utilisation and management of the environment, and promotion of good governance. Pursuant to Section 2 of Article 9 of the Constitution, which directs the State "to promote those conditions that will enable the pursuit of GNH," the operational aspects of GNH have been strengthened, most notably with the introduction of the GNH Index in 2008 and the GNH Policy Screening Tool in 2009. The GNH Index is based on biennial surveys and provides an overview of performance across nine domains of GNH that include health, education, living standards, ecological diversity and resilience, good governance, psychological wellbeing, time use, community vitality, and cultural diversity and resilience. Based on the 2010 GNH Index composite score of 0.743, 41% of Bhutanese were identified as 'happy' having achieved sufficiency in 73% of the domains, while the remaining 59% achieved sufficiency in 57% of the domains [GNHC, 2013a]. The GNH Policy Screening is being used as a tool to assess the impact of new policies on GNH and to mainstream GNH into all new policies being formulated against 22 variables representing the nine domains of GNH. Since its introduction, numerous policies related to human resources, youth, education, health and nutrition, land, natural resources, and industries have been approved.

GNH, thus, can be regarded as an Sustainable Consumption & Production (SCP) indicator developed in response to dissatisfaction with the conventional gross domestic product (GDP) measure, which does not capture many aspects that are central for people's wellbeing. For example, GDP does not include unpaid work in households or communities, which plays a significant role in traditional Bhutanese village life where people have a custom of helping each other without expecting any monetary compensation. Bhutan's focus on happiness and the approach of directly collecting information from households on aspects related to happiness have inspired a number of other countries, including OECD member countries such as Japan, to develop their own indicator systems for wellbeing [UNEP, 2012].

The 11th Five-Year Plans (FYP) (2013–2018) is the second FYP to be implemented since the introduction of Democratic Constitutional Monarchy in 2008. It builds on the strong foundations that have been laid since the inception of planned development in 1961. The Plan's underlying objective of "Self-reliance and Inclusive Green Socio-Economic Development" is underpinned by a results-based planning framework that articulates clear national outcomes and outputs. Three main strategic thrust areas have been identified in order to achieve these outcomes and outputs, viz. inclusive social development, accelerated green economic development, and strategic infrastructure development. Through these strategic thrust areas, the government aims to achieve an annual average economic growth rate of 10% or more over the 11th Plan period and reduce the poverty level to less than 5% by 2018 [GNHC, 2013a].

The majority of Bhutan's population is reliant upon agriculture and forestry. India is the nation's closest trading partner, and increasing hydropower exports are expected to drive Bhutanese employment and economic growth. Bhutan currently exploits only an estimated 5% of its total hydropower generation capacity and plans to have 10,000 MW of hydropower generation capacity by 2020. The electricity sector's share of the economy has reached almost 20%, outstripping agriculture as the single largest contributor to GDP. There are also concerted efforts to promote tourism, agro-industries, socio-cultural industries, and local construction materials. Cottage and Small Industries (CSI) constitute more than 96% of total industry in Bhutan. In December 2014, there were 15,193 operational CSI in the country as compared to 12,548 during December 2013 [DCSI, 2015], which underscores the importance of this segment in self-employment and income generation. Bhutan's CSI is dominated by the services and contracts industries with a very small production and manufacturing sector base.

Bhutan has placed environmental conservation at the centre of its development strategy, being one of the four pillars of GNH. In addition, the Constitution mandates that at least 60% of the country remain forested for all time (currently 72.5%). Bhutan is one of the few countries in the world with net GHG sequestration capacity largely due to its vast forest cover and widespread use of hydropower and biomass energy. Due to its geographical location, Bhutan is also especially vulnerable to the adverse effects of climate change.

There are several policies and legal instruments that promote SCP in Bhutan. More specifically, the National Environment Commission Secretariat (NECS) is working with UNEP on SCP-related policy initiatives in Bhutan, such as mainstreaming SCP, greening hotels, greening public procurement, greening products and introducing an SCP curriculum. An energy-labelling programme is currently being reviewed by the Department of Renewable Energy (DRE) and an Integrated Energy Master Plan is in place. Furthermore, there has been a recent push by the government to move towards an electric-powered transport sector including levying a 5% green tax on fossil fuels and also a 5% green tax on import of fossil fuel-based vehicles. In 2008, Bhutan's tourism policy changed from "high value — low volume" to "high value — low (environment) impact" indicating a strategic direction towards sustainable tourism. The Economic Development Policy (EDP) 2010 aims to enhance the productive capacity of the economy and provide a strategic direction for economic development up to 2020. With a vision to promote a green and self-reliant economy sustained by an IT-enabled knowledge society, the EDP's objectives are to achieve economic self-reliance and full employment of 97.5% by 2020. The strategies set out to achieve the objectives include diversification of the economic base with a minimal ecological footprint, harnessing of and adding value to natural resources in a sustainable manner; and increase in and diversification of exports, promoting Bhutan as an organic brand, promoting industries that build "Brand Bhutan" and reducing dependency on fossil fuel.

With the present government's focus on promoting private sector development, an enabling environment to better businesses is foreseen, such as simplification of licensing procedures, enhancement of productivity and efficiency, enforcement of conducive legislation and policies, and facilitation of infrastructure investments to promote ease of doing business. These favourable conditions, coupled with the strategic thrust towards accelerated green socio-economic development, provide a real opportunity for sustainability and promotion of sustainable industries in Bhutan, especially in the cottage-, small-, and medium-sized enterprise (CSME) sectors. However, the inherent limitations to scale up production and manufacturing, small market size, limited human resources, and inconsistencies in the quality of goods, services and infrastructure pose challenges to fostering SCP practices in Bhutan. The country's dependence on its development partners and donors for funding and technical assistance has been declining over the years. Apart from the European Union (EU), major development partners and donors include the Government of India (GOI), the World Bank Group, the Asian Development Bank (ADB), United Nations (UN), etc. The EU funds the government directly as well as providing funds through the SWITCH-Asia Programme. Three projects are being implemented in Bhutan under the SWITCH-Asia Programme: (i) "Sustainable & Efficient Industrial Development in Bhutan and Nepal" (SEID), 2012–2015, (ii) "Tourism in Bhutan: An Integrated Approach to Sustainable Production (SP), Consumption, and Livelihood Development", 2012–2015, and (iii) "Green Public Procurement in Bhutan (GPP Bhutan)", 2014–2017 (see Table 6.1).

6.2 Major Industry Structures and Situation of SMEs

Bhutan's economy is driven mainly by hydropower, construction, services, and power-intensive manufacturing sectors. All have low employment elasticity and minimal linkages in the domestic economy. Due to this, the spillover effects of structural changes and economic modernisation have not been able to tackle challenges related to poverty alleviation, rising income inequalities and unemployment. While the government recognises that private sector development is important for economic diversification and generating employment, the sector remains underdeveloped and is dominated by CSMEs.

Table 6.1: Overview of SWITCH-Asia projects in Bhutan [www.switch-asia.eu]

Name of Project	Period	Main Implementing Organisation	Places of Implementation	SCP Practice	Brief Description of Objectives or Impact
SEID in Bhutan and Nepal	2012–2015	Center for Appropriate Technology (GrAT), Austria	Bhutan and Nepal	Appropriate technology, resource efficiency	To contribute to sustainable development of Nepal's and Bhutan's economy with a clear focus on industrial sectors that impact environment, generate employment, and alleviate poverty
Tourism in Bhutan: An Integrated Approach to Sustainable Production (SP), Consumption and Livelihood Development	2012–2015	Association of Bhutanese Tour Operators (ABTO), Bhutan	Bhutan	Sustainable tourism, sustainable consumption	To promote SCP practices across the tourism value chain of Bhutan coupled with sustainable livelihood development
(GPP Bhutan): A Cross-sectoral Strategy for Sustainable Industrial Competitiveness	2014–2017	International Institute for Sustainable Development (IISD), Canada	Bhutan	Sustainable consumption, GPP	To implement GPP practices in Bhutan, enabling the procurement cycle to be used as a driver for green growth

Industries in Bhutan are categorised by two parameters — employment size and capital investment — as reflected in Table 6.1.

Under the 11th FYP, private sector development policies are being reviewed and appropriate interventions designed and implemented to bring the vulnerable and the poor into mainstream socio-economic development. Special emphasis is being accorded to CSMEs and rural enterprises, as they are deemed crucial for fostering entrepreneurship and innovation, creating employment, generating income, and helping engender pro-poor growth with equity and inclusion. Hence, the success of CSMEs contributes meaningfully towards realising the tenets of GNH.

The Bhutan Vision 2020 and the EDP 2010 identify and deem "small and cottage industries" as a priority sector. The CSMI Policy 2012 provides the necessary enabling and conducive policy environment for the promotion of CSMI development in Bhutan. The Department of Cottage and Small Industries (DCSI) is the line agency mandated to promote CSI development while the Department of Industry (DOI) is responsible for medium and large industries in Bhutan. Both departments are placed under the Ministry of Economic Affairs (MOEA).

According to the National Statistics Bureau (NSB), 99.4% of the 26,807 industries registered in 2013 fall into the cottage (23,324), small (3,053), and medium (268) category, which underscores the importance of the CSME segment in self-employment and income generation. In 2013, out of the 2,485 production and manufacturing registered industrial establishments, 44% (1,094) were forest-based, 14% (348) were agro-based and 10% (248) were mineral-based establishments [NSB, 2014b] (see Table 6.3). CSMEs face various constraints and challenges that prevent their full development and limit a more meaningful contribution to the national development goals including sustainability targets. These include diseconomies of scale, lack of infrastructure, difficulties in accessing finance, inadequate marketing facilities, non-standardisation of products, uncertainty in raw materials procurement, use of obsolete machinery, difficulty in retaining trained personnel, and limited business development services. Industrial establishments in Bhutan can be categorised based on ownership, size, and type (see Table 6.2).

With seven new mega hydroelectric projects planned for the 11th FYP, the construction sector provides an excellent opportunity for Bhutan to

Table 6.2: Industry categorisation in Bhutan

Industry Category	Parameters[1]	
	Employment Size	**Investment (BTN)**
Large	100+	> 100 million
Medium	20–99	10–100 million
Small	5–19	1–10 million
Cottage/Micro	1–4	< 1 million

Source: Cottage, Small, and Medium Industry (CSMI), Development Strategy (2012–2020), and Action Plan (2012–2014) [Ministry of Economic Affairs, 2012].

Table 6.3: Number of industrial establishments by ownership, size, and type (2009–2013)

Industrial Establishment	**2009**	**2010**	**2011**	**2012**	**2013**
Ownership	30,317	32,360	34,692	37,282	39,951
(a) Private	30,207	32,218	34,550	37,155	39,814
(b) Joint	14	46	46	27	29
(c) Public	96	96	96	100	108
Size	19,472	21,008	22,776	24,605	26,807
(a) Large	103	114	133	141	162
(b) Medium	156	201	220	240	268
(c) Small	2,330	2,878	2,649	3,014	3,053
(d) Cottage	16,883	17,815	19,774	21,210	23,324
Type	30,317	32,360	34,692	37,282	39,951
(a) Production and Manufacturing	1,565	1,777	1,977	2,240	2,485
– Agro-based	252	287	291	325	348
– Forest-based	651	733	831	954	1,094
– Mineral-based	163	178	209	236	248
– Others	499	579	646	725	795
(b) Contract	10,845	11,352	11,916	12,677	13,144
(c) Services	17,907	19,231	20,799	22,365	24,322

Source: DOI, MOEA, Thimphu [NSB, 2014b].

[1] In the event of conflict in the usage of the two parameters, capital investment would take precedence over employment size.

realise the goal of full employment. In order to make it an attractive sector for youth employment, mechanisation of the construction industry is being promoted, together with improved working conditions, and higher remuneration gained by enhancing productivity through skills development. Additionally, initiatives are being undertaken to promote the use of local materials to reduce imports and strengthen the capacity of local construction industries to participate in large infrastructure projects.

The following sections focus on food and agriculture, tourism, and renewable resources.

6.2.1 *Food and agriculture*

Agriculture is an important economic sector in Bhutan, particularly as a source of livelihood for the rural poor. The 11th FYP objectives for the agriculture sector include, among others, meeting a greater share of the demand through local production, and hence increasing self-sufficiency in food production. Even though only 2.93% of the land area in Bhutan is classified as agricultural, crops and livestock's share in GDP stood at 13.29% in 2013 and provided employment to over 56% of the total population. Paddy, maize, apple, oranges, and potatoes are the major crops, and cattle, and poultry the major livestock. Given the predominance of subsistence farming, 60% of cereals, vegetables and animal products, and 95% of fruit and nuts are domestically produced while 97% of fish, 80% of beef, 77% of pork, and 90% of oils and fats demands are met from imports.

The sector continues to grow, although slowly, and faces a number of challenges. Studies indicate that yield per hectare has been on the decline at a compound annual rate of 1.84% over the last 27 years [World Bank, 2014]. A lack of sufficient farmer labour is considered a constraint because of out-migration in rural areas. This is compounded by inadequate access to markets due to limited number of farm road linkages. Lack of irrigation is another constraint; agriculture is still dominated by rain-fed dry land farming. Other challenges include high soil erosion rate, vulnerability to various pests and diseases, crop loss to wild animal invasion, and lack of good storage and processing facilities.

In order to meet these challenges, through the 11th FYP, Bhutan aims to shift from subsistence to commercial farming, and develop agri-business enterprises to increase rural livelihoods and facilitate economic growth.

Mechanisation will be promoted to help address labour shortages, and large-scale irrigation schemes will be developed with watershed management plans implemented to make water resources available. A comprehensive strategy to address potential human-wildlife conflict is also being developed and the country hopes to work towards ensuring sustainability at the same time as improving productivity, through soil and water conservation, natural resources restoration, and appropriate farming systems. Five advanced cold storage facilities are being established across the country to retain home-grown vegetables, especially potatoes, to make them available to Bhutanese consumers during the lean season, and also to help reduce vegetable imports. These measures aim to support SCP practice in the food and agriculture sector in Bhutan. For example, cold storage and processing facilities play a vital role in the food harvest, preservation, and distribution system. The establishment of advanced cold storage facilities would help people to consume what they produce and cut down on imports and help the country meet its goal of self-sufficiency in domestic vegetable production. Today, self-sufficiency in rice is 48%, beef 39%, pork 40%, chicken 76%, fish 2%, egg 63%, and vegetables 56% [GNHC, 2013b].

6.2.2 *Tourism*

Tourism is an important sector in Bhutan, which has the potential for further growth. The industry began in 1974 and was privatised in 1991. There were 116,209 tourists in 2013 including international, regional, business, official and familiarisation visitors, about 10% higher than in 2012 [NSB, 2014b]. Culture and nature have been the two main attractions for tourists, making this an important sector for green growth. Approximately 22,045 employment opportunities were created in 2011 through this sector [GNHC, 2013b]. The sector is considered an important source of foreign exchange earnings. Gross earnings from international leisure tourism reached USD 63.89 million in 2013, an increase of 0.69% compared to 2012 [NSB, 2014b].

Challenges faced by the tourism sector include accessibility, seasonality, and product diversification. The capacity of air transport services puts constraints on visitors, and there is also a shortage of trained guides and skilled workers in the hospitality sector. Product development and destination marketing are also required. During the 11th FYP, Bhutan plans to increase tourist arrivals to more than 200,000, raise the sector's contribution to GDP almost four times, and employment to 40,000. Bhutan aims to improve product diversification so that regional and seasonal variations are smoothed out and standards of services are improved. New product development is planned in categories including wellness, cultural tourism, sports, adventure, eco-tourism, and MICE (meetings, incentives, conventions, and exhibitions). Based on concerns that too much of the income from eco-tourism is channelled to the government and tour operators, efforts are being made to ensure that local communities also benefit from tourism. To cope up with the increasing tourist arrivals, the Tourism Council of Bhutan (TCB) is continuing to diversify the tourism offering, encourage visits to less-visited districts and to encourage activity throughout the year. The Council is also working on an integrated approach to sustainable tourism development and destination management at the district level. Measures for monitoring by stakeholders are also being strengthened.

Bhutan has always sought to sell tourism as an exclusive product since the country's opening up in the early 1970s. Over the years, the country has migrated from a policy slogan of "High Value, Low Volume" to "High Value, Low Impact" in 2008, suggesting a larger focus on increasing arrivals while ensuring minimal (ecological) impact. The TCB together with other stakeholders have been instrumental in the development and launch of new eco-tourism products, such as the Nabji-Korphu community-based trail in Jigme Singye Wangchuck National Park, the community-based trail in Merak Sakteng in Trashigang, and various farm stay programmes. Furthermore, the country has opened up some of its national parks for tourism and infrastructure development. While the number of tourists has increased following the move to boost economic growth through tourism, the government has been mindful of the low impact goal. The impacts from the sector are recognised, thus policies in the tourism sector promote and provide incentives to the different stakeholders in order to become more sustainable and to adopt green practice, be they in hospitality, transport and tourism products. Along the hospitality front, the Bhutanese Government has been working on the classification of hotels, which also establishes standards for a green hotel and the incentives accorded. The increasing number of tourists results in higher consumption levels as well as creating much needed employment in the country.

Box 6.1 SWITCH-Asia case study: Tourism in Bhutan: An Integrated Approach to Sustainable Production (SP), Consumption, and Livelihood Development

This first SWITCH-Asia project in Bhutan started in January 2012 and ended in October 2015 after securing a three-month implementation extension. The overall project objective was to contribute to economic prosperity, poverty reduction and climate change mitigation in Bhutan, by promoting sustainable tourism development. The specific objective was to promote SP and consumption practices across the tourism value chain of Bhutan, coupled with sustainable livelihood development. Some of the specific goals of the project were:

- Environmental Information System (EIS) for the tourism industry (first of its kind in the country).
- Reduction in GHG emissions from the operation of tourism business.
- Overall reduction in resource utilisation and an increase in tourism sector income.
- Low carbon (LC) tourism products & packages (20 products and packages offered).
- Promote and adopt LC & SCP measures in tourism operations.
- Facilitate public–private partnerships (PPPs) and policy interventions to improve LC & SCP practice by the industry.
- Improve opportunities for rural communities (capacity building, platforms, and linkages).
- Capacity building of the key government stakeholders and intermediary sectors in LC & SCP.
- Capacity building of service providers and industry staff along the supply chain.
- Awareness creation for industry, general citizens, and tourists on GHG, LC, and SCP.

(*Continued*)

Box 6.1 (*Continued*)

By the end of January 2015, the project had achieved key results, listed in brief below:

- PPPs and policy dialogues:
  - Skills development and market linkages for the cooperatives and farmers' groups of five tourist districts (Thimphu, Paro, Punakha, Wangdue, and Tsirang) with industry consumers, mainly hoteliers, in coordination with the Department of Agricultural Marketing and Cooperatives, Ministry of Agriculture and Forests.
  - Support and interventions in the incorporation of environmental and LC components into the hotel classification system of the TCB.
  - Elaboration and inclusion of two modules on LC and energy management in the curriculum of the Royal Institute of Tourism and Hospitality (RITH), the premier government-run tourism and hospitality training institute.
- Capacity-building of government and intermediaries:
  - About 20 local trainers trained to ensure project objectives continue beyond the funding period.
  - More than 70 key government stakeholder staff and intermediary organisations trained.
- Capacity-building and support to industry and rural communities:
  - 33 case studies completed and one-to-one support for high impact industry entities.
  - 620 industry staff and rural community suppliers trained in 19 training programmes with 13 different sector-specific training themes.
- Development of 20 LC tourism products/packages.
- Development of:
  - the first EIS for the industry and creation of an environmental database (based on a comprehensive baseline survey covering eight subsectors of the industry),
  - LC benchmarks for the tourism industry,
  - support centres in industry associations,
  - a carbon calculator specific to Bhutan.

(*Continued*)

Box 6.1 (*Continued*)

At the time of going to press, with a few months left to run of the project, most set targets have been achieved. The next step is to implement the recommendations and mitigation measures identified during the survey analysis and industry case studies, thus reduce GHG emissions and the industry's carbon footprint, and following a comparative re-survey of the industry entities. Facilitating green finance and credits from Bhutanese financial institutions was problematic due to the general moratorium by the central bank on general loans because of the economic situation in Bhutan.

Some of the challenges stated by the project implementers were:

- Overall incentives permissible within the regulations of the EU SWITCH-Asia Programme were not persuasive enough for a full commitment of the industry for maximum investment and change, especially as the tourism industry was granted stronger incentives from the government. However, much was achieved through one-to-one training sessions, consultations, and expert support;
- Lack of vital data about Bhutan's tourism industry required a commitment of almost 1.5 years from the project start just to conduct the comprehensive baseline survey (covering almost all sub-sectors and industry entities throughout the country);
- Limited pool of local experts and resources in specific fields, plus the seasonality of tourism business, gave the project only a six month window for scheduling programmes and industry initiatives, somewhat limiting the scope and span of interventions.

Overall, the project has been successful in raising awareness on GHG, LC, and SCP aspects in the tourism industry, and in promoting changes towards improving energy efficiency and resource use, and lowering the overall carbon footprint of the industry. In order to achieve continuity in the concepts of LC and SCP and sustainable tourism, capacity building of industry stakeholders, as well as provision of tools and the skills to do so efficiently and effectively, were achieved beyond the set target figures (targeted 500, achieved 620). To ensure sustainability of the objectives beyond the project period, recommendations were made to incorporate and further LC and SCP concepts and practices in tourism, such as: establishment of linkages between cooperatives and farmers' groups with hoteliers; incorporation of environmental and LC components in the Hotel Classification System; and inclusion of two modules on LC and energy management in the curriculum of the RITH.

6.2.3 *Renewable resources*

Forests are an important natural resource in Bhutan. The Constitution of Bhutan stipulates that the country maintain a "minimum of 60% of the total land area under forest cover for all time to come." In addition to this Constitutional mandate, since the 1960s regulations do not allow for the export of raw timber out of the country [RGOB, 2012].

As a share of GDP, the forestry and logging sector accounted for only 2.89% in 2013 as compared to 4.24% in 2009. This figure, however, does not do justice to the importance of the sector in the livelihoods of the poor: rural people rely heavily on functioning forest eco-systems for subsistence goods, including fuel wood, non-wood forest products (NWFPs), construction timber, etc. In Bhutan, firewood constitutes about 57% of total energy consumption. Households account for 95% of total fuel-wood consumption, while the government, commercial sector, and industry consume the balance. Stones and sand are the most important NWFPs followed by woodchips, bamboo, resin, and cordyceps.

Although deforestation is not considered to be a major problem in Bhutan, urban expansion and the establishment of new infrastructure, such as roads and hydropower projects, have had a negative effect on forests. Another potential challenge is low productivity, a challenge that is particularly relevant for promoting green growth in this sector. Wood charcoal was one of the top 10 commodities imported into the country from 2008 to 2012, despite the large forested areas in the country. Aside from productivity differences, this partly appears to reflect reluctance to accept the nearby presence of charcoal kilns. Under the 11th FYP, Bhutan hopes to overcome some of these challenges and manage its forest resources in order to supply economic goods and services through the establishment of Forest Management Units, Working Schemes, Community Forests (CFs), plantations, and NWFP user groups. The number of CFs in particular is to be increased to help empower rural communities to manage forests sustainably and alleviate poverty. The plan also emphasises biodiversity conservation and the maintenance of ecosystem services through protected area management, watershed management, and wildlife management. Bhutan is also conducting Reducing Emissions from Deforestation and Forest Degradation (REDD+) readiness activities, and hopes to be ready for implementing REDD+ activities by the end of the 11th FYP, by which time it is hoped that there will be clarity on the availability of global funds to support these activities.

Another crucial element to promote green growth and sustainability in renewable resource sectors such as forests is to ensure that the resource is managed to enhance productivity and prevent resource rent dissipation, given its common property nature. A package of measures is often needed to realise green growth outcomes: to reap higher and sustainable economic returns from natural forests, for example, requires aligning policies, incentives, capacity, and governance. Enforcing access rights, to avoid over-exploitation given the open access nature of forests, for example, will be as important as developing markets for forest products.

6.3 Policies for SCP

As previously mentioned, Bhutan's pursuit of GNH since its inception in the early 1970s has had the intention for Bhutan to be on the path to becoming a country that is holistic, inclusive, and sustainable in its development. There is a close relationship between GNH policies and those promoting SCP, described in this section. Bhutan has been guided by GNH in implementing its FYP for development. The 11th FYP is currently being implemented and the document centres on the goal of "Self-reliance and Inclusive Green Socio-economic Development" [GNHC, 2013a]. Since 2009, the GNH philosophy has been translated into a Policy Screening tool that is used to align all development policies and activities in Bhutan to the GNH philosophy within which environment and social aspects are carefully considered. There remain challenges in enforcement due to a lack of financial resources to monitor effectively the implementation of activities and developmental programmes.

6.3.1 *National policy framework relating to SCP*

UNEP has defined a Green Economy as "one that results in improved human wellbeing and social equity, while significantly reducing environmental risks and ecological scarcities" and this fits in very well within the framework of GNH pursued by Bhutan. The concept of GNH, based on the premise that true development takes place when social, economic, spiritual, and environmental wellbeing occur side by side (complementing and reinforcing each other), has been the principal driving force behind the growth and development agenda in Bhutan. The GNH development philosophy is the Bhutanese version of the global concept of sustainable development with the Constitution of the Kingdom of Bhutan enshrining it as a state policy [RGOB, 2008a]. The Constitution also spells out the duties and rights of the parliament, the government and the people to safeguard and protect the environment, and establishes the need for intergenerational equity for natural resources. The GNH framework in the sphere of public policy is based on the four main pillars of:

a. Equitable socio-economic development;
b. Conservation of the environment;
c. Preservation and promotion of culture; and
d. Promotion of good governance.

Bhutan currently subjects all national and sectoral policies to the GNH policy screening tool, which currently covers 23 determinants relating to nine GNH domains (see Figure 6.1) identified from the four pillars.

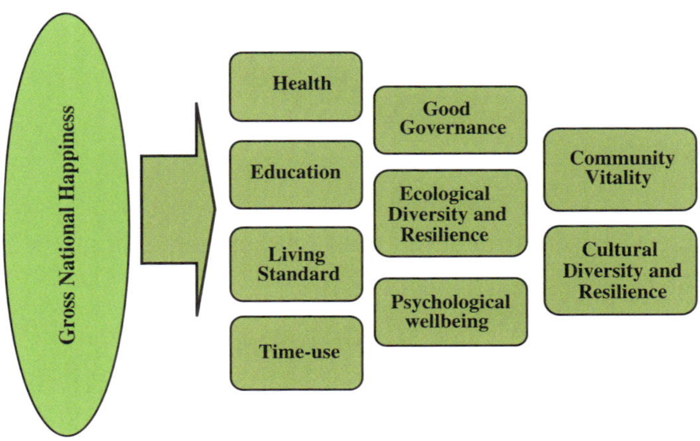

Figure 6.1: The nine domains of GNH

Source: Authors representation adapted from www.grossnationalhappiness.com/ninedomains.

Policies that do not sufficiently meet GNH criteria are reverted to the proponent agencies for review and improvement.

The National Environment Commission (NEC) signed an agreement with UNEP in November 2014 under the 10 Year Framework of Programme (10YFP) with the objective of "mainstreaming SCP into policy making for achieving sustainable development" [Tshering, 2015]. Under the programme, five activities have been prioritised for implementation. These activities, which started in February 2015, are:

Activity 1: Mainstreaming SCP into national policy and plans. Under this activity, the NEC is expected to deliver four outputs to be able to carry out mainstreaming into national policy and plans. Output 1 is a baseline report on SCP in the Bhutanese context, Output 2 assigns the review of policy protocol and policy review tool to identify the gaps, while Output 3 focuses on integrating SCP into the National Environmental Strategy, and Output 4 will provide advocacy and capacity building for conducting Life Cycle Assessments (LCA) and life cycle management. This mainstreaming is being carried out to ensure the sustainability of SCP policies.

Activity 2: Supporting sustainable tourism through the development of green hotel guidelines and provide recommendations for the integration of sustainable tourism into the five-year tourism strategy.

Activity 3: Supporting sustainable public procurement (SPP) through the revision of national procurement rules and regulations (PRR) in partnership with the EU SWITCH-Asia funded "GPP Bhutan" Project and carrying out Training of Trainers on SPP to both procurers and suppliers (see Box 6.2).

Activity 4: Integrating SCP learning materials in technical and vocational education training, tertiary level, civil servant, and continuing education curricula.

Activity 5: Developing guidelines for paperless operations in the public sector and providing "training of trainers" on paperless office operations to managers across agencies and to showcase the benefits of SCP, a pilot project will be identified and paperless operations implemented to document the benefits of such a transition.

Box 6.2 SWITCH-Asia case study: GPP in Bhutan — A Cross Sectoral Strategy for Sustainable Industrial Competitiveness (GPP Bhutan)

This SWITCH-Asia project started in January 2014 and will continue until June 2017. The project aims to establish a strategic approach for the government to scale-up public demand for environmentally and socially preferable goods, services and infrastructure, and utilise GPP as a tool to drive green growth. Specifically, it seeks to:

- lower the direct impact of state's consumption,
- incentivise SP among suppliers,
- build demand-side and supply-side capacity, and
- trigger private sustainable consumption and green economic transformation.

To date, quantitative mapping of public procurement, analysis of legal procurement documents, mapping of institutional arrangements and procedures for public procurement, assessment of supplier pre-qualification requirements, and market assessment for green goods, services, and infrastructure have been completed. Based on the findings, the project will provide policy recommendations, design preferential programmes, train public procurers and suppliers to respond to 'green' tenders, mentor pilot tenders, and finally establish a GPP knowledge platform and curriculum in Bhutan.

Additionally, in its capacity as the SWITCH-Asia Regional Policy Support Component (RPSC), UNEP has signed a Small Scale Fund Agreement (SSFA) with Bhutan's NEC to mainstream SCP into GNH-guided development, in which one of the activities is supporting SPP. In order to avoid duplication, the *GPP Bhutan* project has agreed to take on most of the activities related to SPP, while NEC will provide guidance and serve as the government associate. Their other activities under the SSFA include mainstreaming SCP into policy and plans, developing green hotel guidelines, and incorporating sustainable tourism into the tourism policy, integrating SCP in technical, vocational and continuing education curricula, and developing guidelines for paperless offices.

6.3.2 *Other policies relevant for SCP*

In addition to the overarching guiding principle of GNH in public policy, the Royal Government produced the National Environment Strategy, titled "The Middle Path" (the equivalent of a National Sustainable Development Strategy), some 15 years ago as a strategic document to guide the country in its development. The Middle Path identifies three main avenues for sustainable development in Bhutan and remains relevant to this day with its thrust in developing hydropower based on integrated watershed management, agricultural development based on SP practice, and industrial development based on effective pollution controls and enforcement of environmental standards [NEC, 1998].

With the GNH screening tool and the Middle Path guiding development in Bhutan, in 2010, a new EDP was launched with the vision "to promote a green and self-reliant economy sustained by an IT-enabled knowledge society guided by the GNH philosophy" [MOEA, 2010]. The key strategies towards this end are geared to diversify the country's economic base with a focus on harnessing the natural resources in a sustainable manner, reducing the need for fossil fuels in the economy (especially with regard to transportation), promoting Bhutan as an organic brand and as an eco-tourist destination, with the overall end goal of minimising ecological damages. This is being effected through targeted interventions in the form of tax holidays, tax exemptions, and subsidies.

The Royal Government of Bhutan (RGOB) also formulated and launched "the National Strategy and Action Plan for LC Development" in June 2012, following its declaration to remain a carbon neutral country at the 2009 Conference of Parties of the UNFCCC in Denmark which further reinforces and strengthens Bhutan's commitment to develop with the principles of sustainable development. The National Strategy and Action Plan for LC Development comprises various scenarios analysing development paths until the year 2040. The strategy includes a number of short and medium-term policies regarding residential, commercial, and industrial energy consumption, as well as addressing transport. Non-energy related sectors are also addressed, and further categorised into industrial processes, agriculture, land use and forestry, and municipal waste. The overall objective is to achieve carbon neutrality while still pursuing sustainable economic development based on baseline information provided by the NEC and the NSB.

At the same time, the country is working towards formulating standards; the Bhutan Standards Bureau (BSB) was thus established in 2010. Its aims are to foster and promote standards and standardisation activities as a means of advancing the national economy, benefiting the health, safety and welfare of the public, assisting and protecting consumers, protecting the natural environment, promoting industrial efficiency and development, and facilitating domestic and international trade [BSB, 2010]. This coupled with the launch of work being carried out at the DRE on energy efficiency standards, the launch of the green building design guidelines by the Ministry of Works and Human Settlement, and the development of the Green Hotel Guidelines (under the NEC Secretariat — UNEP 10YFP) provides room for SCP standards in the energy and construction sectors.

Similar to most countries, RGOB also spends a major chunk of its GDP in the procurement of goods, works and services. Public procurement is governed by the PRR 2009 (Revised 2014). Although current practices do not necessarily prioritise sustainability, the PRR provides space for the government to consider value for money and expressly provides that the lowest evaluated bid is not the only criteria for making procurement decisions. The PRR also provides for a 5% award to local vendors and local goods [MOF, 2014].

With the GNH philosophy that guides sectoral policy development through the GNH screening process (an iterative process between the sector and the Gross National Happiness Commission) and a National Environment Strategy and the declaration to remain carbon neutral — there exists a well formulated policy premise for pursuing SCP through green economic development in Bhutan, which is covered in more detail below.

6.3.3 *Sectoral policies related to SCP*

As previously mentioned, all sectoral policies in Bhutan are formulated with the GNH philosophy and screened by the GNH Commission before implementation. The Middle Path also plays a vital role in the development agenda and was a guiding document for policy makers and planners in Bhutan in developing sectoral policies before the introduction of the

GNH screening framework in 2009. Against this background, the 2010 EDP also provides incentives and subsidies to the following targeted sectors. The policies governing the major sectors of revenue and costs for Bhutan are discussed below.

6.3.3.1 Energy

Hydropower has been the primary driver of economic growth in the country since the 1960s. Hydropower generation potential is tremendous in Bhutan with a total generation potential estimated at 30,000 megawatt (MW). Currently, several hydropower projects are under construction or at the planning stage in order to harness additional power to achieve the target of total installed capacity of 10,000 MW by 2020. In 2013, the Government announced a subsidy of 100 units of free electricity to rural households in the country in addition to the already progressive power tariff, which was designed with the objective of ensuring affordable energy for all users and higher tariffs to deter wasteful consumption. The power tariff decisions are mandated to the Bhutan Electricity Authority and made with the objective to ensure affordable energy rates as well as to reduce the use of non-renewable and polluting sources of energy. To ensure the sustainability of the hydropower plants, the country has demarcated approximately 52% of the country as national parks, protected areas or biological corridors. This is necessary to protect not only the rich biodiversity, but also the watershed quality, which has a direct impact on the generation potential and the lives of communities downstream in Bhutan, India, and Bangladesh. To this effect, the government mandates that a minimum of 1% of the royalties of hydropower sales will be reinvested into integrated watershed management through the Ministry of Agriculture and Forests, making resources available for pursuing alternative payment models for eco-system services in the management of natural resources [RGOB, 2008b].

Furthermore, the EDP clearly lays down numerous incentives and tax breaks for investment in other renewable sectors, such as wind and solar farms. The Government has undertaken assessments on solar and wind energy potential in Bhutan, although no major projects are yet planned. Approximately 4,000–5,000 rural households currently use solar power for lighting their homes through government-funded projects. On the wind energy front, the first 600 kW farm was initiated in 2014 by the DRE, MOEA, feeding the electricity generated into the National Grid. At the same time, the Ministry of Agriculture and Forests has been closely working with the Stichting Nederlandse Vrijwilligers (Foundation of Netherlands Volunteers — SNV Netherlands) to implement biogas initiatives in rural households in the country.

6.3.3.2 Agriculture, forests, and biodiversity

Approximately 69% of the country's population lives in rural areas and are primarily dependent on agriculture for their livelihood. The 11th FYP identifies the agriculture sector as critical for pursuing equitable socio-economic growth. Agriculture has always been a priority area under the FYPs and the 11th FYP has expanded programmes to scale up crop productivity and reduce environmental risks. To this end, the Government continues to provide mechanised equipment, tools, seeds, saplings, and livestock at a subsidised cost in addition to professional human resources in agriculture and livestock to all *gewogs* (smallest administrative unit) across the country. To ensure a competitive advantage, the Government established the Department of Agricultural Marketing and Cooperatives with the goal to implement the Cooperatives Act and provide support to farmers for formation and management of these agricultural enterprises. With the objective of SP and consumption in agriculture, the Government launched the National Framework for Organic Farming in 2007 with the vision of developing widespread organic farming and to become fully organic by 2020.

In the forestry and biodiversity sector, in addition to the constitutional mandates of forest coverage and GNH guiding the principles of state policy as laid out in the Constitution of the Kingdom, the forestry sector is managed through a well-established structure of Forest Management Units under the Department of Forests. These units have been established with the purpose of production forestry and the implementation of sustainable forestry practice in the country. Another major programme under the Department of Forests has been the community forestry programme, which integrates community development and forest conservation, allowing members of the community to avail themselves of the economic opportunities afforded by the forest and continuity in the age-old community practices of drawing resources from the forest. However, with development and forest conservation policies, these rural communities have faced difficulties in accessing forest resources. The community forestry programme has bridged the needs of the community in a sustainable manner, also ensuring the conservation of forests in Bhutan. In 2012, there were roughly 14,000 rural households engaged and benefitting from the 340 or so CFs [GNHC, 2013b].

Bhutan, as a signatory to the Convention on Biological Diversity, requires the formulation and implementation of a National Biodiversity Strategic Action Plan, the most recent launched in 2014. At the same time, Bhutan recognises the importance of non-wood forest products as an opportune sector for poverty eradication. To this end, the Government allows for the collection of non-wood forest products by local people, subject to product specific regulations in the locality.

The RGOB in recent years has been driving the establishment of rural enterprises that promote and sustain the value of agriculture, livestock, and forest products. In 2014, the micro and small business tax exemption programme benefitted 11,122 rural business enterprises. In the same year, the Government's programme for boosting domestic production, import substitution, and employment generation, through the Business Opportunity and Information Centre, resulted in the registration of 589 new businesses and the creation of 905 jobs. Based on the EDP and the Foreign Direct Investment Policy (revised to allow investments in bioprospecting and agro processing), the government is pursuing these sectors with the goal of product diversification/improvement and market access. To this end, the Government has been implementing skills development programmes and support for formation of farmers groups and cooperatives for improved market access.

6.3.3.3 Transportation

Although Bhutan is a net exporter of energy, the import of fossil fuels to power the transportation sector is a significant contributor to the drain on the national exchequer. In 2013, the country imported 7.882 billion

Bhutanese Ngultrum (BTN) (approximately EUR 112.6 million) worth of fossil fuels against power exports of BTN 11.2 billion (EUR 160 million), a major portion of which goes to the transportation sector. This was driven by the huge growth in the number of vehicles on roads, which in 2012 increased from approximately 40,000 vehicles to 67,500 vehicles [Kuensel, 2015]. To counter this, the country implemented a controversial "pedestrian day policy" — requiring all people to not drive their cars on Tuesdays in 2012, later rescinded in 2013 due to a lack of public support. However, to tackle this huge dependence on fossil fuel, the Government introduced a new tax bill in 2013, which increased the customs duty and sales tax of vehicles significantly; progressive tax rates based on the capacity of the engine [Kuensel, 2014]. The same bill also defined electric vehicles as tax-free and a lower tax regime for hybrid cars. The concept of a Green Tax was also introduced on fossil fuels (paid for by the consumer) citing the "polluter pays" principle. The green tax has been built into the taxes paid for when a vehicle is imported and also is progressive in nature.

6.4 Status of International Aid Cooperation for SCP

In Bhutan, most international agencies work directly with the RGOB, along the FYP activities that align with the donor agencies' focus areas. The EU provides funds in the form of direct budgetary support to the government, while the EuropeAid SWITCH-Asia Programme provides funds through the not-for-profit track, such as academic institutions and international and national NGOs, and work in mutually agreed and targeted areas at all levels from the grassroots to policy interventions. To date, the EU has focused on intensive support for Bhutan's efforts towards poverty reduction, food security, and democratisation. The development programme was worth EUR 14 million in the period 2007–2013, mainly providing support for renewable natural resources and enhancing good governance. The new EU–Bhutan cooperation programme, known as the Multi-annual Indicative Programme (MIP), amounts to EUR 42 million and runs from 2014 to 2020. The assistance to the RGOB will focus on moving towards Bhutan's overall goal of achieving self-reliance and inclusive socio-economic development as identified in its 11th FYP [EC, 2014]. The identified priority sectors are (1) Civil Society and Local Authorities and (2) Sustainable agriculture and forestry.

6.4.1 *International aid-cooperation programmes in Bhutan*

Apart from the EU, Bhutan's major development partners and funders include the GOI, Danish International Development Agency (DANIDA), World Bank Group/IFC, ADB, various UN organisations participating in the "Delivering as One" programme (including the Food and Agriculture Organisation (FAO), UN Development Programme (UNDP), UN Population Fund (UNFPA), UN Children's Fund (UNICEF), World Food Programme (WFP) and World Health Organisation (WHO), Swiss Development Cooperation, Austrian Development Cooperation, Helvetas Interco-operation, Japan International Cooperation Agency (JICA)/Japan Overseas Cooperation Volunteers (JOCV), and SNV Netherlands Development Organisation. Development assistance in the form of grants and credits are given for various programmes and projects that align with both Bhutanese development priorities as well as the focus areas identified by donors. The GOI continues to be Bhutan's largest grant donor and most important development partner, accounting for 81% of all grant inflows in 2013–2014 DANIDA, with 3.6%, was the second largest grant donor for the year, followed by the EU at 2.6%. In 2013–2014, GOI was also Bhutan's largest creditor, followed by the ADB, the World Bank, and the Government of Austria.

6.4.2 *Current aid-cooperation landscape in Bhutan for sustainable development*

Hydropower, health and education, communications, and agriculture sectors have been the largest recipients of international grant assistance since the 1990s. However, over the years, there has been a discernible — albeit marginal — expansion in the direction of grant aid towards other sectors, such as trade and industry and autonomous agency activities, including information technology, environment, good governance, and women's empowerment programmes. Apart from the EU's support through the SWITCH-Asia Programme, there are no other international aid cooperation programmes directly supporting initiatives for SCP. However, since all aid-cooperation is granted against Bhutan's FYPs guided by the GNH development philosophy, themes of sustainability are indirectly incorporated into most, if not all, development activities. The goal of current FYP is "self-reliance and inclusive green socio-economic development" which is very favourable for promoting SCP. While the most significant aid-cooperation to Bhutan is through support to the government, some international and regional agencies working in environment-related areas such as the World Wide Fund for Nature (WWF) and the International Centre for Integrated Mountain Development (ICIMOD) support various projects and programmes in Bhutan, which have aspects of sustainability built into them.

Due to Bhutan's significant achievements thus far, development cooperation has begun to phase-out its support, such as the most-notable conclusion of support from Danish Government to RGOB. Bhutan is also enlisted in the UN as a potential country to graduate from the list of Least Developed Countries (LDCs) in the next 5–6 years. Although the graduation from LDCs is not certain, its considerable social, economic, and political progress in the last 50 years could mean that the scale, scope, and nature of international aid-cooperation will change. However, it is very important to note that as a small, landlocked country, Bhutan continues to face various development challenges. Examples of these are limited scope in economic activities, heavy import dependence on India for food and non-food items, vulnerability in the agriculture sector, rapid urbanisation coupled with inadequate urban planning, varying levels of opportunities in different districts and for different segments of society (which could lead to rise in inequality) and dependence on revenue generated from hydropower. While Bhutan's vision, policies, and plans are very conducive to SCP, local capacity and expertise need to be strengthened in order to ensure development activities and economic growth adequately address both the social development needs at hand as well as the environmental conservation needs for sustainability.

6.5 Conclusions

While there is no stand-alone national SCP policy or framework currently being pursued in Bhutan, the recent agreement between UNEP 10YFP and the NEC Secretariat marks the interest and the will of the government to streamline and integrate the compartmentalised pursuits of sustainability right across the Bhutanese economy. The introduction of activities under the UNEP 10YFP and the mainstreaming of SCP into national policies will allow for the integration of various sustainability initiatives that the RGOB has been pursuing under the umbrella of sustainable development. Over the last two decades, Bhutan has been consciously moving towards more sustainable policies for development, which is evident from the country's commitment to pursuing development based on GNH, which places environmental conservation at the centre of its development strategy. The GNH development model uses the GNH framework for both planning and evaluation in the form of a policy-screening tool and a GNH Index for evaluation. This in itself ensures that policies are formulated and evaluated along the lines of sustainability and provides a chance for correction after evaluation if desired outcomes are not being achieved. Thus, Bhutan's current policies, which focus on priority areas like hydropower, sustainable tourism, value-added agriculture products, and other environmentally friendly businesses, provide a firm foundation for SCP-based growth. Some key growth-related challenges facing Bhutan include macro-economic imbalances created by hydropower-led development, stagnation in agricultural productivity, rising youth unemployment, constraints to diversification of the economy, and increasing tensions between infrastructure development and environmental conservation. In the long term, the increasing vulnerability in the hydropower sector due to climate change could have serious implications for the Bhutanese economy. In order to address urgent growth needs while pursuing sustainability, SCP strategies in energy efficiency and transportation need to be complemented by other strategic policies and interventions. These include institutional reforms to improve the investment climate, infrastructure upgrading in particular, and increased availability of skilled labour. Policies for spending revenues from hydro exports and how tourism is expanded are key issues to be addressed in making growth more sustainable and inclusive. NEC is currently reviewing and updating the Middle Path document, which has been the primary document guiding sustainable development in Bhutan. The partnership NEC has with UNEP under the 10YFP will likely contribute to the revised Middle Path document, bringing SCP into national policies. While SCP is not necessarily mentioned explicitly in Bhutan's national policy documents, all sectoral policies include sustainability at the core of their objectives and this is also reflected in Bhutan's 11th FYP with its vision of green growth and self-reliance. With the EU already promoting sustainable tourism and SPP in Bhutan through the SWITCH-Asia Programme, the transportation sector and energy efficiency sector provide major opportunities for Bhutan to further pursue its sustainable development through SCP measures.

References

Bhutan Standards Bureau (BSB) (2010). *Bhutan Standards Act 2010*. Royal Government of Bhutan.

Department of Cottage and Small Industries (2015). *Cottage and Small Industry Report 2014*.

Ea Energy Analyses (2012). *A National Strategy and Action Plan for Low Carbon Development: Final Report.*

European Commission (EC) (2014). *MEMO/14/596: EU development cooperation with Bhutan.* Available on: https://ec.europa.eu/europeaid/countries/bhutan_en.

Gross National Happiness Commission (GNHC) (2013a). *Eleventh Five Year Plan, Volume I: Main Document (2013–2018).*

Gross National Happiness Commission (GNHC) (2013b). *Eleventh Five Year Plan, Volume II: Programme Profile (2013–2018).*

International Monetary Fund (IMF) (2014). World Economic Outlook — *Legacies, Clouds, Uncertainties*. October 2014.

Kuensel (2014). *Vehicle ban lifted from July 1, new taxes levied.* Retrived March 21, 2015. Available on: http://www.kuenselonline.com/vehicle-ban-lifted-from-july-1-new-taxes-levied/#.VRK3XfmUfT8.

Kuensel (2015). *Energy Trade Balance records Nu. 120 million surplus.* Retrieved on March 21, 2015. Available on: http://www.kuenselonline.com/energy-trade-balance-records-nu-120m-surplus/#.VRKzY_mUfT8.

Ministry of Economic Affairs (MOEA) (2010). *Economic Development Policy 2010.*

Ministry of Economic Affairs (MOEA) (2012). *CSMI Development Strategy (2012–2020) and Action Plan (2012–2014).*

Ministry of Finance (MOF) (2014). *Public Procurement Rules and Regulations.*

National Environment Commission (NEC) (1998). *The Middle Path — National Environment Strategy for Bhutan.*

National Statistics Bureau (NSB) (2014a). *Bhutan Poverty Assessment 2014.*

National Statistics Bureau (NSB) (2014b). *Statistical Yearbook of Bhutan, October 2014.*

Royal Government of Bhutan (RGOB) (2008a). *The Bhutan Sustainable Hydropower Development Policy.*

Royal Government of Bhutan (RGOB) (2008b). *The Constitution of the Kingdom of Bhutan.*

Royal Government of Bhutan (2012). *Bhutan: In Pursuit of Sustainable Development.*

Royal Monetary Authority (2014). *Annual Report 2013/14*, Bhutan.

The Bhutanese (2014). *Bhutan's First Wind Power Project in Rubessa to power 600 households.*

Tshering, K. (2015). *Presentation on Sustainable Consumption and Production in Bhutan, Life Cycle Management Workshop,* April 13, 2015. Thimphu, Bhutan.

United Nations Development Programme (UNDP) (2014). Human Development Report 2014 — *Sustaining Human Progress: Reducing Vulnerabilities and Building Resilience.*

United Nations Environment Programme (UNEP) (2012). *Sustainable Consumption and Production: A Handbook for Policy Makers, with cases from Asia and the Pacific.*

World Bank (2014). *Note on Green Growth for Bhutan.*

Chapter 7

Sustainable Energy through SCP in Cambodia

R. de Jong

7.1 Introduction

This chapter addresses the economy, sustainability challenges and sustainable consumption and production (SCP) practices in Cambodia. It focuses in particular on renewable energy, energy efficiency, and providing energy access, which are also priority areas of the country's Green Growth policy for 2013–2030.

Cambodia is located in Southeast Asia bordering Vietnam in the East, Lao PDR in the North, and Thailand in the West, and has a total land area of 181,035 km^2. The country's population grew from around 9 million in the 1960s to 15.14 million in 2013. The capital, Phnom Penh, has 2.2 million inhabitants with reasonable access to modern services like healthcare, education, and energy. However, approximately 80% of Cambodians live in rural areas with limited access to clean and affordable energy and water.

Cambodia is one of the poorest countries in Southeast Asia and is classified as a Least Developed Country (LDC) by the United Nations and as a low-income country by the World Bank. With a Human Development Index (HDI) of 0.584, Cambodia ranks 136th out of 187 countries. The HDI differs greatly depending on the area: Generally, the urban populations are better off than the rural populations, with Phnom Penh having the highest HDI of the country at 0.936, and the worst indicator for Mondulkiri, which has a HDI of only 0.220. However, Cambodia has experienced rapid economic growth since 1999, with annual growth rates of between 6 and 10%. Between 1999 and 2011, GDP per capita has more than tripled and it is expected to continue to increase [Small-Scale Sustainable Infrastructure Development Fund, 2015]. This leads to the expectation Cambodia will soon move towards becoming a low–middle income country.

Cambodia has a tropical climate and is subject to both Southeast and Northwest monsoons. The Southeast monsoon, which coincides with the rainy season, extends from May to October. The Northwest monsoon brings a cool but drier period from November to April. The average annual rainfall is about 1,500 mm, with the heaviest rainfalls of up to 4,000 mm per year occurring along the southwest coastal line. The Tonle Sap River drains the Tonle Sap Lake from the northwest before it continues further to the south east to its lower delta in Vietnam. The Tonle Sap Lake is the largest freshwater body in Cambodia, serves as a buffer in the Mekong River system for flood mitigation, and is the source of beneficial dry season flows. The monsoon amplifies the inflow of water volume from the upper Mekong region. As result, hydropower plants face a significant decrease in their generation capacity during the dry season, illustrating one of the challenges Cambodia faces in providing stable electricity supply.

7.2 Economy, Employment, and SMEs

Export of goods and services contributed 66% of Cambodia's GDP in 2013, with the main export destinations being the European Union (EU), China and the United States of America (USA). Around 70% of total export comes from textile goods; other exports include vehicles, footwear, natural rubber, and fish, while the service sector accounts for 40.8% of GDP [UNDP, 2015], with tourism as one of the most important service sectors. In 2013, over 4 million tourists visited Cambodia, providing an accumulation of foreign currency earnings and employment for the Cambodian workforce. The sector faces two main challenges, being revenue leakage and human resources issues. According to the Ministry of Tourism (MoT), 25% of revenue was leaked out of the country due to the country's dependency on foreign goods to supply the needs of hotels and restaurants. Secondly, there is a lack of human resources and professionalism in the sector. Cambodia's sustainable tourism, which should help to minimise the impact of tourism on the local environment and culture, is not yet well established and investment is needed to build and maintain the hard and soft infrastructure to support the development of this sector. Soft infrastructure refers to human resources, and hard infrastructure refers to transportation, telecommunications, and electricity, including renewable energy technologies. Cambodia's Tourism Strategic Development Plan is mostly oriented towards improving tourism infrastructure (road, airport, water supply, and electricity), simplifying visa services and travel facilities, and diversifying its tourist products and locations to Siem Reap, Phnom Penh, the coastal zone, and the Northeast region. However, the focus is not so much on developing sustainable tourism but rather to take full account of current and future economic, social, and environmental impact, while helping to generate future employment for local people.

The agricultural sector accounts for 33.5% of GDP and is mostly based on crops, livestock, poultry, fisheries, forestry, and logging. Export goods are pigs, fish, livestock fish, and beef. Another 25.6% of GDP comes from the industrial sector, within which textiles are the largest industry with 19% of GDP. Regarding employment, the unemployment rate was estimated at 1.7% in 2013. Nearly half of the total labour force was employed in the agriculture sector, see Table 7.1 [NIS/MOP, 2014]. Table 7.1 also shows that in 2013, the service sector required 67.9% of the workforce in urban areas and 31.5% nationwide. Among the employed labour force, the proportion employed in the agricultural sector has fallen

Table 7.1: Employment by sector (%)

Sector	**Cambodia**	**Urban***	**Rural**
Agriculture	48.7	13.4	60.4
Industry	19.9	18.8	19.2
Services	31.5	67.9	20.4
Total	100.0	100.0	100.0

*Excluding Phnom Penh.
Source: NIS/MOP [2014].

from nearly 60% in 2009 to 48.7% in 2013. One out of five people in the employed labour force works in the industrial sector (see Table 7.1).

Spread over all economic sectors, Cambodia has 505,134 enterprises, most within the wholesale sector (57.9% of enterprises), followed by the manufacturing sector with 14.1% of enterprises [NIS/MOP, 2011]. The small- and medium-sized enterprise (SME) sector, defined as enterprises with 11–100 employees, measured 10,809 in 2011 [NIS/MOP, 2011]. Most (80.7%) of these SMEs have between 11 and 30 employees. Within the SME sector, the education sector is largest (31.5%), followed by the accommodation and food service sector (18.9%), then the manufacturing sector (13.1%). Zooming in on the structure of Cambodia's enterprises, 89% are small businesses with fewer than five employees. This is also expressed in the location of the establishments: 64.7% are home businesses and 8.3% street businesses. Of the 28% in rented business premises, the area required for the enterprise is less than 10 m^2 in 52.5% of the cases [NIS/MOP, 2011]. In terms of SCP, these enterprises lack the necessary funds and skills to promote medium and high cost sustainability activities or cleaner production. The concept of SCP is still new for most Cambodian SMEs and in the absence of a national policy framework and promotion of sustainability, their acceptance of this approach will take time.

7.3 Cambodia's Energy Situation

Cambodia's power sector is small by regional and international standards, but demand has been growing rapidly over the last decade. The annual energy growth rate from 2002 to 2011 was 16.3 and 17% for the country's capital Phnom Penh; it is anticipated to show an annual growth of 9.4% until 2020. However, demand has outpaced supply, and electricity shortages and power outages negatively impact the country's economic development [Open Development Cambodia, 2014], illustrating the link between access to energy and development on a macro level.

Wood fuel plays a large role in the energy mix of Cambodia. Of total energy consumption in 2012, only 6% was electricity, 24% oil products, and 70% biomass energy, e.g., agricultural by-products (rice husk, corn cob), and wood fuels like firewood, charcoal, saw dust, wood pellets [IEA, 2015]. Within the wood fuel consumption, 85% can be attributed to domestic cooking, and 15% to industry and SMEs. While the dependence on firewood reduced from 90.4% in 1998 to 79.5% in 2010 [Kingdom of Cambodia, 2012], wood fuel consumption still asserts pressure on the forests: annually 3,400,000 tonnes of wood fuel originate from Cambodia's forests, and deforestation continues to be a serious problem. Cambodia's forested land area, as a percentage of total land area, declined rapidly due to industrialisation, energy need and a lack of forest conservation. Total forest cover declined from 59 to 57% between 2006 and 2010, equivalent to 366,993 ha of the total land area. Only 18% of Cambodia's forests are considered protected and even protected areas are vulnerable to illegal logging. Despite measures taken, the rate of deforestation and restocking of trees is not enough for Cambodia to meet its MDG target of 60% forest cover by 2015. The percentage of forested land area even declined to 55% in 2013 [WB, 2015b].

Likewise, charcoal production and use contributes to deforestation and causes black carbon emissions. Charcoal for cooking is generally produced and sold by informal SMEs, and these entrepreneurs do not necessarily know or care about producing it sustainably. Since these enterprises operate in the informal sector, their prices are lower than prices of formal and/or sustainable businesses. For Cambodia's transition towards more sustainable energy practices, it is necessary for sustainable businesses to become more competitive by reducing the price differential between the formal and informal sectors. This can only happen when some regulatory measures are put into place, for instance with measures like VAT exemption for formal/sustainable businesses. Strategies like these are currently missing in policies and regulations, but would certainly encourage the development of sustainable energy sources and the formalisation of SMEs in the renewable energy sector.

Hydropower dams, currently providing 3% of Cambodia's electricity supply, could provide more power; however, a huge issue is the mitigation of social and environmental impacts on the Mekong River and its tributaries (e.g., fisheries, resettlement, land issues, changes in flood patterns, less sediment, greenhouse gas/GHG emissions, etc.). In the commissioning of hydropower dams, there generally is a lack of transparency, environmental and social impact assessments, and community consultations, all of which make large-scale hydropower dams highly controversial [Energypedia, n.d.].

Additionally, these hydropower projects are usually implemented with foreign investment, and therefore revenues, for instance from the export of electricity, go to foreign investors and not to national coffers.

The efficient use of agricultural biomass residues offers solutions to address the issues of affordability and access. In 2013, the Cambodian Ministry of Industry, Mines and Energy launched a project with the support of UNIDO, to promote the development agricultural-residue biomass utilization. One specific example is rice husks of which Cambodia has significant amounts available for utilisation. It is estimated that if all risk husk resources from mills were used in gasifiers to generate electricity, up to 30% of Cambodia's current electricity demand could be met [Larasaty, 2015]. Rice processing plants can achieve significant savings with gasifiers, similarly large rice mills. Rice Husk Gasification (RHG) technology in the rice-milling sector has been in use in Cambodia since 2006 with over 100 examples currently in operation, but with gasifiers not always of the highest quality or safety. These low quality RHG systems have negative environmental impacts associated with them. The SWITCH-Asia project "Waste-to-Energy in the Rice Milling Sector" addressed these issues (see Box 7.1).

Box 7.1 Case study of the SWITCH-Asia project "Waste-to-Energy in the Rice Milling Sector"

The Cambodian rice milling industry faces challenges to compete with neighbouring countries due to the high cost of processing and logistics — within which energy prices play a significant role. The rice milling sector in Cambodia potentially has 1.6 million metric tonnes of rice husk available that could be converted into energy. However, currently only about 10% of the rice husk is utilised as fuel biomass for waste-to-energy (WtE) technologies. Of the over 100 Cambodian RHG systems in use today, there are significant concerns over the negative environmental impacts from low-quality RHG systems.

The main goal of the "WtE in rice milling sector" project, implemented from January 2012 to December 2015, was to promote sustainable production (SP) of milled rice through the replication of existing RHG technologies. The project

(*Continued*)

Box 7.1 (*Continued*)

promoted a standardised RHG technology and its application by 150 rice mills (30 rice mills with existing WtE installations and 120 new installations).

Three project components were implemented:

1. Technological improvements and the establishment of essential business services that support increased application of standardised WtE technologies over nine target provinces.
2. Development and implementation of a national standard for WtE technology and a licensing procedure that will encourage millers to switch to WtE.
3. Essential investment in business planning and the promotion of WtE, so that rice millers and WtE manufacturers have better access to investment credit. As banks and financial institutions (FIs) see the benefits, they will be better able to provide tailored financial packages to the sector.

Under Component 1, the project carried out Internal Management System to test some tools and templates on rice milling production at a number of selected mills (in terms of book and record keeping, operation and management of the mill, sales inventory, administration tasks, etc.). Training was also provided during testing and the project reached out to other relevant organisations (rice export and import organisations) in Cambodia to disseminate the templates and tools in order to capture a broader audience and introduce the applications.

Based on the project's experiences, basic safety procedures, operation and maintenance procedures and handling have proved to be a real challenge for most of the mills to abide by, which requires a gradual process and steady approach in order to change the present behaviour. The rice milling sector will need further supported in order for them to seamlessly adopt the proposals and create the necessary change.

During 2015, the project's focus was on blackwater assessments, disposal and management, and wastewater treatment plant improvements for three rice mills. A number of new activities related to turning waste into another source of biomass energy (e.g., pellets of rich husk char and other organic solid waste) and formulating a mixture of rice husk char with organic and slurry waste to create an organic fertiliser for agriculture crops.

(*Continued*)

Box 7.1 (*Continued*)

The development and implementation of a national standard for WtE technology and a licensing procedure under component two was still underway when the project was concluded at the end of 2015. The project has established cooperation with the Institute of Standards of Cambodia (ISC) under the Ministry of Industry and Handicrafts (MIH), who will establish an implementation body at the provincial level for the standard. They have committed to appoint one officer in each province. It can be expected that this effort will garner attention from the industry, despite being a voluntary initiative. As the development of the standard is being organised in a transparent manner, the process of adopting the standard is expected to be seamless.

The project has published a final document on the Baseline Standard on Health, Safety and Environment at workplace, where ISC and MIH will extend the baseline standard into a more detailed technical standard for manufacturing and production of RHG. The Health, Safety, and Environment baseline will be applied to rice mills and manufacturers while the standard for the RHG system is to be adopted by the manufacturers, both local and imported technology providers. The development of the business support services that the project provided under Component 3 have shown some positive signs that the technology suppliers, rice milling equipment suppliers, and commercial banks will work together to provide rice millers the equipment they require at competitive loan terms. Both the local Cambodian banks Canadia and Acleda have participated in most of the project's awareness raising events with attendance from the rice millers and other key sector players. Both banks have their own existing loan and credit structures for the rice sector, with an interest rate between 10% and 12%, and typically the mill's land title and other physical assets are required as collateral. The only downside of the existing loan structure was that millers take out loans for facility improvements and stocking paddies and very few would use the loans for RHG installations or upgrades to create the necessary energy switch at their facility.

More project information is available on: http://www.switch-asia.eu/projects/w2e-in-rice-milling-sector/.

7.3.1 *Electricity access and poverty*

From 1990 to 2010, worldwide access to electricity in urban areas increased by around 1.1 billion people, while the total global population increased by 1.27 billion; at the same time both total population and people with access to electricity in rural areas increased by around 0.3 billion people. As we see, rural electrification has increased in line with population growth, but the number of people without access to electricity has not changed [IRENA, 2015]. Cambodia is no exception to this and compared to its neighbours has the lowest electrification rate in the region: while almost all households in urban areas are connected to the national grid, only 14% of rural households are connected. In 2012, 31% of Cambodia's population had access to electricity [World Bank, 2015]. Even though GDP per capita increased between 2000 and 2009, the growth in electricity access did not keep track with this development (see Figure 7.1).

From the perspective of SCP, the challenge for Cambodia is how to provide access to affordable and sustainable energy sources, thereby enable leapfrogging of unsustainable energy generation infrastructures and unsustainable energy consumption patterns of industry and households. Until 2007, Cambodian energy supply was almost entirely generated from oil-fired power stations. Domestic generation was replaced by imports from Thailand and Vietnam with the commissioning of inter-connectors in 2007 and 2009 respectively [Cambodia Chamber of Commerce, 2015]. Supply and demand continue to have mismatches at different times of the year and day. Because of expensive imported diesel and fragmented power supply systems, electricity prices in Cambodia are amongst the highest worldwide.

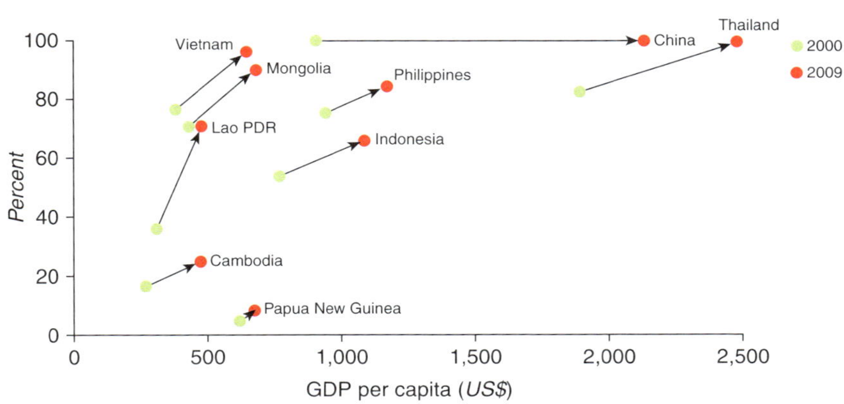

Figure 7.1: Growth in electricity access versus GDP in Asia (per capita, 2000–2009)
Source: [World Bank, 2011].

The Cambodian population suffers from having high electricity tariffs and energy costs. Paradoxically, prices per kWh are the highest in the areas where the poorest people live: in Phnom Penh, households pay USD 0.18 per kWh and businesses USD 0.19 per kWh. In grid-connected towns and urban areas, prices can be as high as USD 0.25–USD 0.40 per kWh.

Even though the Millennium Development Goals (MDGs) did not explicitly address the need for access to energy, particularly modern energy, the need to improve overall welfare were well recognised by the development community [World Bank, 2011]. The UN Sustainable Development Goals (SDGs), in particular SDG7, specifically addresses the need of access to "affordable, reliable, sustainable, and modern energy for all." The targets of SGD7 entail not just increased access to energy, but also to increase the share of renewable energy solutions in the energy mix and the improvement of energy efficiency. Here are clear overlaps and synergies with SDG12 on SCP. Realising the targets of the SGD framework requires new strategies to ensure affordable, sustainable energy especially for the poor through SCP, which encompasses issues such as energy efficiency and renewable energy.

7.3.2 *Sustainable energy policies*

Policy frameworks play an important role to enable the development of an effective sustainable energy supply and demand system. Cambodia has abundant renewable energy resources, such as hydropower, biomass, and solar, however, the development of renewable energy sources is slow and their contribution to the total energy supply mix is still small. This is partly due to the lack of experience and funds, coupled with inadequate data, but more importantly, the country's legal, regulatory, and policy framework regarding renewable energy is nascent and has not yet facilitated the uptake of renewable energy sources. The policies and laws which have been implemented so far to address the supply side and rural electrification are listed below (see Table 7.2).

Furthermore, the energy demand side has so far not been addressed sufficiently. Until 2013, Cambodia did not have a policy for energy efficiency to reduce energy consumption while increasing energy availability, when the EU Energy Initiative Partnership Dialogue Facility (EUEI PDF) assisted the Ministry of Industry, Mining and Energy (MIME) to develop

Table 7.2: Cambodia's key laws and policies related to sustainable energy development from 1998 to 2008

Year	Laws, Policies, and Action Plans Related to Cambodia's Sustainable Energy Development
1998	National power development plan
1999	Cambodia power sector strategy
2001	Approval of electricity law
2002	Renewable Electricity Action Plan 2002–2012
2005	Sub-decree on electricity tariffs
2006	Rural Electrification by Renewable Energy Policy
2008	Master Plan Study on Rural Electrification by Renewable Energy

Source: [Kingdom of Cambodia, 2012].

such a strategy. This resulted in the draft National Policy, Strategy, and Action Plan on Energy Efficiency in Cambodia (CNEE) that contains an action plan for promoting energy efficiency in industry, including raising awareness of good energy management, funding energy audits for SMEs and providing loans for improvements in energy efficiency [Cambodia Chamber of Commerce, 2015].

Development and energy efficiency, especially industrial energy efficiency, are clearly linked. Remarkably, even though energy prices are high in Cambodia, energy management practices are not widespread and even in the industry and service sector, energy audits are sparse. Even if actors are aware of the disproportionate consumption of high cost energy and the potential of energy efficient products and services, they have so far failed to achieve significant energy efficiency. Reasons for this lack of progress could be linked to insufficient technical capacity, lack of human and financial resources, lack of qualified local suppliers, or financing constraints.

7.4 Towards SCP in the Energy Sector

Since 2004, Cambodia's long-term socio-economic energy development vision has been detailed in the 'Rectangular Strategies for Growth, Employment, Equity and Efficiency.' The National Strategic Development Plans (NSDP) set out the implementation of the Rectangular Strategies and align sectoral planning as well as guide external development partners to align their efforts to enable better aid effectiveness. In the first NSDP (2004–2008), environmental issues or energy efficiency were not yet mentioned specifically. However, the 2009–2013 NSDP started to include a focus on the environmental and social effects of energy consumption. The current 2014–2018 NSDP takes this further by referring to strategies and policies for green development and climate change — topics that are overlapping with the SCP agenda.

For the development of these strategies and policies, the Royal Government of Cambodia (RGC) works together with a number of organisations, such as the Global Green Growth Institute (GGGI). In 2012–2013, the GGGI supported the RGC with adopting the National Policy and Strategic Plan on Green Growth 2013–2030, and establishing the governance structures, such as for the coordination of green growth sector strategies and activities. Currently, GGGI works together with Cambodia's National Council for Sustainable Development (SD) and the General Secretariat for Sustainable Development (SD) to develop the Green Urban Development Plan, which aims to help integrate green growth into the planning processes of Cambodia's cities.

In 2012–2013, the National Council on Green Growth was established with 57 members, with core responsibilities to prepare legal norms, policies, strategic plans, activity plans and programmes related to green growth and to integrate green growth principles into all aspects of the national development strategies. The National Green Growth Road Map 2010 has been integrated into the National Policy on Green Growth (2013–2030), aiming at developing the economy with consideration for the environment and sustainability of natural resources. With the national policy targeting a balance between economic development and environmental protection, culture preservation, social stability, and sustainable consumption of natural resources to improve people's living conditions and welfare, the Green Growth plan aims at developing a green economy by the effective use of natural resources, environmental sustainability, and green economy and finance. While pursuing its Green Growth strategies, the RGC has also embraced the MDGs and, more recently, the SDGs, where SCP has become a standalone goal (SDG 12) which links to other SDGs. There are numerous potentials to link SCP with Cambodia's National Strategic Development Plans and the Green Growth Road Map.

7.4.1 *The SWITCH-Asia programme in Cambodia*

The central question of this book, and this chapter on Cambodia is no exception to this, is how to reduce environmental impacts such as GHG emissions, water pollution and unsustainable use of natural resources while sustaining the growth of the economy and reduce poverty. Regarding Cambodia's energy sector, the essential approach is to balance the use of energy resources alongside the increasing demand for goods and services, which can be partly achieved by increasing energy efficiency; or by increasing the efficient use of biomass as energy resource.

The SWITCH-Asia Programme has so far co-funded seven projects in Cambodia (see Table 7.3), including the "MEET-BIS" project, which focused on increasing energy efficiency by improving SMEs' access to energy efficient and renewable energy technologies through business innovation packages (see Box 7.2).

7.5 Summary and Conclusion

In this chapter, Cambodia's economy, sustainability challenges and energy-related SCP policies and practices were introduced, illustrated by two SWITCH-Asia projects implemented in Cambodia, which demonstrate the development of SCP in the country.

Cambodia is still one of the poorest countries in Southeast Asia, but it has seen a rapid economic growth in the first decade of the 21st century. If current trends continue, Cambodia will soon be classified as a low–middle income country. With the increase of wealth, energy consumption has also risen and the energy growth rate is expected to grow annually by more than 9% until 2020. Unfortunately, the country's energy demand has outpaced supply, resulting in high energy prices, electricity shortages, and power outages which has a negative impact on the country's economic development. The implementation of SCP practices for energy efficiency is likely to contribute solutions which will ensure sustainable and affordable energy for many and sustainable economic growth, especially in the SME sectors.

Table 7.3: Overview of SWITCH-Asia projects in Cambodia

Name of Project	Period	Main Implementing Organisation	Places of Implementation	SCP Practice	Objectives or Impact
Sustainable Freight & Logistics	2016–2019	GIZ, Germany	Cambodia, Laos, Myanmar, Vietnam, Thailand	Sustainable transportation, supply chain	To increase sustainable freight transport and logistics in the Mekong Region mainly through energy efficiency and safety measures in at least 500 SMEs in Cambodia, Lao PDR, Myanmar, Vietnam (CLMV), and Thailand
Efficient Air Conditioners	2013–2016	European Copper Institute (ECI)	Cambodia, Indonesia, Laos, Malaysia, Myanmar, The Philippines, Thailand, Vietnam	Energy efficiency	Increasing the market share of higher efficient air conditioners in ASEAN, through harmonisation of test methods and energy efficiency standards, adoption of common Minimum Energy Performance Standards (MEPS), and changing consumer purchasing attitudes in favour of energy efficient ACs

AEMAS	2010–2014	ASEAN Centre for Energy	Cambodia, Indonesia, Laos, Malaysia, Myanmar, The Philippines, Thailand, Vietnam	Energy efficiency accreditation	Reducing energy consumption in the manufacturing and industrial sectors in ASEAN and to cut greenhouse gas emissions
MEET-BIS Cambodia	2014–2015	ETC foundation	Cambodia	Energy efficiency	Promoting economic prosperity and poverty reduction in Cambodia with reduced adverse environmental impact of SMEs in selected sectors
Reducing plastic bag waste	2014–2017	Fondazione ACRA — CCS	Cambodia	Waste Management	Promoting sustainable growth and environmental sustainability in the country, by changing consumption patterns and consumer behaviour to order to reduce plastic bag use and waste in major Cambodian cities
SPIN-VCL	2010–2014	Delft University of Technology	Cambodia, Laos, Vietnam	Product design for sustainability	Promoting sustainable product innovation as a proven approach in at least 500 companies in five of the most relevant industrial sectors in Vietnam, Laos, and Cambodia

Box 7.2 Case study of the SWITCH-Asia project "Mainstreaming Energy Efficiency through Business Innovation Support" (MEET-BIS Cambodia)

The MEET-BIS project promoted SP by SMEs in Cambodia by ensuring that they have access to affordable energy efficient and renewable energy technologies through scalable, commercially viable business innovation packages. The project did not target SMEs directly, but aimed to mobilise Cambodian suppliers of state-of-the-art and proven clean technology products, as well as (inter)national FIs that can offer financial services to SMEs to invest in these energy efficient technologies, if required. The project built on the experiences of the MEET-BIS Vietnam project, which was implemented from 2009 to 2013, also part of the SWITCH-Asia Programme. Trying to promote energy efficiency in a country with a low price of electricity (USD 0.06 per kWh) is a well-known challenge. As a first step, a baseline survey was conducted to investigate the experience of SMEs and identify the main obstacles encountered by SMEs regarding energy efficiency issues. The main barriers are summarised in Table 7.4.

Table 7.4: Four barriers to energy efficiency in Cambodian SMEs

Identified Barrier	Proportion of Respondents
Too busy with other business issues	69%
Lack of authoritative information	43%
Cost of implementing new measures	41%
Too much information available to select the best option	8%

Note: Information is based on a MEET-BIS survey with 172 respondents could choose more than one option.

For SMEs, energy efficiency is mostly a marketing challenge, and the MEET-BIS project activities focused on supporting suppliers to enhance their marketing and sales capacity, in order to build their market share among SMEs. To demonstrate this to SMEs, an audit was carried out in a garment factory to assess its energy saving potential, as well as showing the payback periods of the potential investments in new technology. The payback period is

(*Continued*)

Box 7.2 (*Continued*)

short for many simple measures, making energy efficiency an interesting cost saving measure for the majority of SMEs.

The project strategy was to develop partnerships with suppliers of energy efficiency products at the beginning of the project, lead the market research, execute the marketing and sales campaigns, and build capacity of suppliers. To facilitate these marketing and sales campaigns, MEET-BIS developed a Business Support Toolkit — based on a needs assessment of the partner suppliers — linked to the marketing and sales cycle, and specifically targeted to the SME sector. Figure 7.2 shows the different business support tools that have been developed as part of two different types of roles that MEET-BIS has used to build capacity and increase sales to SMEs:

1. MEET-BIS as facilitator: market creator, business connector, capacity developer, international matchmaker.
2. MEET-BIS as innovator & initiator: developing marketing and sales tools for suppliers to approach SMEs profitably.

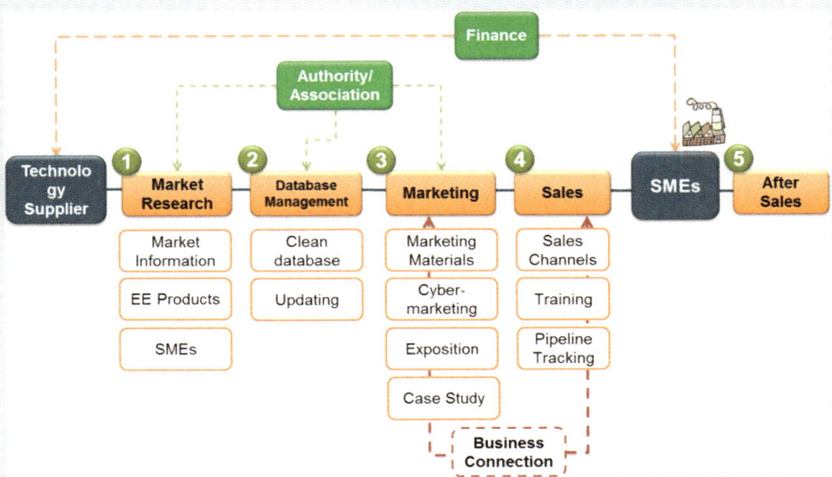

Figure 7.2: MEET-BIS project business support tools for SMEs

The project conducted research into relevant product/market combinations, resulting in insights into the landscape of relevant SME sectors, existing FIs

(*Continued*)

Box 7.2 (*Continued*)

operating in Cambodia and available green credit lines. Secondly, partnerships were developed with six suppliers of energy efficient and renewable energy products such as solar water heaters; variable speed drives/inverters; lighting (T5, LED); heat pumps gas water heaters, boilers, sensors and compressors; motors and pumps; and single split and multi-split air-conditioning.

An initial version of the Business Support Toolkit Manual in English and Khmer was provided to the suppliers. They were also supported with commercial and promotional materials specifically targeted towards their energy efficient and renewable energy products, which leverages their marketing approach to potential customers.

In terms of access to finance, two memoranda of understanding (MoU) were concluded with Acleda Bank and Mega Leasing Ltd. With the two FIs, five pilot financing models were developed: (SME) banks, lease firms, donor energy and climate funds, vendor leasing and ESCO structures, and crowd-funding type structures. Upon the conclusion of the MEET-BIS project in 2015, one pilot on product finance has been implemented with a leasing firm.

At the policy level, an MoU was signed with the Ministry of Mines and Energy, who made a valuable contribution to the project implementation.

Besides capacity building, the project also organised events in order to start the sales process for suppliers. Eight events have been held (workshops, business connection events, and sales training), involving and attracting 201 participants from project stakeholders, plus two seminars engaging 114 SMEs. Awareness has been raised among 765 SMEs through surveys, energy efficient and renewable energy technologies promotion, and providing information via newsletters. A total of 115 SMEs showed interest in energy efficient and water saving products and services by attending the seminars or by approaching the suppliers' sales agents at meetings organised by MEET-BIS project. Seven SMEs decided to invest in the energy efficient technologies.

More project information is available on: http://www.switch-asia.eu/projects/meet-bis-cambodia/.

Addressing the gaps in Cambodia's SME and energy sectors as a way of contributing to the country's SD, the SWITCH-Asia projects have introduced SCP practices in various industry sectors. The "MEET-BIS" project has worked to mainstream energy efficient technologies among SMEs and the "WtE in Rice Milling Sector" project promoted RHG as alternative, sustainable biomass energy source. Both projects have achieved substantial results by combining technical input, education and awareness-raising, and financing options that could be replicated in other sectors or industries.

7.5.1 *Recommendations for SCP in Cambodia*

The topic of SCP is relatively new in the Kingdom of Cambodia. Even though there are many existing laws, legislation, policies and strategies on energy, development and environmental protection, a solid policy that combines all these topics has not yet been issued. Considering the focus on energy that the Government placed on the implementation of SD, SCP can pave the way towards a more integrated policy addressing both supply and demand side, due to the cross-cutting nature of SCP itself.

The development of a quality control label for different renewable energy sectors would be recommendable to help raise awareness and trust amongst potential users of renewable energy technologies. As in the case of the "WtE in Rice Milling Sector" project, low quality gasifiers spoil the market and the same trend occurs in the solar sector with low quality panels and products flooding the market.

In the absence of a strong coherent network of specific policies, strategies and tools for SCP, projects like "MEET-BIS" and "WtE in Rice Milling Sector" are crucial in pioneering and promoting SCP practices amongst SMEs and providing examples for policymakers. The SWITCH-Asia projects have shown that industrial development, technology innovation and environmental sustainability can develop hand in hand.

References

Cambodia Chamber of Commerce (2015). *Cambodia — In Depth Study on Electricity Cost and Supplies (TDSP/2012/081/02/1)*. March 2015.

Energypedia (2016). Cambodia Energy Situation. Retrieved on October 13, 2015. Available on: https://energypedia.info/wiki/Cambodia_Energy_Situation#Hydro.

International Energy Agency (IEA) (2015). Energy and climate change. *World Energy Outlook Special Report*. IEA, Paris.

International Renewable Energy Agency (IRENA) (2015). *Off-grid Renewable Energy Systems: Status and Methodological Issues.* IRENA, Abu Dhabi.

Kingdom of Cambodia (2012). The Cambodian Government's achievements and future direction in sustainable development. *National Report for Rio+20 United Nations Conference on Sustainable Development.*

Larasaty, I. (2015). WTE - Gasification for the rice milling sector in Cambodia. *Project presentation during SWITCH-Asia networking event, "Advancing Energy Efficiency through SCP and Green Finance" Jakarta, Indonesia,* 7–8 July 2015. Retrieved on March 3, 2016. Available on: http://www.switch-asia.eu/news/energy-efficiency-in-asia-switch-asia-highlights-best-practices-in-policy-finance-and-smes-in-ja/.

National Institute of Statistics and Ministry of Planning (NIS/MOP) (2011). *Economic census of Cambodia 2011.* Retrieved on September 13, 2015. Available on: http://www.stat.go.jp/english/info/meetings/cambodia/census11.htm.

National Institute of Statistics and Ministry of Planning (NIS/MOP) (2014). *Cambodia Socio-Economic Survey 2014.* Retrieved on September 13, 2015. Available on: http://www.nis.gov.kh/index.php/en/find-statistic/publications/reports/cses-reports.html.

Open Development Cambodia (2014). *The Cambodian Energy Sector.* Retrieved on September 13, 2015. Available on: http://www.opendevelopmentcambodia.net/briefing/the-cambodian-energy-sector/.

Small-Scale Sustainable Infrastructure Development Fund (2015). *Social Merchant Bank Approach: Opportunities for dissemination to Cambodia.*

United Nations Development Programme (UNDP) (2015). *Energy efficiency NAMA in the Garment Industry in Cambodia.*

World Bank (WB) (2011). *One goal, Two paths: Achieving Universal Access to Modern Energy in East Asia.* World Bank, Washington DC.

World Bank (WB) (2015). *World Bank indicators — access to electricity (% of population).* Retrieved on October 1, 2015. Available on: http://data.worldbank.org/indicator/EG.ELC.ACCS.ZS.

Chapter 8

Sustainable Consumption and Production in Lao PDR

T. Phonsavath

8.1 Introduction

8.1.1 *Geography*

The Lao People's Democratic Republic (Lao PDR) is a landlocked country in Southeast Asia, bordering with Myanmar and the People's Republic of China in the Northwest, Vietnam in the East, Cambodia in the South, and Thailand in the West, and has an area of 236,800 km^2. Lao population was estimated to be around 6.8 million in July 2014 [World Bank, 2015a]. Since 1975, the numerous ethnic groups are often distinguished into three categories according to the geographic areas they occupy: The lowland ethnic groups known as Lao Loum (68%), the midland groups known collectively as the Lao Theung (22%), Lao Sung, including the Hmong and the Yao (9%), and the ethnic Vietnamese/Chinese (1%) [CIA World Factbook, 2007]. The population consists of 49 ethnic groups, in four main linguistic families, according to preliminary figures given to a symposium on the names of ethnic groups on 13–14 August 2000 [Asia Pacific Parliamentary Forum, 2009]. The main languages are Lao, in the Mon-Khmer language group. The leading religion is Buddhism with 67% adherents. About 85,000 or 1.5% declare themselves as Christians, Muslims, and

Bahai represent less than 1%. Animism was not regarded as a religion and included in "Other" which accounted for about 30.9% of the population. About 80% of the population live in rural areas within 18 provinces.

8.1.2 *Economy*

The economy of the Lao PDR has been growing rapidly since the government began to decentralise control and encourage private enterprise through the New Economic Mechanism (NEM) in 1986. Currently, the economy grows at about 8% per year, and the government is pursuing poverty reduction and education for all children as key goals. The country opened a stock exchange, the Lao Securities Exchange, in 2011, and has become a rising regional player in its role as a hydroelectric power supplier to neighbours such as China, Vietnam, and Thailand. Over the past 27 years, annual per capita gross domestic product (GDP) has fluctuated between USD 1,319.60 in 2011 compared to USD 151.15 in 1988 [The World Bank, 2015b]. The UN data economic indicator shows per capita GDP of USD 1,369 in 2012 and the Lao Statistical Bureau shows the latest per capita GDP of USD 1,628 in 2013.

8.1.3 *Human resource development and gender equality*

Human resource development is a main strategy to achieve a higher standard of living for Lao people and to eradicate poverty, thus is a priority for the Lao government. The government also promotes educational activities, human rights, and gender equality. In 2006, the government announced the National Educational System Reform Strategy 2006–2015. The Lao government has also been committed to gender equality and gender mainstreaming. In May 2000, the Prime Minister's Office issued a directive on the integration of sex-disaggregated statistics in policy and planning of gender-sensitive development programmes/projects. In 2002, the government established the Lao National Commission for Advancement of Women (NCAW). The government's commitment to gender equality is also expressed in a number of policy documents, including those on population, health, and human resources [GRID, 2005].

8.1.4 *Human Development Index*

Development progress in the Lao PDR has been recognised by a rise in the country's Human Development Index (HDI). From 2010 to 2011, the HDI improved from 0.520 to 0.524 [UNDP, 2014]. The Lao PDR has seen a 39% rise in its HDI since the first Human Development Report was published in 1990. In 2014, the Lao PDR sits in the medium human development category, ranking 139th out of 187 countries and territories in the world. The average HDI for countries in the medium human development group is 0.614 and 0.703 for countries in East Asia and the Pacific region. The Lao PDR's HDI for 2013 is 0.569, which is an increase from 0.565 in 2012. However, when the value is discounted for inequality, the HDI falls to 0.430, a loss of 24.5%. This is a similar rate of loss to the other countries in the medium human development grouping, but higher than the average for the countries in the region [UNDP, 2014].

8.1.5 *Energy and water consumption*

In the Lao PDR, domestic electricity consumption continues to grow. In 2013, households accounted for 38% of the Lao PDR's total electricity consumption. The public sector accounts for 6% of national electricity use, and has shown rapid growth over the past years [Lao DSM, 2013], whilst the industrial and commercial sectors account for a combined 55% of Lao's electricity demand [RESDALAO, 2005]. In 2010, the total electricity consumption was 2,230,000 MWh/year, equivalent to 39 Watt per capita per hour [Lao DSM, 2013], while the total energy consumption per capita was 110 kg oil equivalent in 2010 and correspondingly the annual carbon dioxide emissions generated per capita were very low at 0.3 metric tonnes per capita [UNdata, 2015].

The water sources in Laos comprise the Mekong tributaries, which contribute 35% to the whole Mekong Basin, supplying 270 billion cubic meters or about 600,000 m^3 per person. Only 2% or about 5.7 billion cubic meters is used for agriculture and irrigation, equivalent to approximately 850 m^3 per capita, while current demand is only 259 m^3 per capita. Water usage is predominantly agricultural at 82%, followed by industrial at 10%, and domestic at 8% [WEPA, 2015].

8.1.6 *Sustainability challenges*

The Lao PDR faces a challenge to balance its rapid economic growth without causing further environmental damage. Forest cover in the country has declined from 49.10% in 1982 to 40.34% in 2010. This is down from some 70% forest cover several decades prior. When combined with further industrial activity, the decline in forest cover transformed the country from a net sequester of CO_2 in 1990 to a net emitter in 2000 [UNDP, 2013]. The main causes of forest reduction are the shifting of rice cultivation in the northern part of Laos and the unsustainable forest exploitation in the past to cover economic balance. Since 2000, the Lao Government has issued policies to stop shifting rice cultivation and reverting to previous agricultural practices.

The construction of hydropower dams and the inefficient industrial use of forest resources are further reasons for the decline in forest cover. The biggest challenge facing the Lao PDR is the goal to lift up the country from the list of least developed country by 2020 and to develop in sustainable ways as described in the Millennium Development Goal (MDG) 7 of Laos. State policies and strategies have been issued and implemented in order to attain these goals, including:

- The national Growth and Poverty Eradication Strategy.
- Lao Tourism Strategy 2006–2020.
- Renewable Energy Development Strategy in Lao PDR 2025.
- Forestry Strategy to the Year 2020 of the Lao PDR.
- The National Socio-economic Development Strategy 2011–2020.
- Strategic Framework for National Sustainable Development Strategy for Lao PDR (2008).
- National Environment Strategy toward 2020.
- Industry and Commerce Development Strategy 2016–2020.
- Industry and Handicraft Development Strategy toward 2020.

So far, no specific policy framework or national strategy has been established that specifically addresses sustainable consumption and production (SCP).

8.2 Major Industry Structures and Situation of SMEs

Lao PDR has relatively little industry, no heavy industry and much of the country's industry is comprised of small companies. These small establishments are involved primarily in the production of textiles and handicrafts. Laos is well known for the high quality of its aesthetically attractive textiles.

Even though industry plays a relatively minor role in the Lao economy, its importance has increased significantly. In 1987, industry represented only 11% of GDP, while in 2013 it represented 33.2%, a threefold increase since the introduction of the NEM policy. The number of enterprises increased from about 25,200 in 2004 [Kyophilavong, 2008] to about 124,567 enterprises in 2013, of which 99% are small- and medium-sized enterprises (SMEs) [Department of Small and Medium Enterprise Promotion, 2013].

SMEs are independent enterprises that are legally registered and operate according to the prevailing laws of the Lao PDR and are classified into the following size categories:

Small enterprises are those having an annual average number of employees not exceeding 19 persons or total assets not exceeding KIP 250 million (USD 31,875) or an annual turnover not exceeding KIP 400 million (USD 50,000).

Medium-sized enterprises are those having an annual average number of employees not exceeding 99 persons or total assets not exceeding KIP 1.2 billion (USD 150,000) or an annual turnover not exceeding KIP 1 billion (USD 125,000).

Lao SMEs play an important role in the country's economic development. The industries which contribute most to Lao economic development are mainly electricity generation, mining, garments, wood, coffee, and other agricultural products. In addition, tourism has become an important sector for the Lao economy. The agriculture and forestry sector saw average annual growth of 4.1% over the period 2005–2010, accounting for 23.5% of total GDP, while the industry sectors of mining and hydropower grew by 12.5% annually over the same period, and account for 33.2% of total GDP. The service sector also grew by 8.4% per year over the same period, accounting for 37.4% of GDP [Lao Statistics Bureau, 2013].

8.3 Sectoral Analysis

8.3.1 *Industry*

The main industry sectors in Laos to be suitable for economic development, as declared by the Lao government in 2014 are:

1. Manufacturing with a GDP share of 10.3% and average annual growth rate of 14.5%.
2. The mining sector with a 10.0% GDP share and average growth rate of 8.1% per year.
3. The construction sector with a GDP share of 6.7% and average yearly growth rate of 19.2%.
4. Electricity and water supply with a 4.2% GDP share and average growth rate of 0.2% per year.[1]

The number of factories as recorded in 2010 stood at 35,948 and in 2012 at 38,126, a 5.7% increase in this two-year period. The number of employees in industry was recorded in 2010 at 116,826 and in 2012 at 135,273, showing a 13.6% increase in the two-year period. More information and historical data from 2010 to 2012 are presented in Table 8.1.

Worth mentioning, although the growth rate of the electricity sector in 2012 is negligible with only 0.2% compared to other industries, the GDP remained stable and value was created within the industry. It is known that electricity from hydropower has a significant export potential, where most of large-scale hydropower schemes are funded by foreign investment. It is thus assumed that revenues from electricity export go directly to foreign investors and are not counted as national revenue.

---

[1] *Source*: Unpublished data obtained by author from the Lao PDR Ministry for Industry and Commerce.

Table 8.1: Data of industry 2010–2012

Description	Units	2010	2011	2012	Remarks
No. of factories	factory	35,948	34,623	38,126	
No. of employees	employees	116,826	123,414	135,273	
Total GDP by Industry Manufacturing	Million LAK	15,618,293	19,781,187	22,677,289	Value of the
Mining Electricity and water supply		5,440,923	6,246,070	7,456,422	same year
Construction		5,157,997	6,833,713	7,285,994	
		2,135,261	2,851,839	3,048,872	
		2,884,113	3,849,565	4,886,000	
Total industrial Growth Rate Manufacturing	%	17.5	14.6	11.4	Constant value
Mining Electricity and water supply		7.0	9.7	14.5	of 2002
Construction		12.6	5.2	8.1	(refer to total
		63.1	29.5	0.2	GDP)
		20.0	24.8	19.2	
Total GDP Share to National Economy	%	28.0	30.6	31.2	Value of the
Manufacturing Mining Electricity and		9.8	9.6	10.3	same year
water supply Construction		9.3	10.6	10.0	
		3.8	4.4	4.2	
		5.2	5.9	6.7	
Percentage of GDP to total industry	%	100	100	100	Value of the
Manufacturing Mining Electricity and		35	31	33	same year
water supply Construction		33	35	32	
		13	14	13	
		19	19	21	
Total investment in industry	Million* Million LAK	170	150	140	

Note: The exchange rate was approx. 8,000 LAK (Lao kip currency) per USD 1 in 2012.

8.3.2 *Sustainable tourism*

Apart from the four key industry sectors, tourism and its related products and services are among the fastest growing sectors, which create jobs and revenue and therefore contribute significantly to the Lao economy. Thus, the government has placed tourism as the first out of 11 priority sectors contributing to economic development. The tourism sector is now a major contributor (second biggest revenue source after manufacturing and mining) to national income (7–9% of GDP) and employment [Lao Statistics Bureau, 2013].

The Lao PDR opened its doors to tourism in 1989 and ever since the number of tourist arrivals has risen annually. From 2002 to 2011, the total number of visitors grew by an annual average of 14%, from 735,662 to 2.7 million. In 2011, the total contribution of tourism to GDP was USD 1.4 billion, and the sector was responsible for 461,500 jobs, accounting for 16% of total employment in the country. No sector other than tourism has an equally positive combination of high GDP contribution with 37.4% of GDP in 2013 [Lao Statistics Bureau, 2013] and high employment generation with 16% of the workforce, and high growth rate 14% [Swiss Cooperation in the Mekong Region, 2013]. In 2012, the number of international tourists visiting Laos reached 3.3 million, which generated revenue of almost USD 517 million. The number of foreign visitors arriving in Laos in 2014 exceeded 4.15 million. The government therefore targeted 5 million international tourists for 2015 and expected revenue of around USD 1 billion [Cleaner Production Center Laos, 2012].

As numbers of tourists continue to increase every year and tourist sites are developed, there are concerns about the sustainability of tourism sector, and this issue has been addressed since the early 21st century. The government has developed strategies to promote and develop sustainable tourism, as outlined in the Lao PDR Tourism Strategy 2006–2020, and undertaken participatory ecotourism projects, often through international cooperation. A good example is the Nam Ha Ecotourism Project Phase I, which was established and implemented from early 2000 to 2004 in the Luang Namtha province by Lao National Tourism Authority (NTA) and the UNESCO-Lao NTA, in cooperation with the Ministry of Agriculture and Forestry and the Ministry of Information and Culture. The project's main donors were the Government of New Zealand, through NZODA, and the Government of Japan, through the International Finance Corporation's Trust Funds Programme [Lyttleton and Allcock, 2002].

The Nam Ha Ecotourism Project Phase II was launched in January 2005, providing support to the Provincial Tourism Office to identify new products and strengthen project management systems. In Luang Namtha province, the German development agency, GIZ, and the European Union (EU) are supporting ecotourism planning and management activities in Muang Singh and Vieng Phoukha districts [Lao National Tourism Administration, 2005].

Another example is the GMS Sustainable Tourism Development Project (2009–2013), which was mainly financed by the Asian Development Bank with additional budgetary resources from the Lao government. The Lao National Tourism Administration was the executive agency responsible for the coordination, management, and implementation of the project in the nine target provinces of Champasack, Salavanh, Savannakhet, Vientiane Province, Houaphanh, Oudomxay, Xayyabouly, Bokeo, and Luang Namtha. The main goal of the project was to contribute to the sustainable socio-economic development of Lao PDR with an aim to reduce poverty, contribute to the sustainable development and protection of natural and cultural heritage, and protect vulnerable groups from exploitation [ADB, 2008]. The main result of this project was the increase in ecotourism locations, especially in the area of Siphandone. Tourist guides were trained through intensive capacity-building courses and the income and livelihood of local communities were improved. Another important aspect of the project was the reduction of environmental impacts through better management of projects and involvement of local communities.

8.3.3 *Agriculture and forestry*

Agriculture, mostly subsistence rice farming, dominates the Lao economy, employing an estimated 85% of the population and producing 51% of GDP during the 1900s. The Lao government has committed to improving food security as part of its efforts to graduate from the category of least-developed countries by 2020 [FAO, 2015]. As recorded by the Lao Statistics Bureau in 2013, agriculture (including plantation, livestock, forestry, and fishery) contributed 23.5% to the GDP. The agricultural land as recorded in 2000 was 18,360 km^2 equal to 8% total area; arable land is

Table 8.2: Lao top 10 food and agricultural commodities production in 2012 (FAOSTAT, 2013)

Rank	Commodity	Production (int. prices $1,000)	Production (MT)
1	Rice, paddy	865,350	3,489,210
2	Vegetables, fresh	171,497	910,085
3	Bananas	102,823	365,100
4	Cassava	99,740	1,060,880
5	Maize	98,677	1,125,485
6	Coffee, green	93,824	87,330
7	Meat indigenous, pigs	88,814	57,775
8	Meat indigenous, cattle	71,238	26,371
9	Tobacco, unmanufactured	64,666	40,600
10	Meat indigenous, buffalo	52,704	19,580

8,770 km^2, which increased to 10.7% in 2012 [World Bank Indicators, 2014]. The latest record of the Lao Statistical Bureau shows a cultivated area of 14,280 km^2. The agricultural products consist of rice, sweet potatoes, various types of vegetables, and meat (see Table 8.2).

As already mentioned above, deforestation has been a pressing environmental issue for Laos. Underlying this chapter and the approach employed by a SWITCH-Asia project is promotion of rattan as a non-timber forest product and sustainable rattan management to address deforestation. The case study of SWITCH-Asia project "Sustainable Rattan" is described in Box 8.1.

8.3.3.1 Cleaner production and sustainable rattan harvesting

Implemented in 2009–2011 by the Lao National Chamber of Commerce and Industry (LNCCI) in collaboration with world wide fund (WWF) and the Vietnam National Cleaner Production Centre, the Lao Cleaner Production Centre played a role in providing cleaner production (CP) assessments to rattan factories and creating CP awareness to staff in three rattan factories: Daenlao in Vientiane province, Chaemchanh in Vientiane, and Phonemyxay in Bolikhamxay. Taking the Daenlao as an example, like

Box 8.1 SWITCH-Asia Case Study: Sustainable Rattan Project

The first phase of Sustainable Rattan project was implemented by WWF Laos in partnership with local communities and national stakeholders, such as Lao National Agriculture and Forest Research Institute (NAFRI), Lao Forest Research Centre, Department of Forestry, Ministry of Commerce and Industry, and Faculty of Forestry at Lao National University, with donor support from IKEA, a global furniture company. Phase I was a three year project (2006–2008) that implemented a sustainable rattan harvest and production model in the Vientiane and Bolikhamxay provinces to support local livelihoods, conserve nature, and capitalise on the rapidly growing rattan export market by establishing full-scale production and manufacture of rattan products within the country. The second phase of the project which focused on cleaner production and sustainable rattan harvesting was co-funded by the EU SWITCH-Asia Programme, titled "Establishing the sustainable production system for rattan products in Vietnam, Laos, and Cambodia." Overall, the project strengthened small- to medium-sized rattan enterprises by improving the processing and supply chain, including the introduction of certification, and implemented and enforced national and regional policy to support sustainable rattan management, marketing and regional/international trade [Campbell and Knowles, 2011].

other rattan factories, it faced the problem of high loss of rattan as waste. End-cuttings of rattan and the short lengths, which were stored to make other products, were not used. The waste from processing, like peeling, splitting, sanding, and cutting also were not used. This gives the company a high potential to save money and improve production efficiency, where existing waste was used as raw material for new products, such as small chairs, bins, drawers, trays, etc. These products opened new markets and required new design or re-design of existing products which included process control, modification of equipment, and use of new processing technology.

The project's main improvements were:

- Redesign of furnace: the usual furnace had two firing gates which necessitated much fuel for burning. The CP experts recommended to close one firing gate and replace it with chimney, making it higher than the length of the pan.

Table 8.3: Specific consumption for semi product at Daenlao rattan company before and after CP measures (CP assessment report Daenlao rattan factory, CPC-L 2012)

No.	Input	Unit	Jan–June 2010 Before CP	Jan–June 2011 After CP
1	Raw rattan *Calamus poilanei* (for semi product production)	tonne/tonne raw rattan	3.4	3.4
2	Fuel wood (for boiling)	kg/tonne	983	936
3	Diesel oil (for Rattan boiling)	litre/tonne	148	139
4	Electricity	kWh/tonne	525	528
5	Water for washing	m^3/tonne	17.4	16.4
6	Rattan waste (*Calamus poilanei*)	kg/tonne	32	30

- Optimisation of feeding system: the feeding system was rebuilt to utilise waste of rattan sawdust as fuel, in combination with firewood.

The results of CP implementation in rattan factories are presented in the following tables. Table 8.3 shows the resource consumption before and after CP practice through the implementation of low-cost and no-cost options, most in the category of good housekeeping and process control. Reductions were achieved in the fuel wood and diesel oil consumptions, which were followed by a decrease in the electricity and water consumptions. Table 8.4 shows a significant reduction of rattan waste in semi-finished product and furniture production.

8.3.3.2 CP practices for villagers

The challenges that the project faced were low product quality, with mould and fungi affecting rattan baskets produced by villagers to be exported to European market. Thus, the CP Centre was involved to provide technical assistance. The training course for villagers was to provide knowledge of CP techniques in rattan processing, including certain techniques for products destined for the European market.

Following the CP training, the communities saw an increase in villagers' income from sustainable rattan harvesting and production (weaving, splitting),

Table 8.4: Resource consumption of furniture production at Daenlao rattan factory before and after CP measures (CP assessment report of Daenlao, CPC-L 2012)

No.	Input	Unit	Jan–June 2010 Before CP	Jan–June 2011 After CP
1	Raw rattan *Calamus poilanei* (for furniture production)	kg/tonne	1.48	1.48
2	Varnish only for furniture	litre/tonne	—	—
3	Thinner (for painting furniture)	litre/tonne	—	—
4	Rattan waste *Calamus palustris* (as compared to the input material, i.e., small rattan *C. palustris*)	kg/tonne	327	367

better rattan forest management through Forest Stewardship Council (FSC) certificates, and better relationships between the project, local authority, and local community. The companies engaged in the project took the role of buyers for the villages, strengthening the export of Lao rattan products to Europe (see Figure 8.1).

Results achieved by the SWITCH-Asia project "Sustainable Rattan":

- Systematic involvement and training of all actors along the rattan supply chain, from village producer groups to buyers.
- 12 contracts with international retailers were signed and 46 were drawn up after the project completed.
- 22,000 villagers increased their income by 5–45%.
- The world's first FSC certified rattan plantations of 19,000 ha were under responsible forest management.
- 220 SMEs were introduced to CP practices.
- Policies were reviewed and piloted to support community-based rattan processing and to promote a green rattan industry.
- 38 SMEs started to amend their production systems taking into consideration environmental and social standards.
- 5,774 households (rattan pre-processors) improved rattan production skills.

Figure 8.1: Poungpatao villagers making rattan baskets, Bolikhamxay province, Lao PDR

Due to its success, the project was continued in phase III until 2014 with funding from IKEA. The objective was to strengthen the project's achievements through the following main activities:

- Strengthen village-level rattan management groups.
- Expand the FSC-certified sustainable forest resource management areas.
- Establish strong linkages with IKEA and other companies.
- Improve research on rattan ecology and biodiversity.

The social benefits of the project consist of increased number of secure jobs as well as revenue generation for villagers.

8.4 SMEs, Policies, and Strategies for SCP

In the Lao PDR, SMEs represent 99% of all enterprises. They are small even in comparison to SMEs in other ASEAN countries. Regarding sustainability, Lao SMEs lack funds and skills to promote sustainability activities or CP in the medium and high cost options. From the national authority or government side, there is still a lack of awareness about the necessity to establish a national policy framework and marketing for sustainability. The concept of SCP is still new for Lao SMEs, even though the CP concept has been introduced to Laos and implemented since 2005. In this context, there is an urgent need for:

- Creating national public awareness on SCP.
- Formulating a national policy framework on SCP.
- Human resource and skill development for SMEs.
- Information on best available technologies (BAT) and best available environmental practices (BEP), innovation on technology, product and process.
- Financial support for new BAT/BEP for SMEs and research.
- Marketing and tools for new market development.

As SCP is a new topic for Lao PDR, there is still lack of policy promotion. However, the government has agreed to contribute to related activities. With support from the SWITCH-Asia Programme, UNEP and the 10 Year Framework of Programmes on SCP (10YFP), a training on "SCP — the 10YFP and SCP within Southeast Asian Policies — Building Sustainability into Southeast Asian Policies Together" was held on 21–23 October 2014 in Vientiane. The event was an important milestone for the country to start SCP activities and later to develop its own SCP policy. The sectoral strategies described below will provide the backbone for SCP in Lao PDR.

8.4.1 *Lao Tourism Strategy 2006–2020*

The 2006–2020 Lao Tourism Strategy is a master plan document to define policy, guidelines, and the overall goal of the development and promotion of tourism which will be in line with the party congress resolution, national socio-economic plan and strategy in order to strengthen and develop tourism to become an industrial sector that generates foreign exchange revenue for the country. Sustainable development of tourism destinations is mentioned together with the objectives of providing more employment, promoting cultural conservation and preservation of the nation's good norms and customs, including the protection of abundant natural resources, promotion of local products in order to contribute to poverty reduction of all ethnic groups [Lao People's Democratic Republic, 2005]. Based on the strategy and the sustainable tourism pilot projects described above, sustainable tourism offers strong potential to support the overall sustainable development of the Lao economy.

8.4.2 *Renewable energy development strategy in Lao PDR*

Lao PDR has a high potential for renewable energy, especially from its hydropower resources. It is the most important energy resource in the country. The technical potential was estimated at around 26,000 MW. In Lao PDR, hydropower schemes with a capacity below 15 MW are classified as small-scale schemes. Only 10% of the produced electricity is used domestically. The government's energy strategy focuses on renewable energy resource development for the following technologies: biofuels, small-scale hydropower plants, solar, biomass, biogas and wind, and other alternative fuels for transportation [Vongchanh, 2012].

In 2011, the Ministry of Energy and Mines issued a Renewable Energy Development Strategy intending to make 30% of the country's energy sources renewable by 2025 [Lao People's Democratic Republic, 2011]. The main priorities include biofuels, small hydroelectricity schemes, and biomass. To reduce fossil fuel imports, the government has outlined a tentative vision to reach 10% of the total transport energy consumption to be derived from biofuels. The strategy aims to develop renewable energy resources which have not yet been widely explored in the Lao PDR. These are to replace resources that will be exhausted in the future ("non-renewable energy" such as fossil fuels, coal, natural gas), in order to ensure an adequate supply of energy, energy efficiency (EE), and conservation, to bring socio-economic benefits and finally to ensure environmentally and socially sustainable development through enforcement of adequate safeguards [Lao People's Democratic Republic, 2011]. According to Vongchanh [2012], the potential of biomass includes energy crops, such as oily crops (palm, *Jatropha*, *Veronica montana*, sunflower, beans, coconut), sugarcane, cassava, corn, and quick-growing tree, and aquatic cultures. Other sources of biomass are organic waste which includes residues from agriculture-forestry production, by-products from agro-forestry industry (e.g., sawdust, wood chips, rice husks, corncobs, livestock residue, and manure); and municipal waste (household waste, communal waste, food-processing waste). It was estimated that utilisation of livestock wastes for biogas production could generate around $2.8 \times 108\ m^3$ of biogas per year or equivalent to 5×108 kWh electricity (about 216

Name	Improved Cookstove	Tao Payat	Tao Dam	Tao Cement
Efficiency	39%	32%	28%	24%
Estimated savings	N/A	18%	28%	39%

Figure 8.2: Test result of the ICS

Source: SWITCH-Asia "ICS" Project.

million tonnes of oil equivalent/MTOE). Currently, most Lao households use firewood, charcoal and other biomass as cooking fuels. Biomass accounts for almost 70% of the nation's overall energy consumption [Lao People's Democratic Republic, 2011], resulting in high external costs, environmental degradation and an estimated 2,000–3,000 annual premature deaths from indoor air pollution. Most of the traditional and old cook stoves currently in use are very inefficient. Improved cook stoves (ICS) can better efficiency by up to 10–15% compared to conventional cook stoves (see Figure 8.2).

The new (improved) cook stove model is being promoted by the SWITCH-Asia project "ICS" which is described in Box 8.2.

8.5 Status of International Aid Cooperation for Sustainability

Lao PDR receives support from many international organisations to pursue a sustainability development pathway. UNEP works closely with the government on environmental, climate change and poverty issues, and the United Nations for Industrial Development Organisation (UNIDO) on industrial pollution issues. Another leading organisation which has an increasing role in Lao PDR on sustainable development is

Box 8.2 SWITCH-Asia Case Study: ICS Project

As in many countries, the fuel mix used in Lao kitchens consists of a variety of sources primarily comprised of biomass, wood, and charcoal. Charcoal prevails in 88% of kitchens in the intervention area, with an average monthly consumption of 40 kg, for some 10 USD/month. Wood is used in 48% of households and, with a large variation, this is in the range of 150 kg/month. Wood is normally collected rather than purchased, a task that requires 13.5–16 hours per month. Availability and affordability of wood and charcoal are highly variable. Charcoal is the preferred fuel for several speciality meals, and is therefore used regardless of the availability of clean cooking options, even in higher-end households.

Over the last decades, there have been attempts to design new, energy efficient cook stoves in Lao PDR with some success. One such is the *ICS* project, carried out by Oxfam Novib in close collaboration with SNV Netherlands Development Organisation and a local NGO, NORMAI in 2013 with funding from the EU SWITCH-Asia Programme and Blue Moon. The project is actually a continuation of an initiative started in 2010, to support further ICS uptake. The ICS project is one of the few initiatives in the Mekong sub-region that aims at mass dissemination of ICS, while contributing towards poverty alleviation in Lao PDR through the development of a SCP chain of fuel-efficient cook stoves. The ICS also reduces the use of wood and charcoal and lower greenhouse gas emissions.

The ICS project's key objectives for 2013–2017 include:

1. 15 producers sustainably produce 100,000 ICS.
2. 150 SME retailers successfully promote the ICS.
3. Lao Women's Union assumes its role as promotional partner.
4. Five testing agencies are operational.
6. A national standard of stoves is endorsed.
7. Establishment of a multi-stakeholder partnership.

Achievements as per December 2014 are as follows:

1. 16 producers are actively producing ICS.
2. 375 retailers are selling ICS in their local shops.

(*Continued*)

Box 8.2 (*Continued*)

3. The Lao Women Union conducted 26 demonstration workshops.
4. The Ministry of Science and Technology operates three test labs.
5. National standards are under preparation.
6. Multi-stakeholder meetings conducted twice a year.

The improved cook stove was tested for its EE and offered to project staff and officers from the Ministry of Science and Technology. Three test labs across the country are now operating; the tests evaluated fuel savings realised by ICS compared to various stoves commonly seen on the market (see Figure 8.3). The version of 'Tao Payat' improved cook stove has the potential to save 18–39% fuel. Apart from the economic benefit, the social benefit, which is sometimes hard to quantify, is better indoor air quality resulting in housewives' health improvement due to less smoke, while ICS also creates jobs for villagers, producers, and traders who are working in charcoal production supply chains. Further benefits are the energy saving potentials, which can be quantified in terms of greenhouse gas emission reduction [Teune, 2015].

Figure 8.3: Testing and production of the ICS

Further project information is available on: www.switch-asia.eu/projects/cook-stoves-programme-laos/www.snvworld.org/en/countries/lao-pdr.

the EU and through its SWITCH-Asia Programme, the EU promotes SCP implementation in the country. The EU's support and contributions are described in more detail below.

8.5.1 *Development cooperation with the EU*

In recent years, Lao PDR has increasingly received support from the EU. The EU has allocated up to EUR 60 million to Laos under its bilateral cooperation programme over the period of 2014–2015 to improve basic education, food and nutrition, security, and strengthen good governance as well as the rule of law and human rights. The EU and Laos have engaged in the Forest Law Enforcement, Governance, and Trade (FLEGT) process to reduce illegal logging. This bilateral cooperation programme has continued into 2015, but environmental sustainability is not one of the main topics. Cooperation also covers other topics such as human rights. For this purpose, the 5th Meeting of the Informal Bilateral Working Group on Governance and Human Rights was held in May 2014 in Brussels to promote information exchange on human rights in both Laos and the EU. In October 2014 the 7th EU–Lao PDR Joint Committee meeting was held in Brussels on a broad range of issues, including political and economic developments [European Union External Action, 2014]. Laos also engages in the regional SWITCH-Asia Programme (see Table 8.5) and the SCP initiatives held through UNEP. The majority of SWITCH-Asia projects implemented in Laos are multi-country led by either European or ASEAN institutions. An important partner for the projects has been the LNCCI. The sectors and technologies addressed include EE appliances, efficient cook stoves, rattan products, production, and marketing of organic food and innovative handicrafts. The following table provides an overview of current and completed SWITCH-Asia projects implemented in Laos.

To promote SCP policies in Laos, the SWITCH-Asia Programme's Regional Policy Support Component coordinated by UNEP, worked together with the Lao Ministry for Natural Resources and Environment (MONROE) to initiate national policy on SCP. For this purpose, a three-day workshop on SCP was organised in October 2014, involving the International Resource Panel Secretariat.

The event consisted of the following two workshops:

1. The Rio+20 10YFP on SCP: Building the knowledge of National Focal Points on SCP (held on 21–22 October 2015 in Vientiane); and

Table 8.5: Overview of SWITCH-Asia projects in Laos (www.switch-asia.eu)

Name of Project	Period	Main Implementing Organisation	Places of Implementation	SCP Practice	Brief Description of Objectives or Impact
ASEAN Energy Manager Accreditation Scheme (AEMAS)	Feb 2010–Jan 2014	ASEAN Center for Energy	Laos, Cambodia, Indonesia, Malaysia, Myanmar, the Philippines, Thailand, Vietnam	EEaccreditation	Established EMAS National Councils in Indonesia, Malaysia, Myanmar, the Philippines, Thailand, and Vietnam with a total membership of 74 organisations. Lao PDR and Cambodia memberships are under preparation. Brought about a total reduction in CO_2 emissions of up to 55,000 tonnes
ICS Programme Laos PDR	Feb 2013–Jan 2017	Oxfam Novib (lead); Association for Rural Mobilisation and Improvement (NORMAI) (Lao partner)	Vientiane, Savannakhet, Khammouane, and Champassak	Sustainable consumption	The project aims at introducing cleaner and fuel-efficient ICS by the end of 2016, aiming for 50% of the market share of cook stoves.

(Continued)

Table 8.5: (*Continued*)

Name of Project	**Period**	**Main Implementing Organisation**	**Places of Implementation**	**SCP Practice**	**Brief Description of Objectives or Impact**
Eat Greener — Changing Food Consumption Patterns: A Sustainable Approach towards Economic Development in Lao PDR	2014–2015	VZW Oxfam Solidariteit (lead); Phone Soung Agricultural Development Project (PSADP) (Lao partner)	Vientiane, Luang Prabang, Champassak, Khammouane, Xieng Khouang	Sustainable consumption, eco-labelling	The Project sought to boost national, ASEAN and European consumption of Lao sustainable food products (organic rice, tea, etc.). Increased demand for Lao greener processed food products will increase their market share and have a positive impact throughout the value chain stakeholders in a sector with high poverty alleviation potential.

Promotion and deployment of energy efficient air conditioners in ASEAN	Jan 2013–Dec 2016	European Copper Institute	Laos, Cambodia, Indonesia, Malaysia, Myanmar, Philippines, Thailand, Vietnam	EE, energy standard	The project aims at increasing the market share of higher efficient ACs in ASEAN through harmonisation of test methods and EE standards, adoption of common Minimum Energy Performance Standards (MEPS), and changing consumer purchasing attitudes in favour of energy-efficient ACs.

(Continued)

Table 8.5: (*Continued*)

Name of Project	Period	Main Implementing Organisation	Places of Implementation	SCP Practice	Brief Description of Objectives or Impact
Sustainable Product Innovation in Vietnam, Cambodia, and Laos (SPIN-VCL)	April 2010–Sept 2014	Delft University of Technology (lead); LNCCI (Lao partner)	Cambodia, Vietnam, and Laos	Product design for sustainability	The project set up a sustainable product innovation network to improve innovative power of industry, and improve environmental and societal quality of products made in Vietnam, Cambodia, and Laos. Activities included marketing skill training sessions for SMEs, marketing access via fairs and product catalogues.

Sustainable Rattan Industries	Jan 2009–Dec 2011	WWF Austria (lead); LNCCI (Lao partner)	Multi-country project in Laos, Vietnam, and Cambodia	CP, eco-certification	This project supported the sustainable rattan industry by introducing CP, a credible chain-of-custody certification and by establishing links to European and other international markets, thereby delivering a measurable improvement of the sector's environmental performance. Direct results include 22,000 villagers increased their income by 5–45%; the world's first FSC certified rattan and 19,000 ha under responsible forest management; 220 SMEs were introduced to CP.

2. Sustainable Resource Management Science — Policy Seminar conducted by UNEP's International Resource Panel (held on 23 October 2015).

Both workshops aimed to support Southeast Asian policy makers and stakeholders to build their knowledge on how SCP policies could support the region's sustainable development and meet the needs of the expanding consumer and producer base in Southeast Asian countries, especially Laos. Another policy project to formulate SCP at national level is currently undertaken with the support from the SWITCH-Asia Programme, as reported by the Department of Pollution Control of the Lao MONRE. The project, titled "Quality support programme," is being implemented from 2015 to 2017. The objective of the project is (1) creating awareness on SCP, (2) developing indicators on SCP for Laos, and (3) developing an SCP curriculum at the National University of Laos. This SCP policy project will contribute to sustainable development in Laos as well. However, it is just a start compared to SCP activities in other ASEAN countries. Thus, there is need for stronger support from the EU SWITCH-Asia Programme to advance the SCP policy agenda in the country.

8.6 Summary and Conclusion

This chapter reviewed the state of SCP in the Lao PDR. It is one of the South East Asian countries undergoing rapid economic development since the announcement of the New Economy Mechanism in 1986, especially from the 1990s when the Lao government opened the country to foreign investment. The main industries which contribute to the Lao economy are manufacturing, hydropower, construction, and mining sectors with high growth rates, but the latter has caused increasing concern for its environmental and health impacts. The manufacturing sector is dominated by SMEs and has grown continuously with an average annual growth rate of 14.5%, providing foodstuffs and consumer goods for the Lao people, reducing import dependency and creating jobs locally. Apart from the four main industry sectors, tourism is an important service sector industry, which creates jobs and revenue.

Simultaneously to rapid economic growth, concerns about social, and environmental impacts are mounting. Sustainability is becoming an increasingly relevant theme for policy and industry. Despite many existing laws, legislation, policies, and strategies related to environmental protection, there is still a need to have specific policies, strategies and tools for SCP implementation, partly because SCP concept is still new for the country. The policy initiatives on SCP have only begun in October 2014 through a workshop supported by the SWITCH-Asia Regional Policy Support Component/UNEP and the Ministry of Natural Resources and Environment. To move SCP further up the government's agenda, more support is needed from international organisations to run projects on development of SCP policy and strategy. This is vital so that Laos will not lag far behind other ASEAN countries, many of which have already established their national SCP frameworks.

The two case studies from the SWITCH-Asia projects implemented in Laos demonstrate the success of SCP promotion, especially in sustainable rattan processing and harvesting and energy-efficient cook stoves at household level. The success of the SWITCH-Asia projects is based on strategic collaboration of various stakeholders on national, regional, and local levels. It is suggested that the SWITCH-Asia Programme and the 10-Year Framework Plan on SCP could also support the promotion of sustainable production among SMEs in the field of manufacturing, agro-industry, renewable energy, and for sustainable consumption in the field of trade, consumer education, and eco-tourism.

References

ADB (2008). *Proposed Grant to the Lao People's Democratic Republic and Loan to the Socialist Republic of Viet Nam: Greater Mekong Sub-region Sustainable Tourism Development Project*. Available on: http://www.ecotourismlaos.com/downloads/GMS_STDP_Project%20Document.pdf.

Asia Pacific Parliamentary Forum (2009). *17th Annual Meeting of the Asia Pacific Parliamentary Forum (APPF)*. Vientiane Capital, Lao PDR, 11–15 January 2009.

Campbell, R. and Knowles, T. (2011). *Project Evaluation of WWF Sustainable Rattan Project Lao PDR*. Final report. October 2011. Retrieved on May 5, 2015. Available on: http://www.ecolarge.com/wp-content/uploads/2012/07/WWF-rattan-project-evaluation-Lao-PDR-FINAL.pdf.

CIA World Factbook (2007). *The World Factbook. Central Intelligence Agency (US)*. Retrieved on May 01, 2015. Available on: https://www.cia.gov/library/publications/download/download-2007/.

Cleaner Production Center Laos (2012). *Annual Report 2012*. Retrieved on May 5, 2015. Available on: www.laocpc.org.

Department of Small and Medium Enterprise Promotion (2013). *Unofficial record 2013 of SME Data Obtained by Author from Department of Small and Medium Enterprise Promotion (DOSMEP)*.

European Union External Action (2014). *The European Union will provide up to EUR 60 million in grants to Laos in 2014–2015*. Press Release 8 December 2014. Retrieved on May 15, 2015. Available on: http://eeas.europa.eu/statements-eeas/2014/141208_02_en.htm.

FAOSTAT (2013). *Lao PDR Commodities Production Data 2012*. Retrieved on May 14, 2015. Available on: http://faostat.fao.org/site/339/default.aspx.

FAO (2015). *Lao People's Democratic Republic and FAO*. Available on: http://www.fao.org/3/a-av023e.pdf.

Gender Resource Information & Development Center (GRID) (2005). *Lao PDR Gender Profile 2005*. Available on: http://siteresources.worldbank.org/INTLAOPRD/Resources/Lao-Gender-Report-2005.pdf.

Kyophilavong, P. (2008). SME development in Lao PDR. In Lim, H. (ed.), *SME in Asia and Globalization, ERIA Research Project Report 2007–5*, pp.191–215. Available on: http://www.eria.org/SMEs%20Development%20in%20Lao%20PDR.pdf.

Lao PDR Lao National Tourism Administration (2009). *Project Baseline Report — November 2009, GMS Sustainable Tourism Development Project*.

Lao People's Democratic Republic (2011). *Renewable Energy Development Strategy in Lao PDR*. October 2011. Available on: http://www.asialeds.org/sites/default/files/resource/file/LIRE-Renewable_Energy_Development_Strategy_in_Lao_PDR.pdf.

Lao People's Democratic Republic (2005). Lao PDR Tourism Strategy 2006–2020. Available on: http://www.tourismlaos.org/files/files/Lao%20PDR%20Tourism%20Strategy%202006-2020%20in%20English.pdf.

Lao National Tourism Administration (2005). *National Ecotourism Strategy and Action Plan 2005–2010*. Retrieved on May 14, 2015. Available on: http://www.ecotourismlaos.com/directory/publications/lao_nta_ecotourism_strategy.pdf.

Lao Statistics Bureau (2013). *Statistical Yearbook 2013*. Retrieved on May 20, 2015. Available on: http://www.lsb.gov.la/en/Statisticalyearbook2013.php.

Lao DSM (2013). Overview of energy consumption 2013. *Lao Demand Side Management Project*. Retrieved on May 12, 2015. Available on: www.laodsm.net/index.php/en/energy-use-statistics.

Lyttleton, C. and Allcock, A. (2002). *External review 'Tourism as a Tool for Development' UNESCO-Lao National Tourism Authority Nam Ha Ecotourism Project*, July 6–18, 2002. Available on: http://unesdoc.unesco.org/images/0014/001448/144843e.pdf.

RESDALAO (2005). Final report on energy status in Lao PDR. *Renewable Energy for Sustainable Development Association (RESDALAO)*. Available on: http://www.sunlabob.com/data/documents/energy_issues/O-05-11-Laos_Energy_Status.pdf.

Swiss Cooperation in the Mekong Region (2013). *Supporting the Tourism Sector to Alleviate Poverty in Lao PDR*. July 23, 2013. Available on: http://www.sdcmekong.org/tag/tourism/.

SWITCH-Asia Programme (2014). 80 projects at a glance. *Fact Sheet Brochure SWITCH-Asia Programme*. Available on: http://www.switch-asia.eu/publications/2014-project-fact-sheet-brochure/.

Teune, B. (2015). A Recipe for Success in the Dissemination of Improved Cookstoves. *A Case Study from Lao PDR*. SNV Lao PDR, February 2015.

UNDP (2013). *The Millennium Development Goals, Progress Report for the Lao PDR 2013*, *United Nations Development Programme*. Available on: http://www.la.undp.org/content/lao_pdr/en/home/library/mdg/mdgs-progress-report-lao-pdr-2013.html.

UNDP (2014). The Global Human Development Report. *United Nations Development Programme*, 2014.

UNdata (2015). Data for Lao PDR. Available on: https://data.un.org/CountryProfile.aspx?crName=Lao%20People%27s%20Democratic%20Republic.

UNEP (2014). Sustainable consumption and production — the 10YFP and SCP within South East Asian Policies —Building sustainability into South East Asian Policies together. *Training Workshop Agenda*. Available on: http://www.unep.org/10yfp/Portals/50150/downloads/Agenda_SCP_10YFP_IRP_Vientiane_21–23October.pdf.

Vongchanh, K. (2012). Lao PDR country report: the need for sustainable renewable energy in Lao PDR. *Report from SUSTAINABLE FUTURE ENERGY 2012 and 10th SEE FORUM*, 21–23 November 2012, Brunei Darussalam. Retrieved on April 30, 2015. Available on: http://www.seeforum.net/countryreport/laopdr.html.

WEPA (2015). Laos database. *Water Environment Partnership in Asia*. Available on http://www.wepa-db.net/policies/state/laos/overview.htm.

World Bank (2015a). World development indicators — GDP ranking. Updated 1 July 2015. Available on: http://data.worldbank.org/data-catalog/GDP-ranking-table.

World Bank (2015b). Lao PDR country profile. Available on: http://www.worldbank.org/en/country/lao.

World Bank Indicators (2014). *Laos Agricultural Land % of Land Area*. Available on: http://data.worldbank.org/indicator/AG.LND.AGRI.ZS.

Chapter 9

Promoting Sustainable Consumption and Production for a Better Future in Nepal

R. P. Chhetri

9.1 Introduction: Nepal's Development Challenges

Nepal is a small landlocked sovereign state located in South Asia. It lies in the Himalayas and is bordered between two giant neighbours — China in the North and India in the other three directions. The total area of the country is 147,181 km^2 consisting of 83% mountains and hills and 17% the flat terrain of Terai. Nepal is rich in natural resources and biodiversity with plenty of flora and fauna [Worldatlas, 2015]. High snow-capped mountains in the North, green terrace farms in the mid hills and fertile plains in the South provide untapped opportunity. Nepal is home to Mount Everest, the tallest mountain in the world with a height of 8,848 metres above sea level. It is also rich in cultural diversity, language, ethnicity, and is home to some of the best World Heritage sites according to UNESCO.

The total population of the country is around 28 million with an average annual per capita income of USD 730. The literacy rate of Nepal is 57.4%, out of which male literacy is 71.1% and female 46.7% [UNESCO, 2015]. The life expectancy of an average Nepali is 67 years. According to the World Bank, Nepal has achieved remarkable progress over the last years, where it managed to halve the percentage of people living on less than USD 1.25 a day in only seven years, from 53% in 2003–2004 to 25% in 2010–2011 and is continuing to make progress [World Bank, 2015a, 2015b]. Several social indicators in education, health, and gender have also improved. However, according to the Human Development Index (HDI) report, Nepal stands 145th in the world. Nepal needs to do more in the areas of education, health, income generation, infrastructure development, and food security. Nearly one quarter of the population still lives in extreme poverty.

Agriculture is key to Nepal's economy as the majority of the population relies on it for livelihood, work and subsistence. Production is largely for household consumption and the country has yet to progress into commercial agriculture. Promotion and development of the agricultural sector is imperative to Nepal as it continues to import food. Tourism is an important sector that promotes small enterprises and is a significant contributor to Gross Domestic Product (GDP). Many tourists are attracted to Nepal due to its natural scenic beauty; nature tourism is a huge attraction, catering for trekking, mountaineering, white water rafting, wildlife safaris, etc. Many tourists are also attracted to cultural, traditional, and religious activities. According to immigration office at Tribhuvan International Airport in Kathmandu, 585,981 foreign tourists came to Nepal via air in 2014 [NepalTourNews.com, 2015]. Nepal, as the birthplace of Lord Buddha, also attracts a large number of pilgrims.

Nepal is rich in hydropower resources, which are the major source of energy. Yet, the huge potential for generating hydro energy is still untapped. Therefore, the country suffers from an acute energy shortage adding an extra burden to the poverty-stricken country. Since the mid-90s, Nepal has prioritised and implemented a renewable energy model by incentivising investment in other energy sectors, such as solar, biogas, and wind. Rural energy supply continues to rely on agro-forest products, kerosene, and biogas for cooking and lighting.

Nepal envisions upgrading from the status of a Least Developed Country (LDC) to a middle-income country (MIC) by 2022. In order to achieve this target, much planning and investment will be required at the national level, including attracting international investment, and creating enabling environments for business to flourish. Furthermore, Nepal will need to prioritise significant investment in the energy sector, infrastructure development, agriculture, education, health, and industry. Simultaneously, the country will need to devise strong social and environmental friendly policies regarding production and consumption of resources.

In 2015, the Government of Nepal initiated discussion on a low carbon and climate resilient development strategy, within which energy, transportation, and industry, and commerce are prioritised. With a growing population and simultaneously degrading environment, it is urgent for Nepal to produce and consume more sustainably. In a small and emerging economy, small- and micro-enterprises have a crucial role in leading the country to sustainable development pathways.

In April 2015, Nepal was hit by a magnitude 7.6 earthquake, resulting in over 8,000 fatalities and more than 20,000 injured [UNHCR, 2015]. The earthquake also left hundreds of thousands homeless, and the government estimated the overall damage to be about USD 10 billion with rebuilding estimated at nearly USD 7 billion. This disaster left the country paralysed in its economic activities, having lost infrastructure, and other essential services, as well as causing severe damage to Nepal's cultural heritage sites, which are major attractions for tourists.

Nepal relies on international support for the implementation of its plans and programmes. According to the Ministry of Finance (MoF) [MoF, 2013], foreign aid plays a significant role in the country's socio-economic development, contributing nearly 26% of the national budget. Donors such as the European Union (EU), the United Kingdom (UK), Germany, Norway, the United States (US), and Denmark are development partners of Nepal; multi-lateral agencies like the World Bank, Asian Development Bank, and various UN agencies also provide significant assistance. The presence of international non-governmental organisations (INGO) is also important; in recent years, neighbouring countries like China and India, and new partners like Saudi Arabia and South Korea, have assisted Nepal in its economic development efforts. The MoF has, therefore, created an online Aid Management Platform for transparency and accountability, and to measure the effectiveness of an aid in the country. Substantial foreign assistance is directed towards projects for sustainable consumption and production (SCP) and environmental integrity [MoF, 2015].

9.2 Opportunities for SCP in Nepal

Like other Asian developing countries, Nepal is in the process of modernisation, which creates an unprecedented level of pressure in balancing the socio-economic growth with environmental conservation. To mitigate negative impacts on Nepal's natural resources and environment, there is an immediate need to change the way that goods and services are currently produced. Sustainability cannot be attained within the present context of over-production and over-consumption. Nepal's use of resources is unsustainable, produces large amounts of waste and rapidly pollutes its environment. In particular, waste generation is increasing at an alarming rate and Nepal does not have modern disposal or recycling facilities yet. In this context, embracing SCP principles is urgently needed.

If the correct development course is chosen, Nepal can put itself on track to achieve SCP principles. For this purpose, Nepal needs to learn from other countries and decouple its rapid economic growth from resource depletion. However, targeting double-digit economic growth has hitherto not been sustainable and often been detrimental to the environment. Over-extraction of natural resources, extreme business competition, and over production of goods and services can lead to low quality of human life both in the short and long run. Serious air pollution in Kathmandu and its impact on health are often taken as pertinent example. SCP principles promote quality of life, doing more with less, and preserving environment for future generations. Embracing SCP principles would help tackle poverty in the country, for example, by creating new (green) jobs, enabling resource management on local level, promoting local production of organic food, generating renewable energy, and attaining fair trade. Nepal has already taken some constructive steps towards SCP implementation, which should be built on.

Against this backdrop, the EU SWITCH-Asia Programme is currently supporting Nepal to switch to SCP patterns through several grant projects. The SWITCH-Asia projects implemented in Nepal have attempted to promote behavioural and technological changes in order to produce goods and services more sustainably. In general, these projects aim at small- and medium-sized enterprises (SMEs) and the way they do business, which in turn affect the consumers. Table 9.1 gives an overview of the SWITCH-Asia projects implemented in Nepal.

Table 9.1: SWITCH-Asia projects implemented in Nepal

Name of Project	Period	Main Implementing Organisation	Places of Implementation	SCP Practice	Brief Description of Objectives or Impact
METABUILD	Mar 2016–Feb 2020	The Energy and Resources Institute (TERI), India	Nepal, Bangladesh, Sri Lanka	Resource efficiency and cleaner production (RECP)	To implement sustainable production processes and practices in 400 SMEs and to create a conducive environment for further adoption of sustainable production processes in the metal products supply chain for the building and construction sector.
Up-Scaling the Production and Consumption of Bio-Energy to Reduce Carbon Emissions and Enhance Local Employment	Jan 2014–Dec 2017	HELVETAS Swiss Inter-cooperation	Nepal	Sustainable/bio-energy	Contribute to the national goal of poverty reduction through up-scaling the production and industrial consumption of bio-energy, thereby increasing employment and reducing carbon emissions.

(*Continued*)

Table 9.1: (*Continued*)

Name of Project	Period	Main Implementing Organisation	Places of Implementation	SCP Practice	Brief Description of Objectives or Impact
Green Homes — Promoting Sustainable Housing in Nepal	Jan 2013–Dec 2015	United Nations Human Settlement Programme Nepal (UN-Habitat)	Nepal	Sustainable building	Create an enabling policy environment to promote sustainable housing; strengthening supply chains for sustainable housing and building capacity of SMEs to deliver household-level green technologies and services.
Sustainable Production of Commercially Viable Products from Municipal Waste through Public–Private Partnerships in Green SMEs, Green City, Green Agro Products, and Green Employment Generation (PPP for 4Gs)	Jan 2014–Dec 2018	Winrock International	Nepal	Sustainable waste management	Enable a sustainable waste management system, construction and management of compost plant through Public–Private Partnership approach, promotion of compost use for organic tea and vegetable farming, and mobilisation of financial institutions to increase access to credit for the enhancement of organic farming.

Enhancing Sustainability and Profitability of the Carpet and Pashmina Industries in the Kathmandu Valley	Jan 2014–Jul 2017	Mercy Corps	Nepal	Cleaner production, resource efficiency	Increase resource efficiency, profitability, and sustainable growth by mobilising private sector and relevant public sector authorities to reduce fuel and water use, and water pollution in the Nepali carpet and pashmina industries.
Sustainable and Efficient Industrial Development in Nepal and Bhutan/ SEID (a multi-country project)	Feb 2012–May 2015	Centre for Appropriate Technology (GrAT)	Nepal, Bhutan	Appropriate technology, resource efficiency	Contributes towards sustainable development of Nepal's and Bhutan's economy with clear focus on industrial sectors that impact environment, employment generation, and poverty alleviation.

(Continued)

Table 9.1: (*Continued*)

Name of Project	Period	Main Implementing Organisation	Places of Implementation	SCP Practice	Brief Description of Objectives or Impact
VSBK — Vertical Shaft Brick Kilns and Other SCP — Sustainable Construction Practices	Jan 2012–Apr 2015	Deutsche Management Akademie Niedersachsen (DMAN)	Nepal	Cleaner production, resource efficiency	Promotion of SCP patterns in the construction industry, by raising awareness of private sector stakeholders for green building materials and solutions, and by providing consumer information on the benefits of clean energy and energy-saving building material.
Proposal for enhancement of sustainable production of lokta handmade paper production in Nepal	Jan 2009–Dec 2011	Nepal Handmade Paper Association	Nepal	Resource efficiency, sustainable production	

Source: SWITCH-Asia Project Fact-sheet Brochure (2014).

9.3 Nepal's Industry Structure

The industrial sector in Nepal is still small but growing steadily, being placed under the administration of the Ministry of Industry (MoI). Two other major bodies, the Department of Industry (DoI) and the Department of Cottage and Small Industry (DCSI), fall under its remit. With these dedicated institutions and their policies, Nepal is steadily progressing towards industrialisation. It was only after 1951 that Nepal started to look outward for its sustainable economic growth, liberalising its economy and inviting international investors. Economic growth grew rapidly after 1990, but was soon hindered by the civil war that lasted for nearly a decade. Nepal is now gradually attracting international investment, yet various political and socio-economic issues hinder more sustainable economic growth and progress. Nepal's distinct feature of being a landlocked country is also often perceived as an obstacle for industrial growth. Consequently, a large number of workers migrate to the Middle East, India and other countries in search for work and livelihood. In 2012, remittance was the largest source of foreign exchange income, amounting to 25% of GDP.

Nepal's Industrial Policy from 2011 categorises enterprises into various scales (see Table 9.2). Large enterprises are categorised as those with investment over NPR 150 million (USD 1.4 million) including land and buildings. Medium enterprises are those with investment of less than NPR 150 million and over NPR 50 million (USD 0.47 million) including land and buildings. Small-sized enterprises are those with investments less than NPR 50 million including land and buildings. Micro-enterprises are

Table 9.2: Number of enterprises registered by scale (up to financial year (FY) 2012–2013)
USD 1 = NPR 100 (approximation)

Scale	Number of Enterprises	Total Capital (in Million NPR)	Fixed Capital (in Million NPR)	Working Capital (in Million NPR)	Employment
Large	614	475,319.78	430,863.21	44,456.57	100,729
Medium	1,254	97,767.85	63,899.85	33,868.00	127,648
Small	3,406	45,995.56	27,944.23	18,051.33	229,901
Total	5,274	619,083.19	522,707.29	96,375.90	458,278

Source: Department of Industries [2013].

categorised with investment up to NPR 200,000 (USD 1,900) excluding land and buildings.

9.3.1 *Large enterprises in Nepal*

Nepal's large industrial enterprises contribute about 20% to the national GDP. Through its five-year development plans, the country has devised various programmes and policies to emphasise economic growth and promote industrial sectors. The government has prioritised sectors such as agriculture, tourism, energy, telecommunications, and industry (see Table 9.3). Infrastructure is developed within dedicated industrial zones in various parts of the country. The carpet and garment industry is growing rapidly and represents an estimated 70% of the total exports. Nepal's industry needs to produce quality products in order to compete in the international market, which is even more important after joining the World Trade Organisation (WTO). Nepal lags behind in many of its own targets in helping the industry to grow and flourish. The major of industries in Nepal are agro-based, manufacturing, energy or tourism.

9.3.2 *Cottage and small-sized enterprises in Nepal*

As Nepal is a rural and agrarian country, cottage- and small-sized enterprises play an important role in the provision of employment and income within

Table 9.3: Number of enterprises registered by category (up to FY 2012–2013) USD 1 = NPR 100 (approximation)

Category	Number of Enterprises	Total Capital (in Million NPR)
Agro-Based	271	13,419.44
Construction	40	6,219.03
Energy-Based	184	269,736.65
Manufacturing	2,319	181,076.15
Mineral	52	4,010.91
Service	957	45,784.74
Tourism	957	45,784.74
Total	5,274	619,083.17

Source: Department of Industries [2013].

society; this is in part due to the relatively low start-up costs requiring less capital and minimal expertise. These enterprises are seen as family businesses where capital is obtained from personal savings and family property. Realising its importance, the government in 1974 set up the DCSI to promote and foster this sector. The intention was to enhance productivity and create a favourable environment for investment, whilst increasing contributions to the national economy. Since then, the government has launched several programmes and projects funded by national budget. Cottage industries are expected to promote indigenous skills, foster traditional industries, and create local employment.

Most of the enterprises are involved in the manufacture of consumer and household goods, textile-related products, and food processing. Activities include weaving, handicrafts, woodcraft, pottery, leatherwork and handmade paper, and the making of noodles, candy, and biscuits. Since many of these goods are for export, Nepal's industrial policy puts a special focus on the micro-, cottage, and small-sized enterprises. This focus includes upskilling and improved access to loans. However, there is a clear need for more enabling environment that promotes the utilisation of local resources and skills. Therefore, to increase the sustainability of this sector, both skills and business capacity are of paramount importance to remain competitive in the international arena. There is also a need to identify new products for export and maintain quality control. Attracting foreign investment and the adoption of modern technology may also contribute to the development of this sector in Nepal.

9.4 Policy Perspective on SCP

Nepal has formulated several national plans and policies to accelerate its socio-economic development. Although it does not have yet a specific policy addressing SCP practice, Nepal is recently making efforts to encourage SCP of goods and services through an environmental legislation. The 2007 interim constitution of Nepal states that every person shall have the right to live in a healthy environment as a fundamental right. It also states that priority shall be given to the prevention of adverse impacts on the environment from physical development activities. Previously Nepal has issued an Environmental Protection Act (1997) that mandates different types of enterprises based on their size and nature to conduct mandatory Initial

Environment Examination (IEE) or Environment Impact Assessments (EIA). The Ministry of Science, Technology and Environment (MoSTE) oversees this via a dedicated division.

The established Industrial Policy has provision to promote sustainable production and consumption through good business practice. One objective states "Establish industrial entrepreneurship as a sustainable and reliable sector by utilising the latest technology and environment friendly production process" [Industrial Policy, 2010]. The policy also highlights the need for enterprises to conduct IEEs and EIAs. It offers support to small and sustainable enterprises that use local resources and are less harmful to the environment and the economy. The National Agriculture Policy (2004) emphasises the conservation, promotion, and utilisation of natural resources and the environment. The provision of environmental protection also exists in other policies and laws such as the Forest Act (1993), Water Resources Act (1993), Tourism Act (1978), Mines and Minerals Rules (2000), and Hydropower Development Policy (2001).

MoSTE has recently started formulating a strategy on low carbon economic development. This is an encouraging step, despite the fact that Nepal has less than one per cent global share in greenhouse gas emissions. Addressing climate change is of huge national interest as it is regarded as one of the most vulnerable countries to its impact. For instance, Himalayan glaciers are melting fast and there is a sharp increase in natural disasters such as landslide and flooding. Adopting SCP principles will contribute to reducing the climate vulnerability of Nepal through forests preservation, sustainable use of natural resources, improved food security, increased income for the poor, reduced negative environmental impact that lower disaster risk, as well as the adoption of low carbon development pathways.

9.5 Opportunities and Challenges for SCP

As Nepal is in its early stages of development, there are many opportunities for the country to move ahead in a sustainable and environmental friendly manner from the outset. Nepal can learn from other countries' experience to not pursue unsustainable development paths. Due to significant damage caused by the 2015 earthquake, Nepal will have to undertake a massive rebuilding process; this can be used as an opportunity to establish eco-friendly and sustainable policies. In fact there are policies and regulations already in place, which Nepal can further strengthen and implement to be a model for sustainable development. Embracing SCP would support Nepal's target to become a MIC by 2022.

Comparatively speaking, human-induced damage to the environment in Nepal is currently not so high and still relatively easy to mitigate. Urban growth and planning in cities like Kathmandu still lack coherence, which can be corrected given the necessary political will. Recently Nepal is in the process of writing a new constitution and this again provides opportunities to envisage a nation that is more sustainable, responsible, and environmentally conscious.

As Nepal is an economically poor country, sustainable development comes with many challenges. Issues like poverty, food security, sustainable infrastructure, health, and education already pose a huge challenge, not yet to mention the unstable political situation in the country. Nepal still lacks effective implementation and monitoring of the policies supporting SCP and sustainable development. Lack of competent human resources and the ability to bring in modern technology is also a big hindrance. Hence, implementation of policies that support sustainability is a challenge for Nepal.

9.5.1 *Agriculture, rural livelihoods, and food consumption*

Agriculture still dominates Nepal's economy and is considered to be the backbone of the country. According to the Ministry of Agriculture Development [MOAD, 2014], 66% of the country's population relies on agriculture for income and employment. Agriculture alone contributes 33% to the national GDP. The Statistical Pocket Book 2010 states that the total agricultural land is 24.97 million hectares of which 6.8% is in the mountains, 40.4% in the hills and 52.9% in the plains. Out of the country's total land area, 27% is arable, forest covers 39.6%, pastures occupy 12%, 17.2% is covered by snow and rocks, and the remaining 2.6% by water [Central Bureau of Statistics, 2010].

In Nepal, paddy, wheat, maize, millet, and potatoes are grown as major food crops. Only a bit later, the government gradually promoted cash crop farming, such as sugar cane, jute, tobacco, tea, and coffee. The cropping pattern is based on climatic conditions and topography of the country. Farmers still use traditional methods and outdated technology. Nepali farmers lack modern farming techniques, skills, and tools to improve seed varieties and lack adequate knowledge required for commercial agriculture. Due to this, the agricultural production rate is declining and farmers are even struggling to meet their own needs. Migration of youths to urban areas and to the Gulf countries also greatly affects agricultural production. Furthermore, agriculture provides only seasonal employment for rural population, which constitutes 88% of the total population. Hence, off-season and off-farm activities, such as weaving, knitting, basketry, teashops, and roadside shops, complement rural incomes [Ghimire, 2011].

Despite being an agrarian country, Nepal suffers from food insecurity. Multiple factors like low production and lack of access to health services, knowhow, infrastructure, and knowledge in food management make the country vulnerable to food insecurity. The high hills and mountainous regions are particularly susceptible to hunger. According to the World Food Program (WFP), 41% of children under five are stunted, 29% are underweight and 11% are classified as wasted. The prevalence of stunting in the hills and mountains of the mid and far western regions is extreme with rates above 60% [World Food Program, 2015]. Nepal is not in a position to match agriculture production with that of population growth. Furthermore, frequent natural disasters saddle the already poor population. According to the Food and Agriculture Organisation [FAO, 2014], despite a declining trend over the last decade, 4.5 million Nepali people are still undernourished (see Tables 9.4 and 9.5).

Agriculture is one of the sectors where SCP can be promoted in Nepal. Different from the industrialised countries, sustainable food consumption in Nepal requires *increasing* consumption rates and calorie intake to overcome undernourishment. National agriculture policy places an emphasis on the conservation, promotion, and utilisation of natural resources and the environment to minimise the negative impact of modern agriculture practices. The policy also motivates farmers to continue organic farming and support biodiversity. With the awareness level rising among citizens against the use of inorganic chemicals, a movement

Table 9.4: Nepal per capita food supply

	Quantity [kcal/capacity/day]			
Year	1996	2001	2006	2011
Food Supply	2,220	2,281	2,400	2,580

Source: FAO [2014].

Table 9.5: Prevalence of undernutrition in Nepal

	Prevalence (%)			
Year	1999–2001	2004–2006	2007–2009	2010–2012
Undernutrition	25	22	20	18

Source: FAO [2014].

towards organic agriculture and products is increasing. As the majority of Nepal's agricultural products are from traditional farming methods, imbedding SCP practice is feasible.

9.6 Forestry Sector

Forest is an important natural resource, which is managed by the Ministry of Forests and Soil Conservation (MFSC). Communities, international donors, and civil society organisations also play a crucial role in managing the forests. According to the Government of Nepal, forests cover 39.6% of the country, which is about 5.83 million hectares. This constitutes 29% of dense forest and the remainder shrub habitat. The Forest Act identifies two primary kinds of forest — national forest and private forest. It has further categorised national forest into five secondary types: Government Managed, Community Managed, Protected Forests, Leasehold Forest, and Religious Forest. Many rural and agriculture dependent populations rely heavily on forest for fuel, fodder, and agricultural activities. According to an MFSC report, forestry contributed 9.5% of GDP in 2008 with its direct products and 27.5% through its environmental services. Community-managed forest is hugely successful in the mid hills of Nepal. The Department of Forests (DoF) reports that 17,685 Community Forest User Groups (CFUGs) consisting of 1.45 million households or 35% of the population are involved in the community forestry management programme, managing about 1.65 million ha of forest to date. Under the community forestry management programme, members of community who have rights over the nearby public areas of forest can form a group. This group manages the entire forest, plants trees, saves it from fire, and shares the forest products and benefits. Apart from the increasing forest cover, the community forestry management programme has helped rural people increase their income and expand forest-based enterprises. The programme has helped increase greenery and biodiversity, and restored degraded forestland, and in return has served communities by supplying forest products and improving livelihoods.

According to Department of Forests [2015], between 1990 and 2005, Nepal lost 42,000 ha of its primary forest cover. The forest cover loss in the plains (Terai) alone from 1991 to 2010 was found to be about 32,000 ha. The annual rate of decrease in forest cover was 0.44% and 0.40% during the periods of 2001–2010 and 1991–2010 respectively. However, despite the issue of deforestation, a recent study by MFSC revealed that the rate of forest cover was slightly increasing at an annual rate of 0.06% during 1990–1991 to 2000–2001. The community forestry intervention has significantly improved Nepal's forest coverage. An example of sustainable forest in Nepal practice is demonstrated by the SWITCH-Asia project, which promoted Lokta handmade paper (see Box 9.1).

Box 9.1 SWITCH-Asia Case Study: Enhancement of Sustainable Production of Lokta Handmade Paper Production in Nepal

The SWITCH-Asia project, "Lokta Handmade Paper" aimed at addressing social and environmental issues related to the handmade paper sector in Nepal. The process of preparing handmade paper from a plant, *lokta*, is very popular in Nepal. Lokta (*Daphne bhoula* or *Daphne papyracea*) is an indigenous plant of Nepal, found at an altitude ranging from 4,500 feet to 10,000 feet. There are over 170 enterprises employing thousands of rural people to produce such paper. Lokta handmade paper has been a good source of income generation for poor people, especially women. For many, the sector also provides an additional revenue stream, which they make during their free time.

(*Continued*)

Box 9.1 (*Continued*)

During the project implementation from 2009 to 2011, various activities were implemented including training for the makers of lokta paper, especially in sustainably harvesting and forest management. Altogether, 1,195 lokta cutters and 727 paper makers have benefited from the training. Through a training of trainers programme, the project prepared a pool of local trainers who were equipped with knowledge and skills to implement SCP in the lokta paper industry. Thirty entrepreneurs were trained to reuse wastewater and help reduce environmental pollution. They also learnt to prepare lokta paper in a sustainable manner and how to market the green products.

The project sought to provide additional benefits by preparing guidelines for lokta plant cutters and paper makers, similarly, codes of conduct for the lokta entrepreneurs. The project promoted cost minimisation among paper producers and entrepreneurs through reduced consumption of fuel wood, paper drying, and water whilst maintaining the quality of end product. The project also provided many stakeholders with exposure visits and networking opportunities with national and international entrepreneurs. Overall, the project has helped build capacity among lokta cutters, entrepreneurs and its association, and develop more sustainable and environment friendly practice.

9.7 Tourism Sector

Tourism is one of the largest industrial sectors in Nepal that contributes to the economic development. It is the country's main foreign exchange earner, creates jobs, provides an economic alternative to the people of both rural and urban settings, and generates revenue. According to World Travel and Tourism Council [WTTC, 2014], in 2013 travel and tourism directly supported 504,000 jobs, which is 3.2% of total employment. In a country where unemployment rate is about 45%, this sector indeed has something to offer to the unemployed. In 2013, tourism has direct contribution of 3.9% of GDP. The major attractions of tourism in Nepal are mountaineering, adventure, and eco-tourism. Tourists come from all over the world, but the top five countries are India, China, US, Sri Lanka, and UK. Besides nature, Nepal is attractive for tourists because of its cultural, traditional, and religious aspects. To support the tourism sector, the Government of Nepal had organised tourism promotion programmes such as "Nepal Tourism Year 2011," "Visit Lumbini Year 2012," and "Everest Diamond

Jubilee 2013." However, Nepal continues to face multiple problems in the tourism sector due to its political instability, low product diversity, and seasonality. Since the 2015 earthquake, tourist numbers dropped by around 80%, jeopardising the entire sector [Deccan Chronicle, 2015]. Instilling SCP in the tourism sector is therefore imperative, so Nepal may continue generating revenues the long run. The SWITCH-Asia project, SEID, can be an example of how a sustainable and efficient industrial development supports tourism sector (see Box 9.2).

Box 9.2 SWITCH-Asia Case Study: Sustainable and Efficient Industrial Development in Nepal and Bhutan (SEID)

The SWITCH-Asia Programme has supported a bi-country project which was implemented in Nepal and Bhutan from early 2012 to November 2015. The project sought to contribute to the sustainable development of economy with a focus on national industrial sectors impacting the environment and which have a huge potential for employment generation and poverty alleviation. This was, among others, achieved by reducing operational costs and pollution, and improving health and safety measures in the tourism and agro-based sectors. The project stakeholders included SMEs, workers, experts, government authorities, and policy makers.

To meet its objectives, the project conducted training to enhance SMEs' capacity, promoted resource and energy efficiency, built networks, and mainstreamed relevant policies. In Nepal, the project focused more on tourism sector. An awareness campaign and in-house training were organised for business associations, whilst exchange of best practice was also encouraged to enhance national and international learning. The project provided knowledge and skills to more than 40 local consultants as well as representatives from industry and academia through a series of training sessions. The project worked with about 200 micro-, small-, and medium-sized enterprises (MSMEs) helping them to acquire skills, making them environmentally sensitive, and building knowledge on managing wastewater. Global best practice was also introduced to local companies and institutions, which resulted in the establishment of new academic curricula and Green Eco Clubs at colleges. The students from the Eco Club then acted as social agents to promote environmental protection and raise public awareness.

To mainstream SCP practice, the project has worked with the Federation of Nepal Cottage and Small Industries (FNCSI), Nepal Tourism Board (NTB),

(*Continued*)

Box 9.2 (*Continued*)

Sustainable Tourism Network of Nepal, and Hotel Association of Nepal (HAN). The objective was to bring about behavioural changes among the entrepreneurs. SEID project has helped MSMEs generate financial savings of around 10–15% through an enhanced efficiency in the production and operation. This has led to a reduced energy consumption by 10–25%. Similarly, the use of hazardous materials such as pesticides and inorganic fertilizers used in the production was reduced by 50%, whilst the practice of managing waste, pollution and water has improved the living environment around the MSMEs.

9.8 Renewable Energy Sector

Hydropower is the major source of energy in Nepal with a huge potential to generate electricity of approximately 40,000 MW. However, it has only managed to develop around 600 MW [IPPAN, 2011]. Until 1990, hydropower development was under the domain of the state-run Nepal Electricity Authority (NEA). However, in 1992 the government enacted a new Hydropower Development Policy to open up the sector to private operators. Since then private entities have commissioned several hydropower projects, which contributed about 148 MW of power to the national grid. In Nepal, 44% of the energy is used by domestic sector, while 37% and 8% is used by the industrial and commercial sectors respectively.

Nepal faces acute energy shortages. Although only 70% of the population has access to energy, a shortfall of about 40% results in severe power cuts (see Table 9.6). With the 2015 earthquake, the situation has worsened with 14 hydropower projects were damaged out of the 23 in operation, according to the Nepal Economic Forum. This is a loss of 150 MW of power. These situations make people in rural areas continue to rely on forest products, kerosene and biogas for cooking and lighting. In order to address this problem, Nepal is currently prioritising an energy mix model by investing in various renewable energy sources.

In 2012, Nepal launched a five-year programme called the National Rural and Renewable Energy Programme (NRREP) with the objective to improve the living standard of rural people and reduce dependency on traditional energy. The targets of this programme include producing

Table 9.6: Nepal energy demand–supply gap

Energy Gap (2011 Figures)	
Annual Peak Demand	946.10 MW
Dry Season Generation	450 MW
Deficit (Gap)	500 MW
Annual Total Energy Demand	4,833.35 GWh
Generated Energy from Available Source	3,850.87 GWh
Yearly Energy Gap	982.48 GWh (20.33%)

Source: HIDCL [2013].

Table 9.7: Installed renewable energy technology in Nepal (Until July 2011)

	Renewable Energy Technology	Total Installation		Unit	District Covered
		No.	Capacity		
1	Hydropower	40	14.95	MW	31
	Mini hydropower	999	18.65	MW	59
	Micro hydropower	1,480	3.18	MW	53
	IWM	7,959	—	—	46
2	Biogas				
	Household plant	258,642	—	—	72
	Institutional plant	111	—	—	25
	Community plant	61	—	—	20
3	Solar				
	HH Solar PV	284,097	7.44	MW	74
	Institution Solar PV — for computers, FM radios and Vaccine refrigerators	299	—	—	42
	Solar Pumps	81	—	—	22
	Solar cookers/dryers	1,920	—	—	30
	Small Solar Home System	11,687	0.05	MW	49
4	Biomass				
	ICS	619,816	—	—	52
5	Wind	21	—	—	12

Source: AEPC [2011].

25,000 kW of energy from mini and micro hydropower and distributing 600,000 solar photovoltaic systems and 475,000 improved cook stoves for rural villagers (see Table 9.7). According to NEA, energy demand is increasing and is likely to grow at an average annual rate of 8.34%.

Nepal's energy is largely green and renewable. However, with the growing focus on building mega hydropower, producing this green energy may not necessarily be sustainable and environment friendly. Therefore, it is mandatory to undertake an EIA before constructing large-scale hydropower schemes. Nepal's hydropower policy has actually stringent environmental protection safeguards during the development of any scheme. However, provisions in the policies to protect the environment are much weaker, though the government has allocated substantial resources for small-scale renewable energy sources and been launching programmes in rural areas. The SWITCH-Asia Bio-energy project provides an example of the implementation of SCP in energy sector (see Box 9.3).

Box 9.3 SWITCH-Asia Case Study: Bio-energy Project

The SWITCH-Asia Programme is supporting a project in Nepal with the aim to contribute to the national goal of poverty reduction through upscaling the production and industrial consumption of bio-energy, thereby increasing employment and reducing carbon emissions. Energy demand is increasing in Nepal for both industrial and domestic purposes. Though rich in hydropower, the country has not been able to supply adequate energy; hence, many rely on diesel generators for household energy. Therefore, this Bio-energy Project is designed to meet the increasing energy demand by replacing fossil fuels with locally-produced charcoal that helps to reduce carbon emissions. Though developed countries are the largest consumers of fossil fuels and developing countries like Nepal have low carbon footprints, choosing the right path from the onset will help to contribute in addressing climate change. This project helps create local employment for poor people by engaging them in the collection of biomass residue from forests and charcoal production and marketing.

Being implemented in 16 districts of Nepal, the project aims to increase the production and processing capacity of bio-energy enterprises. Over 10,000 local jobs are planned to be created where charcoal will be produced by sustainably harvesting forest products as part of forest management. Through the project's intervention, the capacity of SMEs will be enhanced and income

(*Continued*)

Box 9.3 (*Continued*)

increased. The project also aspires to reduce 74,000 tonnes of CO_2 by replacing fossil fuel consumption with charcoal. To create sufficient demand, the project helps SMEs to market charcoal to local hotels, restaurants, and brick industries. The project contributes to establishing the value chain by strengthening network among SMEs and increasing local business through a sustainable production and consumption of charcoal.

Various project activities are planned, where local entrepreneurs and businesses are supported to make a business plan and operate bio-energy projects. The project helps establish links between the SMEs and financial institutions for potential financing. SMEs are also trained on and equipped with the appropriate technology to increase their production. Information and learning exchange will expand the SMEs' activities and shift use from fossil fuels to bio-energy. Training and capacity building conducted stakeholders will ensure cordial relations between charcoal producers and consumers.

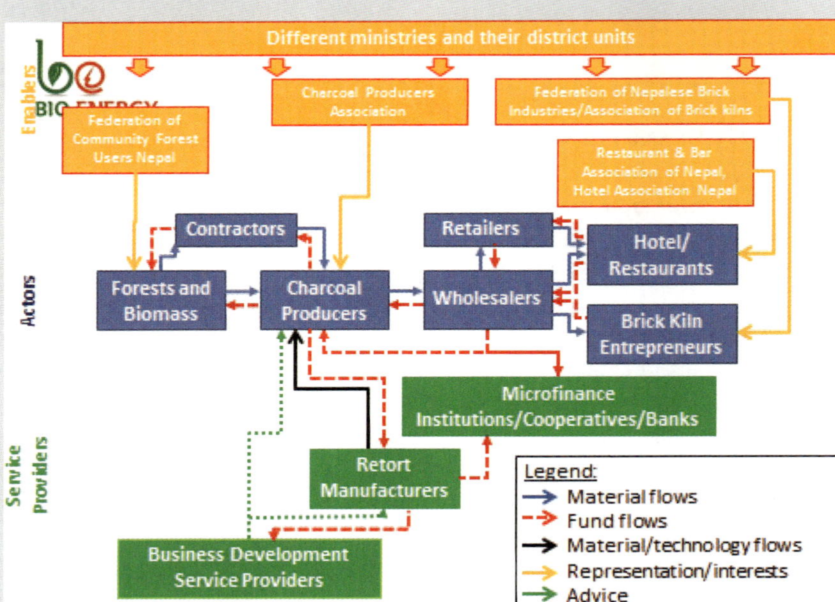

Source: SWITCH-Asia Bio-energy Project.

(*Continued*)

Box 9.3 (*Continued*)

In 2014, 14 Business Development Service Providers benefitted from procurement contracts. Another 29 Business Development Service Providers had been trained in entrepreneurship skills and business planning, so they can provide training and consultation to SMEs. Also, 43 new charcoal enterprises had been established in 2014. This initiative will not only help increase the income of the target groups, but also contribute to environmental protection. In its nascent stages, the project has yet to have concrete results. However, there are goods signs as one SME already produces around 10 tonnes of charcoal.

9.9 Conclusions

Nepal still lacks a single and coherent policy that promotes and protects SCP practice. However, the prospect looks promising when the available policies, laws and strategies supporting sustainable development are gathered for a more synchronised implementation. These instruments serve as the building blocks for a successful SCP implementation. Lack of skilled human resources as well as low awareness of and insufficient incentives to adopt SCP practice have hindered its implementation in Nepal. The low level of policy monitoring and implementation is also a major hurdle. The government will need to ensure an effective implementation of its policies. Many encouraging steps have already been taken in sectors like renewable energy, agriculture (the use of organic fertilizers and reduction in the use of harmful chemicals), air quality, sustainable tourism, waste management, and forest and environment conservation. These are progresses that Nepal can build upon, while moving towards a low carbon economic development. If this can be realised, Nepal will enjoy a sustainable development, which at the same time help tackle the issue of climate change. The SCP concept is relatively new in Nepal with industrialisation just taking its first steps. The industries and entrepreneurs will have to be aware of and then embrace the SCP principle seriously. There will need to be significant international assistance in terms of awareness, skills, knowledge, access to finance and technology. However, there is also a vibrant civil society and media in the country that can advocate and promote this principle.

Acceptance of SCP principle will not come without challenges. There is a huge pressure on the government to deliver socio-economic development and to pull people out of poverty. It will also need to meet the demands of gradually incubating businesses and industries in the country. Lack of adequate infrastructure, energy, and an enabling environment for industry is considered to be a big setback for the economy. In this context, SCP will have to be pitched as an approach that will address poverty, meet the basic needs of the people and protect the environment all at the same time. The government will also have to strengthen existing policies or formulate new ones through a participatory process and then enforce them. In the present context, the SWITCH-Asia Programme is financing projects under diverse areas to promote SCP concept. This is a positive and timely start to lead by example. The success of these grant projects can further motivate the government and other stakeholders to adopt SCP practice. In the future, the SWITCH-Asia Programme could launch more projects that target strategic issues in Nepal such as air and water pollution, low-carbon development, pesticide and inorganic fertiliser management, waste management, and organic agriculture, which will concurrently promoting sustainable production and consumption. Overall, specific policy influence at national level to promote SCP would be a crucial forward step for Nepal. The SWITCH-Asia Programme could help promote these policies through facilitating the exchange of lessons learnt from other countries' good practice. Learning, sharing and networking could be promoted among like-minded stakeholders within the country and beyond.

References

Alternative Energy Promotion Centre (AEPC) (2011). *Summary of Installed RETs in Nepal (Till July 2011)*. [online] Retrieved on October 19, 2015. Available on: http://www.aepc.gov.np/?option=statistics&page=natstats&mid=6&sub_id=45&id=1.

Deshar, B. D. (2013). *Global Journal of Economics and Social Develop* 3, 1.

Bhatta, G. R. (2014). Structural changes in a small and open economy: Evidences from Nepal. *NRB Working Paper* No 23. Nepal Rastra Bank, Kathmandu, Nepal.

Central Bureau of Statistics (2010). *Statistical Pocket Book 2010*. Thapathali, Kathmandu, Nepal.

Deccan Chronicle (2015). *Nepal's Tourism Industry in Jeopardy, 80 per cent Tourists Cancel Trip to Quake-Hit Country: Report*. 5 May 2015. Retrieved on October 19, 2015. Available on: http://www.deccanchronicle.com/150505/world-neighbours/article/nepal%E2%80%99s-tourism-industry-jeopardy-80-cent-tourists-cancel-trip-quake.

Department of Forests (2015). *Community Forestry*. Retrieved on July 26, 2015. Available on: http://dof.gov.np/dof_community_forest_division/community_forestry_dof.

Department of Industries (2014). *Industrial Statistics, Fiscal Year 2012/2013*. Kathmandu, Nepal. Available on: http://doind.gov.np/documents/pdf/industrial_statistics_2069_70.pdf.

Food and Agriculture Organisation (FAO) (2014). *FAOSTAT Nepal*. Retrieved on July 24, 2015. Available on: http://faostat.fao.org/CountryProfiles/Country_Profile/Direct.aspx?lang=en&area=149.

FRA/DFRS (2014). *Terai Forests of Nepal (2010–2012), Forest Resource Assessment Nepal Project/Department of Forest Research and Survey*. Kathmandu, Babarmahal. Availableon: http://www.franepal.org/wp-content/uploads/downloads/publications/TeraiForestsofNepal_23April2014_LowResolution.pdf.

Ghimire, R. (2011). Micro and small enterprises in Nepal: Prospects and challenges. *Journal of Finance and Management Review*. March 2011, 2(2). Available on: http://www.academia.edu/5589600/Micro_and_Small_Enterprises_in_Nepal_Prospects_and_Challenges.

Government of Nepal (2010). *Industrial Policy*. Kathmandu, Nepal.

Government of Nepal (2004). *National Agriculture Policy*. Kathmandu, Nepal.

Government of Nepal (2001). *The Hydropower Development Policy*. Singhadurbar, Kathmandu, Nepal. Available on http://www.nea.org.np/images/supportive_docs/hydropower_development_policy_2001.pdf.

Government of Nepal (1997). *Environment Protection Act*. Kathmandu, Nepal.

Hydroelectricity Investment & Development Company Limited (HIDCL) (2013). *Nepal Hydropower Overview*. Retrieved July 23, 2015. Available on: http://www.hidcl.org.np/nepal-hydropower.php.

Independent Power Producers Association Nepal (IPPAN) (2011). *Hydropower in Nepal*. Retrieved on July 19, 2015. Available on: http://www.ippan.org.np/HPinNepal.html.

Institute for Integrated Development Studies (2014). *Nepal Economic Outlook - 2013/14, Summary Report*. Kathmandu, Nepal. Available on: http://iids.org.np/wp-content/uploads/2014/07/Economic-Outlook-2013-14-Summary-Report.pdf.

Katmandu University (2009). *Journal of Science, Engineering and Technology*. 5(II). Available on: http://www.ku.edu.np/kuset/vol5_no2/17_Ramesh_EIA%20Article%20Revised%20Final.pdf.

Ministry of Agricultural Development (MOAD) (2014). *Statistical Information on Nepalese Agriculture 2013/2014*. December 2014. Retrieved on July 20, 2015. Available on: http://www.moad.gov.np/uploads/files/Year%20book%202014.pdf.

Ministry of Finance (MoF) (2015). *Nepal Aid Management Platform*. Retrieved on July 26, 2015. Available on: http://amis.mof.gov.np/portal/.

Ministry of Finance (MoF) (2013). *Foreign Aid in Nepal*. March 2013. Retrieved on July 26, 2015. Available on: http://www.mof.gov.np/uploads/document/file/second(1)_20130715031659_20130813114805.pdf.

NepalTourNews.com (2015). *Tourist arrivals by air decreased in 2014*. 12 March, 2015. Retrieved on October 19, 2015. Available on: http://www.nepaltournews.com/news/14-nepal-news/42-tourist-arrivals-by-air-decreased-in-2014.

SWITCH-Asia Programme (2014). *80 Projects at a Glance, Fact Sheet Brochure SWITCH-Asia Programme*. Available on: http://www.switch-asia.eu/publications/2014-project-fact-sheet-brochure/.

UNESCO (2015). *Family Literacy Programme*. Country Profile: Nepal. Retrieved on October 16, 2015. Available on: http://www.unesco.org/uil/litbase/?menu=14&programme=206.

UNHCR (2015). *Nepal: 2015 Earthquakes*. Retrieved on August 13, 2015. Available on: http://data.unhcr.org/nepal/.

Worldatlas (2015). *Nepal Geo Statistics*. Retrieved on October 19, 2015. Available on: http://www.worldatlas.com/webimage/countrys/asia/nepal/nplandst.htm.

World Bank (2015a). *Nepal Country Data*. Last updated 19 June 2015. Retrieved on October July 16, 2015. Available on: http://www.worldbank.org/en/country/nepal.

World Bank (2015b). *Nepal Overview*. Retrieved on August 13, 2015. Available on: www.worldbank.org/en/country/nepal/overview.

World Food Program (2015). *What are the Current Issues in Nepal*. Retrieved on October 16, 2015. Available on: https://www.wfp.org/countries/nepal.

World Travel & Tourism Council (WTTC) (2014). *Travel and Tourism, Economic Impact 2014, Nepal*. Available on: http://www.wttc.org//media/files/reports/economic%20impact%20research/country%20reports/nepal2014.pdf.

Chapter 10

Sustainable Consumption and Production in the Philippines

Leonardo L. Sta. Romana

10.1 The Philippines and the Path to Sustainable Development

In the years from 2010 to 2015, the Philippines economy has been recovering from its unenviable reputation as the "laggard of East Asia." It is now exhibiting rapid rates of economic growth — 7.1% in 2013 and 6.1% in 2014 [National Statistical Coordination Board, 2015b] — and improving its ranking in global competitiveness reports. The Philippines ranks as a promising newly-industrialised country, with its export economy moving away from agriculture to electronics and labour-intensive manufactured goods (like garments, footwear, processed foods, and furniture). Its credit rating has also been upgraded by international rating agencies to the level of sovereign investment grade.

While that has been a worthwhile achievement in itself, some thoughtful observers have raised the question about the apparent stubbornly-high incidence of poverty that has remained, despite the evident economic expansion. Another question about the economic growth is the continued deterioration of the environment, felt especially in Metro Manila and the country's other big cities.

In this chapter, environmental issues will be considered as well as — partially — poverty alleviation. Firstly, various concepts will be clarified, despite being further elaborated elsewhere in the book, as they form the context of the discussion.

Sustainable development refers to the development of a country that meets the needs of the present without compromising the ability of future generations to meet their own needs [UNEP, 2010]. In this specific sense of having a regard for the needs of future generations, sustainable development is, in part, equivalent to an environmentally-sustainable development. The concept of sustainable development consists, however, of two other aspects, namely, the well-known (though still elusive to some) notion of economic progress, and that of socially inclusive growth and poverty eradication (as opposed to the traditional "grow first, redistribute later" policy mind-set). This leads to the concept of "green growth," which is an environmentally-sustainable economic progress that fosters low-carbon, socially inclusive development [OECD, 2014; GGBP, 2014]. Green growth is the opposite of the prevailing "grow first, clean up later" type of economic growth [UNESCAP-ADB-UNEP, 2012]. The concept of sustainable consumption and production (SCP), with its various approaches, is a major element of green growth and an important means to achieving it [UNEP, 2012a, 2012b].

10.2 Are the Consumption and Production Patterns of the Philippines Sustainable?

This section starts with a brief look at some of the main policies in the country relating to SCP, then an introduction to the promotion of SCP in the country by the SWITCH-Asia Programme. This is followed by a review of a number of indicators of the overall state of the environment in the Philippines.

10.2.1 *Policies for SCP in the Philippines*

The Philippines is known as a leader in the region regarding laws that provide the legal and policy framework for protecting the environment, for example, the Clean Air Act 1999, the Ecological Solid Waste Management Act 2000, the Clean Water Act 2004, the Biofuels Act 2006, and the Renewable Energy Act 2008 (see Table 10.1).

Table 10.1: Selected Philippine laws on the environment

Designation of the Law	Purpose of the Law
Philippine Environmental Impact Statement System (PEIS) of 1978 (Presidential Decree 1586)	A Decree providing the legal and procedural framework for conducting Environmental Impact Assessments (EIA) for projects likely to have significant environmental impact. This has been updated by several DENR administrative orders.
Clean Air Act of 1999	An Act providing for a comprehensive air pollution control policy and a national programme to prevent, manage, control, and reverse air pollution through both regulatory and market based instruments.
Ecological Solid Waste Management Act of 2000	An Act setting up a national programme for managing the transfer, transport, processing, and disposal of solid waste. It calls for a phasing out of open dump sites and converting them into sanitary landfills.
Clean Water Act of 2004	An Act providing for a comprehensive water quality management, with the aim of protecting the country's water bodies from pollution from land-based sources.
Biofuels Act of 2006	An Act establishing the framework for the promotion of the use of biofuels in road transport (biodiesel and gasoline blended with bioethanol).
Renewable Energy Act of 2008	An Act establishing the framework for the accelerated development of renewable energy resources.
Climate Change Act of 2009	An Act establishing the Climate Change Commission, tasked to coordinate, monitor and evaluate programmes, and action plans.

Sources: DENR website (denr.gov.ph); NEDA [2014]; and Philippine Senate [2011, 2014].

Regarding SCP, the Philippines has not yet enacted a single policy or plan specifically for SCP. The country has stated its vision of a green economy in the Philippine Development Plan 2011–2016, which emphasises the need for inclusive growth as well as "sustainable use of resources to benefit the present and future generations." A specific sector outcome goal is defined as improving environmental quality for a cleaner and healthier environment with reduction targets for air pollution, water pollution and waste generation [NEDA, 2014].

To advance SCP, the Philippines is also using an enhanced national Agenda 21 plan as part of the national development strategy, which includes six key actions:

1. Need to increase economic ecological activities and opportunities for green markets.
2. Need to increase awareness of consumer options for sustainable consumption.
3. Businesses must be able to receive assistance to change to better production practice.
4. Life cycle assessment (LCA) must be brought down to a level the consumer understands.
5. Accelerate the establishment of a government green public procurement system.
6. Need to assess policy options for promoting SCP, especially an incentive structure for green production [IGES, 2010].

This environmental policy framework, including those policies relating to SCP, is an important starting point, yet policy implementation is less clear. The Department of Environment and Natural Resources (DENR) is the agency tasked with implementing the country's environmental policy, however, it performs this task through regional offices in the country's 13 administrative regions. The enforcement of environmental laws has been devolved to local government units (LGUs), but despite this devolution of power, LGU enforcement remains subject to the supervision of the DENR.

For example, the local heads of the country's smallest administrative units, called the *Punong Barangay*, are tasked to enforce laws relating to pollution control and environmental protection, while municipal mayors are mandated to safeguard and conserve land, mineral, marine, forest, and other resources of the municipalities [Lerma and Batan, 2015]. As a result, multiple issues including political interference, corruption, lack of coordination, lack of support from the community, and lack of logistical and financial resources have hindered the enforcement of environmental policies.

The actual environmental situation (or "outcomes") experienced by the ordinary citizens is covered in the following sections below.

10.2.2 *Promoting SCP in the Philippines through the SWITCH-Asia Programme*

The SWITCH-Asia Programme has been implementing projects in the Philippines since 2009, all of which are aimed at facilitating and supporting the shift to SCP.

The programme is implemented on two levels: firstly, policy support at the national government level; secondly, pilot projects at the enterprise level. The preceding section covered the national environmental policy framework; this following section covers the SWITCH-Asia *National Policy Support Component* (NPSC) (see Box 10.1).

Box 10.1 The SWITCH-Asia NPSC

The SWITCH-Asia Programme's involvement in the Philippines includes technical assistance to support the national government's implementation of policy instruments related to the "switch" towards SCP.

The Philippines is one of the five countries receiving this technical assistance, namely SWITCH-Asia National Policy Support Component (NPSC). The NPSC in the Philippines was implemented by a consortium consisting of GFA Consulting Group (Germany) as the leading organisation, Ecorys (Netherlands), Milieu (Belgium), and ASSIST (Philippines).

The technical assistance project started in July 2012 and continues until December 2016, thus the present discussion involves a project that has not yet finished.

With the objective of supporting the government in implementing SCP policies, the project focuses its efforts in three areas: (1) clean energy and energy efficiency; (2) green procurement and eco-labelling; and (3) capacity-building at the DENR in order to be able to address cross-cutting SCP issues, including the Clean Air Act. The other government agencies that receive

(*Continued*)

Box 10.1 (*Continued*)

technical assistance from the project are the Department of Energy (DOE), the Department of Trade and Industry (DTI), the Climate Change Commission, and the Philippine Council for Sustainable Development.

One recent project achievement was the approval in July 2014 by the DOE secretary of the Energy Efficiency and Conservation Roadmap 2014–2030, whose development was supported by the technical assistance team [Lister, 2013]. Several consultation meetings were held earlier to obtain inputs from relevant government agencies and stakeholders, including professional organisations, and development partners. After extensive discussions, the roadmap was revised incorporating pertinent inputs and recommendations from these stakeholders.

When technical assistance from a foreign donor to a government is involved, a major concern is the issue of "buy-in" by the respective government agency of the policy support. This is often referred to as the degree of "ownership" manifested by the recipient agency regarding the technical support being provided. This has been addressed successfully by the project, as the most recent half-yearly progress report states "the project is well integrated in the partner institutions [...] There is a high level of ownership among the main partners, especially at the DOE, DTI, and DENR" [Bischoff and Balamiento, 2015].

At the enterprise level, in 2015 there are nine SWITCH-Asia grant projects either completed or operational in the country (see Table 10.2). We used two criteria to "triangulate" on which projects to select as case studies. One criterion was that the project focused solely on the Philippines, since some involve a number of other countries in the region. This criterion reduced the number of projects to four. A second criterion was that the projects should already be completed, rather than on-going. At the time of writing, three projects had already been completed. The *Zero Carbon Resorts* is already discussed in this book's chapter on sustainable tourism (see Chapter 14). We therefore focus on the two other completed projects as case studies, namely, the projects *GPIoS* and *SMART Cebu*. Both projects are presented below in text boxes, but they do not involve a detailed *ex post* evaluation (i.e., performance evaluation and/or impact evaluation).

Table 10.2: SWITCH-Asia projects in the Philippines, 2015

Name of Project	Period	Implementing Organisations	Places of Implementation	SCP Practice	Brief Project Description
Philippines Only					
Completed					
(1) GPIoS	2009–2013	VSB-Tech Univ Ostrava, GrAT, AREC, ASSIST, ECCP	Metro Manila, CALABARZON	Cleaner production, resource efficiency	Green Philippines Islands of Sustainability
(2) SMART Cebu	2009–2013	SEQUA, EFA, ECCP, ADFIAP	Cebu	Cleaner production, eco-design	SMEs for environmental Accountability, Responsibility, and Transparency
(3) Zero Carbon Resorts, ZCR	2009–2014	GrAT, PCSD, PSA-CIEMAT, ASSIST	Palawan	Resource efficiency, 3R (reduce, replace, redesign)	Building Energy Autonomous Resorts, Creating Appropriate Technology Solutions
On-going					
(4) High-Efficiency Motors	2014–2018	IIEE, ICASEA, ASSIST, ECCP	Various areas	Energy efficiency	Increasing the Uptake of High Efficiency Motors and Drive Systems in Philippine Industries

(Continued)

Table 10.2: (*Continued*)

Name of Project	Period	Implementing Organisations	Places of Implementation	SCP Practice	Brief Project Description
Including Other Countries:					
Completed:					
(5) AEMAS	2010–2014	ASEAN Centre for Energy, ASD, ENPAP	7 ASEAN nations	Energy efficiency accreditation	Establishment of the ASEAN Energy Manager Accreditation Scheme
On-going:					
(6) Efficient Air Conditioners	2013–2016	Europe Copper Inst, UNEP-DTIE, IIEE	7 ASEAN nations	Energy efficiency	Promotion and Deployment of Energy Efficient Air Conditioners in ASEAN
(7) Hand-Woven Eco-Textiles	2013–2017	Hivos, NTFP-EP	Indonesia	Sustainable consumption, eco-design	SCP of Hand-Woven Textiles (Songket, Ulos, Lurik, Abaca, Ikat), Female Entrepreneurship in Indonesia and the Philippines

(8) Lead Paint Elimination Project	2011–2015	IPEN, Arnika-Toxics & Waste Programme, EcoWaste Coalition	6 Asian nations	Eco-labelling	Elimination of lead in paints through awareness raising and standard setting
(9) ZCR for Sustainable Tourism	2014–2018	GrAT, PCSD, PSA-CIEMAT,	Thailand	Resource efficiency	Zero Carbon Resorts towards Sustainable Development of the Tourism Sector in the Philippines and Thailand

Source: European Union [2014], SWITCH-Asia's 80 Projects at a Glance: Fact Sheet (2014).

10.3 Indicators on the Impact on the Environment and Climate

In this section, selected indicators to evaluate the impact of unsustainable consumption and production patterns on the environment and society in the Philippines are discussed.

There has been growing literature regarding appropriate indicators to use to monitor green growth towards the green economy [UNEP, 2015; GGKP, 2013; UNESCAP, 2013]. While the tendency is to propose a dashboard of socio-economic and environmental indicators, there is also the need to have a single so-called "headline" indicator (parallel to the Gross Domestic Product) that will communicate easily the state of green growth to policy makers and to the educated layperson.

But problems with both concept and measurement exist, and while the search for such an elusive indicator continues, there the Environmental Performance Index (EPI) exists which offers a summary index for the "green" aspect of growth. The EPI, updated every two years, is a joint project of the Yale University Center for Environmental Law and Policy and the Columbia University Center for International Earth Science Information Network [Hsu *et al.*, 2014].

The EPI ranks how well countries perform on high-priority environmental issues in two broad policy areas: protection of human health from environmental harm and protection of ecosystems. Within these two policy objectives, the EPI scores country performance in nine issue areas comprised of 20 indicators. The nine areas are health impacts, air quality, water and sanitation, fisheries, water resources, agriculture, forests, biodiversity and habitat, and climate and energy.

Based on the EPI, the Philippines ranked 114th out of 178 countries in 2014, while 2012, it ranked 42nd out of 132 (see Table 10.3). Its EPI ranking thus fell from the 68th percentile in 2012 to the 36th percentile in 2014, i.e., only 36% of countries are now ranked below the Philippines.

Refinements in the methodology and underlying data perhaps make the comparison of rankings over time an exercise of limited validity, yet the 2014 ranking represents the best estimate of the country's environmental performance, as they have been calculated using latest iteration of this measure. Since 2006, the EPI has been recalibrated, refined and updated every two years.

Table 10.3: Selected sustainability indicators: Philippines

Indicator	Latest	Previous	Source
GDP growth rate	6.9 (2014 Q4)	5.3 (2014 Q3)	NSCB [2015a]
Poverty incidence (% of population)	25.8 (2014 H1)	24.6 (2013 H1)	NSCB [2015a]
Environmental Performance Index (ranking among nations)	114 out of 178 (2014)	42 out of 132 (2012)	EPI [Hsu, 2012, 2014]
Protected forest land area increase (hectares)	333,160 (2014 Q3)	221,763 (2013)	NEDA [2015]
Households with electricity (% of total)	79.1 (2013)	76.7 (2012)	NEDA [2015]
Households with access to safe water (% of total)	83.8 (2013)	N.A.	NEDA [2015]
Households final consumption expenditure (annual % growth)	5.4 (2014)	N.A.	World Bank [2015]

Source: The respective data source is indicated on the right-hand column above, with the full reference given at the end of the chapter.

This survey of selected indicators of the unsustainable patterns of consumption and production in the country would not be complete without some discussion of the threat of global warming and climate change. In terms of emissions of greenhouse gases (GHG), the country accounts for only 0.4% of global emissions, and is therefore not a major emitter of GHGs [ADB, 2011]. A recent report [World Bank, 2013a], however, identifies that the country's GHG emissions are increasing rapidly compared to other low and middle-income countries, and can be expected to increase further, as the economy continues its recent rapid growth.

Another way of looking at the same issue is through the lens of a country's Ecological Footprint. It measures the amount of biologically productive land and sea area that a country needs to produce the resources it consumes, provide room for its infrastructure, and absorb its waste [WWF and ADB, 2012].

As people consume resources from around the world, the Ecological Footprint adds these areas together regardless of where they are located on the planet. Because trade is global, a country's footprint includes land or sea from all over the world. The footprint is usually measured in "global hectares" (or gha), a unit that encompasses the average productivity of all the biologically productive land and sea area in the world in a given year.

One estimate puts the per-person Ecological Footprint of the Philippines at 1.3 gha in 2008, within the limits of the world average available biocapacity of 1.8 gha [Global Footprint Network, 2012], and one of the smallest-footprint nations in the region. For Asia-Pacific as a whole, the footprint is 1.6 gha, while Australia and Singapore are in the largest-footprint category of nations, with a range of 5–7 gha [WWF and ADB, 2012].

However, in 2008, there was only 0.6 gha of biocapacity per person available in the Philippines [Global Footprint Network, 2012], indicating that although consumption levels are relatively low, the demand exceeds the country's biocapacity. The report also shows that 61% of the ecological footprint of households comes from the food sector, which highlights the limited contribution of other sectors, like construction, transport, goods, and services. It also highlights the Philippines' dependence on "food biocapacity" imports from other countries.

To return to our point of the country's minor role as a global emitter of GHGs, the Philippines, however, is one of the most highly vulnerable countries to existing climate risks and future climate change. To be specific, four Philippine cities — San Jose, Manila, Roxas, and Cotabato — are among the top 10 cities in the East Asia/Pacific region most vulnerable to the climate-related impacts of intensified storm surges and sea-level rise [Dasgupta *et al.*, 2009].

The Philippines is ranked second country in the world most at risk from natural hazards (i.e., earthquakes, storms, floods, droughts, and sea-level rise) including the adverse effects of climate change, according to the latest World Risk Index [Welle, Birkmann, and Rhyner 2014]. And in a related study but with a focus on coastal areas, the Philippines is among the top 10 countries in the world with the highest risk from coastal hazards (i.e., storms, floods, surges, tsunamis, and sea-level rise), according to the Coasts@Risk Index [Beck, 2014].

The next sub-chapter will address the implications of a shift to a sustainable pattern of consumption and production on the issue of global warming and climate change.

10.3.1 *Indicators on air pollution, human health, and municipal waste generation*

Unsustainable patterns of consumption and production contribute to air pollution. Industries, households, and cars, trucks, and other vehicles emit various mixtures of air pollutants, many of which are harmful to human health. Among these pollutants, fine particulate matter has the most harmful effects.

Most fine particulate matter results from fuel combustion, both from "mobile" sources (i.e., vehicles), and from "stationary" sources (i.e., smoke stacks). Some major sources include exhaust fumes from vehicles, emissions from manufacturing facilities (e.g., factories) and power generation (e.g., smoke stacks of coal-fired power plants) [WHO, 2014].

High concentration of small and fine particulate pollution is particularly associated with high numbers of deaths from heart disease and strokes, as well as respiratory illnesses and cancers. Measurement of fine particulate matter of 10 micrometers or less (also known as microns) in diameter ("PM10") is one indicator of the level of health risks from air pollution. The most health-damaging particles are those with a diameter of 10 microns or less, which can penetrate and lodge deep inside the lungs.

Air quality measurements are typically reported in particles per cubic meter of air volume. Following the WHO's Ambient (outdoor) Air Pollution Database Update 2014, the PM10 reading for the country was 50 (in 2010), which would indicate a level of pollution that is 2.5 times higher than the WHO air quality guideline value of 20 [WHO, 2014]. This value was taken from four stations in the three cities of Manila, Cebu, and Baguio. The major contributor to air pollution is the transport sector (mainly the ubiquitous jeepneys, buses, and tricycles) [ADB, 2011].

Levels of pollution have to be seen in its context, as some advances have already been made in air quality parameters. Lead concentrations have dropped since the complete phase out of lead in petrol/gasoline in December 2000. The lead concentration in the ambient (outdoor) air in Metro Manila was monitored in 2003 to be much lower than the national air quality guideline value of 1.0 microgram per cubic metre. This compares with a value in 1992 of around 1.7 [ADB and Clean Air Asia, 2006; World Bank, 1997]. The closure of some coal and oil-fired power stations has also reduced sodium dioxide concentrations, and there is much lower consumption of ozone-depleting substances.

Another indicator of the consequences of unsustainable patterns of consumption and production is municipal solid waste generation and its disposal. The issue of appropriate solid waste management is particularly important in highly urbanised areas, where an effective waste management system will determine of the level of impacts on public health, environmental quality, and the resulting quality of life.

When the waste management works well, residents give it little thought: out of sight and quickly out of mind. Discarded materials are collected, some are recycled or composted, and most are landfilled or incinerated. However, the problem soon rears its ugly head when there is poor disposal of collected and uncollected waste. Indiscriminate dumping of solid waste onto open areas and watercourses and unsanitary methods of final disposal are major factors behind the deterioration of urban environment.

The Philippines generates about 30,000 tonnes of garbage per day, only half of which is collected. Even in Metro Manila, only 70% of the 8,000 tonnes of garbage generated each day is collected [ADB, 2011]. The rest often winds up on the streets and in local rivers. The waste that is collected is taken to open dump sites that often catch fire or contaminate local water supplies. The waste decomposes and produces methane, a GHG that is 21 times more potent than carbon dioxide and is a major cause of climate change [World Bank, 2012]. The country also remains inadequately equipped to deal with hazardous waste.

When the collection of waste material is difficult, as is the case in many cramped settlements of informal settler families, nearby watercourses such as creeks and rivers become convenient dumping grounds, ultimately hampering water discharge during the rainy season and thus contributing to flooding. The waste materials also causes damage to pumping stations, thereby affecting their function of pumping out floodwater. Hence, a city's ability to keep solid waste out of drainage ditches can influence whether a neighbourhood floods after a heavy storm.

LGUs, responsible for the collection and disposal of solid waste material, generally have little capacity to plan, develop, operate, and maintain sanitary landfills and have difficulty in complying with the Ecological Solid Waste Management Act [ADB, 2012].

City dwellers have a role to play regarding the problem of solid waste, as they consume and discard resources at an ever-increasing rate. The responsible authorities will need to develop more effective programmes to reduce, reuse, recycle, and recover waste. While recycling helps to manage solid waste, reducing consumption, and minimising waste based on principles of reduce, reuse, or recycle (3Rs) should be the ultimate goal (see also Chapter 15). By minimising waste, the demand for landfill space can be reduced, which in turn will save resources and energy, reduce pollution, and increase the production efficiency of industries.

As simple as it sounds, however, waste minimisation is difficult to achieve because it requires a change in people's mindset. Simply expecting people to reduce, reuse, or recycle simply because it is the right thing to do is an ideal, since most are caught up in the culture of consumerism.

The persistent challenge is how to remove and manage waste in a safe, environmentally sound, and cost-effective manner. If done well, municipal waste management practices can contribute to the reduction of GHG emissions of a city, also short-lived climate pollutants such as methane that is far more potent than carbon dioxide. Under the SWITCH-Asia Programme, the "*Green Philippines Islands of Sustainability*" (GPIoS) project carried out a number of activities and initiatives to address the issue of waste management and recycling (see Box 10.2).

Box 10.2 The Case Study of SWITCH-Asia project Green Philippines Islands of Sustainability (GPIoS)

The objective of the GPIoS project was to contribute to an overall improvement of the environmental situation of a strategic area of the country, namely, Metro Manila and its linked regions, the CALABARZON, Subic, and Clark areas [Labodova, 2014].

In order to attain the objective, it aimed to achieve the reduction in pollution level, as well as the reduction in: (1) waste water, (2) hazardous waste, (3) raw and auxiliary materials, and 4) energy consumption for a significant number of SMEs and other specific companies in the targeted regions.

The GPIoS project was the successor to a pilot project, the *Green Philippines* project, which ran from 2006–2009. While the pilot was focused in the Pampanga, Subic, and Clark regions, GPIoS extended its scope to Metro Manila and CALABARZON regions. The pilot project was limited to only 30 companies, several of which continued on to the *GPIoS*.

The GPIoS's main instrument for attaining its objectives involved workshops and individual consulting by experienced consultants. The project transferred know-how through training workshops and coaching, combined with a system of quality assurance and monitoring. At the core was a 12-month capacity-building programme of workshops offered on a periodic basis to help interested companies clean up their production processes. In order to do this, it had the benefit of several European partner organisations, namely the Center for Appropriate Technology (GrAT) in Austria. GrAT provided the technical know-how with its expertise in environmental solutions as well as international experience.

(*Continued*)

Box 10.2 (*Continued*)

Using the 'training the trainers' approach, GrAT shared European best practice to local consultants, also through coaching in on-the-job training. Another organisation, Austrian Recycling (AREC), contributed expertise in waste management and recycling. AREC assisted in the validation of environmental recommendations implemented by SMEs involved in the project. Collaboration between VSB-Technical University of Ostrava in the Czech Republic, as the lead organisation, with GrAT and AREC had resulted from their participation in the GPIoS project.

Locally, the Asia Society for Social Improvement and Sustainable Transformation (ASSIST) mobilised local stakeholders for the implementation of the project. The Philippine Chamber of Commerce and Industry (PCCI), the European Chamber of Commerce of the Philippines (ECCP), and the Philippine Business for Environment (PBE) were partner organisations who spread the word about the project among local firms and helped recruit the target number of SMEs.

As a result, over the course of 2009–2013, the project had involved around 400 SMEs within its geographical scope, thus raising environmental awareness among the participating SMEs. To create an enabling policy environment, the project worked in close collaboration with the DNER, which increased legal compliance of the participating SMEs. The project also established a relationship with two municipalities of Pasig City and Angeles City. At the end of the project, a training and consulting centre was established as a joint activity of project partner ECCP and a local consultancy, which employs six consultants trained within the project. A detailed business plan has been created, which included a number of companies in need of a good financial base to become self-sustaining.

10.4 Micro, Small, and Medium-sized Enterprises and the SWITCH-Asia Projects

Another source of pollution and resource consumption in the Philippines is the industrial sector. Of the 944,897 business enterprises operating in the country in 2012, 99.6% are micro-, small-, and medium-sized enterprises

Table 10.4: Definition of micro-, small-, and medium-sized enterprises

	Number of Employees	Amount of Assets (PHP)
Micro	1–9	Less than or equal to 3 million
Small	10–99	More than 3 to less than 15 million
Medium	100–199	15 to less than 100 million

Source: Employment — *Magna Carta for MSMEs of 2008*; and Assets — *MSME Development Plan 2011–2016*.

(MSMEs) [Department of Trade and Industry, 2014]. In the following Table 10.4, the definition of MSME as defined by the Philippine government is described [World Bank, 2013b].

Looking at each category of the MSME sector, micro firms account for 89.4% of all enterprises, small firms for 9.7%, while medium firms for 0.4%. Given that only 0.4% of all enterprises are large firms, it is not surprising that the average employment per establishment in the country is 25 [National Statistics Office, 2015].

According to the Micro, Small, and Medium Enterprise Development Plan for 2011–2016 [MSMEDC, 2011], in terms of total employment of all enterprises, in 2008 the MSME sector contributed 64.9% of the total jobs, which can be broken down into 30.5% from micro firms, 27.2% from small firms, and 7.3% from medium firms. In terms of value-added, in 2006, the MSME sector contributed 35.7% for all enterprises, which can be further broken down to 4.9% from micro firms, 20.5% from small firms, and 10.3% from medium firms.

In terms of the location of the MSME sector, 22.4% of the enterprises are located in Metro Manila, and 15.4% are in the CALABARZON region. (CALABARZON is an acronym for the group of adjacent provinces of CAvite, LAguna, BAtangas, Rizal, and QueZON.) 11.2% are located in the rest of Central Luzon. Making up the rest of the top five geographical areas are Central Visayas with 7% of the enterprises, followed by Western Visayas with 5.7% of the firms. These top five regions accounted for 61.7% of the MSME sector.

10.4.1 *SMEs, inclusive growth, and poverty alleviation*

It has become an important development goal for policy makers to design and implement policy initiatives, which ensure that economic growth is broad-based and reduces the incidence of poverty. Yet, the grim reality is that poor people do not, and cannot, fully participate in and enjoy the fruits of the current economic growth in the Philippines.

As mentioned, SMEs contribute nearly 65% of the total employment of all enterprises in the country due to the less sophisticated and labour intensive production systems. SMEs tend to have lower entry requirements in terms of skills, education, and qualifications. They are also likely to employ marginalised groups who may otherwise have difficulties finding jobs in large enterprises. As such, some SMEs are "survival enterprises," operating out of necessity, rather than with the intention to grow, providing incomes, and livelihoods to the majority of the poor who are faced with the absence of any real alternative due to a lack of sufficient wage employment [ILO, 2015].

At the same time, though, it is important to note that SMEs and large enterprises do not exist in isolation, but form part of an interacting system, where large enterprises provide SMEs with markets. SMEs require access to credit, new inputs, technology, and services that lead to improved products that large enterprises are looking to purchase [Habito, 2010; Paderanga, 2011].

This suggests the need to focus on creating openings for small enterprises to integrate into domestic value chains or in the different stages of production and trade of goods and services. This is the means for SMEs to develop linkages with large enterprises in the economy, expanding the business scope of the SME sector and enhancing competitiveness.

The substantial share of jobs that come from the SME sector would seem to provide a pointer to an alternative path leading to a more inclusive type of economic growth. An example of achieving sustainable development and more inclusive growth, by supporting SMEs, has been demonstrated by the SWITCH-Asia *SMART Cebu* project (see Box 10.3).

Box 10.3 The Case Study of SWITCH-Asia project: Small and Medium Enterprises for environmental Accountability, Responsibility, and Transparency (SMART Cebu)

The objective of the SMART Cebu project was to increase the competitiveness of SMEs in the home and lifestyle industries through cleaner production processes of eco-friendly products, thereby contributing to the cleaner environment in the Cebu province [Ritter, 2014]. Three industries of the home and lifestyle sector were engaged in the course of the project's life over three-and-a-half years (2009–2013), namely: (1) furniture and furnishings, (2) gifts, toys, and housewares, and (3) fashion accessories. These have been long-standing industries in Cebu, for which the province is renowned, and constitute an important element of the local economy.

However, the sectors were having a negative impact on the environment, since energy and raw materials were not being used in an efficient manner. Production processes released dust and fumes from sanding, cutting and paint spraying, exposing those workers with inadequate protection to unhealthy indoor pollution.

To reach the SMEs, the business membership organisations (BMOs) of the three industries became the vehicle, namely: the Association of Cebu Gifts, Toys, and Hardware (Cebu GTH), the Cebu Furniture Industries Foundation (CFIF), and the Association of Cebu Fashion Accessories Manufacturers and Exporters (Cebu FAME). The project sought to instil a *SMART Cebu* mind-set (i.e., resource efficiency and cleaner production, or RECP).

The project's lead organisation, SEQUA, a non-profit development organisation from Germany, teamed up with experts from Energy Efficiency Agency (EFA) in North Rhine-Westphalia, Germany, to train and coach local experts and staff of the BMOs. They first trained six counsellors to provide advisory services to member companies of the BMOs. Then a pool of 30 clean production experts is trained to guide the SMEs on the technical aspects of how to make the manufacturing processes cleaner and more efficient.

In total, the project conducted 150 walk-through eco-assessments and coached SMEs on the use of metrics in production operations and proper costing. RECP actions led to savings in energy and water, lower use of chemicals, less in-factory pollution, and improved operational efficiencies. Around 1,000 participants from close to 300 SMEs were involved in more than 30 training sessions on eco-design, SCP, RECP, as well as other SCP-related conferences.

(*Continued*)

Box 10.3 (*Continued*)

For the first time, Cebu's home and lifestyle sector was able to participate in international trade fairs in Europe and Asia, presenting the sector as a global partner for sourcing and designing eco-friendly products. Marketing of these products was undertaken at these trade fairs and a new line of eco-friendly products was launched on the international market.

About 12 fashion accessories companies, 12 GTH companies, and nine furniture companies promoted their newly developed eco-product lines at trade fairs in Paris, Cologne and Frankfurt. The participating companies can now claim that they are utilising natural and renewable resources more efficiently in its production process, while reducing the carbon footprint of the products as they reach the world market.

Another key aspect of the SMART Cebu project was its pair of local partners, the European Chamber of Commerce in the Philippines (ECCP) and the Association in Development Financing Institutions in Asia and the Pacific (ADFIAP), a regional organisation based in Manila. After the project was completed, its website became the responsibility of ECCP. The project also collaborated closely with the Department of Science and Technology; one result of this collaboration is the eventual accreditation of most of the local trainers coached by the project.

Given the relative success of this project, other sectors in Cebu were quite eager to be the beneficiaries of a similar SMART project (e.g., hotels, resorts, restaurants, and food companies), as well as BMOs in other regions (e.g., other provinces in the Visayas and Luzon).

10.5 Conclusions

This chapter gives an overview of the SCP patterns in the Philippines, within the framework of its sustainable development. The search for simple and understandable indicators for the environmental impacts of the prevailing patterns of consumption and production in the country initially has yielded few results. Indicators that attempt to assess the overall state of environment in the Philippines were reviewed, together with those that indicate the country's ecological footprint and emissions of GHGs, as well as indicators on air pollution and the generation of waste material. The indicators show environmental degradations in all domains assessed.

Environmental policy and the legal framework that pertains to the country's laudable endeavours to switch from its unsustainable patterns of consumption and production were addressed, but the indicators suggest a considerable gap between the rhetoric of the stated policies and laws versus the environmental outcomes. This indicates that there is room for improvement in the implementation of existing policy frameworks at various levels of environmental governance.

One explanation for such a wide gap between policy design and implementation is the persisting lack of political will and bureaucratic inertia, which results in the weak — or worse, lack of — enforcement of the laws. There is, however, some attempt to improve the state of affairs, as discussed above in the case of SWITCH-Asia NPSC, which works to promote and strengthen the adoption of SCP-related policies.

The SWITCH-Asia NPSC provides technical assistance and policy support to the Philippine national government. Its three selected priority areas are the constituent elements of the country's efforts toward SCP, namely, clean energy and energy efficiency, green procurement and eco-labelling, and capacity-building at the DENR in order to enable it to address cross-cutting SCP issues, including the Clean Air Act.

To date, the NPSC has progressed well, with the recent approval of the Energy Efficiency and Conservation Roadmap by the DOE cabinet secretary. However, challenges continue, which is common with any other foreign donor's technical assistance, regarding the degree of "ownership" of the technical support being provided by the recipient agency.

Being the backbone to the economy, MSMEs were also addressed. The MSME sector makes up 99.6% of all enterprises and contributes almost 65% of jobs. A policy direction was identified by which MSMEs can be assisted as part of the national effort towards more inclusive growth and poverty alleviation.

In the context of the Philippines' pursue of sustainable development, case studies of two completed SWITCH-Asia projects were described, with a focus on SMEs and their industrial processes, and how they may contribute to the objectives of reducing poverty and environmental degradation. Both projects had advocated a switch from business as it is to a more resource efficiency and cleaner production. By doing so, the projects contributed to a cleaner environment in their implementation areas in the

Greater Manila/Luzon and Cebu regions. To sustain the results, the projects had embarked on an outreach programme involving a large number of SMEs to further promote the adoption of RECP techniques and practices.

As with all projects that run for a limited period of time (whether foreign or domestic), the long-term desirable effects of the SWITCH-Asia projects on the target groups, especially SMEs, may not be immediately apparent.

Two final remarks can be made of this chapter. Firstly, the search for indicators that are understandable to policy makers and educated laymen has to continue — the indicators discussed in this chapter can serve as a starting point for such a search. Only through such indicators can progress in green growth and SCP implementation be monitored, and with monitoring comes the resulting pressure from citizens for further environmental action from government and companies. Secondly, there is a relationship between the push for a shift toward SCP and the climate change. As the Philippines has minor role as a global emitter, this seems to suggest the need for a rethinking of priorities in environment-related programmes. It suggests there is a "double dividend" for the country from any action to shift consumption and production to more sustainable patterns.

One dividend will be felt in the not-so-distant future — less fossil fuel fumes, pollution, waste and garbage, environmental degradation, and perhaps even less floods in cities. The second dividend is the country's contribution toward a reduction in the emission of GHGs and its ecological footprint, which already exceeds its national biocapacity. It would seem to be the equivalent of hitting two targets (or birds) with one policy instrument (or stone), with due apology for the metaphor to the conservationists looking after the country's national bird, the critically endangered Philippine eagle.

References

Asian Development Bank (ADB) (2011). *Philippines 2011–2016 Country Partnership Strategy*. Manila. Retrieved on May 1, 2015. Available on: http://www.adb.org/documents/philippines-country-partnership-strategy-2011-2016.

ADB (2012). *Philippines: Urban Sector Assessment, Strategy, and Road Map*. Manila, May. Retrieved on July 5, 2015. Available on: http://www.adb.org/publications/philippines-urban-sector-assessment-strategy-and-road-map.

ADB–Clean Air Asia (2006). *Country Synthesis Report on Urban Air Quality Management: Philippines*. Discussion draft. Retrieved on August 1, 2015. Available on: http://cleanairasia.org/portal/sites/default/files/documents/philippines.pdf.

Beck, M. (ed.) (2014). *Coasts at Risk: An Assessment of Coastal Risks and the Role of Environmental Solutions*. UN University — Institute for Environment and Human Security, Nature Conservancy and University of Rhode Island Coastal Resources Center. Retrieved on July 14, 2015. Available on: http://collections.unu.edu/view/UNU:2049#viewAttachments.

Bischoff, J. and Balamiento, M. (2015). *Six-Monthly Progress Report for July–December 2014: Technical Assistance to the Government of the Philippines for the Implementation of the SWITCH-Asia Policy Support Component*. GFA Consulting Group, Hamburg and Manila.

Dasgupta, S., Laplante, B., Murray, S. and Wheeler, D. (2009). Sea-level rise and storm surges: A comparative analysis of impacts in developing countries. *World Bank Policy Research Working Paper* No. 4901, April. Retrieved on July 10, 2015. Available on: http://documents.worldbank.org/curated/en/2009/04/10446662/sea-level-rise-storm-surges-comparative-analysis-impacts-developing-countries.

DTI (Department of Trade and Industry) (2014). *Micro, Small, and Medium Enterprise Statistics*. Philippines, February. Retrieved on May 1, 2015. Available on: http://dti.gov.ph/dti/index.php/msme/msme-statistics.

European Union (2014). *SWITCH-Asia's 80 Projects at a Glance*: Fact Sheet. Europe Aid Development and Cooperation Directorate-General, Brussels, July. Retrieved on March 28, 2015. Available on: http://www.switch-asia.eu/publications/2014-project-fact-sheet-brochure/?tx_switchasia_publications%5Bcontroller%5D=Publication&cHash=a8fcc34cb5e2ecb9329979aa612dea0b.

Global Footprint Network (2012). *A Measure for Resilience: 2012 Report on the Ecological Footprint of the Philippines*. Retrieved on August 24, 2015. Available on: http://www.footprintnetwork.org/images/article_uploads/Philippines_Footprint_Report_2012.pdf.

Green Growth Best Practice (GGBP) (2014). *Green Growth in Practice: Lessons from Country Experiences*. Retrieved on April 26, 2015. Available on: http://www.ggbp.org/sites/all/themes/ggbp/uploads/Green-Growth-in-Practice-062014-Full.pdf.

Green Growth Knowledge Platform (GGKP) (2013). Moving towards a common approach on green growth indicators. *With the Global Green Growth Institute, OECD, UNEP, and World Bank*. Scoping Paper, April. Retrieved on April 26, 2015. Available on: http://www.greengrowthknowledge.org/node/4620/.

Habito, C. (2010). *An Agenda for High and Inclusive Growth in the Philippines*. Asian Development Bank, Manila. Retrieved on June 18, 2015. Available on: http://www.adb.org/sites/default/files/publication/27470/agenda-high-inclusive-growth.pdf.

Hsu, A. and Emerson, J. (2012). *Environmental Performance Index and Pilot Trend Environmental Performance Index*. Yale Center for Environmental Law and Policy, New Haven. Retrieved on May 1, 2015. Available on: http://epi.yale.edu/.

Hsu, A. and Emerson, J. (2014). *2014 Environmental Performance Index*. Yale Center for Environmental Law and Policy, New Haven. Retrieved on May 1, 2015. Available on: http://epi.yale.edu/.

Institute for Global Environmental Strategies (IGES) (2010). SCP policies and national strategies. *Report on an IGES-UNEP Joint Roundtable Session at the 9th Asia Pacific Roundtable on SCP*. Retrieved on August 20, 2015. Available on: http://www.iges.or.jp/en/archive/wmr/activity20100611.html.

International Labour Organization (ILO) (2015). *Small and medium-sized enterprises and decent and productive employment creation. Report (IV) submitted to the International Labour Conference, April*. Retrieved on August 7, 2015. Available on: http://www.ilo.org/ilc/ILCSessions/104/reports/reports-to-the-conference/WCMS_358294/lang--en/index.htm.

Labodova, A. (2014). *Creating Green Philippines Islands of Sustainability (ECOSWITCH-GPIoS): Final Narrative Report submitted to the EU Delegation to the Philippines*. VSB — Technical University of Ostrava, Czech Republic.

Lerma, B. and Batan, T. (2015). Philippines — environment & climate change law 2015. *International Comparative Legal Guides*. Retrieved on August 20, 2015. Available on: http://www.iclg.co.uk/practice-areas/environment-and-climate-change-law/environment-and-climate-change-law-2015/philippines.

Lister, M. (2013). An energy efficiency roadmap for the Philippines 2014–2030: Final Report. *SWITCH-Asia Policy Support Component in the Philippines*. Manila, December. Retrieved on July 11, 2015. Available on: www.switch-asia.eu/fileadmin/user_upload/PSCs/DOE_Energy_Efficiency_and_Conservation_Roadmap_2014-2030.docx.

Micro, Small, and Medium Enterprise Development Council (MSMEDC) (2011). Micro, small, and medium enterprise development plan 2011–2016. *Bureau of Micro, Small, and Medium Enterprise Development, Department of Trade and Industry, Philippines*. Retrieved on May 1, 2015. Available on: http://dti.gov.ph/dti/index.php/msme/smed-plan.

National Statistical Coordination Board (NSCB) (2015a). *StatWatch*. Philippine Statistics Authority, Manila. Retrieved on April 27, 2015. Available on: http://nscb.gov.ph/stats/statwatch.asp.

National Statistical Coordination Board (NSCB) (2015b). *2014 Annual Growth Rate Still at 6.1 Percent*. Press Release, May 25. Philippine Statistics Authority, Manila. Retrieved on September 8, 2015. Available on: http://www.nscb.gov.ph/announce/2015/27May_revisedQ42014.asp.

National Statistics Office (2015). *2012 Census of Philippine Business and Industry — Final Results:* Economy-Wide Total Employment of 20 and Over. Philippines, April. Retrieved on May 1, 2015. Available on: http://census.gov.ph/content/2012-census-philippine-business-and-industry-cpbi-final-results-economy-wide-total-0.

National Economic and Development Authority (NEDA) (2014). *Philippine Development Plan 2011–2016*: *Midterm Update*. Philippines. Retrieved on April 27, 2015. Available on: http://www.neda.gov.ph/?p=3989.

NEDA (2015). *Socioeconomic Report 2014*: *Assessment and Implications for 2015–2016*. Philippines, March. Retrieved on April 27, 2015. Available on: http://www.neda.gov.ph/?p=5212.

Organization for Economic Cooperation and Development (OECD) (2014). *Towards Green Growth in Southeast Asia*. OECD Green Growth Studies, OECD Publishing, Paris. Retrieved on April 27, 2015. Available on: http://www.oecd-ilibrary.org/development/towards-green-growth-in-southeast-asia_9789264224100-en.

Paderanga, C. (2011). Private sector assessment: Philippines. *Asian Development Bank*. Retrieved on August 9, 2015. Available on: http://www.adb.org/documents/private-sector-assessment-philippines-2011.

Philippine Senate (2011). *Updates on the Implementation of Laws*. Fourteenth Congress, May. Retrieved on June 27, 2015. Available on: http://www.senate.gov.ph/publications/Book-MONITORING%20OF%20IMPLEMENTATION%20OF%20LAWS%20%2814th%20Congress%29.pdf.

Philippine Senate (2014). *Updates on the Implementation of Laws*. Fifteenth Congress, July. Retrieved on June 27, 2015. Available on http://senate.gov.ph/publications/Updates%20on%20the%20Implemention%20of%20Laws%20%28as%20of%20July%2028,%202014%29.pdf.

Ritter, T. (2014). *SMART Cebu — Small and Medium Enterprises for environmental Accountability, Responsibility and Transparency*: *Final Narrative Report*. SEQUA, Germany.

United Nations Environment Programme (UNEP) (2010). *ABC of SCP*: Clarifying Concepts on Sustainable Consumption and Production. Retrieved on April 26, 2015. Available on: https://sustainabledevelopment.un.org/content/documents/945ABC_ENGLISH.pdf.

UNEP (2012a). *Capacity Building and Policy Needs Assessment for Sustainable Consumption and Production*: Final Report. Retrieved on April 16, 2015. Available on: http://www.switch-asia.eu/fileadmin/user_upload/RPSC/policy-assessment/2015/Policy-Needs-Analysis-Final-report.pdf.

UNEP (2012b). *Capacity Building and Policy Needs Assessment for Sustainable Consumption and Production*: Executive Summary. Retrieved on April 16, 2015. Available on: http://www.switch-asia.eu/fileadmin/user_upload/RPSC/policy-assessment/2015/Policy-Needs-Analysis-Exec-Summary.pdf.

UNEP (2015). Sustainable Consumption and Production Indicators for the future SDGs. *With the International Institute for Sustainable Development and the Commonwealth Scientific and Industrial Research Organisation. Discussion Paper*, March. Retrieved on April 27, 2015. Available on: http://sd.iisd.org/news/unep-proposes-indicators-of-progress-toward-scp/.

UN Economic and Social Commission for Asia and the Pacific (UNESCAP) (2013). *Green Growth Indicators*: *A Practical Approach for Asia and the Pacific*. Thailand, December. Retrieved on April 30, 2015. Available on: http://www.unescap.org/resources/green-growth-indicators-practical-approach-asia-and-pacific.

UNESCAP–ADB–UNEP (2012). *Green Growth, Resources and Resilience: Environmental Sustainability in Asia and the Pacific*. Bangkok and Manila, January. Retrieved on April 26, 2015. Available on: http://www.unescap.org/resources/green-growth-resources-and-resilience-environmental-sustainability-asia-and-pacific.

Welle, T., Birkmann, J. and Rhyner, J. (2014). The world risk index 2014, in *World Risk Report 2014*. Bündnis Entwicklung Hilft (Alliance Development Works) and UN University-Institute for Environment and Human Security. Retrieved on July 14, 2015. Available on: http://ehs.unu.edu/news/news/world-risk-report-2014.html#info.

World Bank (1997). *Urban Air Quality Management Strategy in Asia* (*URBAIR*): *Metro Manila Report*. Shah, J. and Nagpal, T. (eds.). Retrieved on August 2, 2015. Available on: http://www-wds.worldbank.org/external/default/WDSContentServer/WDSP/IB/2003/08/02/000094946_03072204051061/Rendered/PDF/multi0page.pdf.

World Bank (2012). *Philippines*: *Toward Greener Waste Management*. Press Release, October 24. Retrieved on July 5, 2015. Available on: http://www.worldbank.

org/en/news/press-release/2012/10/24/philippines-toward-greener-waste-management.

World Bank (2013a). Getting a grip on climate change in the Philippines: Climate public expenditure and institutional review. *Extended Technical Report*. Retrieved on April 25, 2015. Available on: http://www.worldbank.org/en/country/philippines/publication/getting-a-grip-on-climate-change-in-the-philippines.

World Bank (2013b). *Philippine development report: Creating more and better jobs*. *Working Paper*, Philippine Office, September.

World Bank (2015). *Global Consumption Database Philippines*. Retrieved on February 20, 2016. Available on: http://datatopics.worldbank.org/consumption/country/Philippines.

World Health Organization (WHO) (2014). *Ambient (outdoor) Air Pollution Database 2014*. May. Retrieved on May 1, 2015. Available on: http://www.who.int/phe/health_topics/outdoorair/databases/cities/en/.

World Wildlife Fund for Nature (WWF–ADB) (2012). *Ecological Footprint and Investment in Natural Capital in Asia and the Pacific*. Manila, June. Retrieved on April 26, 2015. Available on: http://www.adb.org/publications/ecological-footprint-and-investment-natural-capital-asia-and-pacific.

Chapter 11

Linking Tourism, Energy and Agriculture through Sustainable Consumption and Production in Sri Lanka

M. Tissera, D. Samarakoon and G. Senanayake

11.1 Introduction

Sri Lanka is an island nation 65,610 km^2 in size, located off the southeast coast of India and home to a multi-ethnic population of around 20 million, according to the 2012 census [Department of Census and Statistics, 2012]. The per capita GDP of Sri Lanka is approximately USD 3,200/year with an incremental HDI of 0.715 [UNDP Human Development Report, 2013] and in the decade from 2002 to 2013, Sri Lanka achieved an average real GDP growth rate of 5.5% per year, with the national poverty rate falling from 22.7 to 6.7% [Department of Census and Statistics, 2015]. The economy relies heavily on the service sector with almost a 60% share in GDP, followed by the industrial sector with a 37% share. Sri Lanka's leading foreign exchange earners include the garment industry, foreign remittances, and the rubber and tea industries. Compared to countries of similar GDP and HDI rankings, Sri Lanka boasts a high literacy rate (91%), sound education and health care systems, and low carbon emissions of 0.7 metric tonnes CO_2 annually per capita in 2011 [World Bank Data, 2015].

Since the end of the 30-year conflict in 2009, Sri Lanka has experienced significant changes in consumption and production (SCP) patterns influenced by unprecedented development, economic growth, and a tourism boom. A number of environmental challenges and priority concerns have emerged resulting from the fast economic development. These include key impact areas, such as urbanisation, management of solid waste, conservation of biodiversity, degradation of land, fresh water and marine resources, abatement of air and noise pollution, and energy conservation [Ministry of Environment and Natural Resources and UNEP, 2009].

SCP approaches are being adopted by the government and business to address the emerging environmental challenges. The following sections discuss Sri Lanka's evolving policy frameworks relating to SCP and the role of the SWITCH-Asia National Policy Support Component (NPSC) for Sri Lanka. This section is followed by an overview of the role of SMEs in the Sri Lankan economy, focusing on three interlinked sectors of renewable energy, agriculture and food systems, and tourism, which are presented together with SWITCH-Asia project case studies.

11.2 Policies for SCP

Sri Lanka is not without adequate national policy on environmental protection and conservation, land use and conservation, forest protection, soil conservation, wastewater treatment, and air quality — some of the policies have been relatively successful compared to other countries in Asia. The Yale University Environment Performance Index (EPI) from 2016 [Hsu *et al.*, 2016] revealed that Sri Lanka had the highest performance score in South Asia. Examples are effective air quality management tools that are used in the country, including vehicle emissions testing and industrial emission control.

Sri Lanka has also developed a number of national policies and guidance documents, which are closely related to SCP, and which could be used as the basis to develop a comprehensive national SCP framework. An example is the Haritha (Green) Lanka Programme, launched by the

Ministry of Environment (MoE) in 2009, with the objective to incorporate sustainable development principles in all relevant sectors of the economy. This Programme is implemented under the direct guidance of the National Council for Sustainable Development (NCSD), set up under the Presidential Secretariat. The National Action Plan for the Haritha Lanka Programme is being implemented and aims at greening the development of all-important economic sectors, ensuring that these sectors implement their activities within the framework of sustainable development.

SCP pattern is a crosscutting theme that is mentioned throughout the Haritha Lanka Programme. In particular, under "Mission 3: Meeting the Challenges of Climate Change" the plan emphasises the strategy to "Optimise energy consumption through energy efficiency in enterprises." Under "Mission 6: Doing Away with the Dumps," the plan highlights the strategy to "Promote life cycle management in designing, manufacturing, consumption and disposal of products, based on principles of SCP." Under "Mission 10: Knowledge for Right Choices," SCP is mentioned specifically to "promote behavioural changes amongst youth towards sustainable production and consumption" and "Promote women to become change agents towards sustainable production and consumption practices" [National Council for Sustainable Development, 2009]. The MoE has taken steps to do a comprehensive forward-looking evaluation with the objective to undertake participatory refinement of the programme and to prepare the National Haritha Lanka Action Plan 2012–2022 to development vision by 2022. In addition to this development vision, a number of different policies are relevant for the promotion of SCP (see Table 11.1).

As Table 11.1 demonstrates, whilst the MoE, Ministry of Agriculture and Ministry of Energy are the main drivers of sustainability in Sri Lanka, a number of other government agencies are also involved in the design and implementation of SCP relevant policies, which requires cross-coordination among ministries for effective implementation. Development plans of these ministries do have some key components addressing sustainability through SCP, but, in order to be effective, the development plans need to be institutionalised as policies and guidelines to be implemented by local authorities. Furthermore, most sustainability strategies in the country are driven by key individuals who champion the cause of

Table 11.1: Major environmental policies in Sri Lanka relating to SCP

Name of National Policy	Main Objectives of the Policy	Main Implementing Bodies	State of Implementation of National Policy
National Agriculture Policy	Implement technically sound, economically viable, environmental friendly, and socially acceptable programmes to promote sustainable agricultural development with efficient and effective utilisation of resources. Increase productivity of water and land by enhancing crop production through the application of sustainable cultivation practice. Promote production and utilisation of organic and bio-fertilisers and gradually reduce the use of chemical fertilisers.	Ministry of Agriculture; Provincial Agriculture Departments; Irrigation Department	The Divineguma scheme was partially successful in the promotion of home gardening. The Government banned the sale of two types of pesticides proved to be contributing to water contamination. The strategies on organic fertiliser production and promotion have so far failed to gain any momentum due to the policy of subsidising chemical fertilisers.
National Energy Sector Development Plan — 2015	Increase the share of electricity generation from renewable energy sources from 50% in 2014 to 60% by 2020 and finally to	Ministry of Power & Energy Sustainable Energy Authority	Good guidelines and approval mechanisms to set up renewable energy power plants

	meet the total demand from renewable and other indigenous energy resources by 2030. Reduce the technical and commercial losses of the electricity transmission and distribution network from 11% to 8% by 2020. Reduce annual energy demand growth by 2% through conservation and efficient use. Reduce the carbon footprint of the energy sector by 5% by 2025.		that feed the national grid have been established. Active engagement with industries to increase energy efficiency and renewable energy share in the sector. Tariff structure to reduce excessive usage of electricity. A counterproductive measure was to reduce the petroleum prices, which resulted in increase in usage of petrol for less productive activities.
National Land Use Policy	Land suitable for non-agricultural activities has to be identified and development plans prepared for such land. In order to improve land management and productivity through land use planning, the	Ministry of Planning and Development; Ministry of Agriculture; Ministry of Urban Development.	Since 2010, the key mash lands and water retention areas have been identified and named as protected areas. If agricultural land greater than 10 acres is to be used for habitat development, special approval has to be obtained.

(Continued)

Table 11.1: (*Continued*)

Name of National Policy	Main Objectives of the Policy	Main Implementing Bodies	State of Implementation of National Policy
	laws and regulations related to land have to be reviewed and a new legal framework introduced. While adopting an integrated approach to land resources management, all stakeholders in land use will be consulted and decisions taken via a participatory process.		Laws on soil protection have not been implemented successfully; across the island, industries neglect the laws and are not penalised.
Tourism Development Plan 2010	The development plan refers to strategies of increasing numbers of international arrivals and product diversification, but does not refer to concrete strategies on sustainability or SCP.	Ministry of Tourism, Sri Lanka Tourism Development Authority, Sri Lanka Tourism Promotion Bureau	The development plan is expected to change with the new government headed by the President Maithripala Sirisena.

sustainability. However, the foremost issue for promoting sustainability at the policy level in a systemic way is to enhance strategic level knowledge and capacity within the country and administrations. The SWITCH-Asia Programme's NPSC for Sri Lanka aims to address this issue (see Box 11.1).

Box 11.1 Case Study of the SWITCH-Asia SCP-NPSC Sri Lanka

The EU-funded "SWITCH-Asia SCP-NPSC" for Sri Lanka was launched on 9th April 2015. As a cooperation between the European Union (EU) and Government of Sri Lanka, the project aims at supporting the Sri Lankan Government in selecting, adapting and implementing a suitable economic and regulatory policy framework to promote SCP, thereby enhancing the long-term SCP patterns in the country.

With a budget of EUR 1.87 million, the key focus areas of the four year project include the following aspects:

- developing an overall SCP policy framework, enhancing the economic, social and environmental benefits of SCP, and providing further direction for upgrading the national policies in Sri Lanka,
- strengthening the institutional mechanism for enhancing the capacity of the government to promote SCP (also via the establishment of an Inter-agency Working Group),
- facilitating SCP implementation in selected sectors, including fostering eco-innovation,
- providing capacity development support,
- raising awareness through a knowledge development platform and facilitating inclusion of SCP in educational programmes.

The project has commenced the national SCP policy formulation, which was expected to be completed by mid-2016, followed by provision of training and capacity development for the main beneficiary: the staff of the Sustainable Development Division of the Ministry of Mahaweli Development and Environment, and the Project Steering Committee members. Additionally, the development of a knowledge platform and e-learning 'training of trainers'

(*Continued*)

Box 11.1 (*Continued*)

tools and courses, as well as media campaigns will support public awareness raising on SCP.

The project is implemented by a consortium led by Application Européenne de Technologies et de Services (AETS) in partnership with the Ministry of Mahaweli Development and Environment selected as the key national agency. The consortium brings together local and international organisations, including the Industrial Services Bureau (ISB), Global Sustainability Solutions (GLOSS), the United Nations Economic and Social Commission for Asia and the Pacific (ESCAP), the Regional Environmental Centre for Central and Eastern Europe (REC), and the BIO Intelligence Service (BIO).

Formulation of an overarching national policy on SCP is one of the major objectives of the SWITCH-Asia NPSC Sri Lanka. A search was initiated to collate existing national policies and related materials that had some relevance to the SCP policy to be formulated. During the process of collecting the policy documents, it was realised that there was an urgent need for a central depository system. To date, the project team has collected nearly 80 policy documents.

To formulate a national SCP policy, a three-pronged strategy has been adopted:

1. review of existing national policies that have some relevance to the SCP policy to be formulated,
2. align the national SCP policy with Sustainable Development Goals (SDGs) of the 10 Year Framework of Programmes on SCP (10YFP) and other multinational agreements, treaties and covenants,
3. learn from similar experiences in the region and EU countries.

Sri Lanka does not have a standardised policy formulation process and hence different policy proponents follow different procedures. A deficiency in the process often results in suboptimal policies and eventually weaker implementation. Therefore, it is important to adopt a standardised process of policy formulation and make it mandatory so that policy proponents have to follow a unified system. This would make the task easy for the Ministry of National Policies & Economic Affairs, which is responsible for assessing policy proposals while ensuring the adoption of robust and effective policies. Once this has been established, the SCP policy framework will be developed using this process.

(*Continued*)

Box 11.1 (*Continued*)

The SWITCH-Asia NPSC Sri Lanka has also developed a comprehensive tool for the selection of sectors for deeper project interventions. Accordingly, the three sub sectors of dairy processing, tea manufacturing and rice processing of the food and beverages industry have been selected; baseline conditions shall be established shortly before SCP policy tools are applied to these sectors.

11.3 Sri Lanka's Industry Structures and Current State of SMEs

Small- and medium-sized enterprises (SMEs) contribute significantly to Sri Lanka's economy, accounting for 80% of all businesses [Secretariat for Senior Ministers Sri Lanka, 2012]. According to the Sri Lanka Industry Survey from 2008, over 18,000 companies were operating in the country, of which about 91% are SMEs [World Bank, 2011]. SMEs provide employment for the skilled, semi-skilled, unskilled, and the differently abled. SMEs are found across the primary, secondary, and tertiary sectors of the Sri Lankan economy. No unified definition of an SME exists in Sri Lanka; the Department of Small Industries defines an SME as an enterprise with fewer than 50 people and capital investment less than LKR 5 million (USD 34,400). For the Export Development Board, an SME is an enterprise with less than LKR 8 million (USD 55,000) investment and less than LKR 50 million (USD 344,000) annual turnover [Jayasekara and Thilakarathna, 2013]. The SME sector is a core segment of economic development in the country. SMEs account for 70% of enterprises in the plantation sector, 85% of rubber producers are SMEs, 100% of paddy cultivators, and 90% of coconut smallholdings. SMEs' contribution to Sri Lanka's total GDP is growing and has increased to 52% in 2011 from 40% in 2010 [Jayasekara and Thilakarathna, 2013].

SMEs play an important role in promoting inclusive and economic growth, developing entrepreneurial skills and innovation, as well as promoting social cohesion. SMEs in agri-business engage in growing spices, fruits, and vegetables, whilst SMEs in the manufacturing sector engage in numerous industrial activities accounting for about 20% of industrial establishments. Sri Lanka has recognised the importance of a healthy SME sector and vibrant industry for ensuring competitiveness of the economy internationally. An SME Task Force was established in 2002 with the goal of strengthening the institutional framework for SME development. In order to create an enabling environment for globally competitive SMEs, inter-institutional coordination, developing staff and institutional capacities, and reforming and restructuring existing SME development institutions are all required. The SME Task Force recommended the establishment of an apex agency to undertake the institutional reforms required for SME development. Accordingly, in 2006 the National Enterprise Development Authority (NEDA) was established to promote, support, encourage and facilitate enterprise development within Sri Lanka, with special emphasis on SMEs [Ministry of Environment, 2012]. Also, the Science, Technology & Innovation Strategy for Sri Lanka (2011–2015) proposed a mechanism to support SMEs to innovate and transfer technologies, giving priority to high-end technologies [Secretariat for Senior Ministers Sri Lanka, 2012].

Furthermore, the National Human Resources and Employment Policy of Sri Lanka in its website states that there is room for improvement in the operating environment of SMEs in the following key areas [Secretariat for Senior Ministers Sri Lanka, 2012]:

- Gender bias — Workers employed in SMEs are predominantly men. Good gender balance in employment practice is required to correct this bias and attract, recruit, retain, and promote women in SME employment.
- SME entrepreneurs lack knowledge and experience in good personnel management practice. Most entrepreneurs do not like to provide training, health, and welfare facilities for employees due to the resulting increase in the cost of production.
- A common feature found in SMEs is the high degree of absenteeism among SME workers. This leads to loss of productivity and staff morale. Attendance improvement policies and programmes require implementation.

The following sub-sections will introduce the three sectors of renewable energy and energy efficiency, agriculture and food, and tourism, highlighting challenges and opportunities for SCP and case studies from SWITCH-Asia projects.

11.3.1 *Renewable energy and energy efficiency*

Energy independence is seen as a key contributor to Sri Lanka's national security; around 50% of Sri Lanka's electricity is generated from imported fossil fuels such as oil and coal, and the transport sector is almost fully dependent on petroleum imports. At present, Sri Lanka's energy mix of approximately 3,600 MW is made up of 51% thermal, 37% large hydro and 12% renewables [Samarasekara, 2014]. With ambitious targets of achieving 100% electrification by 2015 (over 95% has been achieved; the balance may not be possible solely via national grid expansion due to technical reasons, hence the need to use standalone renewable options) and achieving a target of 30% of non-conventional renewable energy in the country's energy mix of wind, solar, and biomass by 2030 [Daily Mirror Sri Lanka, 2015]. The cost of energy in Sri Lanka is rapidly increasing and with it the dependence on imported fossil fuels. Rural communities on the island still use biomass as the main cooking fuel; this resource is fast depleting which is a major concern for rural households. Not surprisingly, given the statistics above, the most common issue facing SMEs is the increasing cost of energy. Progress in the SME sector has also been hampered by the lack of appropriate technologies to overcome the challenges posed by climate change.

The EU-funded SWITCH-Asia project on "*Promoting Renewable Energy as a Driver for Sustainable Development and Mitigation of Climate Change in Sri Lanka*," is a timely and necessary intervention. The project focuses on up-scaling biogas technologies for sustainable development, responsible tourism, economic growth contributing to poverty reduction, and climate change mitigation in Sri Lanka. The project targets tourism SMEs, households and public authorities in the country while building the technical capacity of manufacturing and construction SMEs in biogas technologies. The project also supports micro-finance institutions to develop financial schemes providing loans for biogas installations to SMEs and households. Furthermore, the training and capacity building component of the initiative assists local construction sector to enhance its technical and entrepreneurial competences regarding manufacturing and installation of biogas systems (see Box 11.2).

Box 11.2 Case Study of the SWITCH-Asia Sri Lanka Renewable Energy

In 2014, SWITCH Asia launched the "*Promoting Renewable Energy as a Driver for Sustainable Development and Mitigation of Climate Change in Sri Lanka*." The three-year project implemented by People in Need (PIN), Czech Republic, and local partner, Janathakshan, aims to create an enabling environment for the large-scale dissemination of biogas as a reliable source of clean energy for the hospitality industry and households in Sri Lanka. With this project, SWITCH-Asia Programme continues its focus on the hospitality industry, highlighting the significant role the hospitality industry plays in contributing to economic growth and poverty reduction through a shift to energy efficiency, renewable energy, and environmental practices in the tourism sector.

Biogas technology has had a presence in Sri Lanka since the 1970s, reaching a peak in the early 1980s when electricity was scarce and costs associated with the construction of biogas units was affordable due to low cost of labour involved. Regrettably, the adoption of biogas technology has remained more or less stagnant since the late 1980s. Biogas technology in itself is an ideal solution with benefits to three pertinent issues currently facing Sri Lanka, that of energy security, sustainable waste management, and the overuse of chemical fertiliser, which has contributed to environmental pollution and a rise in kidney disease. Biogas technology converts waste into sustainable clean energy improving environmental stewardship by reducing greenhouse gas (GHG) emissions, energy costs and dependence on imported fossil fuels and producing organic fertiliser as a bi-product.

The SWITCH-Asia project aims at developing biogas as an industry focusing specifically on improving the availability of technical knowhow and skilled personnel; developing financial tools and resources to disseminate biogas units; improving the policy and regulatory framework for dissemination and increasing public awareness and acceptance of the technology. After two years in operation, the project reached the following milestones:

- A training manual on the construction of the *SiriLakUmaga* biogas unit.
- Training workshops across five provinces where 35 masons received a comprehensive scientific training on the construction of a biogas unit.
- 20 SMEs trained and capacitated to provide services to install biogas units in five provinces.

(*Continued*)

Box 11.2 (*Continued*)

- Set up Provincial Biogas Promotion Committees in three provinces with the inclusion of key government institutions, banks, and private associations.
- Developed long term Biogas Promotion Plans for three provinces.

A collective effort by various stakeholders in the industry has seen the development of a Nationally Appropriate Mitigation Action Plan for Biogas, under which around 1,000 biogas units will be constructed across the country at all levels but mainly focusing on four provinces; Uva, Central, North Western, and Southern. Additionally, the Sri Lanka Sustainable Energy Authority (SEA) is currently in the process of developing a national programme for biogas development. The relatively high cost of construction is one of the major obstacles for the up scaling of biogas at the domestic level, with progress further restricted by a recent government reduction in the price of liquid petroleum gas (LPG), which is sure to be short-lived. These are a few of the challenges that lower middle-income countries such as Sri Lanka face when addressing issues of SCP practice. Awareness of sustainable development and responsible tourism is key to thwarting short-term benefits that could jeopardise sustainability in the long term.

More information about the project is available at: http://www.switch-asia.eu/projects/sri-lanka-renewable-energy/.

11.3.2 *Sustainable agriculture and food systems*

SCP practice can play an important role to change current unsustainable practices in Sri Lanka's agriculture and food sector. This section will look at two particular issues: On the production side, the overuse of agrochemicals and fertilisers in food production, and on the consumption side, the growing trend towards consumption of unhealthy fast foods.

The Sri Lankan food industry is very diverse: small-scale farmers produce primary goods, 80% of distribution and sales is handled by medium and large-scale institutions, with small scale entities accounting for about 20% of the market share. The processed food sector is mainly driven by large companies and multinationals achieving growth from exports and local market expansion. Rice continues to be one of the main agricultural crops in Sri Lanka and accounts for about one fifth of total agricultural output. Excessive use of chemical fertiliser and pesticides in agriculture has resulted in contamination of ground water and deteriorating soil conditions. Starting in the mid-1960s, successive governments and the agricultural department have encouraged Sri Lankan farmers to use chemical fertilisers and pesticides by giving heavy subsidies. Instead of the natural methods farmers have been using for centuries, they were encouraged to use chemical fertilisers and other agrochemicals. As a result, green and sustainable agricultural methodologies employed in the past, such as cascade tanks and the use of compost and animal dung as organic fertilisers, have diminished rapidly in rice cultivation. According to Wimalawansa and Wimalawansa [2014], Sri Lankan farmers currently use around 600,000 tonnes of solid fertiliser and 250,000 tonnes of liquid fertiliser annually. Fertiliser use in the three largest provinces in Sri Lanka is as follows: North Central Province, 130,000; North Western Province, 96,000; and Eastern Province, 100,000 ha (see Figure 11.1).

Although fertiliser consumption has been on a steady downwards trend over the last decade (see Table 11.2), current usage levels are still unsustainable and Sri Lanka uses more phosphate fertilisers and certain other toxic agrochemicals than any other country in the Southeast Asia [Wimalawansa and Wimalawansa, 2014].

Notorious environmental pollutants, these agrochemicals and petrochemicals are key contributors to soil infertility and have been linked to the steep rise in the incidence of chronic kidney disease in Sri Lanka.

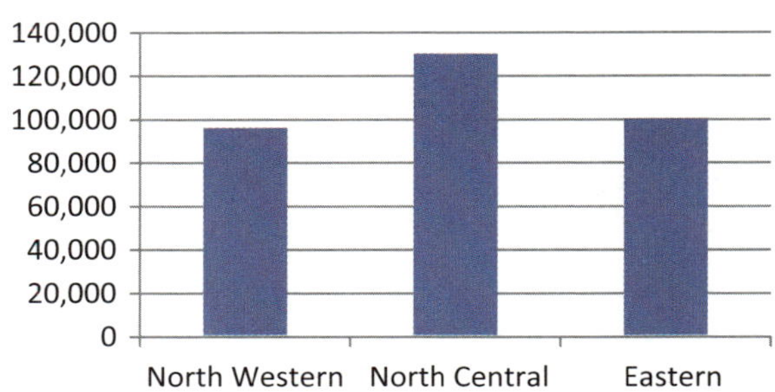

Figure 11.1: Geographic distribution of fertiliser use in Sri Lanka (tonnes per year)

Source: Wimalawansa and Wimalawansa [2014].

Table 11.2: Fertiliser consumption in Sri Lanka [World Bank Data, 2013]

Year	2006	2007	2008	2009	2010	2011	2012	2013
Kg per hectare of arable land	291.3	288.5	311.7	281.4	229.0	256.1	198.4	160.0

The number of affected people in the country has grown to an estimated 450,000 [Handunnetti, 2013]. This has posed a major threat to farming communities and many leave rural areas looking for alternative livelihoods and opportunities [Daily Mirror Sri Lanka, 2014]. Some producer groups have made efforts to grow organic and eco-friendly produce. However, the lack of awareness about organic produce among consumers, the lack of standards for organic labels, limited certification systems at affordable prices and the lack of third party verification [Ranaweera, 2008] have so far hindered the switch to environmentally sustainable and healthy practices in the agriculture sector.

Sri Lanka is also an example of how fast food is becoming part of developing countries' diets. Sri Lanka's food consumption pattern is gradually shifting to a more processed food consuming market. In the early 1980s, processed food consumption was limited to powdered milk and a few items purchased at the local bakery such as bread, a daily staple. The common practice was to purchase fresh produce and prepare everything at home. Increasing urbanisation and the introduction of global fast food chains such as Mac Donald's, KFC, and Pizza Hut are beginning to change consumer patterns as people are more likely to opt for items that are ready to eat off the shelf or can be prepared with minimal time and effort. The seemingly appealing nature of junk food including its time-saving factor, attractiveness in packaging, advertising and addictive taste all play a key role in causing negative impacts to an individual's health. The health risks twofold: first, there are the more pronounced health risks, such as cholesterol from the consumption of high fat content and obesity from high sugar. Second, there is the incidence of dental cavities, type 2 diabetes and certain ingredients that negatively impact pregnancies and existing health conditions, like asthma [Ashakiran and Deepthi, 2012].

These changes have created varying structures across the entire food supply chain. The production pattern of raw food items remains unchanged;

from rice to vegetable and fruits, the majority of producers are smallholder farmers. A few large companies engage in the production of these items, however, the overall share remains low. Dominated by SMEs only a few decades back, the sourcing and processing sectors have seen a major shift now equally shared by large companies. Large multinationals and their Sri Lankan agents dominate the support service sector, comprising fertiliser, chemicals, and equipment.

11.3.3 *Sustainable tourism through SCP*

As trends in consumption and production are changing in the country along with economic development, sector-specific government policy and industry regulation need to be implemented to ensure a balance is struck between development and preservation of natural resources. This is especially significant in the tourism sector, which has over the last three years experienced exponential growth, putting increasing pressure on natural resources and energy consumption, an issue which needs to be remedied urgently. A blueprint document, the '*Sri Lankan Tourism Development Strategy 2011–2016*,' whose objectives are to distribute national economic benefits through tourism to economic development and national social cohesion, is at the time of writing guiding tourism development for the country's tourism sector.

The 26-year civil war conflict was evidently unfavourable for tourism. Prior to the end of the conflict in 2009, the average volume of international tourist arrivals into the country remained stagnant at around 400,000–500,000 per year. Post-conflict, dividends of peace resulted in a tourism boom with 1.5 million tourist arrivals recorded in 2014 alone. The Central Bank of Sri Lanka Annual Report [2013] states that total tourist earnings increased from USD 1,039 million in 2012 to USD 1,715 million in 2013. Cashing in on the huge potential of its tourism sector, Sri Lanka is aiming to make it the largest foreign exchange earner increasing total room capacity to 35,000 and attracting 2.5 million tourists in 2016 [Wickramasinghe, 2012], by launching tourist development zones in Kalpitiya, Kuchchaveli, and Yala. Both international hotel chains and medium and small-scale hotels are clamouring to cater to the increasing demand for services. The unprecedented demand for services, however, is not without teething problems, as it struggles to deal with the lack of support services such as uninterrupted supplies of quality food, transportation, community-managed tourism such as day tours and other activities, training, supplier development, and environmental restoration and protection.

The newly elected President, Hon. Maithripala Sirisena, who took office in January 2015, has shifted focus to strengthening relations with Sri Lanka's top bilateral trade partner India, which would ensure Sri Lanka's development continues and offsets any deteriorating ties with China, which has emerged as a major investor in Sri Lanka's infrastructure. An example is the USD 1.4 billion Colombo Port City project [Springer, 2014]. Sri Lanka's strategic position in the Indian Ocean and along major trade routes means it will likely remain an attractive destination for investment, including the tourism sector. As Sri Lanka experiences its tourist boom and the demand for services and infrastructure increases, regulatory mechanisms need to be bolstered to ensure transparency, accountability, and quality of service, which if ignored could pose a serious threat to the future of the industry. The Sri Lankan tourism sector is a mix of private sector and public sector entities where large-scale and small-scale service providers play an equally prominent role. The hospitality industry is widely known to be one of the most energy-intensive industries in the country. The cost of energy accounts for nearly 18% of the total cost in a hotel and the percentage would be higher for smaller entities due to low economies of scale [Wickramasinghe, 2012]. Small-scale hoteliers and related service providers such as restaurants, food suppliers, and transport service providers have long faced financial difficulties related to high operating costs owing to increasing energy prices. Not surprisingly, the main environmental management practices implemented by hotels are use of energy-efficient lighting methods (used by 88% of hotels) and use of solar power (used by 69% of hotels) [Wickramasinghe, 2015].

Tourism development also puts pressure on natural resources when it increases consumption in areas where resources are already scarce. In a country that endures annual droughts in the dry zone and certain areas still lack water piping supply, the tourism industry already overuses water resources for hotels, swimming pools, gardens, and personal use of water by tourists. Many hotels do not maintain monthly records of their water consumption and the lack of data on water consumption remains a barrier for taking necessary water management decisions [Wickramasinghe, 2013]. Excessive water consumption could result in water shortages and degradation of water supplies, as well as generating a greater volume of wastewater.

The sustainable disposal of degradable and non-degradable waste is another serious issue, improper disposal being a major despoiler of the environment. In the last few years, numerous large and medium scale constructions without proper environment impact assessments (EIAs) have mushroomed, increasing pressure on natural resources and attractive landscapes and forcing the local population to compete for critical resources. Uncontrolled conventional tourism can put enormous pressure on an area leading to negative impacts such as increased pollution, soil erosion, water pollution, natural habitat loss, increased pressure on endangered species, and deforestation.

For the Sri Lankan tourism sector to compete with the global hospitality market and meet the Global Sustainable Tourism Criteria, a shift to energy efficiency, sustainable practice and the use of alternative energy sources needs to be a key focus. This also includes tropical alternatives such as the rattan industry for furniture and construction, which represents 30% of the world's supply along with Malaysia, the Philippines, and Bangladesh. Likewise, Sri Lanka's bamboo industry can contribute to sustainable tourism, which presently has 5,166 ha in coverage and is valued at USD 1.19 million, and aims to expand to 10,000 ha coverage by 2018 [Ministry of Industry and Commerce, 2012].

Linked closely to the tourism industry, the Sri Lankan food industry has policy and regulations on food safety but lacks the same with regard to sustainable food systems, which take into account production, processing, distribution, consumption, and waste disposal. Ambitious in its targets for infrastructure and human resource development, the current tourism blueprint falls short of ensuring sustainable tourism goals, in particular environmental and social issues such as distribution of benefits, and taking into account the interests of all stakeholders such as indigenous groups, the local population, tourists, SMEs, and local government [Kamble and Bouchon, 2014]. For instance, regarding environmental criteria, of the three areas across the country covering 1,500 acres designated

Box 11.3 Case Study of the SWITCH-Asia Project "Greening Sri Lanka Hotels"

Funded by the SWITCH-Asia Programme with key implementing partner the Ceylon Chamber of Commerce, the "Greening Sri Lanka Hotels" project was launched in 2010 and completed in 2013. The project's main objective was to support the hotel sectors in Sri Lanka to reduce their carbon footprint by implementing environmentally sound energy and waste management practices. As key implementing partner, the Ceylon Chamber of Commerce played a significant role connecting business institutions in the country to key government partners including the SEA, the Institute of Environmental Professionals and the responsible tourism partnership (a consortium set up by the Ministry of Tourism together with private sector partners).

In an unprecedented feat, the "Greening Sri Lanka Hotels" project connected over 250 of the 358 registered hotels across the country through awareness creation workshops, technical training sessions, energy audits, and a national competition. The project was well received by the majority of hotels further bolstered by government regulation, implemented at the time, requiring high energy consuming entities to have a compulsory on-site energy manager.

Initially, it was the larger hotels that seemed to embrace the concept of the project because they could allocate the necessary resources, and the savings garnered were clearly visible. In time, the enthusiasm shown by larger hotels and awareness programmes conducted under the project attracted the interests of the small and medium hotel sector and they too began to participate actively, reaping the benefits of environmentally sound energy and waste management practices. There still remains a gap in lack of affordable technical guidance and financial tools for small and medium hotels to achieve their targets. The basic action plan of the project included initial awareness creation workshops for key decision makers in the hotel sector at identified zones, followed up with walk through site audits promoting awareness on the potential savings and preservation a hotel could achieve with minimum investment.

Walk through audit information was subsequently used to develop essential technical training programmes for delivery. Designed with the concept of an on-site "energy manager" responsible for implementing, monitoring and sustaining government-introduced renewable energy schemes and regulations, the project has helped institutionalise the majority of knowledge transferred during the project activities. A handbook on "good practice guidelines" developed

(Continued)

Box 11.3 (*Continued*)

under the project continues to be used by most hotels in the country for training purposes.

Additionally, the project introduced the "SWITCH-ASIA — GREENING SRI LANKA HOTELS" awards programme, which recognised and awarded the best practising hotels. An annual event held continuously for the past three years since its inception in 2012, the "SWITCH-ASIA — GREENING SRI LANKA HOTELS" awards programme has become a trademark competition in which hotels vie for the prize of best energy and environment practices in the country. At the conclusion of the project in 2013, the awards programme continues to be taken forward by the Ceylon Chamber of Commerce in partnership with other stakeholders in the tourism sector.

More information on the project is available at: http://www.switch-asia.eu/projects/greening-sri-lankan-hotels/.

for the development of resorts, the only criteria covering the aspect of sustainability was the EIA conducted prior to the pre-construction stage. There are challenges associated with using EIAs as effective conservation and sustainable development tools because they fail to take into consideration the cumulative impacts of natural resource drainage and long-term ecological damage. The tourism blueprint also does not consider any sustainability criteria for the operation of hotel and tourism facilities.

11.4 Conclusions and Recommendations

SMEs contribute significantly to Sri Lanka's economy, accounting for 80% of all businesses. Sri Lanka has experienced significant changes in consumption and production patterns influenced by unprecedented development and a tourism boom since the end of the conflict in 2009. Today, Sri Lanka is in a state of rapid economic expansion. However, integrating environment and development at the policy, planning, and management levels that account for the economic and environmental impact in the long-term, the large-scale extraction of natural resources and generation of unmanaged waste are still to be achieved. It is the households and hospitality sector in Sri Lanka that will be most affected if efficient systems are not established for integrated environmental and economic accounting. Though the government has made some headway in addressing issues of sustainability, there remains much to be done in this regard. SCP can play an important role in guiding national development if it is included in national policy documents, such as tourism sector development plans. Furthermore, the more active involvement of international donor agencies could play a significant role in guiding local implementing organisations towards sustainable development practice. The SWITCH-Asia projects serves as key learning experiences for this sector, creating compelling case studies for the furtherance of sustainable development practice. Currently, SMEs suffer from a lack of information exchange, leading to conflict, dissonance, and other industrial relations issues. More systematic cooperation and consultation with stakeholders could be addressed through new SME policy. Taking this into account, the EU-funded "SWITCH-Asia SCP-NPSC" for Sri Lanka was launched on 9th April 2015. A partnership between the EU and the Government of Sri Lanka, the project aims at supporting the Sri Lankan Government in selecting, adapting and implementing suitable economic and regulatory policy framework to promote SCP, thereby enhancing long-term sustainability of consumption and production patterns in the country. The project recommends the development of a national level action plan, with the inclusion of government and support of donor agencies, for SCP that will contribute to environmental integrity, social justice, and economic development.

References

Ashakiran and Deepthi, R. (2012). Fast foods and their impact on health. *Journal of Krishna Institute of Medical Sciences University* 1(2), p. 277.

Central Bank of Sri Lanka Annual Report (2013). *Chapter 5 External Sector Developments and Policies Chart 5.2*. Retrieved on December 7, 2015. Available on: http://www.cbsl.gov.lk/pics_n_docs/10_pub/_docs/efr/annual_report/AR2013/English/9_Chapter_05.pdf.

Daily Mirror Sri Lanka (2015). *Sri Lanka self-sufficient in energy by 2020*: *Champiaka*. Retrieved on October 12, 2015. Available on: http://www.dailymirror.lk/67265/sri-lanka-self-sufficient-in-energy-by-2020-champika.

Daily Mirror Sri Lanka (2014). *Water pollution and chronic kidney disease in Sri Lanka*. 22 April 2014. Retrieved on November 12, 2015. Available on:

http://www.dailymirror.lk/43526/water-pollution-and-chronic-kidney-disease-in-sri-lanka.

Department of Census and Statistics (2012). *Sri Lanka 2012 Census Final Report*. Department of Census and Statistics, Colombo.

Department of Census and Statistics (2015). *The Spatial Distribution of Poverty in Sri Lanka. Department of Census and Statistics — Sri Lanka and Poverty Global Practice, World Bank Group*. August 2015.

Handunnetti, D. (2013). *Agrochemicals Blamed for Chronic Kidney Disease in Sri Lanka. SciDev.Net*, 12 April 2013.

Hsu, A. *et al.* (2016). *2016 Environmental Performance Index*. Yale University, New Haven, CT.

Jayasekara, J. P. D. R. and Thilakarathna, A. (2013). *Government Policy and Strategy for SME Development*. Ministry of Finance and Planning, Sri Lanka Presentation at the Fourth IMF-Japan High-Level Tax Conference for Asian Countries in Tokyo April 2–4, 2013.

Kamble, Z. and Bouchon, F. (2014). Tourism planning and a nation's vision: A review of the tourism policy of Sri Lanka. *Procedia — Social and Behavioral Sciences* 144, 229–236.

Ministry of Environment (2012). *Sri Lanka's Middle Path to Sustainable Development through 'Mahinda Chintana — Vision for the Future'*. Country Report of Sri Lanka for United Nations Conference on Sustainable Development/(Rio +20). Sustainable Development Division, MoE, June 2012.

Ministry of Environment and Natural Resources — Sri Lanka (MENR — SL) and the United Nations Environment Program (UNEP) (2009). *Sri Lanka Environment Outlook 2009*. Retrieved on November 10, 2015. Available on: http://www.environmentmin.gov.lk/web/pdf/annual_reports/Book-1.pdf.

Ministry of Industry and Commerce (2012). *UNIDO's first Lankan Bamboo Industry Initiative*. Available on: http://www.industry.gov.lk/web/index.php?option=com_content&view=article&id=176%3Aunidos-first-lankan-bamboo-industry-initiative&catid=44%3Aindustry-events&Itemid=194&lang=en.

National Council for Sustainable Development (2009). *National Action Plan for Haritha Lanka Programme*. Ministry of Environment and Natural Resources, Colombo, January 2009.

Ranaweera, S. (2008). Development of organic agriculture sector in Sri Lanka. *Asian Tribune*. 25 March 2008. Available on: http://www.asiantribune.com/?q=node/10186.

Samarasekara, B. (2014). Status, Plans and Challenges. Ceylon Electricity Board, 16 September 2014. Retrieved on January 09, 2015. Available on: https://

www.google.ae/url?sa=t&rct=j&q=&esrc=s&source=web&cd=3&ved=0ahUKEwj-tbGS2LHOAhXFcRQKHVa7C4sQFggnMAI&url=http%3A%2F%2Fwww.costi.gov.lk%2Findex.php%2Fen%2Fenergy-security%3Fdownload%3D163%3Aroundtable-discussion-on-energy-security&usg=AFQjCNEsJVcKjtZB9U3dPG0RkFHZSKQ9mA.

Secretariat for Senior Ministers Sri Lanka (2012). Small and medium sized enterprises (SMEs). *National Human Resources and Employment Policy*. 15 November 2012. Retrieved on October 14, 2015. Available on: http://www.nhrep.gov.lk/index.php?option=com_content&view=article&id=81&Itemid=59&lang=en.

Springer, J. (2014). Ten reasons to invest in Sri Lanka. *Forbes Asia*. October 30, 2014. Retrieved on October 24, 2015. Available on: http://www.forbes.com/sites/jonspringer/2014/10/30/ten-reasons-to-invest-in-sri-lanka/#7c57ef6c5cc5.

UNDP Human Development Report (2013). *The Rise of the South: Human Progress in a Diverse World*. Retrieved on November 6, 2015. Available on: http://hdr.undp.org/sites/default/files/Country-Profiles/LKA.pdf.

Wickramasinghe, K. (2012). *Giving Tourism a Green Shade: Studying Environmental Practices in Sri Lanka's Hotels*. Institute of Policy Studies Sri Lanka, 27 September 2012. Retrieved on January 11, 2015. Available on: http://www.ips.lk/talkingeconomics/2012/09/27/giving-tourism-a-green-shade-studying-environmental-practices-in-sri-lankas-hotels/.

Wickramasinghe, K. (2013). *Tourism and Water Management: Is Sri Lanka Paying Enough Attention*? Institute of Policy Studies Sri Lanka, 27 September 2013. Retrieved on January 11, 2015. Available on: http://www.ips.lk/talkingeconomics/2013/09/27/tourism-and-water-management-is-sri-lanka-paying-enough-attention/.

Wickramasinghe, K. (2015). *Talking Economics Blog. Good Environmental Management Practices in the Hotel Industry in Sri Lanka: Determinants and Barriers*. Retrieved on December 7, 2015. Available on: http://www.ips.lk/talkingeconomics/2015/02/09/good-environmental-management-practices-in-the-hotel-industry-in-sri-lanka-determinants-and-barriers/.

Wimalawansa, S. A. and Wimalawansa, S. J. (2014). Impact of changing agricultural practices on human health: Chronic kidney disease of multi-factorial origin in Sri Lanka. *Wudpecker Journal of Agricultural Research* 3(5), 110–124.

World Bank (2011). *Small and Medium Enterprises: Engines of Growth in Post Conflict Sri Lanka*. Feature Story. September 30, 2011. Retrieved on September 20, 2015. Available on: http://www.worldbank.org/en/news/feature/2010/09/30/small-medium-enterprises-engines-growth-post-conflict-sri-lanka.

World Bank (2013). *Fertilizer consumption (kilograms per hectare of arable land)*. Retrieved on November 20, 2015. Available on: http://data.worldbank.org/indicator/AG.CON.FERT.ZS?locations=LK.

World Bank (2015). *CO2 emissions (metric tons per capita)*. Carbon Dioxide Information Analysis Center, Environmental Sciences Division, Oak Ridge National Laboratory, Tennessee, United States. Retrieved on November 12, 2015. Available on: http://data.worldbank.org/indicator/EN.ATM.CO2E.PC.

Chapter 12

Thailand's Sufficiency Economy and Sustainable Consumption and Production

K. Merle

12.1 Sustainability in Thailand: Sufficiency Economy and SCP

Thailand achieved the status of an upper-middle income economy in 2011 and is the second largest economy in the Association of Southeast Asian Nations (ASEAN) [IMF, 2014]. In 2015, the Thai economy recovered from a slump the previous year when political unrest disrupted the economy: Gross Domestic Product (GDP) grew by 2.9% in the first half of 2015 [ADB, 2015].

Sustainability in Thailand is characterised by the paradox between (i) the national drive to industrialise the economy and (ii) the Thai emphasis on localism, rooted in resistance to globalisation by self-sufficient rural communities. From 1969, King Bhumibol Adulyadej Rama IX of Thailand, the world's longest serving head of state, has spent decades nurturing a philosophy of life in balance with nature, building on traditional Thai values of self-reliance, perseverance, and wise living. The philosophy, promoted as "Sufficiency Economy" has been applied at household levels, in rural areas, as well as being influential at the national level as a guiding principle, particularly since the 1997 global stock market crash and subsequent financial crisis.

Its key principle is moderation, in line with the Buddhist "Middle Way": living within one's means, neither lacking nor excess, and hence being equipped with risk mitigation capacity and increasing resilience, or "self-immunity" as the King's Chaipattana Foundation puts it [Chaipattana Foundation, 2015]. In the early 1990s, the sufficiency economy philosophy led to the New Theory, which His Majesty introduced to be implemented at the royally-initiated Wat Mongkol Chaipattana Area Development Project, to serve as a model of land and water management for farmers based on integrated agriculture and modern agricultural theory [Leaders Magazine, 2006].

Within this approach, farmers are advised to follow three steps. Firstly optimal farmland division is a ratio of 30:30:30:10, being a pond to store rainwater to irrigate the land during the dry season; land for rice cultivation in the rainy season; farmland used to grow fruit and perennial trees, vegetables, field crops and herbs for daily consumption; and finally areas for facilities and infrastructure, such as accommodation, animal husbandry, roads, and other structures. Secondly, grouping farmers for joint initiatives related to production, marketing, welfare (health services, financial services), and societal values. Finally, contacting banks and private funders to develop the farms. The emergency water reservoir, established for times of draught, simultaneously serves as a pond for fish farming. Rice fields, after the gathering season, are used for planting vegetables such as sweetcorn, bitter gourd and green beans. The selection of crops is made on the basis of suitability to the environment and market demand [Tourism Thailand, 2015].

The philosophy of sufficiency economy is very much in line with what was coined "sustainable consumption and production" (SCP) by the Oslo Symposium in 1994. Sufficiency is defined by meeting the needs of wellbeing, ranging within a scope defined by a maximum level of "within the carrying capacity of the planet" and a minimum level of "consuming enough to live well." SCP is a means to sustainable and fair development. It strives at achieving "better and more with less." This can include "consuming more" to meet one's minimum needs (e.g., nutrition, electricity).

SCP aims at decoupling economic growth from its potentially negative effects on the environment and society. The concept acknowledges that everyone in his/her diverse roles in society — e.g., citizen, government, industry — is both a consumer of resources and a producer of goods and/or services, and that sustainable consumption patterns can stimulate green production behaviour, and vice versa. Striving at decreasing the overall negative impact of economic growth, SCP accounts for mitigating potential rebound effects by looking at the optimisation of footprints of the entire product life cycle, i.e., from cradle to cradle (reduce, reuse, recycle) or cradle to grave (see Chapter 2).

A consumerist lifestyle has been adopted by the growing urban elite and upper middle classes [Ünaldi, 2014], and stands in contrast to the sufficiency economy principle of moderation promoted in rural areas. The richest 20% of Thai society make almost 60% of the income and the poorest 20% garnered only 4% (the Gini coefficient which measures inequality, has decreased but remains consistently high; last time estimated in 2010 at 39.37) [Yuthamanop, 2011]. In 2009, compared against Indonesia, Laos, Malaysia, the Philippines, and Vietnam, these figures show the severest gap between rich and poor. Poverty in Thailand is primarily a rural phenomenon, with (in 2013) over 80% of the country's 7.3 million poor living in rural areas. Some regions, especially the North and Northeast, and some ethnic groups, lag behind others, and the benefits of economic success have not been shared equally, especially between Bangkok, Thailand's largest urban area, and the rest of the country [World Bank, 2015]. A differentiated approach to SCP by geographical area is thus expected to have an impact in Thailand.

12.2 Designated Special Economic Zones for Sustainable Tourism

The introduction of individual company-level resource efficiency measures and low carbon development at different stages of product life cycle over the last two decades has advanced sustainable tourism in Thailand. This started in the mid-1990s with the cleaner production movement [UNEP, 2015]. Below, three examples of SCP instruments in Thailand are identified, together with their potential to shape SCP both domestically and globally.

12.2.1 *Tourism and sustainability potentials in Thailand*

Thailand is a veteran among Asian economies when it comes to benefitting from visits of international guests. Starting in the early 1960s, boosted by the presence of US military who arrived for rest and recuperation (R&R) during the Vietnam War [Ouyyanont, 2001], Thailand was one of the first players in Asia to capitalise on the then-new trend of tourism [UNESCO, 2015]. From 1979, tourism was the main contributor to the Thai economy, surpassing exports, textiles, and agricultural goods [Wirudchawong, 2011]. From the 6th National Economic and Social Development Plan (NESDP 1987–1991) onwards, Thailand has given particular attention to the development of tourism, resulting in an additional boost to the sector. Each local administration currently allocates budget for tourism promotion and development, recognising its pivotal role in regional economic development. Arrival figures show a significant rise from 2000 onwards, with a peak of 26.74 million visitors entering Thailand in 2013. This reflects an increase of almost 170% in the last decade, despite several incidents that could have caused a setback for the sector (see Figure 12.1).

The long-term prospects of Thailand's tourism sector look promising, with an estimated annual increase of 7.3% [WTTC, 2014]. The contribution of the tourism industry to GDP is estimated at 9% (THB 1 trillion or about USD 6.8 billion in 2013), and when including the indirect effects of tourism, it accounted for 20.2% of Thailand's GDP (THB 2.4 trillion or about USD 16.5 billion in 2013) [WTTC, 2014]. Worldwide, tourism is considered one of the most resource-intensive industries, so the hidden cost behind these rising numbers is environmental damage, in particular in countries like Thailand where tourism is one of the major industries.

On the other side, the Thai tourism sector has great potential to help reduce GHG emissions and environmental footprints, particularly in hotels and transport. For example, water usage per guest night in hotels in Thailand (800 litres) is currently more than double that of developed

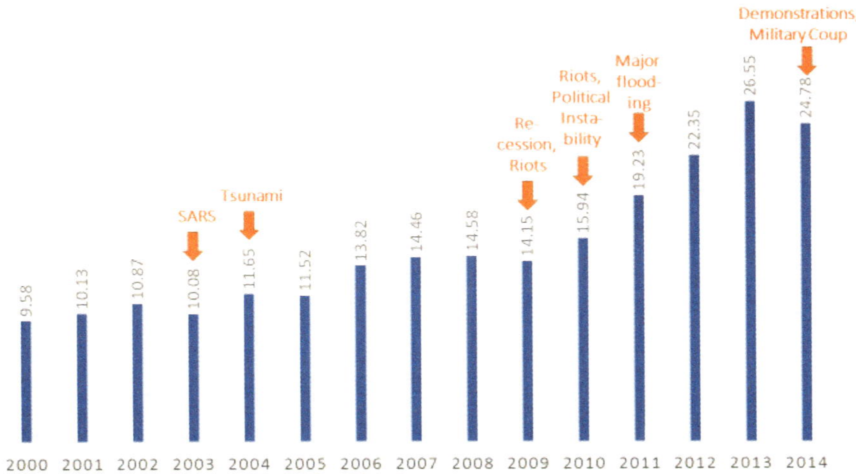

Figure 12.1: International visitors 2000–2014 [in million]

Source: Data from Department of Tourism [2014].

countries (e.g., Australia 350 litres) and eight times the amount used by local Thai people [LightBlue Environmental Consulting, 2015]. The pattern looks more or less the same with respect to energy usage and waste generation, due to the extra comforts expected by guests.

One of the models to be highlighted in Thailand's sustainability landscape is the creation of the Designated Areas for Sustainable Tourism Administration (DASTA) in 2003. DASTA is mandated to establish guidelines for sustainable tourism development and complements Thailand's well-established Tourism Authority Thailand (TAT, established in 1959) — with its 21 international representations — as well as the Ministry of Tourism and Sports (MOTS, established in 2002) and its 73 provincial (Changwat) offices of Tourism and Sports. The Decentralisation Plan and Process Act 1999, responding to the Thai Constitution promulgated in 1997, has expanded the obligations of local government to provide public services, among others in the area of tourism. Furthermore, the Thai institutional landscape includes private sector organisations, such as the Tourism Council of Thailand (2001), the Thailand Community-based Tourism Institute (2006), and several banks and financial institutions which support SMEs in the tourism sector with special interest rates [Wirudchawong, 2011].

As in other parts of the world, increased awareness of the negative impact of tourism in Thailand motivated the search for alternative models of tourism with benefits for both the environment and more equal income distribution. With DASTA's creation, the Thai Government acknowledged the importance of sustainable tourism and its potential to increase and distribute income to local communities (see Chapter 14 on sustainable tourism). The DASTA model designates a special economic zone and creates a specific ad-hoc agency with full authority to act on behalf of local authorities. The model follows a holistic and participative approach, involving local communities and stakeholders, with activities ranging from town and spatial planning, to infrastructure provision (e.g., telecommunications) [Wirudchawong, 2011]. DASTA coordinates with government agencies nationwide, with civil society, businesses, and network partners. It aims at striking a balance between the economic, social, and environmental impact of tourism development, while retaining the natural beauty of the places, as well as their local culture and traditions.

Following a pre-set list of criteria covering destination value, potential for destination development and administrative aspects, regions can apply for registration as designated areas for sustainable tourism. To be selected, the applicant area needs to score a minimum of 75% of the available scores. Between 2004 and 2012, six regions were chosen; two aimed at low-carbon development: the Elephant Island "Koh Chang" (2004) and Pattaya (2009) [Sangsnit, 2013]. Eco-friendly tourism has been extended to other designated areas, such as the development of a DASTA Low Carbon Route in the Designated Area of Loei, and the Green Historical Town development in the Designated Areas of Sukhothai — Si Satchanalai — Kamphaeng Phet Historical Parks [Muqbil, 2013]. Participation in DASTA has contributed to increased income, with gains from tourism-related businesses such as food and souvenirs, e.g., on Chang Islands and Vicinity in three participating communities: Salak Khok (+20% in less than 1 year), Nam Chiao (+130%), Laem Klat (+63.5%) [Sangsnit, 2013].

Koh Chang island cluster in Trat province was promoted as the first climate-friendly tourism destination in ASEAN when the ASEAN

Economic Community (AEC) took effect in December 2015 [Chinmaneevong, 2014]. The project is one of six under the German-sponsored International Climate Initiative in Thailand. The destination has evolved using a holistic approach including community-based solid waste management, training in the tourism sector about climate change, energy and resource efficiency, and organic production. In 2014, 12 tourism-based communities in six special designated areas helped reduce tourism-cased carbon-dioxide emissions. DASTA further emphasises creative tourism and low carbon development as their two key projects for tourism development plans from 2015 [National News Bureau in Thailand, 2015].

The next generation of Thai society will focus less on attracting further tourists and more on sustainability and preservation of environment, culture and heritage. The National Tourism Development Plan 2012–2016 acknowledges, "*tourism development must meet the needs of present tourists and host regions while protecting and enhancing opportunities for the future.*" In line with the King's vision of sufficiency economy, Thailand's vision is to become a quality tourism destination competitive across all provinces, enabling the country to generate more income and distribute wealth on a sustainable basis. The strategy of sustainable tourism is based on four pillars, namely co-creation (community benefit and participation), working together with all partners, creative tourism ("*Thainess*" — local wisdom, way of life, art, culture, and history) and low carbon tourism [Sangsnit, 2013].

Within the AEC, Thailand seeks to maintain its leading position, yet is now competing against Laos, Cambodia, and Vietnam, since they opened up to international tourism in the 1980s and 1990s. Destinations like Angkor Wat, Luang Prabang, and Halong Bay now contest Thailand's former monopoly on tourism in the Indochina region. The AEC will intensify competition in the tourism sector. Thailand needs to understand how to maintain and increase revenue from tourism without overstretching its resources, e.g., by higher spending per tourist per day. The country therefore has been targeting niche markets such as golf holidays, or holidays combined with medical treatment, and international meetings and exhibitions (MICE). The Thailand Convention & Exhibition Bureau TCEB is taking a determined stance on making Thailand the first sustainability hub for MICE in Asia [Rungfapaisarn, 2012]. Thailand also plans on becoming the hub for Buddhist tourism in the region. Eco-friendly and green tourism have become more popular in recent years, and inclusiveness will be supported with community-based tourism (CBT), which counts as a promising approach to increasing local revenue and at the same time improving hygiene, new skills and know-how, and access to finance [Wirudchawong, 2011]. The concept of CBT directly supports community-level social, cultural and environmental initiatives. It is managed and owned by the community, for the community, with the purpose of enabling visitors to increase their awareness and learn about local ways of life. In the event of partnerships with the private sector, community members retain decision-making authority and are able to guide the direction of tourism development in their village [CBT-I, 2012]. Instruments, such as CBT or DASTA, provide the chance for local communities to sharpen their awareness on how important sustainable consumption is for sustained local welfare and prosperity. With this knowledge, it is more likely that all stakeholders collaborate in transmitting the same values when receiving domestic and international visitors.

Many hotels of all sizes in Thailand's major tourism destinations have steered their operations toward green policies, including reducing the use of energy, water and chemicals, and waste reduction programmes. Most efficiency programmes, however, are yet to show the desired results of decoupling growth from total resource depletion. The industry still mainly concentrates on implementing technology-based solutions to reduce energy consumption, water usage, etc. Often the sustainable consumption side and guest engagement are omitted, which results in those policies not yet being sufficiently adopted (including the provision of staff training, incentives for guest engagement, and life cycle aspects such as transport, upcycling, etc.) [LightBlue Environmental Consulting, 2015]. Despite the higher importance of "green" and "eco-friendliness" among certain groups of travellers [Chinmaneevong, 2014], e.g., Europeans, who account for approximately 25% of international visitors [Barnett, 2009], "green" remains widely associated with "less comfort" and "sacrifice." Unless this image can be transformed and 'marketed' as a desirable lifestyle, particularly among the growing middle-income bracket of upcoming Asian economies, including Thailand itself [Thai Department of Tourism, 2014], a mainstream paradigm change will be hard to achieve.

A reduction in impacts from the transport and aviation sector also remains a challenge. Thailand is a hub for travel across Southeast Asia. Globally, the aviation sector alone contributed 2% of total man-made CO_2 emissions in 2013 [ATAG, 2015]. When it comes to transport, most tourists choose speed and price over environment-friendliness. Only a few carriers consider carbon-offsetting or other environmental impact programmes. The Aviation GHG Emissions Reduction Working Group, headed by the Thai Department of Civil Aviation (DCA), acknowledged the importance of the issue, and was trained in 2013 in low emission development strategies and monitoring, reporting and verification approaches (MRV) for the new low carbon regime under the United Nations Framework Convention on Climate Change (UNFCCC) [Verifavia, 2015]. While offsetting does not avoid climate change from happening, it can reduce the overall impact and help raise awareness of the issue. As the most effective way to combat climate change is to reduce emissions, hope remains to capitalise on future fleet fuel efficiency, as forecast by the air transport cluster (25% improvement by 2020) [Chinmaneevong, 2014], and to commercialise renewable energy-based aircraft, such as the current solar-driven airplane "Solar Impulse" [Solar Impulse, 2015].

12.3 Green Industry Mark (GIM) in Combination with a Market for Sustainable Goods and Services

Thailand's GIM certification scheme, initiated by the Ministry of Industry (MOI), is a key tool to drive SCP into practice. Following the Johannesburg Declaration in 2002 and the Manila Declaration in 2009, the Green Industry Project was initiated by the MOI in May 2011, aimed at promoting continuous improvements and sustainable development through green industry operations. The GIM project activities range from creating awareness of reducing environmental impacts, implementation, certifying the environment management system, to network extension of practices throughout the supply chains. The project guideline practices include minimisation of environmental impact, prevention of pollution, resource efficiency, reduction of climate change, and protection and restoration of the ecosystem.

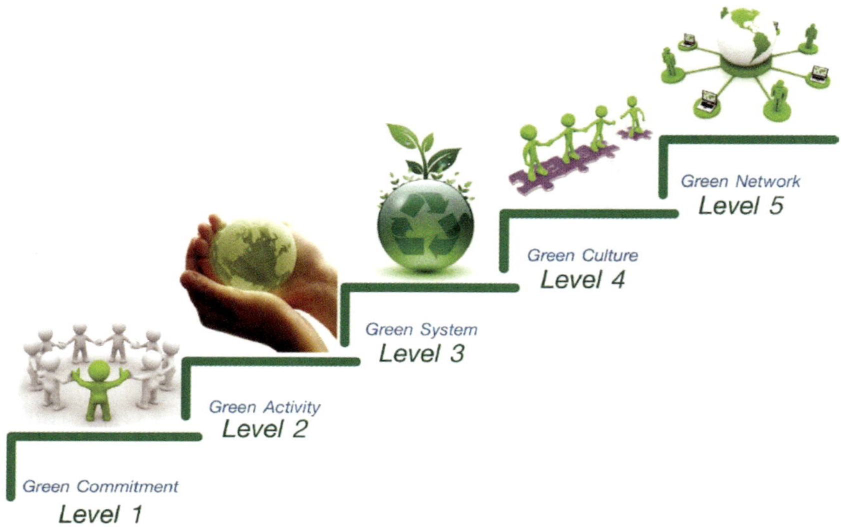

Figure 12.2: Five levels of the GIM

Source: SWITCH-Asia Policy Support Component Thailand (PSCT), [2014].

The Green Industry Award honours sustainability and environmentally friendly production on five levels (see Figure 12.2).

The core elements of green industry are the implementation of green productivity, environmental management systems and corporate social responsibility (CSR) throughout the supply chain, as well as community stakeholders. The GIM is an advanced scheme, which integrates many of the green industry instruments. Four areas link into the GIM, and which result in a reduction of the carbon footprint:

1. Reducing environmental impact and pollution.
2. Improving resource utilisation.
3. Mitigating climate change.
4. Protecting and restoring the natural environment.

The scheme comprises five levels: "Green Commitment" (GIM-1), "Green Activity" (GIM-2), "Green System" (GIM-3), "Green Culture" (GIM-4), and "Green Network" (GIM-5). For GIM-1, GIM-2, and GIM-3

(ISO 14001), only a document submission is required for approval, while for GIM-4 and GIM-5 additional on-site visits by specially trained government auditors are required. A company who wants to achieve the highest level (GIM-5) has to work together with the entire supply chain to get its business partners to level GIM-2 or GIM-3, as well as to gain community acceptance of the company's environmental management performance. Participating manufacturers who can achieve all the steps will be awarded the GIM, which makes them eligible for additional benefits. Such incentives include waivers of membership fees (to the MOI), tax reduction for energy-efficient equipment, being listed in a green directory, and specific green loans.

The green industry certification scheme targets especially those factories whose activities are likely to cause the highest pollution (i.e., large-scale enterprises, machines of more than 50 horsepower, more than 50 staff), which amounts to some 70,000 factories, 50% of the total in Thailand [SWITCH-Asia PSCT, 2014]. The MOI aims at spreading the application of the green industry concept throughout the country, leading to sustainable communities, cities and industries.

In December 2014, after only three years of implementation, there were 17,668 companies certified by the GIM scheme, which represents a share of 25% of the target population [SWITCH-Asia PSCT, 2014]:

At the time of writing, only five companies have reached GIM-5, the level at which companies act as multipliers of the green industry concept (see Table 12.1). One among them is the Siam Cement Group, which has at the same time shown leadership in reacting to new market opportunities

Table 12.1: Share of companies by GIM level

Level	Number of Certified Companies	%
GIM-1	11,532	65.27
GIM-2	3,429	19.40
GIM-3	2,651	15.01
GIM-4	51	0.29
GIM-5	5	0.03

Source: [SWITCH-Asia PSCT, 2014].

offered by Thai Green Public Procurement (GPP): the group pioneered change in one business segment by developing a green product line (recycled paper) so it could be procured by Thai public agencies. By creating a market, the sustainable procurement policy has created an exemplary pull factor for making a sustainable version of an existing product. The inclusion of GIM-certified companies in the approved list of suppliers in the GPP national policy will give competitive advantage to green producers.

The ten pilot projects under the Department of Industrial Works (DIW) and the Green Industry Promotion Office (GIPO), supported by the SWITCH-Asia Programme (in sectors like food, building materials, and automotive parts), have shown that GIM-5 in some sectors can be difficult to obtain even though the applying company tries to educate suppliers. For example, the highly competitive automotive industry is characterised by a large number of service providers involved in the multi-level supply chain, which offers a large potential to impact a great variety of different supply industries. However, suppliers often change from year to year [SWITCH-Asia Automotive SSCM, 2015]. Unless the companies applying for green industry certifications have implemented a green procurement programme to pre-select their "green" suppliers (such as ISO 14001-certified, green label awarded, energy award achieved, total quality assessment awarded, etc.), their effort in meeting the GIM criteria will be low.

The GIM model allows an easy start to participate in greening factories through the relatively simple and self-declaratory steps in stages 1–3. For stages 4 and 5, however, it is mainly the frontrunner companies that have the capacity to implement. Government auditors are also still too few to respond efficiently to the number of applications. Step 5 in particular takes into account the entire supply chain, which supports the spreading of the GIM scheme among the business community. Overall, the measure still focuses on cleaner production; a more streamlined integration of entire life cycle considerations, e.g., design for sustainability, clean mobility, cradle-to-cradle approaches, and respective education of the consumer (industry, government, civil society), is still underway.

The scheme has been vital to create awareness about green growth. It is in line with the framework of the current [NESDP, 2012–2016], which

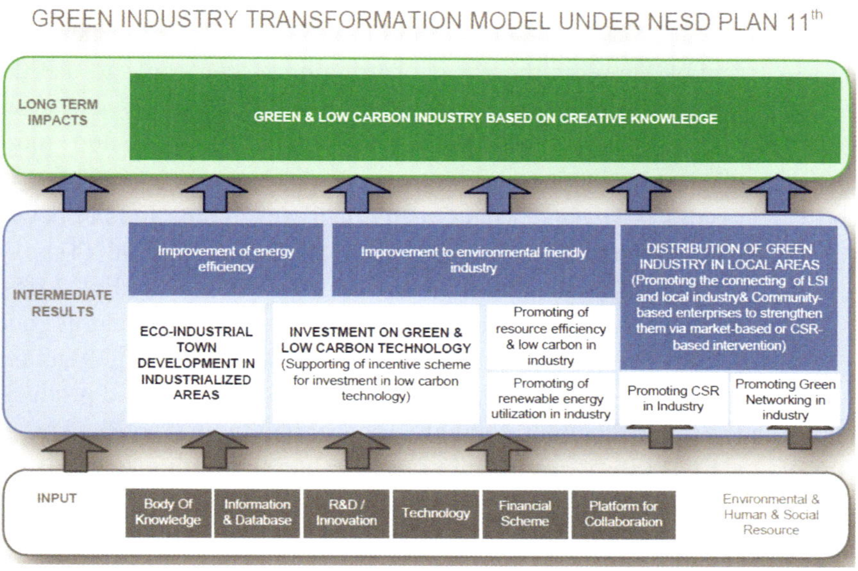

Figure 12.3: Green industry transformation model under the 11th NESDP
Source: [SWITCH-Asia PSCT, 2014].

seeks to transform Thailand into a "green society" (see Figure 12.3). The plan seeks to develop eco-industrial towns and restore the environment in major industrial regions by creating awareness of the need for co-existence between industries and communities.

12.4 Eco-Card and Sustainable Food Industry

Another business model that has the potential to strengthen Thailand's path towards a "Sustainable Society" is the creation of the "Eco-Card." The model brings together a great variety of partners, e.g., retailers like Tesco/Lotus, Big C, Tops, IKEA, Home Pro, 7 Eleven, Central, The Mall, and the Bangkok Mass Transit System BTS, as well as eco-label organisations. The Eco-Card provides points to consumers for the purchase of "eco-products." Those can be redeemed into cash coupons, discounts, free tickets for public transport, etc. This means that the scheme goes beyond classic awareness raising and combines a financial incentive with responsible purchasing. At the same time, offering free tickets for public transport in Bangkok supports the effort of bringing more people to use the capital's low-carbon mobility options. Sustainable consumers and users drive the availability of sustainable goods and services, and more resource-efficient production processes. All products with any kind of eco-label (Types 1–3), e.g., "Thai Green Label" (excluding food & beverages, Type 1), "Chemical-free" (Type 2) and "Carbon Footprint" (Type 3) are classified as "eco-products" in the eco-card scheme [VGREEN, 2015].

Already in 2013, seven large retail chains (Siam Makro, Central Food Retail, CP All, Tesco Lotus, and Big C, 7-Eleven, and Thai Retailers Association) signed an agreement to support and distribute food products with ThaiGAP certifications showing good agricultural practice. This is one of the food safety certifications applicable at farming level [BOT, 2013b], building on earlier initiatives emphasising locally grown food, such the "From Farm to Table" or "From Farm to Forks" initiatives from 2004. When it comes to labelling and carbon footprint mapping, the Thai food industry is also a frontrunner, and hence the eco-card can be an effective tool to educate grocery shoppers. The food industry has further shown pioneering leadership in the Thai Life Cycle Inventory (LCI) database [Mungkung, 2015], carbon and eco-footprint labelling, as well as the GIM scheme [SWITCH-Asia PSCT, 2014].

Thailand's efforts in mapping and calculating footprints (see Table 12.2) have resulted in a relatively good overview of basic products as well as the potential to reduce negative environmental impacts. The carbon footprint labelling takes account of the entire life cycle of the product, including its raw materials, acquisition, manufacture, use, waste management, and final disposal, including related transport at all stages. It also accounts for the impact of food waste, which often is a neglected aspect, but which in Thailand comprises 64% of consumer waste per year (i.e., 17 million tonnes in 2013) [Pattaya Mail, 2014]. Worldwide, it creates an estimated 3.3 billion tonnes of CO_2 equivalent (CO_2e) without accounting for GHG emissions from land use change, according to a recent FAO report (2013) [FAO, 2013].

Thailand's food industry is known as the "*kitchen of the world*" [BOI, 2014]. Since its first National Plan (1961–1966), the Government of

Table 12.2: Four Carbon footprint labels and contribution of the food sector

Label	Definition	Food Sector Contribution
Carbon Footprint (CFP and CFO)	Carbon score of life cycle GHG emissions	Launched in 2009, the food industry helped in drawing up 5 out of 23 national product category rules (PCRs) (22%), namely jasmine rice, fruits and vegetables, chicken meat, livestock products, and 83 of 138 company PCRs (60%). When the Carbon Footprint for Products (CFP) was piloted with 43 products, more than half of them came from the food industry. The Carbon Footprint for Organisations (CFO) was initiated in 2010. Since then, the number of piloting companies increased eightfold from 10 to 79, out of which 18 are in the food sector (23%).
Carbon Offset	Partial carbon offset of life cycle GHG emissions	Thailand Carbon Offsetting Programme (TCOP), with carbon offset and carbon neutral labels, was introduced by TGO in 2013. The first carbon neutral product was again reported to be in the food sector. In total, 3,687 tonnes CO_2e GHG emissions have been offset.
Carbon Neutral	Full carbon offset of life cycle GHG emissions	
Carbon Footprint Reduction	Reduced carbon footprint value by 2% or equal/below the benchmarking value	Since 2014, 10 pilot companies have been involved as demonstration Carbon Footprint Reduction (CFR) projects, which is another advancement of the scheme that started with 25 certified products.

Source: Mungkung [2015].

Thailand has been supportive of developing the food industry. In the current vision 2026 and the 11th NESD Plan, the food sector was identified as one of the most significant. The priority of developing the food industry has been translated into national trade, financial, agricultural, industrial, health, and environmental policies. Supporting policies and significant government and private sector investments in technology, food safety, R&D, and the strengthening of SMEs, have provided effective complementarities to the country's other comparative advantages, such as its geographic centrality and its abundant resources (including GMO-free raw materials). Food is available in a wide variety and at low prices in Thailand. More than 80% of the raw materials used in the food industry are sourced from the domestic market. This gives the industry a comparative advantage and a high level of competitiveness. As a result, Thailand has developed into a strategic hub for food production of both fresh and particularly of processed food [Food Industry in Thailand, 2012; Vanit-Anunchai and Schmidt, 2006; Fernquest, 2011].

The food industry contributes approximately 28% to the Thai GDP and grows at an average of 13% per year. Its value added makes up 19% of the total amount of value added in the industrial sector. The sector provides a market for domestic agricultural products and employment for over 10 million people in over 10,000 food processing companies. In 2014, Japan was Thailand's biggest market for food products, taking 14% of the total the export values, followed by the US at 11.1%, China at 7.6%, and Indonesia 3.8% [BOI, 2014]. With the AEC, the market of Thai food is expanding to around 600 million consumers over Southeast Asia.

Being one of the world's largest producers of food products, such as rice, canned tuna, frozen seafood, chicken, and canned pineapple, Thailand's produce could play an enormous role in minimising resource use in the sector and in influencing sustainable food purchasing and consumption patterns in ASEAN and globally. In the global value chain, the food industry's production patterns, trade flows and worldwide attempts to minimise resource consumption are not yet reflected. Given Thailand's role as a global kitchen, resource-wise the global community could benefit from improving Thailand's water productivity. The country particularly benchmarks poorly in its agricultural production and food processing. In fact, with 51.79 billion m^3 annual quantity of water withdrawn for irrigation purposes and livestock feed, Thailand's agricultural sector takes up 70% of the nation's total water supply. The issue is exacerbated by farmers who have expanded their activities outside irrigated zones. Many do not conserve water and have failed to plan crop production efficiently. The increasing demand for food, feed, and biofuels promises to increase

Table 12.3: Benchmark of virtual water footprints

	World Average (m^3/tonne)	**Thai Average (m^3/tonne)**
Chicken	4,325	5,443
Rice Flour	2,628	3,592
Raw Sugar	1,666	2,049
Cassava	563	467

Source: Yuwanan *et al.* [2011].

pressure on water competition, especially in Thailand with its large agricultural base [Gheewala *et al.*, 2014]. In 2011, Thailand was identified as being a virtual water exporter, which means that the overall amount of exported products have been using more water in Thailand than the imported products sent into Thailand [Mekonnen and Hoekstra, 2011]. As seen in the following overview (Table 12.3) basic food products, only cassava can be processed and exported using less water units in Thailand than the global average.

In 2015, Thailand was certain to reclaim its position as the world's largest rice exporter, with a volume reaching 10.7 million tonnes, valued at USD 5.2 billion (THB 170 billion) [Pratruangkrai, 2014].

With each tonne of rice exported from Thailand to Indonesia, the world loses more than 2,300 m^3 of water [Chapagain and Hoekstra, 2011]. With an annual trade of approximately 416,000 tonnes, this loss translates to almost 1 billion m^3 (1 trillion litres) which compares to 400,000 Olympic size swimming pools and 1% of Thailand's total water footprint every year, for this trade flow of rice alone.

Being positioned at the very interface between consumers and producers, retailers through their procurement and promotion policies become the new powerhouses in fostering eco-friendly purchasing decisions and the availability of sustainable products in the food chain. At the domestic level in Thailand, the eco-card scheme has taken into account this leverage. The effectiveness of labelled products and organisations in decoupling their economic activities from negative environmental impact depends on quality assurance in the food chain. Their success in reaching consumers, both in terms of acceptance and accessibility, will determine the actual leverage of the eco-label. While the importance of supermarkets among Thailand's grocery sales channels is growing in urban areas, and a next trend might be selling food online, a non-neglectable part of Thailand's food trade still happens in wet markets [Ruddick, 2013]. It remains to be seen how the concept and educational purpose of the eco-card will be rolled out to the majority of consumers in order to reach a critical mass in Thailand. Recently undertaken random tests of fresh fruit and vegetables among supermarkets and wet markets in Thailand resulted in a higher probability that products in supermarkets were the ones not meeting the promised food safety standards, which made their credibility questionable [Frederickson, 2014]. In this case, the eco-card would miss its target and suffer from poor credibility, even before its official introduction. Pioneering these labels, the food and retail industry has displayed its commitment to contribute to healthier and more sustainable food value chains. Given the food industry's size of about 10,000 companies, the current number of frontrunners represents a tiny fraction of the sector. The achievements of environmental impact reduction are yet to be implemented at the larger scale.

12.5 The European Union as Partner on SCP in Thailand

SCP is about the promotion of thoughtful and environment friendly choices and behaviour at both the production and the consumption side. However, behavioural change can take generations. To achieve most impact, strategies for change need a mix of short, medium, and long-term instruments ranging from financial incentives to comprehensive educational efforts. Initiatives for change can originate from business, civil society and government. Over the last decades, the Thai government, through its policies, has shown high awareness of the significance of sustainable development. Various international partners have accompanied Thailand in this task with technical and financial assistance dedicated at promoting SCP in the country. Cooperation between the European Union and Thailand started in the 1970s with assisting the Royal Thai Government's crop diversification efforts and improvement of farmers' revenue. The EU changed its role from a "donor of development assistance" to a "facilitator of knowledge sharing" and a "partner for policy dialogue" on key development issues, which are both aligned with Thai development priorities and which serve mutual interest [EUD Thailand, 2015].

Since the start, four regional grants projects of the EU-funded SWITCH-Asia Programme have included Thailand and one grant focused on the Thai automotive industry (see Table 12.4).

Furthermore, Thailand was selected among the first batch of four (Thailand, Indonesia, Malaysia, Philippines) — now five (extending to Sri Lanka) — Asian countries which received a targeted policy support through a national technical assistance component under the SWITCH-Asia Programme, namely the Policy Support Component (PSC) project. The objective was "*To support the Thai government in selecting, adapting and implementing suitable economic and regulatory policy instruments to promote SCP, hereby enhancing the long-term sustainability of Thai consumption and production patterns*", i.e., to develop less polluting and more resource-efficient products, processes and services, and to promote sustainable consumption patterns and behaviour. The SWITCH-Asia PSC Thailand project ran from October 2011 until January 2015.

In line with the Thai 11th NESDP for 2012–2016, the PSC Thailand project encouraged responsible stakeholders to address sustainable development in four components and five work areas (SCP Monitoring, SCP Policy Assessment, Green Procurement, Green Industry, and SCP Awareness) Please consult Table 12.5 for the state of play. The specific objectives were:

- Component 1: To strengthen the institutional framework for SCP in Thailand and develop a national SCP monitoring system.
- Component 2: To update the Green Procurement Policy and develop a green procurement action plan as well as build capacity for implementing the Green Procurement Policy and action plan of target groups.
- Component 3: To conduct a number of pilot projects in order to demonstrate sustainable production principles and approaches in selected sector(s).
- Component 4: To introduce the issues and concepts of SCP, and apply awareness campaigns and driving forces for behavioural change of target group(s).

Table 12.4: Overview of SCP projects by EU-funded SWITCH-Asia Programme in Thailand

Project Title	Period	Main Implementing Organisation	Places of Implementation	SCP Practices	Objectives
Greening Supply Chains in the Thai Auto and Automotive Parts Industries (Automotive SSCM)	02/2012–10/2015	Deutsche Gesellschaft für Internationale Zusammenarbeit (GIZ); Thailand	Thailand	Sustainable supply chain, resource efficiency	To improve sustainable production of SMEs in the Thai auto and automotive parts supply chains.
Establishment of the ASEAN Energy Manager Accreditation Scheme (AEMAS)	02/2010–01/2014	ASEAN Centre for Energy (ACE), Indonesia; Department of Alternative Energy Development and Efficiency (DEDE), Thailand (associate status)	SWITCH-Asia Regional Project including Thailand	Energy efficiency, accreditation	To reduce energy consumption from the manufacturing industrial sector in ASEAN and to cut greenhouse gas emissions in ASEAN member countries.
Lead Paint Elimination	12/2011–06/2015	International POPs Elimination Network (IPEN), Sweden; Ecological Alert and Recovery Thailand (EARTH)	SWITCH-Asia Regional Project including Thailand	Eco-labelling	To reduce childhood lead poisoning in the eight participating countries by decreasing production and use of lead paint with a trend toward their elimination.

Efficient Air Conditioners	01/2013–11/2016	European Copper Institute, Belgium; Electrical and Electronics Institute (EEI), Thailand; International Copper Association Southeast Asia (ICASEA), Thailand	SWITCH-Asia Regional Project including Thailand	Energy efficiency	To increase the market share of more highly efficient ACs in ASEAN through harmonisation of test methods and energy efficiency (EE) standards, adoption of common Minimum Energy Performance Standards (MEPS), and changing consumer purchasing attitudes in favour of energy efficient ACs.
Zero Carbon Resorts for Sustainable Tourism	05/2014–05/2018	Center for Appropriate Technologies (GrAT), Austria; Green Leaf Foundation, Thailand; Healthy Public Policy Foundation (HPPF), Thailand	Philippines and Thailand	Resource efficiency	To contribute to sustainable development of the tourism sector and its value chain in the Philippines and Thailand with a focus on reduction of resource consumption and CO_2 emissions. It targets a critical mass of SMEs demonstrating the value of green tourism by increasing resource efficiency and using renewable resources.
Sustainable Freight & Logistics	2016–2019	GIZ, Germany	Cambodia, Laos, Myanmar, Vietnam, Thailand	Sustainable transportation, supply chain	To increase sustainable freight transport and logistics in the Mekong Region mainly through energy efficiency and safety measures in at least 500 SMEs in Cambodia, Lao PDR, Myanmar, Vietnam (CLMV), and Thailand.

Source: EU SWITCH-Asia website [2015].

Table 12.5: SCP policy advice to Thai national stakeholders

Work Area	Lead Stakeholder	Achievements
SCP Monitoring	Office of Natural Resources and Environmental Policy and Planning (ONEP)	• Importance of SCP institutional framework and monitoring system introduced • ONEP and NESDB took charge of the SCP institutional framework and monitoring system
SCP Policy Assessment	National Economic and Social Development Board (NESDB)	• Road maps for the integration of SCP principles were formulated
Green Procurement	Pollution Control Department (PCD) within Ministry of Natural Resources and Environment (MNRE)	• Starting in 2005, a first phase of GPP was formulated for the Central Administration, and now all departments in Ministries have implemented GPP (primarily (a) office materials e.g., printing paper, pens, makers, light bulbs, and (b) machinery, e.g., photocopiers) • The PCD has developed a second phase to promote GPP focusing at the sub-national level • Seeing the business opportunity, one large supplier company changed production facilities to produce 'green' printing paper (Thai Paper/Siam Cement Group) to supply to the Government. Many smaller creative companies also produce or sell green products, including Concept Tree, Green Cotton Thailand, Eco-Shop and others
Green Industry	Department of Industrial Works (DIW), within the MOI	• Together the DIW and Green Industry Promotion Office (GIPO), within the MOI, assisted 10 leading companies to become certified according to the Ministry's "GIM" • DIW and the Green Industry Promotion Office (GIPO) are in charge of further GIM implementation
SCP Awareness	Department of Environmental Quality Promotion (DEQP)	• Two surveys were conducted on SCP awareness in local communities. Two SCP awareness campaigns were carried out in Phanat Nikhom and Koh Samui in close cooperation with the respective municipal administrations • DEQP has allocated budget for scaling up the SCP awareness model

Source: SWITCH-Asia progress reports [2014].

12.6 Experiences and Impacts of the SWITCH-Asia Programme in Thailand

The SWITCH-Asia Policy Support Component for Thailand has supported cooperation between key stakeholders, a prerequisite for future beneficial planning and implementation of SCP policies and plans [SWITCH-Asia PSCT, 2015].

The PSC Thailand together with the SWITCH-Asia grant project "Automotive SSCM" resulted in the automotive industry approving the GIM certification system, a scheme initiated by the MoI to promote cleaner production processes in companies and their supply chains (for more on the scheme, see Section 12.3). The PSC Thailand supported 10 larger companies and a number of SMEs in gaining certification according to the GIM system. The PSC Thailand focused on companies within three sectors: Food Processing, Building Materials, and Automotive Parts sector. Companies were supported through training and preparation of the necessary documentation. The PSC Thailand also assisted DIW and GIPO in further development of the GIM system, including developing and testing the "opinion surveys", which are part of the criteria for Level 5 certification. Reaching Levels 4 and 5, which requires action at the company's supply chain level, has proven problematic, as it requires resources and time to fulfil the many requirements of the GIM system. By December 2014, only five larger companies, together with their supply chains, had reached Level 5, but many are part-way through the process. In the automotive sector, 46 companies have already complied with Levels 2 and 3 of the scheme [SWITCH-Asia PSCT, 2015].

Thailand is Southeast Asia's largest automotive manufacturer, and has been listed among the 10 most important car producers of the world since 2012 [The Economist, 2013]. In 2012, Thai automotive production capacity was 2.75 million vehicles and the industry employed over 500,000 people; the production capacity is expected to reach 3 million units by 2015 [Sullivan, 2015]. While Thailand has no car brand of its own, many foreign-owned companies produce or assemble cars and car parts in the country. Japan has the highest influence on Thai SMEs as European car makers tend to import parts from Europe and just assemble in Thailand [SWITCH-Asia Automotive SSCM, 2015; TSSD/DoLT, 2014]. The automotive industry is Thailand's second largest export industry after computer parts and components. It is interconnected to local supporting industries of many kinds, e.g., glass, plastic, electronics, textiles, and various assembling steps [The Economist, 2013]. All this shows the potentials of automotive sector to introduce SCP practices and green the industry.

The automotive policies of Thailand have long been more inclined towards growth than towards sustainability. In 2007, an "Eco-Car Programme" was introduced, the first of its kind in Southeast Asia. While the "eco-car" was defined as "fuel efficient" (2nd phase: max. 4.3 litres per 100 km) and "low carbon" (2nd phase: emitting less than 100 grams of CO_2 per kilometre), the policy ultimately aimed at boosting the sector through investment and production of more than 2 million new cars, translating to a minimum of 100,000 units per year per manufacturer. It was combined with a generous investment promotion scheme for "eco-car" manufacturing, granting special incentives and with tax reduced from 30% to 17% [BOI, 2013a].

After the devastating floods of 2011, which forced some manufacturers in central and lower Thailand to temporarily close plants, a "First Car Policy" was introduced by the former Prime Minister Yingluck Shinawatra to jump-start the sector (ending in December 2012). The policy promoted a tax exemption of THB 100,000 (equivalent to approx. EUR 2,500) for the first car, in combination with a cut in interest rates for private lending. It led to an exorbitant domestic demand and production of close to 2.5 million cars in 2012, five times more than the 500,000 units in 1998 [Thai Automotive Institute, 2014].

With the drop in domestic demand in 2014 (exports fell by 1.25%, domestic sales decreased by 34%), lower production (1.88 versus the targeted 2.1 million cars), the political uncertainty in Thailand under the military-led government, paired with banks' unwillingness to approve car loan applications, the question arises whether Thailand's car industry is viable [Sullivan, 2015]. Despite Thailand having long been attractive for car producers due to supply chains established over 50 years, some manufacturers could be tempted to relocate their production to other ASEAN Member States, e.g., Indonesia [The Economist, 2013; Panthong, 2012]. Currently, the bargaining power is clearly in the hands of around ten large car makers. The economy includes approximately 709 Tier 1 auto parts suppliers and 1,700 Tier 2 and 3 suppliers. More than half of the Tier 1

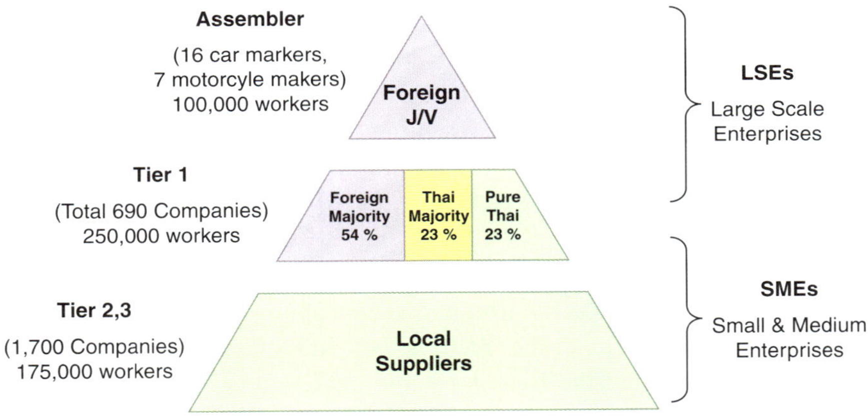

Figure 12.4: Structure of Thai automotive industry

Source: Thailand Business News [2015].

suppliers are car parts companies [Sullivan, 2015]. For an overview on the structure of the Thai automotive industry please see Figure 12.4.

The first priority for many car manufacturers in the region is to guarantee and assure supply 24 hours a day, 7 days a week. Environmental and social aspects clearly come second. While other industries, such as food and beverages, textiles and tourism operate at a high level of awareness, using international state-of-the-art measurements and labels such as carbon footprint and water footprint (see Sections 12.2–12.4), the SWITCH-Asia project "Automotive SSCM" is the first educational project of its kind in Thailand's automotive industry.

Since February 2012, the project has demonstrated through 300 SMEs that:

1. A commercially relevant production cost reduction and increased productivity can be achieved through what is called "good housekeeping."
2. At the same time as economic benefit, the improved production process in all companies resulted in lower consumption of resources such as energy, water, etc. per produced unit.

3. Turnover usually is monitored closely but monitoring savings from resource efficiency has thus far not been a usual business practice, while both parts are equally essential to increasing revenue.
4. Companies (SMEs) were also willing to make higher investments as long as the return on investment could be expected in less than a year [SWITCH-Asia Automotive SSCM, 2015].

With the "Automotive SSCM" project, by February 2014, 83 SMEs participated in Profitable Environmental Management (PREMA) assessments, 92 SMEs joined the Automotive Manufacturing Automation System (AMAS), and the Best Available Technique (BAT) was applied to 20 SMEs. The project offered a thorough consultancy programme of 3–4 days classroom training with a subsequent 5–6 months individual in-company coaching to identify measurable resources for reduction in order to achieve impact [SWITCH-Asia Automotive SSCM, 2015].

The total cost savings from all 289 resource efficiency measures implemented to date amount to over THB 134 million/year (EUR 3.6 million/year) with a total one-off investment required of only THB 22.3 million (EUR 0.6 million). The average annual cost savings achieved per implemented measure was about THB 465,000/year (EUR 12,800/year). The **return on investment** materialised on average after only four months. Many of the measures implemented could be achieved through "good housekeeping", for example, better quality checks and process control, better materials handling, etc., and did not require larger investments from the SMEs [SWITCH-Asia Automotive SSCM, 2015].

The figure below (Figure 12.5) shows the **total environmental savings**, which the SMEs were able to achieve by February 2015, including reductions in energy use, greenhouse gas emissions, water use, raw material use, and waste.

- Energy consumption of about 27,700 GJ per year for participating SMEs. These energy savings translated to about 4,500 metric tonnes of greenhouse gas savings per year.
- The resource efficiency measures have enabled the participating SMEs to reduce the use of raw materials by about 1,140 tonnes per year.

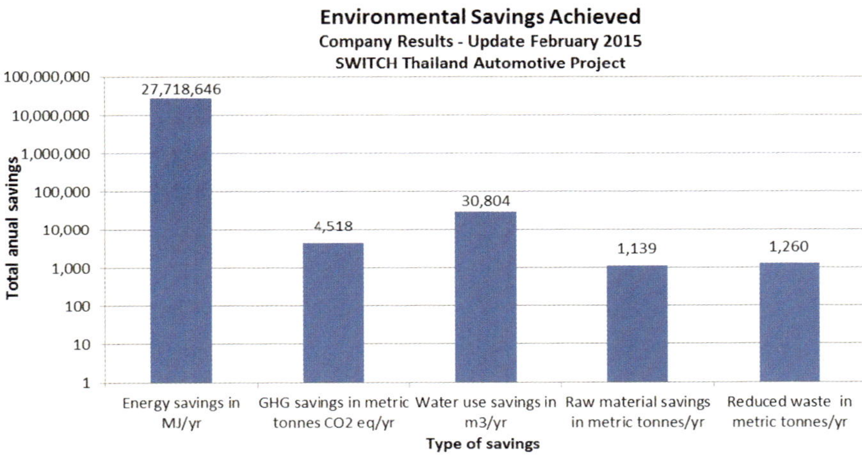

Figure 12.5: Environmental results achieved to date

Source: SWITCH-Asia progress report [2015].

- The SMEs have reduced their waste by about 1,260 tonnes per year [SWITCH-Asia Automotive SSCM, 2015].

In addition to economic and environmental benefits, the PREMA and AMAS assessments undertaken delivered social benefits to the participating SMEs, such as:

- Improved occupational safety and work conditions for SMEs' workers, e.g., less exposure to dust, safer chemical handling, less noise, reduced risk to metal scrap related injuries, etc.
- Easier and less stressful working environment for the company staff, e.g., more efficient material handling, clearer operational manuals, reduced rework, etc.

The clear driver for SMEs to participate in the sustainability measures was the reduced production cost. All resource efficiency measures were economically and technically viable. The assessments delivered very favourable financial results for the participating SMEs [SWITCH-Asia Automotive SSCM, 2015].

Currently, there is no systematic data available of the overall environmental or carbon footprint of the industry. Biking, the most environment-friendly mobility, has become more and more popular. Pun Pun Bike rental stations make biking possible for non-bike owners in Bangkok. Inner-city cycling, however, is still rarely observed due to heavy traffic congestion and health concerns. The lack of alternative modern, safe and comfortable public transport only reinforces the supremacy of the car and motorcycle. The taxis, "tuk-tuks" and "moto-taxis" have been complemented with some car sharing services in recent years (e.g., Uber; Grab-a-Taxi, Easy Taxi) to ensure a safer transport option. Those are limited to the capital city [G2D, 2014]. Car-pooling, which might convince some consumers to use the service when needed rather than investing in car (hence reducing the number of cars on the roads and resulting in less automotive waste) are rare or purely based on a private individual's initiative. The current Thai railway system is safe, affordable, and environmentally friendly but does not address all transport needs, and is usually slow [Thai Railways Website, 2015].

The government coordinated with the private sector to formulate the Master Plan for Automotive Industry (2012–2016). They seek to develop Thailand as a global green automotive production base and to increase research and development for automotive technology. The next plan was due to be launched in early 2016 (Masterplan 2016–2020). While the car specifications are more and more eco-friendly, the production capacity shall be increased to 3 million cars by 2017 according to the plan, a target which might already be reached in 2015 [MPAI, 2012–2016; Sullivan, 2015]. It remains to be seen if, in addition to cleaner production and green(er) products, the next Masterplan will also include sustainable business models that address sustainable consumption, the potential rebound effect, and alternative clean(er) mobility concepts. The latter concept is where the automotive industry collaborates with time-efficient and eco-friendly public transport, such as inner-city BTS/MRT lines or the upcoming Japanese high-speed trains between Bangkok and the northern city of Chiang Mai, and between the capital and the Cambodian border, as well as the separate Chinese scheme to build a medium-speed network [Rogers, 2015].

12.7 Conclusion and Recommendations

Thailand has been among the frontrunners of SCP practice in Asia, both in terms of policy instruments as well as application by consumers, understood as businesses, government, and civil society. Most of the initiatives introduced concentrate on sourcing and production stages. Holistic life cycle approaches with an emphasis on actual reduction of resources by design, as well as consumer contribution to resource reduction — which eventually would lead to a paradigm shift at sector-specific or cross-sectoral levels — have so far been underexplored and/or under-reported.

Selected SCP instruments in Thailand, which include incentivising sustainable consumption, have been discussed here, i.e., DASTA, the GIM, the Eco-Card and LCI, in combination with the respective markets and users. The green industry award is a step forward for green manufacturing in Thailand and can serve as a role model in the Asian region. The GIM scheme has been instrumental in providing easy access to rewarding green intention, and clustering five levels of a continuously growing scope of action, including buyer–supplier cooperation at Level 5, which serves as a multiplier effect. The MOI and MNRE can look back at many years of close collaboration, which has certainly benefitted the linkages of GIM with GPP. First, greener products have been included in the government procurement, which confirmed the viability of eco-friendliness options. Emphasis has been placed on cleaner production. A more streamlined integration of entire life cycle considerations, e.g., design for sustainability, clean mobility, cradle-to-cradle approaches, and education of the consumer (industry, government, private households), is still underway.

With the Eco-Card, an interesting consumer-focused business model has been introduced, but the level of implementation is unclear and clarification is needed on the detailed eligibility of products. The mechanism could motivate consumer contributions to environmental friendliness. However, its effectiveness rises and falls with the scrutiny applied when establishing criteria for the eco-labels, the due diligence undertaken when awarding the eco-label to a product or service, as well as the ultimate outreach to card-carrying consumers. Possible confusion among the many different labels could be lessened through such an accreditation scheme.

In order to emphasise the commercial nature of environmentally friendly measures, detailed implementation should foresee mechanisms to include the most effective green goods and services, looking at the entire life cycle of the products. The LCI has provided an important insight into eco-friendliness and carbon footprints of certain products. Its value is still to be translated for the end-consumer to fully materialise its potential, e.g., following the idea of the eco-card. Globally, Thailand, being the 'kitchen of the world,' has the chance to improve eco-footprints of domestic and international food and beverage consumers by ensuring that their segments of the global value chains are optimised.

Being a world-famous mass tourism destination, Thailand has an enormous potential to shape and educate a large number of domestic and global citizens in what constitutes sustainable tourism. Its role as a regional hub for travel in Asia provides it with the chance to create region-wide lower carbon and eco-friendly travel opportunities in collaboration with tour operators, the transport industry (particularly flight carriers) and tourism destinations in Thailand and the larger region. An increased guest engagement would eventually lead to increased implementation of resource savings and eventually result in world citizens taking home their learnings.

Evidence that SCP can be made as a business case has been shaped and up-scaled with the support of the SWITCH-Asia Programme in frontrunner countries and lesser advanced countries in ASEAN such as Cambodia, Laos, Myanmar and Vietnam (CLMV) alike. Those can now serve as examples from which others can learn, in Thailand, in ASEAN and beyond.

It needs to be acknowledged that sustainability and low-carbon efforts in the automotive sector are limited if an increase in scale is promoted simultaneously. It is recommended, and in line with the original SCP approach, to focus on the need first, and not the product. The need for mobility can be met with different technologies. Given the sensitivity of the automotive production network and the high economic importance of this industry to Thailand, a paradigm shift towards alternative transport technology is not to be expected any time soon. However, a clean mobility movement led by this Southeast Asian production hub could provide new momentum to the economy, which outweighs the eventual losses of a conventional automotive industry.

To solve the paradox of "growth" and "sustainability" would be to start committing — authentically, and with a strong vision — to putting the highest priority on promoting those businesses that follow a cradle-to-cradle approach. This automatically leads to less harmful goods and services or even those with a positive impact on the environment. This would also result in less importance of the potential "rebound effect" which in Thailand, just like anywhere in the world, is the most difficult to address.

References

ADB (2015). Thailand: Economy. *Asian Development Bank Outlook 2015 Update*. Available on: http://www.adb.org/countries/thailand/economy.

Barnett, B. (2009). *Tourism impact on thailand's economy by the numbers. The Phuket Insider (23.06.2009)*. Retrieved on June 5, 2015. Available on: http://www.thephuketinsider.com/tourism/tourism_impact_on_thailands_economy_by_numbers.php.

Board of Investment (BOI, 2013a). *Trade and Investment Report (TIR, December 2013)*. Retrieved on June 25, 2015. Available on: http://www.boi.go.th/tir/issue/201312_23_12/42.htm.

Board of Investment (BOI, 2013b). Traders back farm-produce standard. *Thailand-China Business Link (27/09/2013)*. Retrieved on June 23 2015. Available on: http://www.thailand-china.com/Home/Thailand-China-News/newsthai/BOT,-traders-back-farm-produce-standard.aspx.

BOI (2014). *Thailand's Food Industry*.

Chapagain, A. K. and Hoekstra, A. Y. (2011). The blue, green and grey water footprint of rice from production and consumption perspectives. *Ecological Economics* 70, 749–758.

Chinmaneevong, C. (2014). Koh Chang aims for climate-friendly tag, in: *Bangkok Post* (06/03/2014) Available on: http://www.bangkokpost.com/print/398395/ (retrieved 23.06.2015).

Department of Land Transport/Transport Statistics Sub-Division (TSSD/DoLT, 2014). *Car Brands in Thailand*. Retrieved on November 22, 2015. Available on: http://www.thaiwebsites.com/carbrands.asp.

EUD Thailand (2015). *Political Relations with Thailand*. Available on: http://www.eeas.europa.eu/delegations/thailand/eu_thailand/political_relations/index_en.htm (retrieved on 25.06.2015).

FAO (2013). *Food Waste Worsens GHG Emissions*. Retrieved on April 30, 2015. Available on: http://www.climatenewsnetwork.net/food-waste-worsens-ghg-emissions-fao/.

Fernquest, J. (2011). Food labels for food safety. *Bangkok Post* (*14/03/2011*). Retrieved on April 26, 2015. Available on: http://www.bangkokpost.com/learning/learning-from-news/226657/food-labels-for-food-safety.

Frederickson, T. (2014). Q-mark: Not a guarantee of food safety. *Bangkok Post* (*19/08/2014*). Retrieved on May 1, 2015. Available on: http://www.bangkokpost.com/learning/learning-from-news/427529/q-mark-not-a-guarantee-of-food-safety (accessed 01.05.2015).

Gheewala, S. H., Silalertruksa, T. Nilsalab, P. Mungkung, R. Perret, S. R. and Chaiyawannakarn, N. (2014). Water footprint and impact of water consumption for food, feed, fuel crops production in Thailand. *Water* 6(6), 1698–1718.

IMF (2014). *GDP Estimates of ASEAN Countries*. Retrieved on June 15, 2015. Available on: https://en.wikipedia.org/wiki/List_of_ASEAN_countries_by_GDP_%28nominal%29 (retrieved 15.06.2015).

Jorgensen, G. (2006). (2014). Bring the car around: Uber versus Grabtaxi in Bangkok, in: G2D (April 2014). Retrieved on November 28, 2015. Available on: http:// gregtodiffer.com/bring-car-around-uber-vs-grabtaxi-bangkok/.

MCOT (2014). Every Thai produces 1 kilo of waste daily. *Pattaya Mail* (*15/11/2014*). Retrieved on June 24, 2015. Available on: http://www.pattayamail.com/ news/every-thai-produces-1-kilo-of-waste-daily-42884 — The volume of waste is increasing in Thailand, which generated 26.77 million tonnes of consumer waste in 2013. Some 64% of that waste was food.

Mekonnen, M. M. and Hoekstra, A. Y. (2011). The green, blue and grey water footprint of crops and derived crop products. *Hydrology and Earth System Sciences* 15(5), 1577–1600.

Mungkung, R. (2015). LCI-LCA agri-food product and applications for green policies in Thailand. *4th LCA AgriFood ASIA International Workshop* (*09/03/2015*).

Muqbil, I. (2013). Promoting sustainable tourism via 'designated areas' in Thailand. *Look East* (May 2013). Retrieved on April 24, 2015. Available on: http://www.lookeastmagazine.com/2013/05/promoting-sustainable-tourism-via-designated-areas-in-thailand/.

National News Bureau in Thailand (2015). *DASTA Moves on Low Carbon and Creative Tourism in 2015*. Retrieved on April 24, 2015. Available on: http://thainews.prd.go.th/centerweb/newsen/NewsDetail?NT01_NewsID=WNECO5801270010010.

Ouyyanont, P. (2001). The Vietnam war and tourism in Bangkok's development, 1960–1970. *Southeast Asian Studies* 39(2), 157–187.

Panthong, K. (2012). Indonesia on the road to becoming Thailand's rival. *Jakarta Post (24/05/2012)*. Retrieved on June 25, 2015. Available on: http://www.thejakartapost.com/news/2012/05/24/indonesia-road-becoming-thailands-rival.html.

PEF World Forum (2015). *Thailand's Carbon Labels*. Retrieved on April 26, 2015. Available on: http://www.pef-world-forum.org/initiatives/country-governmental-initiatives/thailand-carbon-labels/.

Pratruangkrai, P. (2014). Thailand set to reclaim top rice exporter title. *The Nation (23/12/2014)*. Retrieved on November 20, 2015. Available on: http://www.nationmultimedia.com/business/Thailand-set-to-reclaim-top-rice-exporter-title-30250443.html.

Rogers, D. (2015). Thailand approves Japanese plan for high speed train. *Global Construction Review* (May 2015). Retrieved on November 28, 2015. Available on: http://www.globalconstructionreview.com/news/thailand-approves-ja8anese-pla4n2-hi0gh6-4s2pe08ed/.

Ruddick, G. (2013). Tesco goes head-to-head with Thailand's wet markets. *The Telegraph (31/03/2013)*. Retrieved on May 1, 2015. Available on: http://www.telegraph.co.uk/finance/newsbysector/retailandconsumer/9963749/Tesco-goes-head-to-head-with-Thailands-wet-markets.html.

Rungfapaisarn, K. (2012). TCEB turns focus on Asian sustainability leadership, in: *The Nation* (09/08/2012), see: http://www.nationmultimedia.com/business/TCEB-turns-focus-on-Asian-sustainability-leadership-30187923.html (retrieved on 14.05.2015).

Sangsnit, N. (2013). Sustainable tourism development in Thailand. *UNWTO Conference on Sustainable Tourism Development* (12/04/2013).

Sullivan, B. (2015). Thailand's auto sales to pick up in 2015 after 33% drop in 2014. *Thailand Business News (22/01/2015)*. Retrieved on June 24, 2015. Available on: http://www.thailand-business-news.com/news/headline/49961-thailands-auto-sales-pick-2015-33-drop-2014.html.

SWITCH-Asia PSCT (2014). English summary report on improving the green industry mark (GIM) programme. *Report SCP Policy Support Component Thailand (December 2014)*, p. 15.

T. J. (2013). Thailand's booming car industry. Detroit of the East, in: *The Economist* (04/04/2013). Retrieved on June 25, 2015. Available on: http://www.economist.com/blogs/schumpeter/2013/04/thailands-booming-car-industry.

Thai Automotive Institute (2014). *Car Manufacturing, Domestic Sales and Exports from Thailand*. Retrieved on June 25, 2015. Available on: http://www.thaiwebsites.com/cars-thailand.asp.

Tourism Thailand (2015). Wat Mongkol Chaipattana royal-initiated area development project. Retrieved on June 15, 2015. Available on: http://www.tourismthailand.org/See-and-Do/Sights-and-Attractions-Detail/Wat-Mongkol-Chaipattana-Royal-Initiated-Area-Development-Project--2607 (retrieved 15.06.2015).

Ünaldi, S. (2014). Thailand: A Coup, the crown, and two middle classes. *The Diplomat*, *(23/05/2014)*. Retrieved on Feburary 10, 2015. Available on: http://thediplomat.com/2014/05/thailand-a-coup-the-crown-and-two-middle-classes/.

Vanit-Anunchai, C. and Schmidt, E. (2006). Consumer Purchase Decisions for Pesticide-safe Vegetables Using Logistic Regression: The Case of Thailand, in: Batt, P. J. (ed.), *ISHS Acta Horticulturae 699*: I International Symposium on Improving the Performance of Supply Chains in the Transitional Economies, Chiang Mai, Thailand. Acta Hort. (ISHS), 457–464.

Verifavia (2015). *MBM Project for Thai DCA*. Retrieved on June 15, 2015. Available on: http://www.verifavia.com/greenhouse-gas-verification/ref-mbm-project-for-thai-dca-293.php.

Wirudchawong, N. (2011). *Policy on Community Tourism Development in Thailand*. Office of the Ombudsman, Thailand, pp. 14–26.

WTTC (2014). *Travel and Tourism, Economic Impact 2014*: *Thailand*. World Travel & Tourism Council, London.

Yuthamanop, P. TDRI (2011). Income inequality in Thailand. Income gap to widen without change, Lower middle-class fails to catch up. *Bangkok Post* (*15/12/2011*). Retrieved on Feburary 10, 2015. Available on: http://www.bangkokpost.com/print/270964/.

Yuwanan S. *et al.* (2011) *Identifying National Science and Technology Development Agency NSTDA R&D Direction on Water Footprint.*

Website references

Air Transport Action Group (ATAG). Retrieved on June 15, 2015. Available on: www.atag.org/facts-and-figures.html.

ASEAN Up http://aseanup.com/thailand-automotive-industry-overview/ — alternatively Thai BOI http://www.boi.go.th/index.php?page=opp_automotive Chaipattana Foundation Website. Retrieved on June 24, 2015. Available on: www.chaipat.or.th/chaipat_english/ (retrieved 24.06.2015).

Solar Impulse Website. Retrieved on April 25, 2015. Available on: www.solar impulse.com.

Thai Railways Website. Retrieved on June 24, 2015. Available on: www.thairailways.com/train-and-travel.map.html.
Thailand Department of Tourism Website. Visitor Statistics 2014. Retrieved on April 5, 2015. Available on: www.tourism.go.th/home/listcontent/11/221/276.
The Thailand Community Based Tourism Institute (CBT-I) Website (2012). Retrieved on June 24, 2015. Available on: www.cbt-i.org/2012/travel.php.
UNEP Website. Retrieved on Februrary 10, 2015. Available on: http://www.unep.fr/scp/cp/.
UNESCO Website: http://www.unesco.org/education/tlsf/mods/theme_c/mod16.html (retrieved 24.06.2015) — specifically "Sustainable Tourism, A Multimedia Teacher Education Programme, Activity 1, The rise of Tourism".
Wiki Website: mw.micronation.org/wiki/Olympic_swimming_pool (retrieved on 03.05.2015) — An Olympic sized swimming pool has a capacity of 2 500 000 litres or 2500 m^3.
World Bank Website: http://www.worldbank.org/en/country/thailand/overview (retrieved 15.06.2015).

Interview reference

LightBlue Environmental Consulting (2015). Benjamin Lephilibert, CEO LightBlue Environmental Consulting, expert interview 05.02.2015.
VGREEN (2015). Dr. Rattanawan Mungkung, Director, Centre of Excellence on enVironmental strategy for GREEN business (VGREEN), Department of Environmental Technology and Management, Faculty of Environment, Kasetsart University, expert interview 24.04.2015.
SWITCH-Asia PSCT (2015). Niels Juul Busch, Team Leader of the former EU SWITCH-Asia Policy Support Component in Thailand, expert interview 25.02.2015.
SWITCH-Asia Automotive SSCM (2015). Wilasinee Poonuchaphai, Project Co-Director, EU SWITCH-Asia — Greening Supply Chains in the Thai Auto and Automotive Parts, expert interview 03.03.2015.

Chapter 13

Sustainable Consumption and Production in Vietnam

N. T. Thong, D. H. Nguyen, P. T. N. Bich and L. T. M. Huong

13.1 Introduction: Vietnam's Economic Reforms and Impacts on the Environment

Vietnam is located on the eastern margin of the Indochinese peninsula, Southeast Asia. The country has a total area of over 332 km^2, along with about 1,000,000 km^2 of exclusive economic zone (EEZ), and a population of 90.6 million (est. 2014). Through the 1986 reform (Đổi Mới), shifting from a highly centralised planned-economy to a social-oriented market economy, Vietnam has enjoyed high growth of 6–7% per year. The country has been transformed from one of the poorest in the world, with per capita income below USD 100 in the early 1990s, to a lower middle-income country with per capita income of over USD 2,000 by the end of 2014. Over the last few decades, Vietnam has made a remarkable progress in poverty reduction. The percentage of people living in poverty dropped from almost 60% in the 1990s to less than 3% today [World Bank, 2015]. Thanks to the economic reform, Vietnam has achieved long-term progress in basic dimensions of human development. The Human Development Index (HDI) value of Vietnam increased from 0.439 in 1990 to 0.638 in 2013, positioning the country in the medium human development category in the world [UNDP, 2013]. Over the last 30 years, life expectancy rose from 61.1 years in 1985 to 75.4 years in 2012, expected years of school from 8.7 to 11.9, and mean years at school from 4.4 to 5.5 [UNDP, 2013]. To date, Vietnam has achieved most and in some cases surpassed a number of the Millennium Development Goals (MDGs), particularly the goals on poverty reduction, education and gender equality [World Bank, 2015]. In the two decades from the 1990s to the 2000s, Vietnam has been one of the fastest developing economies due to rapid export growth and increased investment in the private sector. The country's accession to the World Trade Organisation (WTO) in January 2007 was a key milestone in the economic development path. With its rapid economic expansion and a significant population, Vietnam has become an increasingly important market, as well as gaining importance as a producer in its own right, especially in the garment, rice, pepper, and tea industries. Despite the economic success of the reforms, Vietnam is starting to show signs of falling productivity. The high growth rate of the past, driven by cheap input factors (i.e., low wages), has reached its limit. Symptoms of low competitiveness are poor public service delivery and high costs of doing business. The opaque business environment, gaps in SME access to finance, infrastructure bottlenecks, and the lack of skilled labour and weaknesses in innovation deter the Vietnam's private sector from developing to its full potential [SECO, 2013].

This rapid industrialisation and urbanisation have led to many environmental issues for Vietnam. The significant environmental challenges are deforestation and soil degradation, water pollution and overfishing, groundwater contamination, degrading environment in big cities, loss of biodiversity, air pollution, solid waste problems [The World Factbook CIA, 2015]. Soil degradation has been increasing and degraded land accounts for nearly 50% of the total land area of the country. The 'soil problems' were affected badly by leaching, erosion, degradation, poor fertility, salinisation, acidification, pollution, drought, desertification, inundation, organic reduction, landslide, erosion of river banks and coastline, and losing soil productivity for urbanisation. Regarding forest resources, in the decade from 1980–1990, Vietnam lost an average of 100,000 ha of forest annually for development of industrial zones, and hydropower and irrigation projects. However, since 1995, forest area has increased as a result of forest rehabilitation and plantation programmes. By the end of 2006, forest area in Vietnam was 12.87 million ha, of which 10.41 million ha were natural forest and 2.46 million ha were plantation forest [FAO, 2009]. Vietnam's pollution is among the worst in the world. According to a survey undertaken in 2014 by Yale University, the Environment Performance Index put Vietnam 136th out of 178 nations [EPI, 2014]. The pollution problem has been increasing over the years, driven by industrialisation and urbanisation processes. Air quality, water, sanitation and resources, and biodiversity are the poorest criteria affecting environmental performance. Land for agricultural purposes has been used for construction projects, such as golf courses and new urban centres. The quality of soil faces problems such as erosion, exhaust fumes and pollution due to the use of diesel, and organic and microbiological substances from farming. The ongoing trend of migration from rural regions to cities has also created risks and deteriorated the quality of the environment [Tuoitrenews, 2012]. Furthermore, high exposure to climate change adds to the challenges for Vietnam to cope with environmental issues and natural catastrophes. The factors that obstruct the recovery of the economy also include weakening enterprises, insufficient policy measures and ineffective policy transmission channels. Vietnam needs to develop a concrete action plan to bolster its efforts to strengthen its climate change response and to ensure a climate-resilient future [World Bank, 2015].

Realising the urgent need to promote a shift toward more sustainable industrial development pathways and sustainable consumption and production (SCP) patterns, the Vietnamese government has paid special attention to the promotion of green growth. The government has approved the Vietnam Green Growth Strategy for the period 2011–2020, with a vision to 2050, as "a decisive tendency in sustainable economic development."

The remainder of this chapter is structured as follows: firstly, it provides a detailed introduction of the Vietnamese economy and potential for greening of small- and medium-sized enterprises (SMEs). Secondly, policies for green growth and SCP are introduced, followed by an overview of international cooperation programmes for stimulating green growth. Two projects from the European Union's SWITCH-Asia Programme are highlighted as case studies. The conclusion provides an outlook and recommendations on how to advance green growth and SCP in Vietnam.

13.2 Vietnam's Economy and the Status of SMEs

13.2.1 *The economic structure of Vietnam*

Over the last decades, Vietnam's economic expansion was accompanied by a drastic shift in the composition of gross domestic product (GDP). The economic activities shifted away from agriculture toward services and manufacturing. Key industries in Vietnam currently include food processing, garments and apparel, machinery, mining, coal, steel, concrete, chemical fertilizers, glass, tyres, oil, and paper. National priority is given to application of high and clean technologies in order to promote the production value of these sectors to at least 20% growth per year and contribute at least 35% to the overall national production value [World Bank, 2015].

Vietnam has applied a market-oriented system but the stated-owned enterprise (SOE) is still at the heart of the economy (see Figure 13.1). The non-state enterprises are numerous but small; most are sole traders. Foreign direct investment (FDI) enterprises are extremely important for the Vietnamese economy. Although this block accounted for only 20% of GDP and created 24% of jobs, it contributed nearly 65% of export value for Vietnam in 2014 [FIA, 2015].

Since the Vietnamese government launched its opening policy, its exports have had the opportunity to expand. The traditional labour-intensive manufacturing exports, such as garments, footwear and furniture, continue to grow rapidly (see Table 13.1). Recent new exports, such as

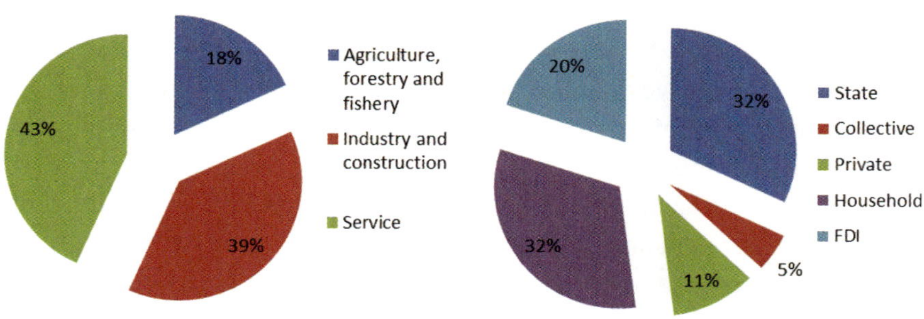

Figure 13.1: GDP structure of 2014 (USD 186.3 billion) by sector and ownership types
Source: GSO [2014].

Table 13.1: Key exported products of Vietnam in 2014 (USD billion) [ITC, 2015]

No.	Products	Exported Value	Trade Surplus
1	Electrical, electronic equipment	46.26	12.18
2	Footwear, gaiters, etc., parts thereof	13.76	12.69
3	Articles of apparel, accessories, not knitted/crocheted	11.53	8.52
4	Articles of apparel, accessories, knitted or crocheted	9.57	5.83
5	Furniture, lighting, signs, prefabricated buildings	6.69	5.78
6	Fish, crustacea, molluscs, aquatic invertebrates	4.96	0.41
7	Coffee, tea, mate, and spices	4.47	4.01
8	Leather, animal gut, harnesses, travel goods	2.84	2.65
9	Wood and articles of wood, wood charcoal	2.67	1.68
10	Edible fruit, nuts, peel of citrus fruit, melons	2.51	0.40
11	Rubber and related articles	2.33	0.91
12	Meat, fish and seafood food preparations	1.73	1.50
13	Other fabricated textile articles, sets, clothing	1.10	0.69
14	Salt, sulphur, earth, stone, plaster, lime, concrete	1.08	0.84

hi-tech and high-value products (cell phones, computers, electronics, and automobile parts), have also maintained rapid growth, and now represent the largest export share.

13.2.2 *Major industries*

Manufacturing sector: The manufacturing sector, including electronics, garments and textiles, and footwear, has a high export turnover, trade surplus, and represents labour-intensive sectors, of international interest given Vietnam's low labour costs. However, given the increasing average salary and changing economic structure among regions, the risk of local labour scarcity affects the competitiveness of all three sectors. Despite being a large exporter of garments and textiles, footwear, and electronic products in the world, Vietnam participated as a subcontractor without creating direct links with export markets; the value added is low. Most added value generated in export turnover is from FDI enterprises. The electronic products and equipment sector currently has the highest export turnover and plays an important role in the economy. Thanks to the participation of many multinational electronics firms (e.g., Samsung, IBM, Canon), and increasing domestic demand for electronic products and services, the annual growth rate was 15–20% in the period 2008–2014; this sector reports the largest export turnover of USD 46 billion in 2014. This sector also attracts unskilled labour to work in assembling factories. According to data from 2012, more than 500 enterprises have over 200,000 direct workers with relatively high incomes and this number will continue to rise in coming years.

Footwear, garment and textile production is considered the most important industry of Vietnam in creating jobs. Annually, the garment and textile sector creates over 2 million jobs, and this number is expected to rise to 3 million in 2020 [MOIT, 2014]. In 2012, Vietnam had 4,654 garment and textile enterprises, of which 85% were SMEs, and 5% large enterprises with over 1,000 workers. Some 850 enterprises engage in manufacturing and exporting footwear, creating jobs for nearly 1 million direct workers and millions of indirect workers [MOIT, 2014]. In 2014, footwear, garment and textile export turnover reached USD 20.9 billion, ranking second after the electronic sector [GSO, 2014]. However, environmental impacts need to be considered, for instance waste discharge and air pollution.

Agriculture, Forestry, and Fisheries: Vietnam is well placed to develop agriculture, forestry, and fisheries due to the climate and diversified topographic conditions. Stretching from 23°23′ to 8°34′, the country has various climates: tropical, sub-tropical, semi-drought climate, and temperate zone. The total soil area used for agriculture, forest, and aquaculture activities in 2014 was 26.1 million ha, making up 78% of the total land area of Vietnam [GOS, 2014]. Plentiful rural labour and low labour cost are also advantageous; Vietnam has 36.1 million labourers aged 15 and above working in rural areas, of which 24.5 million work in agriculture, forestry, and fishery, making up 47.4% of Vietnam's labour force [GSO, 2014]. In the 1980s and before, Vietnam received international aid for national food requirements, but after only a few years of development, the country became an exporter of many agricultural products, such as rice, seafood, coffee, peppercorn, cashew nuts, and tea. Coffee is one of main agricultural products of Vietnam; in 2014, 630,000 ha was under cultivation for coffee cultivation, 1.74 million tonnes of coffee was produced, with an export turnover of over USD 3.6 billion, ranking Vietnam the second largest coffee exporter in the world. Coffee is also a main income source for 540,000 farmer households, with more than 1.6 million labourers in remote areas, contributing considerably to famine elimination, poverty alleviation, and building the sustainable economy of Vietnam. Rice cultivation is a traditional agricultural practice in Vietnam. Rice production, processing, and export are fundamental to national food security, creating rural employment, and stabilising the national macro-economy. The country has 9.27 million households cultivating rice, making up 77.6% of total households with agricultural land [GSO, 2014]. The favourable climate and land conditions help Vietnam to develop rice production and rice exports. Vietnamese rice mainly meets domestic demand, with only about 25% exported [MOIT, 2014].

Vietnam ranks fourth in the world in terms of natural rubber yield and fifth in terms of natural rubber export value, with an export turnover in 2014 of USD 2.3 billion [ITC, 2015]. In 2014, Vietnam used 977,000 ha to produce 953,700 tonnes of rubber [GSO, 2014], mainly in the Southeastern region, the Central Highlands, and North Central Coast. Over 85% of Vietnamese rubber production is exported, of which 60–70% is destined for China. Natural rubber has been identified in the national orientation for sustainable development and facilitating hunger elimination and poverty reduction, however, the natural rubber industry in Vietnam is in the maturity stage of its life cycle. Rubber trees have been planted in the country over 116 years and its industry has a long history of development over 85 years [VTB, 2013].

Forest products (e.g., wood, wooden, and handicraft products) have the largest third export value among agricultural products. Apart from this economic value, the sector plays an important role in environmental protection, biodiversity and contributing to hunger elimination, and poverty reduction, especially for people in mountainous areas. In 2014, Vietnam had an export value for wood and wooden products of USD 2.8 billion in 2014, making up 1.9% of the world's market share, and an annual export growth rate of 25% [MOIT, 2014]. Vietnam has abundant raw materials such as bamboo, rattan, rush, palm leaf, gleicheniaceae, water hyacinth, and banana bark. The handicraft products are diversified, with plaited (baskets) and bamboo products being the most popular. In recent years, the number of workers in craft villages has decreased, by 10–35%. The labour reduction in craft villages is mainly due to low salaries of workers in the arts and crafts sector, as well as weakness in management and the lack of solidarity of enterprises causing the instability of the market.

Fishery is one of the major export sectors of Vietnam. Seafood products were exported to 160 markets in the world, with a total estimated value of USD 7 billion in 2014, representing a 4.3% export share. The main aquatic exported products are shrimp, *Pangasius* catfish, and tuna. Vietnam has innate advantages to develop fisheries and aquaculture, due to its long coast, and many rivers, estuaries, and reservoirs. However, the sector currently faces challenges with fish stock overexploitation and environmental issues in aquaculture. The increasing domestic consumption and export demand have resulted in overexploitation of inshore fishery stocks. Although offshore fishery stock has been considered as under-exploited, the lack of intensive management may cause offshore fisheries to become increasingly over-exploited. In order to exploit the fisheries more sustainably, fisheries management needs to be improved. Some key solutions have been suggested: Integrated coastal zone management, fisheries management in inland, offshore and inshore areas, and diversified aquaculture development in brackish, marine, and freshwater areas. Inland fisheries are an important livelihood for many poor people. However, it is under threat from pollution due to agrochemicals and some flood control projects. To ensure the sustainability of inland fisheries, many issues need to be considered, for instance, assessment the important of inland fisheries, identification of appropriate management measures, such as use of appropriate gear and closed-fishing seasons in selected areas, establishment of sanctuaries to protect key breeding areas and nurturing habitat, etc. Although Vietnam is one of the largest seafood exporters in the world, the sector is less well integrated further down the value chain.

Service Sector — Tourism: The service sector is increasingly important to the Vietnamese economy. In 2014, the services sector contributed an export value of USD 11 billion [ITC, 2015], in which tourism is the main contributor. The sector brought a turnover export value of USD 7.3 billion to 2014's GDP, with an annual growth rate of 17.8%. The number of international visitors in Vietnam in 2014 was 7.9 million, within which tourists from China, Korea, Japan, and US dominate. In 2013, the tourism employed 570,000 direct workers out of 1.8 million, representing 2.5% of the national labour force [ITC, 2015]. It is estimated, by

2020 the tourism sector will employ 870,000 direct workers. Vietnam has enormous tourism potential, particularly ecotourism, due to the spectacular landscape, tropical climate, rich natural resources, long coastline, rich history, and diverse culture. The country is considered one of 16 nations in the world with the highest biodiversity in a wide range of ecosystems [Hong *et al.*, 2002], a very favourable condition for ecotourism development. Vietnam is both a "cradle" of native species and a transitional area of organisms from the biota of the north to the south. In addition, due to its diversity of topography and climatic conditions, Vietnam is rich in floral and faunal species, of which 10% and 11%, respectively, are endemic [Hong *et al.*, 2002]. Vietnam can develop various ecotourism products based on the coastal ecosystem, the limestone ecosystem and the tropical fruit garden. Vietnam is also rich in cultural identity, with 54 peoples whose indigenous knowledge could be made accessible to visitors. Although having much potential for tourism development, the sector is not competitive. The competitiveness indicator of Vietnamese tourism in 2015 ranked 75th out of 141 countries according to the assessment of the World Economic Forum [2015]. In addition, tourism has brought great benefits to the economy, but it has also contributed to environmental degradation, especially biodiversity deterioration. Fully aware of the significance of ecotourism, the government of Vietnam has prioritised ecotourism in its strategy for tourism development to ensure both sustainability and economic benefits. Though ecotourism of Vietnam is nascent, it is expected to grow strongly through support from government and international organisations. Ecotourism needs investment in human resources (tourist guides, tour operators), management, and fundamental research and planning focused on the natural environment of the proposed ecotourism sites.

13.2.3 *Small- and Medium-sized Enterprises*

SMEs have emerged as a dynamic force in the development of the Vietnamese economy since the launching of the reform process in 1986. According to GSO [2014], the number of non-state enterprises in December 2013 represented 96.4% of total enterprises, creating around 60% of jobs, owning nearly 50% of capital (see Table 13.2) and contributing 48% of GDP in 2014. Of this GDP contribution, state enterprises and

Table 13.2: Structure of acting enterprises as of 31 December, 2013 [GSO, 2014]

	Number of Enterprises		Number of Employees		Capital	
	Enterprise	%	Thousd.	%	USD Bills	%
State owned	**3,198**	**0.8**	**1,541**	**13.4**	**257.7**	**30.9**
Central	1,789	0.5	1,155	10.1	235.3	28.3
Local	1,409	0.4	386	3.4	22.3	2.6
Non-state	**359,794**	**96.4**	**6,855**	**59.8**	**416.1**	**49.9**
Private	49,203	13.2	503	4.4	14.5	1.7
Others	310,591	83.2	6,351	55.4	401.7	48.2
FDI	**10,220**	**2.7**	**3,069**	**26.8**	**159.3**	**19.1**
100% foreign	8,632	2.3	2,783	24.3	118.0	14.2
Joint-venture	1,588	0.4	286	2.5	41.2	4.9
Total	**373,212**	**100.0**	**11,464.4**	**100.0**	**833.1**	**100.0**

foreign-investment companies accounted for respectively 31.9% and 20.1% in 2014. Most non-state enterprises are SMEs and have grown rapidly during the past decade.

SMEs are the driver of growth for Vietnam economy and the promotion of SMEs has received strong support from the government. Action plans to improve the business sector have been actively pursued and the priority of private sector and enterprise development is clearly reflected in the socio-economic development strategy. SME promotion, particularly in rural areas, is also regularly referred to as a priority area of the government to underpin the economic growth process. The Vietnamese government has introduced a range of legislation to shore up the private sector's economic success and growth, from a surge in foreign funds, technical assistance and investment. Two groups of interrelated factors, namely market-oriented and business environment reforms, and pro-SMEs policies and programmes [Cuong *et al.*, 2008] have supported the rapid development of SMEs, especially the number of enterprises.

Despite the impressive achievement during the past decades, Vietnam's SMEs remain weak in terms of internal and external networking, competitiveness, innovativeness, human resources, and readiness to globalisation [Cuong *et al.,* 2008]. Apart from the low starting points of SMEs, these shortcomings and weaknesses have been largely due to the prolonged discrimination against private sector's access to capital or credit and land, lack of a pro-private and competitive business environment, and poor quality of human resource and business support services. To strengthen and enhance SME networks, competitiveness, and innovativeness, Vietnam should abandon the position of retaining the lead role of state-owned enterprises in the national economy. There is a pressing need to level the playing field, create solid supporting industries, enhance the quality of human resources, and improve infrastructure.

13.3 Vietnam's Green Industry and SCP Policies

While Vietnam has maintained an intensive focus on a high industrial growth rate for an extended period, productivity remains low, reflecting low labour productivity and the less efficient use of technology, capital, materials, and energy [Ketels *et al.*, 2011]. Outdated and inefficient technologies and equipment are still in operation in many areas of high-energy use, such as power generation, steel, concrete and chemicals, causing significant waste of materials, and fuel. Moreover, enterprises and industrial products are less competitive in comparison with those of other countries in the region, and industry continues to discharge untreated waste, exacerbating environmental pollution and degradation. In the meantime, Vietnamese enterprises invest very little in R&D and technology innovation, on average, only 0.2–0.3% of total turnover [UNIDO, 2012].

13.3.1 *Vietnam's Green Growth Strategy*

Realising the urgent need to promote a shift toward more sustainable industrial development pathways, Vietnam's government has paid special attention to the promotion of green industry. Vietnam signed the Manila Declaration on Green Industry in Asia in 2009, participated in the Tokyo Green Industry Conference in 2011, and the United Nation Conference on Sustainable Development in June 2012 when the government pledged to promote green industrial development. The government has approved the Vietnam Green Growth Strategy for the period 2011–2020, with a vision to 2050, as "a decisive tendency in sustainable economic development." The Vietnam Green Growth Strategy has overall objectives to achieve a low carbon economy, enrich natural capital, and direct sustainable economic development. The objectives would be achieved by accelerating the process of economic restructuring in order to use natural resources efficiently, reducing greenhouse gas (GHG) emissions through research and application of modern technologies, developing infrastructure to improve the entire efficiency of the economy, coping with climate change, contributing to poverty reduction, and driving economic growth in a sustainable manner.

The strategy was approved in September 2012, and it is an effort to synthesise green action plans of major sectors and society. The strategy sets the tasks for the period 2011–2020 are to: (i) reduce the intensity of GHG emissions by 8–10% as compared to the 2010 level; (ii) reduce energy consumption per unit of GDP by 1–1.5% per year; (iii) reduce GHG emissions from energy activities by 10–20%. The orientation towards 2030 is to reduce annual GHG emissions by at least 1.5–2% and to reduce GHG emissions in energy activities by 20–30% (Prime Minister No.1393/QĐ-TTg, 2012).

The Vietnam Green Growth Strategy focuses on three priorities: climate change mitigation, green production, and green lifestyle. The solutions that have been identified include the construction of necessary infrastructure, technological innovation and the creation of an enabling environment through the elaboration of appropriate policy mechanisms, standards, technical regulations, and the rational use of natural resources including fossil fuels [LEDS, 2014]. The mainstreaming of cleaner production is especially endorsed by the Prime Minister in the 2009 Decision no.1419/QD-TTg on "Strategy on Cleaner Production (CP) in Industry Towards 2020." The CP strategy is based on the approach of disseminating the CP concept to 63 provinces and cities nationwide via communication and mass media, technical assistance, CP networking, and financing mechanisms, which are to promote the industrial production facilities to participate in CP application. It targets at least 50% of industrial businesses, who would be made aware of the benefits derived from applying CP methods, and at least half of them would be expected to apply to reduce energy and material consumption by 2015; the strategy also wants to raise the figure to 90 and 50% respectively by 2020.

However, household level enterprises are large in number and as such pose a significant threat to environment, as they have not been considered to be included in the overall efforts to ensure sustainable production. There is a general lack of knowledge on environmental techniques and practices, added to which their limited resources, capacities and infrastructure, and the vulnerability of local communities in which they operate.

Green consumption and sustainable lifestyles refer to the regular practice of consumption of only environmentally friendly products that do not cause any damage to human health and do not threaten the functions and working of any natural ecosystem. Changing today's consumption patterns in order to preserve future opportunities is one of the themes for sustainable development.

The Green Growth Strategy sets the targets and actions for promoting sustainable consumption and building green lifestyle, including:

1. promoting eco-labelling and disseminating information on environmentally friendly products to the entire society (e.g., formulating a roadmap towards 2020 to initiate green procurement),
2. regulating public expenditure leading to the development and use of green economy standards (e.g., from 2015, all public works and projects should adhere to green economy standards, from 2017 all motorised vehicles purchased by public budget will meet emission standards),
3. applying economic and technical instrument to encourage sustainable consumption in the business sector and by people.

Developing greener consumption patterns will require co-operation from consumers, communities, and civil society. However, green lifestyles are not yet topical for research agenda and media programmes in Vietnam. Comprehensive research on aspects of green consumption using various framework approaches is needed, such as economic, psychology, sociology, and culture. In 2012, the European Commission (EC), through its SWITH-Asia Programme, sponsored an initial project of *GetGreen Vietnam* (detailed in Box 13.2) to promote sustainable living and working styles. However, this initial project was limited to consumers in only four cities [Hanoi, Da Nang, Ho Chi Minh City, and Can Tho]. Further efforts are needed to mainstream sustainable lifestyles throughout Vietnam.

13.4 Financing Green Growth in Vietnam

To support sustainable production in Vietnamese industries, some donor organisations have established financial mechanisms, namely The Green Credit Trust Fund (GCTF), Vietnam National Energy Efficiency Program (VNEEP), Vietnam Energy Efficiency and Cleaner Production (EECP) Financing Program, and Vietnam Clean Energy Program (VCEP). These financial mechanisms are described below. ***GCTF*** has the objective to promote long-term investments to SMEs in CP technology with a positive impact on the environment and to contribute to the sustainable development of Vietnam. The GCTF in Vietnam, with a USD 2.1 million guarantee fund, was introduced by the Swiss State Secretariat for Economic Affairs (SECO) through coordination with the Vietnam Cleaner Production Centre (VNCPC) at the end of 2007. The credit size provided by local financial institutions is from USD 25,000 to USD 1,000,000 per project for the SMEs (either private sector or state-owned enterprises) with more than 50% Vietnamese ownership. The Green Credits have a maximum maturity of five years with market-based interest rates.

The Vietnam National Energy Efficiency Program (VNEEP) is the comprehensive programme of work to promote energy efficiency in Vietnam, released in 2005 by the Ministry of Industry and Trade (MOIT) under the framework of the National Strategic Program on Energy Savings and Effective Use for the period 2006–2015. As the first-ever long-term comprehensive plan to institute measures for improving energy efficiency and conservation in all sectors of the economy in Vietnam, VNEEP calls for coordinated efforts for improving energy efficiency, reducing energy losses, and implementing extensive measures for the conservation of energy. The VNEEP aims to reach a certain target of energy saving, which will result in lower investment requirements for the energy supply system and social economic benefits. At the same time, it will contribute to environmental protection and rational extraction of energy resources, moving towards social and economic sustainable development. VNEEP consists of 11 projects within four programme areas, i.e., awareness raising, industry, buildings, and transport. Support to SMEs in the chosen sectors is a priority for the VNEEP.

The Vietnam Energy Efficiency and Cleaner Production (EECP) Financing Program is an integral part of the International Finance

Corporation's (IFC) global Sustainable Energy Finance (SEF) Programme. EECP promotes greater energy efficiency, renewable energy, and CP methods and awareness. It aims to reduce emissions and improve the use of natural resources by increasing available financing for sustainable energy investments. In 2010, with a USD 25 million loan and technical support from IFC, Techcombank became the first bank to launch EECP lending in Vietnam, aiming to build a portfolio of USD 50 million in EECP loans over a two-year period.

The Vietnam Clean Energy Program (VCEP) is a five-year effort (during 2012–2017) to accelerate Vietnam's transition to climate resilient, low-emission sustainable development through clean energy development, by increasing the use of renewable energy technologies and energy efficient practice in the building sector, in close coordination with Vietnam's Ministry of Construction. The programme has been funded by the U.S. Agency for International Development (USAID). VCEP lays the groundwork for an increased private sector engagement by developing public–private partnerships with private sector banks, building developers and owners, as well as industry organisations. In addition, the programme identifies potential funding sources for green buildings that comply with Vietnam's energy code and adopt a green building certification system recognised by the government.

13.5 Status of International Aid Cooperation for Greening Industry and Promoting SCP

The socio-economic development strategy of Vietnam in the period of 2011–2020 will focus on structural reforms, to ensure sustainable environment, social equity, as well as new issues that arise in the process of macro-economic stabilisation. The strategy identifies three "breakthrough areas" including: (i) promoting human resources/skills development (particularly skills for modern industry and employment innovation); (ii) enhancing the institution of market economy; and (iii) infrastructure development. Since 2009, Vietnam has officially shifted into the middle-income country segment and achieved two of the five MDGs; the other two goals will be gained in 2015. However, many development issues and challenges in poverty elimination still exist, which are very complex, and support is still needed from development partners.

The World Bank's Country Partnership Strategy (CPS) to Vietnam ensures the support of investments and policies in three pillars, namely: (i) strengthening Vietnam's competitiveness in the regional and global economy, (ii) increasing the sustainability of its development, and (iii) broadening access to opportunity. Three key cross-cutting themes are: (i) strengthening governance, (ii) supporting gender equity, and (iii) improving resilience in the face of external economic shocks, natural hazards and the impact of climate change. United Nations agencies are working in partnership with the Vietnamese government to develop the One Plan. The One Plan 2006–2011 built on key components of the UN Development Assistance Framework (UNDAF) and harmonised the individual Country Programmes, the Country Programme Documents and the Country Programme Action Plans of individual Participating UN System Agencies (17 participating UN system agencies). The One Plan 2012–2016 identifies the key interventions that will be made over the five years in response to the national priorities established in SEDS 2011–2020 and 2011–2015 SEDP and selected focus areas of UN in Vietnam. The overall budget for the One Plan 2012–2016 is USD 480 million. The UN Agencies system in Vietnam will concentrate on the focus areas: (i) inclusive, equitable and sustainable growth, (ii) assess to quality essential social services and social protection, and (iii) governance and participation.

The joint programme between UN Participating agencies, such as FAO, ILO, UNIDO, UNCTD, and ITC, under the "Development and Private Sector" Thematic Window of the Millennium Development Goals Achievement Fund (MDG-F) on green production and trade, increases income, and employment opportunities for the rural poor in four northern targeted provinces of Vietnam, namely Thanh Hoa, Nghe An, Hoa Binh, and Phu Tho. The joint programme focuses on five value chains: (i) bamboo/rattan, (ii) sericulture and weaving, (iii) sea grass, (iv) lacquerware, and (v) handmade paper. It has the approach of developing a better integrated, pro-poor and environmentally sustainable "green" value chain, enabling poor growers, collectors, and producers to improve the products and link them to more profitable markets. The total MDG-F fund was USD 4,120,000 within which the Vietnamese Government contributed USD 120,000 during 2010–2012.

Vietnam also has development programmes in place with the European Union, which are broader scale and mobilise effective public and private resources for development. Since receiving the first development grants from the EC 20 years ago, Vietnam has achieved in eradicating and eliminating poverty and sustainable development. During the period 2007–2013, EC support to Vietnam focussed on sustainable production in line with the "European Consensus Development", with an indicative allocation of EUR 304 million. The support was divided into two phases: Phase 1 (MIP1) with EUR 160 million (2007–2010) and Phase 2 (MIP2) with EUR 144 million (2011–2013). The objectives of the support were to focus on the implementation of Vietnam's socio-economic development plan (SEDP, 2006–2010), which stressed economic development, poverty reduction, the reform agenda, and reflected new challenges such as WTO accession and the health sector. Additional action funding was provided for trade-related assistance and support to EC-Vietnam strategic dialogue. Based on future "SEDP 2016–2020", the EU has reconfirmed its support for Vietnam as reflected in the overall strategic objective to further develop political, economic and cultural ties and to increase their visibility, understanding and presence in Vietnam. The multiannual indicative programme (MIP) for Vietnam provides financial support of EUR 400 million, of which 86.5% is for sustainable energy, 12.5% for governance and rule of law, and 1% for support measures. This shows the EU's support for the two sectors, making full use of the "leverage effects" of supporting ODA grants and the medium-term support of an enabling environment for private sector investment in sustainable and clean energy. The EU estimates that Vietnam will become a net energy importer in 2015 and will import half of its energy resources in 2030; therefore, cooperation on the development on sustainable energy is an important focus.

13.6 The SWITCH-Asia Programme in Vietnam

As part of the cooperation on sustainable development, the EU has already funded eight projects in Vietnam under the SWITCH-Asia Programme to promote the transition towards SCP patterns. SWITCH-Asia projects have been active in areas such as sustainable use of forest resources, corporate social responsibility (CSR), energy efficiency, sustainable aquaculture, and awareness raising for sustainable lifestyles. A brief overview of these projects is provided in Table 13.3.

Table 13.3: SWITCH-Asia programme overview in Vietnam

Project Name	Period	Main Implementing Organisation	Places of Implementation	SCP Practice	Brief Description of Objectives or Impact
***CSR Vietnam*:** Helping Vietnamese SMEs Adapt & Adopt CSR for Improved Linkages with Global Supply Chains in Sustainable Production	Feb 2009–April 2013	UNIDO	Hanoi, Danang, and HCM City	International standards (CSR)	Awareness of the multidimensional nature of CSR (ISO26000) was improved among SMEs; criteria and the procedures of the 2012 National Vietnamese CSR Award were redesigned — now including the core subjects of ISO26000.
***SUPA*:** Establishing a Sustainable Pangasius Supply Chain in Vietnam	4/2013–3/2017	VNCPC	Vietnam	Sustainable supply chain, resource efficiency, CP	At least 70% of the targeted middle to large *Pangasius* producing and processing SMEs, and 30% of feed producers, hatcheries and small independent production SMEs are actively engaged in RE-CP; and at least 50% of targeted processing SMEs are providing sustainable products with ASC standard to the EU and other markets.
***MEET-BIS Vietnam*:** Mainstreaming Energy Efficiency Through Business Innovation Support, Vietnam	04/2009–09/2013	ETC Energy, the Netherlands	Ha Noi and HCMC	Energy efficiency	The project promoted sustainable production of urban-based SMEs in Vietnam by supporting development of sustainable markets for affordable water & energy efficiency technologies. The project worked with private sector suppliers to develop commercially attractive business innovation packages targeting SMEs. These business innovation packages consisted of both a technical and financial solution.

***GetGreen VN*: Sustainable Living and Working in Vietnam**	4/2012–3/2015	Delft University of Technology	Hanoi, Da Nang, HCM, and Can Tho	Sustainable consumption	The project empowered "Change Agents" to change their consumption behaviour towards sustainability. Actions are taken for big changes for the environment through small shifts in their own habits, which contribute to an increased share of sustainable consumption by Vietnamese consumers by increasing the capacity of consumer organisations and the government in convincing and supporting consumers in making the choice for more environmentally friendly behaviour.
***SPIN-VCL*: Sustainable Product Innovation (SPI) in Vietnam, Cambodia and Laos**	4/2010–3/2014	Delft University of Technology	Vietnam, Cambodia, and Laos	Product design for sustainability	The project contributed to the improved innovative power of industry and the improved environmental and societal quality of products made in Vietnam, Laos, and Cambodia. This was realised by implementing SPI on a significant scale in these three countries. The outcomes of the action contribute to a decrease of environmental impact and improve social sustainability aspects connected to products over their whole lifecycle.

(*Continued*)

Table 13.3: (*Continued*)

Project Name	Period	Main Implementing Organisation	Places of Implementation	SCP Practice	Brief Description of Objectives or Impact
Sustainable and Responsible Trade Promoted to Wood Processing SMEs through Forest and Trade Networks in China, India, and Vietnam	01/2009–01/2013	WWF	Jiangsu province, Jiashan in Zheijang province, Linyin in Shandong province, and Zengding in Hebei province (China), Rajasthan, Kerala, and Uttar Pradesh districts (India), and HCM, Binh Duong, Dong Nai, and Binh Dinh (Vietnam)	Sustainable production, eco certification	This project focused on SME wood processors to build their capacity for responsible sourcing and production of forest products. 600 SMEs in the wood processing sectors of China, India, and Vietnam applied sustainable production techniques and provided certified sustainable forest products to national and international markets.
***Sustainable Rattan*:** Establishing a Sustainable Production System for Rattan Products in Cambodia, Laos, and Vietnam.	01/2009–12/2011	WWF Greater Mekong Laos Country Programme	Cambodia, Laos, and Vietnam	CP, product design for sustainability	By 2015, at least 50% of rattan processing in the region is sustainable, leading to environmental improvements, strengthened competitiveness, poverty alleviation, and national economic benefits. The project sought to address the "Sustainable Rattan Industries" and boosted the export of sustainable rattan products from Cambodia, Laos, and Vietnam.

The following two prominent projects funded by the SWITCH-Asia Programme are taken as case studies (see Boxes 13.1 and 13.2).

Box 13.1 Implementing SPIN — SPI by SMEs in Vietnam, Laos, and Cambodia

SPI is regarded as a significant factor in the approach to SCP, in a broad range in the three countries. Innovation for sustainable product design is the key to create new business activities. The four-year SPIN project with a budget of EUR 2.8 million (80% of funding provided by the SWITCH-Asia Programme and 20% from the project's partners) was implemented in Vietnam, Laos, and Cambodia from April 2010 to March 2014. The lead partner was Delft University of Technology (TU Delft) and other partners were the VNCPC (VNCPC), the Asian Institute of Technology in Vietnam (AITVN), the Lao National Chamber of Commerce and Industry (LNCCI), the Cambodian National Cleaner Production Office (NCPO) and the United Nations Environment Programme (UNEP). Built on the EU Asia-Invest project on SPI in the region (CP4BP — Cleaner Production for Better Products, November 2007 to July 2009), the experiences and lessons learnt brought into the SPIN project included: (i) the concept of Design for Sustainability (D4S) and the possibility to streamline this approach; (ii) added value from the suitability approach for quality products; (iii) the challenges for companies and their intermediaries in integrating sustainability; (iv) the need of companies for technical support to develop sustainable innovation and marketing capacity to sell new products; and (v) the need for strong commitment from companies.

Project objectives and general results

The project aimed to improve the innovative power of industry and to increase the environmental and societal quality of products made in Vietnam, Laos, and Cambodia by implementing the SPIN concept on a significant scale, in five key industrial sectors. Overall, the SPIN project was implemented successfully beyond committed outputs and expected results, especially creating significant impacts and interest from various stakeholders through a regional office called Green Office (GO) and three desk offices (in Ho Chi Minh City, Vientiane, and

(*Continued*)

Box 13.1 (*Continued*)

Phnom Penh) as support centres for companies and independent consultants and designers.

Selected sectors and SMEs

The project reached out to more than 540 SMEs in the region in five relevant sectors with 21 sub sectors. These were food processing, textiles, footwear, handicraft, and furniture sector. These sectors were selected due to their substantial share in the economy of the region, as well as for their overall negative impact on environmental and social sustainability, and as they had a high potential for further multiplication because of their structure and product portfolio.

Methodology and toolkit

Developed by TU Delft, a versatile toolkit was designed for a user-friendly and practical approach (Jansen and Crul, 2012). There were five instant packages for companies to apply. The project addressed not only innovation of products, but also marketing. The documents were made available online as a knowledge base for company consultation, combined with studies on policy and institutional mechanisms.

Training, Capacity building, and stakeholder engagement

SMEs were supported both on-site and remotely by SPIN resource institutions and experts that included 18 international experts, 23 local designers, 25 local experts, 11 Master's students, 2 PhD candidates from TU Delft and 17 international/local volunteers. Various forms of capacity-building activities, such as training, knowledge transfer, and awareness raising workshops were organised. In total, 18 official training courses and 12 other courses regarding SPIN methodology, toolkit, and branding/marketing skills were delivered to over 400 participants from different fields. To increase results, SPIN project established partnerships or cooperation with stakeholders: (i) 14 development

(*Continued*)

Box 13.1 (*Continued*)

organisations such as SNV, GIZ, Oxfam, (ii) 4 design organisations like VietMODE, and (iii) sector associations like HAWA.

Number of SPIN products & sustainable technologies

Over 2,000 new or re-designed sustainable products (in comparison with a forecast of 1,000) in key industries in Vietnam, Cambodia, and Laos were developed by SMEs together with the international/local experts participating in the project. These products covered daily lifestyle topics including living, wearing, working and eating. The products were made available to the public through e-catalogues. One essential factor that helped the SPIN project generate interest from companies was the development of over 30 sustainable technologies. These included technologies for renewable energy, organic farming, green materials, and packaging solutions.

Outreach initiatives

Together with several companies participating, the SPIN project promoted other initiatives including: (i) **i-nature** for sustainable agriculture, (ii) **Green Street**, an outlet and co-creation space connecting sustainable producers and consumers, (iii) **Green designer club** where exchanges took place between designers, and (iv) the **SPIN-e platform,** which helped the project interact online with companies.

Synergies

Within the project implementation period, the SPIN project created synergies with various partners in different fields that helped to strengthen the sustainability of project's results. These included: (i) GetGreen Vietnam for sustainable consumption (see case study in Box 13.2), (ii) Green Credit Trust Fund (funded by SECO) for technology innovation, (iii) One-UN for green production and trade for the rural poor, (iv) Future Living Studio project, (v) VECO

(*Continued*)

Box 13.1 (*Continued*)

for innovating packaging solution, (vi) World Bank for blended training solutions, and (vii) Leapfrog project from Dassault, France, for testing the sustainable design module of SolidWorks design software.

Policy advocacy

The sustainable and replicable outcomes from the project have been used as input for the promotion of sustainable public procurement policies by developing policy advice on favourable policy and institutional mechanisms that encourage proactive and innovative engagement of businesses. This attracted the attention of enterprises to the opportunities of shifting from traditional product processes to innovative approaches. At the national level, Vietnam and Cambodia's commitment to pursue clean and sustainable production (Green Growth strategy) provided the SPIN project with an opportunity for leveraging and advocating its policy recommendations for national strategies.

Remaining challenges for sustainable innovation

Although achieving certain results, the project also found that there were many external and internal challenges and barriers for sustainable innovation in Vietnam.

Internal challenges included: (i) Most SME leaders were aware or conscious about the importance of creativity and innovation, but did not think to transform their awareness into action due to limited knowledge, no methodology or tools, and limited supporting resources, (ii) Cultural and structural barriers in institutions that are managed in a traditional way. Leaders were often not able to share their vision with employees so that the entire organisation does not perceive innovation as strategic for corporate culture, (iii) capacity of accessing, understanding and responding to the market was weak.

External challenges included: (i) the involvement of the whole supply chain in the process of innovation and ability to participate in the global supply chain were limited, (ii) consumption culture and tastes of consumers were not sustainable so that the market for sustainable products was small, (iii) the mechanisms and policies to support businesses with sustainable innovation had not kept pace with the actual situation.

This case study was written by Nguyen Hong Long (Centre for Creativity and Sustainability, Hanoi) and Doan Minh Quang (iNature, Hanoi).

Box 13.2 GetGreen Vietnam — Sustainable Living and Working in Vietnam

The SCP concept has just been introduced to Vietnam recently, and most of the government efforts to promote it are in industrial sectors. Sustainable consumption is still at a very low level even in big cities where the citizens are usually more educated. For this reason, the SWITCH-Asia "GetGreen Vietnam" project aimed to improve the situation (Koning *et al.*, 2015). To promote sustainable living and working lifestyles in Vietnam, the "GetGreen Vietnam" project was implemented during 2012 and 2015 with three partners: Delft University of Technology, the Vietnam Cleaner Production Centre, and the Asian Institute of Technology in Vietnam. Aiming at contributing to an increased share of sustainable consumption among Vietnamese consumers, the "GetGreen Vietnam" project's strategy was to empower consumers to create **behaviour changes** and then become **change agents** who not only move to more sustainable habits themselves, but also inspire and convince their families, friends and colleagues to change. The main target groups of the project were middle class consumers including students, office workers, and community groups. Fifty-six experts from various organisations and different cities were trained on the methodology to become GetGreen trainers. The project developed the GetGreen Guidebook including eight clusters on different working and living topics (e.g., supermarket, kitchen, office, transportation) to serve as the source of information for its trainers and participants. The approach was to target consumers in the same living or working contexts (e.g., workers in the same office, people living in the same community) because Vietnamese people are usually collectivistic (or group-oriented) and tend to act when being supported by the people surrounding them. The group implementation approach combined informative meetings and field trips to enhance consumers' experience of **sustainable lifestyles**. This approach proved to be successful.

After three years of implementation, the project resulted in empowering 1,099 change agents from 52 consumers groups from Hanoi, Da Nang, Ho Chi Minh City, and Can Tho. They were encouraged to share sustainable consumption knowledge with their colleagues, friends, and family members to enhance the impacts of this lifestyle. To illustrate the impact, Mr. Le Viet Hung — a change agent in Hanoi who runs a small cafeteria — shared what he learnt in the project with his family and together they support each other to live

(*Continued*)

Box 13.2 (*Continued*)

sustainably. His electricity bill decrease considerably from VND 3,935,000 VND (EUR 165) per month to VND 3,268,000 (EUR 137) per month. This behavioural change took place only in three months and resulted from applying simple 'green tips', such as switching off lights when leaving the room and using stickers to remind people, unplugging all devices when not in use, avoiding using many electricity devices during the peak hours, etc. The bill, after that first month, continued to go down slightly.

The GetGreen Vietnam project, cooperating with sustainable consumers groups, also created a link between consumers and producers for more sustainable products/services. Sixteen **co-creation** sessions were implemented between consumers and companies in sustainable food processing, transportation, and tourism sectors. The method of the co-creation sessions received much positive feedback from both consumers and companies' representatives. Several achievements were implemented, e.g., by Viet Lien, a company producing organic foods. The company directly implemented suggestions that resulted from the co-creation sessions. Viet Lien developed new packaging designs for its organic tea products. Another example is Tra Que Herb farm (Hoi An, Quang Nam) which successfully organised a green market at their farm with a variety of organic vegetables grown by local farmers. The green market attracted more than 300 local consumers and international tourists. All consumers participating in the co-creation sessions felt more active and empowered to contribute to creating more sustainable products. Overall, the project's review showed that on average, the participants improved from applying 65 to 78% of all suggested sustainable actions. Prior to the project's implementation, the office worker groups were the most sustainable. But after joining the GetGreen project, the student and community groups had the most positive change. The target groups were mostly concerned with energy issues (project cluster "energy efficiency") and food issues (project cluster "in and around supermarket").

The two smaller cities, Da Nang and Can Tho, showed better results in terms of participation and change compared to the other bigger cities of Hanoi and Ho Chi Minh City. The difference occurs probably due to the fact that fewer similar activities are offered in smaller cities, creating relatively higher commitment from the participants to the "GetGreen Vietnam" project.

(*Continued*)

Box 13.2 (*Continued*)

The experience and learning from the project showed that motivations towards sustainable consumption in Vietnam include:

1. Tendency to save: Vietnamese people in general have the habit of saving, not only financially, but also using goods sparingly and keeping good maintenance.
2. Great concern about food safety: food is the first type of product for which consumers are willing to switch to sustainable alternatives, and are also willing to pay a higher price compared to the normal products.
3. High awareness of environmental issues: in recent years, people have become more aware of the severe environmental degradation and they want to do the right thing for the environment.
4. It's a lifestyle trend: living sustainably is a new trend in which young and open-minded people want to be in the lead.

Furthermore, Vietnamese consumers were involved through networking and information dissemination activities, including the website, social networks, brochures, press releases, and events. Other means of communication and behavioural change education, such as promotion and training materials (i.e., "Tips and Tricks" leaflets, short films on sustainable consumption available for Internet/PC use) also have been exploited. Based on the experiences of the "GetGreen Vietnam" project, a handbook for developing and implementing projects on sustainable consumption was published [Marel, Crul and Koning, 2015].

This case study was authored by Ta Huong Thu and Nguyen Thi Phuong Nhung of the SWITCH-Asia GetGreen Vietnam Project.

13.7 Conclusion and Recommendations

With the advantageous conditions of its natural resources, human capacity and geo-political position, Vietnam could be a prosperous nation. However, due to two bloody wars and being trapped in the cold war during the 20th Century, Vietnam is still a developing country with GDP per capita of USD 2,000. Although the country has made great progress through the transition period from a centralised-planned economy to the social-oriented market system, Vietnam faces many challenges to make its development path sustainable. Its population is young, but low skills levels have led to low productivity. Economic sectors are less integrated within the global economy even though Vietnam has participated in many global organisations and regimes, such as WTO, AFTA, bilateral trade agreements (e.g., with EU, Japan, China, U.S.) and the upcoming Trans-Pacific Partnership (TPP). Vietnam has enjoyed successful development of the labour-intensive industries such as food processing, footwear and textiles, and electronic products and equipment. With the export oriented-economy, many of Vietnam's products are exported to various countries, but the added value of the products is low. For over two decades focusing much on labour-intensive and less efficient industries, Vietnamese economy is ranked as less competitive due to the poor governance, weak physical infrastructure, and less innovative activities.

Regarding Vietnam's SMEs, outdated and inefficient technologies and equipment are still in operation in many areas of high-energy use. Aware of the urgent need to promote a shift toward more sustainable industrial development pathways, Vietnam's government has paid special attention to the promotion of green industry. The Green Growth Strategy was approved in 2012 and aims to achieve a low carbon economy, enrich natural capital, and direct sustainable economic development. The strategy focuses on three priorities of climate change mitigation and adaptation, green production, and green lifestyle. In particular, the efforts of greening production and lifestyles are part of SCP practice which is promoted by the SWITCH-Asia Programme. The objectives of the Green Growth Strategy could be achieved by accelerating the process of economic restructuring in order to use natural resources much more efficiently, reducing greenhouse gas emissions through research into and application of modern technologies, and developing infrastructure to improve the entire efficiency of the economy. International aid programmes have provided great assistance for Vietnam's development during its renovation period. In the next decades, the country still needs international assistance to promote economic development towards a more sustainable pathway as specified in the country's development strategy. The areas that need most assistance are rural and agricultural development, renewable energy, climate change adaptation and mitigation, and legislature law reform.

References

ADB (2015). Asian Development Outlook 2015: Financing Asia's Future Growth. *Asian Development Bank, March 2015.*

ADB (2013). Asia SME Finance Monitor, *Asian Development Bank*. Retrieved on October 14, 2015. Available on: http://adb.org/sites/default/files/pub/2014/asia-sme-finance-monitor-2013.pdf.

Binh, L. D. (2013). Investments by SMEs in EE in Vietnam and Main Barriers. Alternative options for financing support for investments in energy efficiency by SMEs in Vietnam. Consultation Workshop. Hanoi, November 13, 2013.

Cuong, T. T., Sang, L. X. and Anh, N. K. (2007). Vietnam's small-and medium-sized enterprises development: Characteristics, constraints and policy recommendations. *SME in Asia and Globalization, ERIA Research Project Report* 5, 323–364.

DANIDA (2012). *Project Document "Low Carbon Transition in the Energy Efficiency Sector"*. Ministry of Industry and Trade, Ministry of Construction of Vietnam, Hanoi.

EPI (2014). *Environment Performance Index*. Yale University. Available on: http://epi.yale.edu/data.

FAO (2009). Vietnam forestry outlook study. *Food and Agriculture Organization of the United Nations. Working Paper* No. APFSOS II/WP/2009/09.

GSO (2015a). Statistics handbook of Vietnam 2014. *General Statistics Office of Vietnam*.

GSO (2015b). Tình hinh kinh tế xã hội 2014 (Status of economics and society in 2014). *General Statistics Office of Vietnam*. Available on: http://www.gso.gov.vn/default.aspx?tabid=621&ItemID=14188.

Hong, P. N., Dao, Q. T. Q. and Thoa, L. K. (2002). *Ecotourism in Vietnam: Potential and Reality*. Kyoto Review of Southeast Asia.

Jansen, G. J and Crul M. R. M. (2012). *Sustainable Product Innovation. A Do-it-yourself Toolkit for SMEs in developing Countries*. TU Delft, the Netherlands.

Ketels, C., Cung, N. D., Anh, N. T. T. and Hanh, D. T. (2011). *Vietnam Competitiveness Report 2010. Central Institute for Economic Management (CIEM) under Vietnam's Ministry of Planning and Investment and the Asia Competitiveness Institute (ACI) of the Lee Kuan Yew School of Public Policy, National University of Singapore.*

Koning, J. I. J. C de, Crul, M. R. M., Wever, R. and Brezet J. C. (2015). Sustainable consumption in Vietnam: An explorative study among the urban middle class. *International Journal of Consumer Studies*, 39(6), 608–618.

LEDS (2014). *Workshop Report on Accessing Finance for Green Growth and LEDS*. Asia LEDS Partnership, Hanoi, March 12–14, 2014 in Hanoi, Vietnam.

Marel, F. van der, Crul, M. and de Koning, J. (2015). *Handbook Changing Behaviour Towards Sustainable Consumption*. TU Delft, the Netherlands.

MOIT (2014). Export potential assessment for Vietnam. *Ministry of Industry and Trade*, Hanoi, 2014.

Prime Minister No.1393/QĐ-TTg, (2012). Decision on Approval of the National Green Growth Strategy. *Prime Minister of Vietnam, Hanoi,* 2012.

SECO (2013). Vietnam Country Strategy 2013–2016. *Swiss Economic Cooperation and Development.*

Tuoitrenews (2012). *Vietnam Air Pollution* among *the Worst in the World* (*05/02/2012*). Available on: http://tuoitrenews.vn/features/482/vietnam-air-pollution-among-the-worst-in-the-world UNDP (2013). Human Development Report 2013, Vietnam. *United Nation Development Program*. Available on: http://hdr.undp.org/sites/default/files/Country-Profiles/VNM.pdf.

UNIDO (2013). Greening Value Chains For Sustainable Handicrafts Production in Vietnam. *Industrial Development Organization, United Nations*.

UNIDO (2012). Towards green growth through green industry development in Vietnam. *Industrial Development Organization, United Nations*.

UNIDO (2000). Assistance to Industrial SMEs in Vietnam: Moving towards a conducive policy framework and improved business development services. *Working Paper* No. 5. *Industrial Development Organization*, *United Nations*.

VEPR (2015). Vietnam Annual Economic Report 2015 "Integration Opportunities, Integration Challenges". *The Vietnam Institute for Economic and Policy Research* (*VEPR*).

VTB (2013). *Natural Rubber Industry in Vietnam, Vietinbank Sc Industry Report*.

WB (2015). Opening remarks at the launch of the climate public expenditure and investment review. *World Bank*, May 21, 2015. Available on: http://www.worldbank.org/en/news/speech/2015/05/21/opening-remarks-at-the-launch-of-the-climate-public-expenditure-and-investment-review.

Part III:

Sectoral Case Studies

Chapter 14

Sustainable Tourism in Asia — Current Situation, Trends, and Existing Practices

E. Kaiwa

14.1 Introduction: Boosting Tourism in Southeast and South Asia

One of the world's fastest-growing industries over the past 10 years has been the travel and tourism sector [WEF, 2013]. As a major contributor to globalisation and local development, tourism has the ability to connect diverse cultures and serve as a bridge between countries. According to the United Nations World Tourism Organisation (UNWTO) Highlights 2014 Edition, one out of every 11 people is employed by the tourism industry. Of the 1.087 million international tourist arrivals worldwide, 248 million (23%) originated from the Asia Pacific region. Of the international tourism receipts, USD 1,159 billion globally, Asia Pacific tourism generated USD 359 billion (31%) [UNWTO, 2014].

International tourism is also a major contributor to climate change. Evidently, 705 million tonnes of CO_2 were produced globally by air operations in 2013 and Asia Pacific's share of global passenger traffic in 2012 was 31.8% [ATAG, 2014]. Tourism growth in Asia is accelerating with a predicted annual growth rate of 6.2% over the period 2014–2018

[PATAmPOWER, 2014]. Recent estimates suggest that 27% of the world's energy-related CO_2 emissions were from Asia. Asia's share is forecast to increase to 44% by 2030 [ADBI, 2013]. The relation between tourist arrivals and CO_2 emissions in selected Asian countries is one of the issues discussed in this chapter.

The formation of the Association of Southeast Asian Nations (ASEAN) Economic Community (AEC) in 2015 brings the region to experience a massive cultural and economic exchange that will influence the tourism industry tremendously. At the ASEAN Tourism Forum in January 2014, the Pacific Asia Travel Association (PATA) revealed that forecasts of international visitor arrivals (IVAs) in Southeast Asia is predicted to increase by almost 10%, from 105 million in 2014 to 173 million by 2018. Southeast Asia is forecast to become the top growth region in the Asia Pacific [PATA, 2014b]. AEC will be the key factor of this growth and the economic transactions will increase accordingly. According to the ASEAN Comprehensive Investment Agreement, the promotion of foreign investment to ASEAN countries is a major priority as it stimulates the growth and development of ASEAN small- and medium-sized enterprises (SMEs) as well as multinational enterprises.

Tourism is also one of the important cooperation areas in the South Asian Association for Regional Cooperation (SAARC). At the time of writing, the most recent 18th SAARC summit was held at Kathmandu in November 2014 with the adoption of the Kathmandu Declaration, where leaders agreed to promote South Asia as an attractive tourist destination in a sustainable manner. The declaration also sets the tone for the implementation of the SAARC Action Plan on Tourism from 2006, particularly through initiating appropriate public and private collaboration [SAARC, 2014]. South Asia is predicted to become the second largest growth region based on its IVAs, increasing by about 7% from 10 million in 2014 to 14 million by 2018 [PATA, 2014]. It is important to note that these forecasts are largely conservative; actual numbers might exceed the forecasts.

From these two regions, the four countries Bhutan, the Philippines, Sri Lanka, and Thailand, in which the SWITCH-Asia Programme implemented sustainable tourism projects, are selected for further discussion. All four countries are tourism destinations with strong growth in IVAs. The Philippines is expecting 4.7 million IVAs and Thailand is expected to receive as many as 36 million in 2015, forecast as the top fastest growth destination in Asia Pacific 2014–2018, with an annual average growth rate of 27.5% [PATA, 2014]. In 2014, Forbes listed Sri Lanka as one of the "10 Coolest Places to Visit in 2015." IVAs to Sri Lanka is predicted to be 1.3 million in 2015 [PATA, 2014], however, that mark was already surpassed with 1.5 million visitors in 2014 [Sri Lanka Tourism Promotion Bureau, 2014]. Bhutan's IVAs were estimated at up to 58,489 in 2015 [PATA, 2014], however, the numbers already reached 116,209 in 2013 according to the Tourism Council of Bhutan (TCB). Despite the relatively small inbound volume in each of the four countries where the SWITCH-Asia tourism project has been implemented, Bhutan was forecast as one of the fastest growth destinations, with its average annual growth rate (AAGR) 12.94% as the highest among South Asian countries [PATA, 2014].

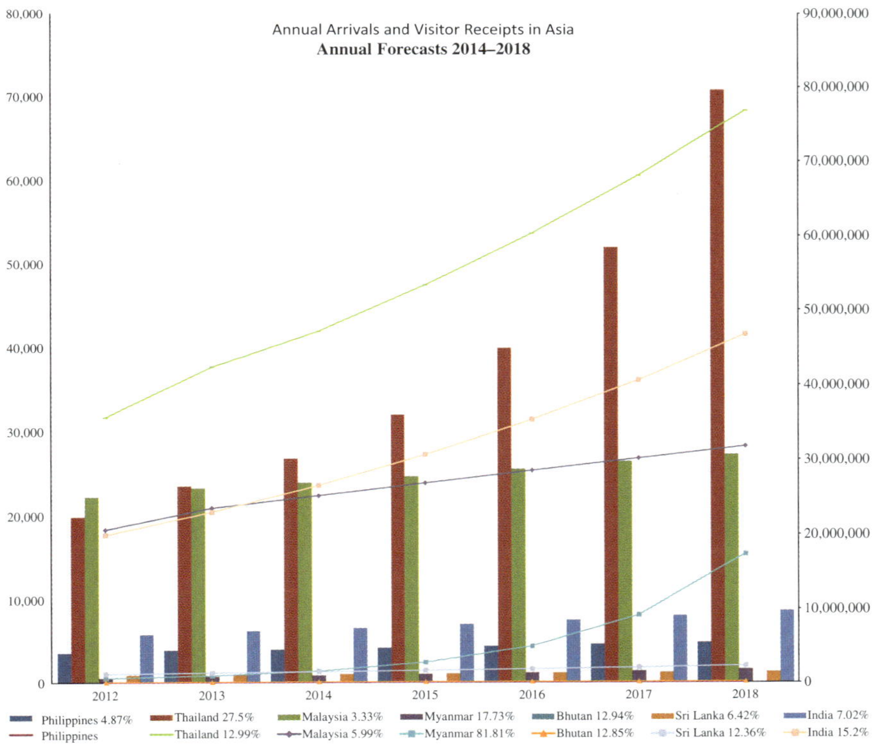

% indicates AAGR (Annual Average Growth)
Arriv Receipt

Source: Asia Pacific Visitor Forecasts 2014–2018 – Volume II (PATA, 2014)

The author's previous qualitative research [Kaiwa, 2014] which analysed Thailand's position on sustainability within the tourism industry and recognised the challenges in promoting it, was used as starting point for this research. In-depth interviews with industry leaders, such as the Tourism Authority of Thailand (TAT), Designated Area for Sustainable Tourism Administration (DASTA), and the Thailand Community Based Tourism Institute (CBT-I) were conducted. The author developed this chapter for the additional countries, i.e., the Philippines, Sri Lanka, and Bhutan, based on desk research and in-depth interviews with SWITCH-Asia project implementers in Thailand, Philippines, Bhutan, and Sri Lanka via teleconferences and emails. Case studies in this chapter were the main results from the interview and used for discovering the uniqueness of each approach.

14.2 The Role of SMEs in Sustainable Tourism

Both Southeast Asia and South Asia are regions with high potential for prosperity and are expected to see further economic growth. However, the manner in which these regions develop their economies and its possible tensions with the countries' sustainable development objectives, will be discussed in the context of sustainable tourism.

Sustainable tourism has gained heightened global attention as a programme initiated in 2014 under the UNEP-led 10 Year Framework Plan (10YFP) on sustainable consumption and production (SCP). The definition of sustainable tourism by the UNWTO [2005] states, "... Sustainability principles refer to the environmental, economic, and socio-cultural aspects of tourism development, and a suitable balance must be established between these three dimensions to guarantee its long-term sustainability."

The involvement of local stakeholders has been emphasised as one of the significant aspects towards sustainable tourism development [UNWTO, 2005; Byrd, 2007]. Among tourism industry stakeholders, SMEs are key players. Out of all firms excluding the agriculture sector, SMEs account more than 90% in most economies, create the high rate of employment and generate both domestic and export earnings. They are the lead player of economic growth and can act as drivers of structural change [Sharafat, Rashid, and Khan, 2014] that contribute to poverty alleviation.

Working closely with SMEs can be very effective and practical in finding solutions to sustainability. Cooperating with SMEs can avoid the bureaucratic procedures that are usually seen in larger enterprises. SMEs can often manage innovations much easier to keep up with the rapid changes in global tourism trends. Travellers looking for something unique often look for SME services, which have the ability to be successful in competing with international competitors through the local connections while being linked to global distribution value chains and networks [Imtiaz, 2008].

Partnering with SMEs also has advantages for potential investors. However, the real challenges SMEs are facing include limited competitiveness in the regional and international market, innovativeness, and most notably the lack of support from their home governments and international organisations. Severe credit conditions compared to large enterprises and equity financing make it difficult for SMEs to participate in international networking opportunities [Imtiaz, 2008].

One of the international cooperation programmes focusing on sustainability of tourism SMEs has been the EU-funded SWITCH-Asia Programme. The SWITCH-Asia projects provide local SMEs with opportunities to try out new sustainable approaches. By joining the SWITCH-Asia projects, several Asian countries have been able to gain access to an international network of sustainable tourism experts. Completed projects had shared their best practice and created positive awareness on SCP among stakeholders. Opportunities for scaling up the SWITCH-Asia project approaches by providing an outlook for the coming years and exploring potential approaches to sustainable tourism for decision-makers in Asia will be discussed below.

14.3 Unsustainable Trends of Mass Tourism

14.3.1 *Socio-economic impacts*

Mass tourism is tantamount to unsustainable tourism [Alampay, 2005; Butler, 1980]. Major challenges of Asia's mass tourism include the degradation of nature, loss of biodiversity, endangerment and extinction of wildlife, and negative impact to local communities. The number of tourist arrival represents a direct economic contribution to national economies;

however, it is important to note that the economic dimension of sustainability does not simply mean that more visitors is equal to more tourism receipts — that is expenditures by international inbound visitors. The tourism economy in total represents about 5% of the world's Gross Domestic Product (GDP) and 8% of total employment [UNEP and WTO, 2012]. However, tourism revenues often do not remain in the country [Diaz, 2001]. For example, about 70% of tourist expenditures flow out of Thailand [UNEP and WTO, 2012], 30% from Sri Lanka [Bowen and Pallister, 2006], and 55% from the typical developing country [FAO, 1997]. Due to international hotel chains, investors and expatriates involved in Asian tourism destinations, the financial leakage occurs and that causes only a low proportion of actual tourism revenue to remain in the host country and benefit local communities. Thus, the linkage between domestic industry and tourism should be tightened to sustain local economies [Situationer, 2006].

A critical point concerning the social unsustainability of mass tourism in Thailand is the *induced effects* of the proportion of the total contribution of travel and tourism to GDP. Induced effects represent the benefits to local community, such as hotel employees spending their income in local regions for food and housing [Stynes, 1997]. In Thailand, out of THB 2,401 billion (approx. USD 71 billion) of total contribution of travel and tourism to GDP, induced effects was only THB 386 billion (approx. USD 11 billion) in 2013 [WTTC, 2014]. Therefore, increasing the proportion of induced effects is an essential factor to be considered for sustainable tourism development. Furthermore, increasing medical tourists as one of the marketing strategies for Thailand [MOTS, 2012] is causing negative effects to local communities. Receiving about 500,000 medical tourists annually causes shortage of staff at local hospitals and the increase of medical fees for self-paying Thai patients makes it more difficult for local communities to obtain quality medical services [NaRanong and NaRanong, 2011].

Due to the emphasis on arrival numbers as an indicator of growth, the Philippines experienced imbalanced marketing and branding as a tourist destination, overriding the promotion of sustainable development. One of the popular 'sun & beach' destinations in the Philippines, Boracay, is an example of a small island facing socio-cultural challenges due to a massive influx of tourists [Ong, Storey, and Minnery, 2011]. With the growing population in the Philippines, labour migration occurs to 'touristy' islands and it creates social tension between locals and migrants. In their fieldwork survey, Ong, Storey, and Minnery [2011] analysed Boracay's economic benefits resulting from tourism. Most of tourism benefits went to non-Boracay individuals, such as 'resort owners' and 'investors from outside.' To avoid such leakage, SMEs having stronger linkage with local communities would need more support in terms of financing and capacity building by the government, to be able to play larger roles in local tourism industries.

Solutions to socio-economic problems caused by mass tourism exist. A case study of Cambodia identified the benefit of rural labour migration into indirect–direct tourism industries in Siem Reap [Biddulph, 2015]. Pro-poor tourism approaches are usually perceived to tighten the link between the tourism industry and local economic benefits and to reduce poverty [Meyer, 2007]. There are strong linkages particularly with micro-, small-, and medium-sized enterprises (MSMEs), which are the focus of pro-poor tourism [Ashley, 2005]. In the case of Sri Lanka, community-based tourism, ecotourism and other alternative tourism are perceived to bring high spending tourists and Sri Lanka focuses on this special interest tourist segment [Kamble and Bouchon, 2014]. Pro-poor sustainable tourism is one of the focused strategies in the Greater Mekong Sub-region (GMS) including Thailand, Cambodia, Lao PDR, Myanmar, Vietnam, and the Yunnan Province of China [ADB, 2011] and are studied well in literature [Hummel, Gujadhur, and Ritsma, 2012; King and Dinkoksung, 2013; Theerapappisit, 2009].

14.3.2 *Mass tourism and climate change*

In addition to the issues of revenue leakage and poverty, tourism also accounts for 5% of global Green House Gas (GHG) emissions. Theoretically, the tourism industry could be seen as a polluting industry mainly through emissions from transport services [UNEP and WTO, 2012; Gössling *et al.*, 2005]. Rapid economic growth and rising household incomes in many parts of Asia motivates people to travel more, and the aviation industry has increased flights and carriers to meet the demand. Low cost carriers (LCC) entering the market have accelerated more tourist arrivals [Duval, 2012] and

CO_2 emissions [Al-Mulali *et al.*, 2014; Peeters and Eijgelaar, 2014; Gössling, Scott, and Hall, 2015; Gössling and Schumacher, 2009]. The relationship between tourist arrival and CO_2 emissions is little studied, but it is critical for policy makers to understand the actual impact originating from national tourism policies towards economic expansion through increasing tourist arrivals. It is important for destination countries to create a sustainable tourism strategy and a monitoring system to minimise the negative impacts of tourism [de Sausmarez, 2007; Choi and Sirakaya, 2006]. The relation between tourist arrivals and CO_2 emissions in the selected countries are examined in more detail in the following section.

Table 14.1 shows a time series of each country from 2000 to 2010 that demonstrates correlations between IVAs, CO_2 emissions and GDP. Among selected countries in Table 14.1, Thailand marked the highest CO_2 emissions from domestic transport, about 55 million tonnes in 2010. Thailand's increment of IVAs of 6.3 million and average CO_2 emission per capita of 1.4 metric tonnes from 2000 to 2010 were also highest among the selected countries. The amount of CO_2 emissions is growing along with the number of IVAs. Interestingly, Vietnam shows the similar time series with Thailand. In fact, Vietnam marked the highest increment of 20 million tonnes CO_2 emission from transport in 10 years. The data indicate that the more arrivals a destination receives, the more CO_2 emissions are continuously produced, not only directly by tourism facilities, but also through additional economic activities.

Having an image of sustainable nation stemming from its policy and resolution that committed to remain a "carbon-neutral" for all times to come [Brown and Bir, 2011], Table 14.1 shows that Bhutan has largely maintained the same level of CO_2 emissions per capita from 2000 to 2010 while receiving 33,000 additional IVAs over this period. With limited carrying capacity as a small country, Bhutan's IVAs was the lowest among the selected countries. However, even small changes in IVAs could have a substantial bearing on the environment, though there were no data to judge Bhutan's overall tourism's impact on the environment. This is compounded by an inadequate awareness in finer distinctions between green tourism and the professional capacity in packaging and providing responsible tourism product options to visitors. Bhutan can take advantage from both the positive and negative experiences of other neighbouring countries

Table 14.1: Comparison of selected Asian countries' tourism arrivals, share of tourism of national GDP and CO_2 emissions

	2000					2005					Increase/Decrease [2000–2005]			2010					Increase/Decrease [2005–2010]			2013	
		CO_2 Emission			GDP [Billion]		CO_2 Emission			GDP [Billion]		CO_2 Emission			CO_2 Emission			GDP [Billion]		CO_2 Emission			GDP [Billion, USD]
Country	IVAs	a	b	c		IVAs	a	b	c		IVAs	a	b	IVAs	a	b	c		IVAs	a	b	IVAs	
Thailand	9.579mil	3	44	28.3%	122.7	11.567mil	3.9	54	25.8%	176.3	1.988mil	0.9	10	15.93mil	4.4	55	23.4%	318.9	4.363mil	0.5	1	26.547mil	387.3
Bhutan	8,000	0.7	n/a	n/a	0.439	14,000	0.6	n/a	n/a	0.818	6,000	−0.1	n/a	41,000	0.7	n/a	n/a	1.585	27,000	0.1	na	116,209	1.781
Sri Lanka	400,000	0.5	5	48%	16.33	549,000	0.6	6	46.6%	24.4	149,000	0.1	1	654,000	0.6	7	51.6%	49.56	105,000	0	1	1.275mil	67.18
Lao PDR	191,000	0.2	n/a	n/a	1.731	672,000	0.2	n/a	n/a	2.735	481,000	0	n/a	1.67mil	0.3	n/a	n/a	7.181	998,000	0.1	na	3,779,490	11.24
Vietnam	2.14mil	0.7	10	23.8%	33.64	3.477mil	1.2	19	23.9%	57.63	1.337mil	0.5	9.0	5.05mil	1.7	30	23.4%	115.9	1.573mil	0.5	11.0	7,572,000	171.4
Cambodia	466,000	0.2	1	67.3%	3.654	1.422mil	0.2	1	56.4%	6.293	956,000	0	0	2.508mil	0.3	2	51.3%	11.24	1.086mil	0.1	1	4,210,000	15.24
Philippines	1.992mil	0.9	24	36%	81.02	2.623mil	0.9	25	35.2%	103	631,000	0	1.0	3.52mil	0.9	24	30.7%	199.5	897,000	0	−1	4.681mil	272.1

Source: The World Bank Data [2013]; TCB [2014]; UNWTO [2014b]. Tourism Development Department, Ministry of Information, Culture, and Tourism Lao PDR.

a: CO_2 emission [metric tons per capita].

b: CO_2 emission from transport [million metric tons].

c: CO_2 emission from transport [% of total fuel combustion].

*b&c emissions excluding international marine bunkers and international aviation.

with mass tourist destinations, especially for Bhutan's tourism promotion programme, e.g., 'Visit Bhutan 2015' [TCB, 2015c].

So far, mass tourism has not yet taken hold of Bhutan, but the industry is growing and becoming more competitive. According to The Bhutanese news [2012], "clean" tour operators are losing out despite the fixed tourist tariff. Tour operators are slashing prices in order to receive more tourists in the competitive market. Regional competition could push Bhutan towards being a mass tourist destination. The challenges are to monitor the real business situation and prevent the influx of insensitive mass tourism to the country. At the same time, the Bhutanese economy does not have many other options to generate income and offer employment, increasing the number of tourists over time seems inevitable [Ethirajan, 2013].

Interestingly, in comparison with Bhutan, Sri Lanka had 0.6 tonnes per capita of CO_2 emission while IVAs tallied 654,000 in 2010 [World Bank data, 2010]. Like Sri Lanka, both Laos and Cambodia had lower CO_2 emission and higher volume of IVAs than Bhutan. Although the CO_2 figures stem not only from tourism, it is meaningful to consider these data. The proportion of CO_2 emission from transport of total fuel combustion shows that the transport sector contributes almost half of total fuel combustion in Sri Lanka, Laos, and Cambodia. It could be argued that the impact from the tourism sector is much powerful in lower GDP countries, and that might also apply to Bhutan.

On the other hand, increasing the frequency of flights to Sri Lanka and attracting more airlines to operate in the country are included in the government's policy towards achieving 2.5 million IVAs by 2016 [Sri Lankan Tourism Development Strategy, 2011]. The more tourists travel to the island, the more accommodation will be needed. Along with the targeted number of tourists, accommodation facilities will need to increase with the construction of 22,500 hotel rooms by 2016. The consumption of water and energy, and production of waste at hotels will increase respectively. That can in turn contribute to climate change that might increase Sri Lanka's vulnerability to extreme weather events affecting tourism [Moore, 2010].

In contrast with Sri Lanka, Laos, and Cambodia, higher GDP countries such as Thailand, Vietnam, and the Philippines have a lower proportion of CO_2 emission from transportation's total fuel combustion (Table 14.1).

This phenomenon shows that the contribution ratio to CO_2 emission from the tourism sector tends to be lower along with economic growth in the country, though the amount of CO_2 emission from transportation tends to be high. The Philippines also have a similar time series compared with Thailand and Vietnam, except for the increment of CO_2 emission. The Philippines maintained the same amount of CO_2 emission during 10 years, whereas Thailand and Vietnam marked high increase along with the high increment of IVAs. High volume of IVAs means high impact in economic figures but also in emissions. Therefore, the Philippines showing slower increment of IVAs than Thailand and Vietnam in the 10 years with less CO_2 emission is an indication that the number of tourist arrivals can have a substantial influence on CO_2 emissions.

14.4 Sustainable Tourism Policies in Asia

The need for sustainable tourism policies and monitoring systems to manage the potential negative impact from tourism has been described above. Initial tourism developments can become a political and marketing promotion to set a pathway for sustainable tourism. Setting down sustainability standards and regulations early on will channel tourism industry in being responsible for the environment, culture and community. Particular sustainable policies under national tourism offices were not yet found in the studied countries, except Bhutan. The sustainability concern in Bhutan's strategy and development plan is clear from the relevant documents of the Ministry of Tourism and the Ministry of Environment.

In addition to policies, sustainable tourism monitoring systems are vital to manage the destinations sustainably [Manning, 1999; Choi and Sirakaya, 2006]. As internationality is an unavoidable notion in the tourism sector, following international sustainable tourism standards is a way forward. Possible standards and indicators on which to base national monitoring systems include the UNWTO indicator system [UNWTO, 2004], Global Sustainable Tourism Council (GSTC) criteria and indicators programme [GSTC, 2012], Global Reporting Initiative (GRI) for sustainable organisations [GRI, 2013] and the European Tourism Indicator System (ETIS) for sustainable destinations [European

Commission DG Enterprise and Industry, 2013]. The following sections discuss national policies and institutions relevant for sustainable tourism development.

14.4.1 *Thailand*

TAT principal role is to guide the direction of tourism industry. As a government body, TAT must follow the appropriate structure, hierarchies, and procedures, which are laid down in the 11th National Economic and Social Development and the National Tourism Development Plan. Common goals of the government are: (1) sustainable tourism, (2) quality tourism, (3) creative tourism, and (4) competitiveness. The government's focus is "quality" rather than "quantity." IVAs of Thailand reached 24.77 million in 2014 [TAT, 2015b] despite the political instability that year. It seems that even without much promotion, Thailand's IVAs as in "quantity" are steadily increasing; whereas the "quality" is harder to promote, to implement and to measure. Therefore, TAT's action plan for 2014 focused on the core theme of "Higher Revenue through Thainess." The plan aimed to attract tourists through an authentic or typical Thai experience, Thai way of life, and Thai culture. Icons such as elephants, for example, represent the image of Thailand for many tourists. However, elephant rides cause the endangerment of Asian elephants and cases of baby elephants having been tortured to let humans ride on top of them have occurred in Thailand [Karsten, 2013].

The key measurement of IVA's "quality" has been the expenditure of tourists. Though this still seems as if the indicator focuses only on profit, the desirable meaning of a quality tourist for Thailand is one who understands and cares about the economy, environment, community, and local culture. The quality tourist would purchase handcrafts at the local market, would not litter at the beach and would not behave disrespectfully to locals. The balanced strategy based on expenditure and behaviour of tourists is important for the socio-economic aspect of sustainable tourism [TAT strategy, 2014]. Awareness of sustainability is a "first step" to become a quality tourist, and for host destinations in harnessing and organising local efforts and attitudes towards sustainable tourism development. Regarding the environmental component, ecotourism is one of the observable elements to raise awareness. A case study of Phuket [Kontogeorgopoulos, 2005] investigated the relation between mass tourism and ecotourism which are inseparable due to the financial factor of the tourism industry. In the past, mass tourism in Phuket began to shift to ecotourism in late 1980s by community-based tourism ventures. Recognition of the harm from mass tourism spurred to create awareness and demand for ecotourism activities among mass tourists. Uncontaminated areas in which ecotourism usually occurs are still close by the areas, which attract mass tourists. Therefore, it is an opportunity and challenge for ecotourism companies and sustainable tourism initiatives to draw attention with innovative ideas by transforming mass tourists into sustainability-minded tourists.

14.4.2 *Bhutan*

Sustainable development can be said to be the core philosophy and component of all of Bhutan's development policies, influenced by the 'middle path' that originates from Buddhism. The Middle Path: National Environment Strategy for Bhutan [1998] stated that the terminology of Middle Path is closely related to the concept of sustainability. His Majesty King Jigme Singye Wangchuck has recognised that Bhutan must follow the middle path to develop, which means integration of Buddhist knowledge into other sectors of society and economy. This stance is represented in Bhutan's existing tourism policy that values both economic benefits as well as environmental and cultural aspect for sustainable growth and development. The Royal Government of Bhutan states strongly that its tourism policy is one of "High Value, Low Impact." The vision of the TCB is "to foster a vibrant industry as a positive force in the conservation of environment, promotion of cultural heritage, safeguarding sovereign status of the nation for significantly contributing to Gross National Happiness (GNH)" [TCB, 2015b].

This policy, so far, appears to be working well; Bhutan has been able to secure tourism benefits while avoiding mass tourism and keeping its natural and cultural resources intact. The principles and purpose of the country's sustainability policy have created an image of exclusivity and high-yield for Bhutan. The Royal Government of Bhutan has set a daily tariff of USD 250 per head to control the number of tourists. Visas and a minimum daily package are arranged through agents. However, there is criticism about this practice and the restrictive policies, which only allow selected high-end tourists to enter the country. As a result, Bhutan saw a relatively low IVAs in 2013, with 116,209 visitors — the smallest number amongst the countries studied (Table 14.1) — though it was the highest tourist number in the country's history. Tourist revenues, however, were overwhelmingly high compared to the number of visitors, at USD 28 million in 2013 [TCB, 2014]. This is mainly due to the 'low volume, high yield' policy that only allows only high-income tourists to visit Bhutan [Dorji, 2001; Richter and Richter, 1985].

14.4.3 *Sri Lanka*

The Ministry of Economic Development in Sri Lanka has laid out a Tourism Development Strategy for the five-year period of 2011–2016. The main target is to achieve 2.5 million tourists annually by 2016. The plan commits to introducing a programme to develop the tourism industry and to fulfil the infrastructure needs amongst other requirements in order to attract tourists. The investment promotion for hotels and other facilities are being made available for potential investors as well. However, sustainability is not explicitly stated in the plan and ecological conservation is only mentioned in the context of wildlife protection. The former president of Sri Lanka, His Excellency Mahinda Rajapaksa previously stated,

> "My intention is to generate environment friendly sustainable tourism instead of relying only on leisure seeking popular tourism."
>
> [Mahinda Chintana, 2005]

The strategies related to the five-year plan are:

1. creating an environment conducive for tourism,
2. attracting the "right type" of tourists,
3. ensuring that departing tourists are happy,

4. improving domestic tourism,
5. contributing towards improving the global image of Sri Lanka.

Creating tourism-related employment is also one of the key objectives in the five-year strategy; the plan aims to increase jobs from 125,000 in 2010 to 500,000 by 2016. By creating employment, the multiplier effect of tourism development is expected. Many of the tourism-related companies are small and medium in size. Thus, SMEs can take advantage from the five-year strategy and link to micro-enterprises as well as to large-scale businesses and corporations through a variety of economic activities. Overall, there is still much room for further specific provisions to promote sustainable tourism in Sri Lanka's future tourism development strategies.

14.4.4 *The Philippines*

The Department of Tourism (DOT) of the Philippines has included a statement on sustainability in the National Tourism Development Plan 2011–2016 [DOT, 2011]. The 2016 target is 10 million IVAs and 35.5 million domestic travellers. A common stakeholders' goal envisions "An environmentally and socially responsible tourism sector that delivers more widely distributed income and employment opportunities." On the national level, sustainable tourism indicators were in place [DOT, 2011]; however, there are still challenges to apply these tourism indicators in practice at the local level.

DOT and the Department of Environment and Natural Resources (DENR) launched the National Ecotourism Strategy and Action Plan (NES) at the 5th World Ecotourism Conference (WEC) in 2014. The NES plan (2013–2022) includes sustainable management of destinations, education and awareness raising, involvement of local communities, development of tourism products, and improvement of tourism infrastructure and services, and human resource opportunities.

The SWITCH-Asia project "Zero Carbon Resorts" is an example of a pilot project for a local sustainable tourism programme in the Philippines, which also contributed to local tourism policy developments in Palawan. The project is now being replicated in Thailand (see Box 14.1).

Box 14.1 SWITCH-Asia project case study — Zero Carbon Resorts

The four-year SWITCH-Asia project "Zero Carbon Resorts" (ZCR) was completed in 2014 as a first phase which focused on switching from the use of fossil fuels to renewable energy for SMEs, such as hotels, resorts, and restaurants located in the Philippines. One of its accomplishments included international recognition of the project and ZCR members.

The first success factor was the selection of the pilot location, selected after careful observation. Palawan is an ecotourism destination and inhabitants are environmentally conscious and protective of their land. The Palawan Council for Sustainable Development (PCSD) is a multi-sectoral and interdisciplinary body composed of representatives from different local government units, NGOs, business, and minority groups. They worked closely with the lead project implementer, the Center for Appropriate Technology (GrAT), where all parties had a common vision of how sustainable development in Palawan should look like. The stakeholders in Palawan were ready to accelerate their sustainable development together with the SWITCH-Asia project.

One of the project aims was to link the tourism industry with the existing Strategic Environmental Plan (SEP) clearance system. In order to participate in the ZCR project, Palawan tourism-related establishments were required to pass through the SEP clearance system. A total of 150 (new or renovated) establishments have already been issued SEP clearance with ZCR terms and conditions. These properties are required to follow the 3R (reduce, replace, redesign) strategy when renovating or establishing a new building. By being a member of ZCR, properties receive guidance on how to become 'zero carbon.' The ultimate goal of the SEP modification is to be able to include efficiency targets as a monitoring instrument.

The second phase of the project, "ZCR towards Sustainable Development in the Philippines and Thailand" (ZCR for Sustainable Tourism) was launched in Thailand in May 2014 and will run till May 2018. This second phase aims to contribute to sustainable development in the tourism sector as well as its value chain in both the Philippines and Thailand. Incorporation of the entire tourism product value chain means that the acquisition and consumption of all resources (energy, water, waste, etc.) are considered, with a focus on the reduction of resource consumption and CO_2 emissions in both countries.

(*Continued*)

Box 14.1 (*Continued*)

Good practice from the first phase of "ZCR" project in the Philippines is now being replicated in Thailand. With the project, these two countries can deepen their understanding through cross-country visits and cross-cultural learning. The Green Leaf Foundation (GLF) in Thailand is one of the project partners and has developed a Green Leaf Certification Programme that can be enhanced further with ZCR measures, for implementation in Thailand, the Philippines, and beyond. During a stakeholders' meeting, the project attracted many participants, ranging from small to large hotels in four locations, Krabi, Kanchanaburi, Hua-Hin (Prachaup Khiri Khan), and Bangkok. The widespread acceptance and enthusiasm for the "ZCR for Sustainable Tourism" project from hotel owners was encouraging. The project also provides capacity building for engineers and professionals, with an additional focus on access to finance, strong policy dialogue, value chain development, and an overall emphasis on the reduction of resource consumption and CO_2 emissions.

The ZCR project implementation in Thailand builds upon previous results through its local partner, GLF, including the 2004 initiative 'Zero Carbon Destination at Kho Chang,' and the joint project, 'Dissemination of experience in the implementation of climate protection policy in nature-oriented tourism,' implemented by the German International Cooperation (GIZ) and DASTA (Guideline Low Carbon Destination Management in Thailand, 2012). Within this "ZCR for Sustainable Tourism" project, the GLF provides an online tool for the Thai tourism industry to calculate its carbon footprint. The project's main activity fields are energy efficient buildings and management, renewable energies, transport, nature conservation, water saving, and waste management.

14.5 Sustainable Tourism Governance: Top-down or Bottom-up?

The following section provides a brief analysis of various governance structures in the four selected Asian countries and shows how these governance approaches influence the development of sustainable tourism.

Table 14.2: Hofstede's power distance indicators for selected Asian countries

Country		2013			Power Distance Indicator [PDI]
		Population	Income Level	Religion	
Kingdom	Thailand	67.01mil	Upper Middle	Buddhism	64
	Bhutan	753,900	Lower Middle	Buddhism	94
Republic	Sri Lanka	20.48mil	Lower Middle	Buddhism	80
	Philippines	98.39mil	Lower Middle	Christianity	94

Source: The World Bank Data [2013]; The Hofstede Centre [2014].

To propel sustainable development through tourism, the contexts of government policies and interventions need to be well structured in accordance with national culture. For both top-down and bottom-up approaches in governance, challenges are commonly unpredictable structural changes, changes in personnel, and shortage of budget; all of which lead to only temporary trends in sustainable tourism, but do not achieve long-term sustainable development. Therefore, Bramwell and Lane [2011] recommend that adaptive governance systems which implies flexibility to changing circumstances and learning by doing, and continuous monitoring shall contribute to success for sustainable tourism in the long run. To navigate the political implications towards sustainable tourism development, communication with tourism stakeholders, especially with local communities, is essential. Many actors should be included in the process as governance has a broader meaning than just government policy. Therefore, participatory planning is an important element. In the broader contexts of participation, cross-border partnerships will help to manage destinations as an end destination of sustainable tourism. ASEAN AEC, GMS, and the SWITCH-Asia Programme are some of the international cross-border affiliations for integrating Asian countries to collaborate in their prosperities, along with environmental stewardship and socio-cultural protection, as well as economic benefits. Interestingly, the four countries studied in this chapter are comparable in terms of governmental approaches towards sustainable tourism development, as detailed below.

14.5.1 *Kingdoms of Bhutan and Thailand*

Thailand and Bhutan are both kingdoms with the majority of the population being Buddhist and the monarchy being especially revered. By using the widely used framework by Hofstede [1983], governmental characteristics of each country have been examined [see also Hofstede, 2011; Lee, Pillutla, and Law, 2000]. Hofstede describes national cultures consisting of four different dimensions, which are individualism versus collectivism, large or small power distance, strong or weak uncertainty avoidance, and masculinity versus femininity. The power distance score is perceived to analyse political systems. High power distance contexts are usually hierarchical and low power distance tends to be more egalitarian [Adaba, Wilson, and Sims, 2014].

The high power distance for Bhutan was shown in Hofstede's study (see Table 14.2) and royalty structures tend to support high power distances. Additionally, low population numbers in Bhutan facilitate a top-down structure. By imposing a high tariff (USD 200/250 per person per night) for international tourists [TCB, 2015a], Bhutan is also able to control the number of arrivals. Pros and cons on the tariff by direct tourism implementers, including tour operators, could be grouped for real need-based proposals as bottom-up approaches that will not be contradictory to the overall national objectives and structures. The efforts would need to have their own "middle path" approaches that combine top-down and bottom-up solutions. While Bhutan is developing and modernising, municipalities and communities with strong private sector stakeholders would need to be given opportunity to apply their bottom-up approaches for sustainable development in the tourism sector.

In contrast, Thailand does not have a high PDI (see Table 14.2), although the King is very well respected by the people. According to the World Bank [2014], Thailand's income level is stated as upper middle, while the rest of studied countries are lower middle. The growth of the middle class leads to more interactions with the world and that can change the perception of the country, which in the end contributes to the perceived PDI. With information from the Internet readily available and no government censorship on social media, most Thai people are closely connected with modern society. The pro-poor sustainable tourism approaches in the GMS Tourism [ADB, 2011] would not have been possible to implement in a top-down approach. Case studies in Northern Thailand have shown the importance of stakeholder commitments, especially at the local level in the process of pro-poor sustainable tourism development [Theerapappisit, 2009]. At the very beginning of tourism planning that should be developed from the grassroots up to global levels, locals need to be involved in order to sustain the sense of community and culture diversity in tourism attractions.

14.5.2 *Republic of Sri Lanka and the Philippines*

The population of Sri Lanka is the second lowest among the four countries, with a higher PDI (see Table 14.2). It seems that the top-down approach would work with a higher power distance and manageable population numbers like Sri Lanka. Income gaps in developing countries like Sri Lanka tend to create an uneven playing field in the market, thus governmental involvement (e.g., policy, regulations, financial support to SMEs) is needed in the process of developing sustainable tourism.

The PDI of both the Philippines and Sri Lanka are high, with the Philippines having the highest population among the four countries (see Table 14.2). With a relatively large population, a high PDI could contribute to effective sustainable tourism policy implementation. Government involvement might cause a slowdown in business activities due to bureaucratic red tape; however, all SMEs would be obliged to comply with national policy and could be required to share their good practice in the context of sustainable tourism development. By sharing their experience and best practice, SMEs or grassroots efforts can have a stronger voice. The Philippine National Eco Tourism Steering Committee stated in the National Ecotourism Strategy (NEC) 2002 that both bottom-up and top-down approaches are important for the country. It remains to be seen how the mixed approach will be realised.

14.6 Outlook for Sustainable Tourism in Asia: Up-scaling of SWITCH-Asia Projects

As discussed earlier, growth in tourism and IVA in Asia are certain. Without regulations to control unsustainable tourism activities in competitive tourist destinations, sustainability of the tourism industry cannot be ensured for the future. This study found that from the four countries studied, Bhutan has a stronger national sustainable tourism development policy than the other three. This policy, with a direct message of sustainable development combined with restrictions on numbers of tourists, could support the creation of demand for sustainability in the mass tourism market, should Bhutan choose to follow this trend. Destination appeal for branding is clear; Bhutan supports spiritual tourism in the 'Visit Bhutan 2015' promotion programme. Through this promotion, the government may increase the tourist tariff in the future, as in the late 1980s [Nyaupane and Timothy, 2010]. In the meantime, Thailand is promoting medical tourism as a main strategy [TAT, 2015a], which has both positive and negative influences on sustainable development. Without appropriate government strategy, locals will suffer from increased medical fees and shortage of quality medical staff (overloaded staff tend to have lowered service quality at hospitals).

In the development of sustainable community-based tourism, it is essential to share the economic benefits with locals. Yet, proactive activities in promoting sustainable tourism with strong economic benefits for communities are barely seen in the industry. It seems that comprehensive understanding of the terminology of sustainability and its environmental benefits is still developing in Asia. Sustainable tourism strategies should address community development issues that normally receive less attention. Therefore, it is crucial for governments to enact policies and regulations to mitigate tourism's negative impacts on communities before pursuing mass tourism pathway. Sri Lanka and the Philippines are recently focusing on increasing the number of IVAs. The window of opportunity to implement strong measures ensuring the sustainability of tourism activities is still open.

Investigation of priority issues of the countries where the SWITCH-Asia projects are implemented might be needed to ensure the projects' effectiveness, e.g., investment priority on sustainable tourism infrastructure along with soft skills components. In order to strengthen the awareness of sustainability issues among tourism stakeholders, it is recommended to enact a sustainable tourism policies based on "tested experiments" or "proven approaches". The SWITCH-Asia projects offer such approaches as they are advancing SCP practice among SMEs in various industries. Voices from 'the bottom' should be considered and taken into account when forming national tourism policy. Financial support schemes for sustainable investment from the government, especially for SMEs embedded in communities, are crucial in order to continue growth in the tourism sector. At the same time, efforts for human resource development in the tourism sector should be considered. Expanding the local network to reach technical expertise is also vital as external experts in many cases do not have sufficient knowledge of local conditions. Persuasive materials based on project lessons to convince decision makers to enact sustainable tourism development policy should be disseminated.

This study also found that there is a lack of an overall comprehensive sustainable tourism monitoring system in the countries where the SWITCH-Asia projects are implemented. The ETIS for sustainable destinations was commissioned by the European Commission in 2013; this system is still evolving, but it could be developed for or adapted to the needs of Asian countries. The Okinawa prefecture of Japan implemented tourism indicators that consist of sustainable tourism principles [Okinawa Prefectural Government, 2014] and the ETIS system was referred to in order to develop those indicators. The SWITCH-Asia projects in the four studied countries have developed indicators to monitor their progress, which are useful and practical for local SMEs. However, a persuasive proof based on a recognised international standard will be required for decision makers to enact national policy.

References

Adaba, G., Wilson, D. and Sims, J. (2014). Power distance and strategic alignment: A case study of a subsidiary of a multinational organisation. Available on: http://www.researchgate.net/profile/Godfried_Adaba/publication/261984392_Power_Distance_and_Strategic_Alignment._A_Case_study_of_a_Subsidiary_of_a_Multinational_Organisation/links/0deec5361024c718d2000000.pdf.

Al-Mulali, U., Fereidouni, H. G. and Mohammed, A. H. (2014). The effect of tourism arrival on CO_2 emissions from transportation sector. *Anatolia* 26(2), 230–243, doi:10.1080/13032917.2014.934701.

Alampay, R. B. A. (2005). *Sustainable tourism: Challenges for the Philippines: Philippine APEC Study Center Network (PASCN) and the Philippine Institute for Development Studies (PIDS)*. Retrieved from: http://dirp4.pids.gov.ph/ris/books/pidsbk05-tourism.pdf

Amnatcharoenrit, B. (2012). Thailand works to preserve 'sustainable tourism' The Nation. Available on: http://www.asianewsnet.net/news-28797.html.

Ashley, C. (2005). *Facilitating Pro-poor Tourism with the Private Sector: Lessons Learned from "Pro-poor Tourism Pilots in Southern Africa"*. Overseas Development Institute London, UK.

Asian Development Bank (ADB) (2011). The Tourism in the Greater Mekong Subregion (GMS). Available on: http://www.adb.org/countries/gms/sector-activities/tourism.

Asian Development Bank Institute (ADBI) (2013). Low-Carbon Green Growth in Asia: Policies and Practices. Available on: http://www.adbi.org/files/2013.06.28.book.low.carbon.green.growth.asia.pdf.

Association of Southeast Asian Nation (2014). *ASEAN Statistic*. Available on: http://www.asean.org/resources /2012-02-10-08-47-55.

Air Transport Action Group (ATAG) (2014). *Aviation Benefits Beyond Borders*. Available on: Switzerland: http://aviationbenefits.org/media/26786/ATAG__AviationBenefits2014_FULL_LowRes.pdf.

Becken, S. (2002). Analysing international tourist flows to estimate energy. Use associated with air travel. *Journal of Sustainable Tourism* 10(2), 114–131, doi:10.1080/09669580208667157.

Biddulph, R. (2015). Limits to mass tourism's effects in rural peripheries. *Annals of Tourism Research* 50(0), 98–112, doi:http://dx.doi.org/10.1016/j.annals.2014.11.011.

Bookbinder, M. P., Dinerstein, E., Rijal, A., Cauley, H. and Rajouria, A. (1998). Ecotourism's support of biodiversity conservation. *Conservation Biology* 12(6), 1399–1404, doi:10.1111/j.1523-1739.1998.97229.x.

Bowen, A. and Pallister, J. (2006). *Understanding GCSE Geography: A For AQA Specification*. Heinemann, Oxford

Bramwell, B. and Lane, B. (2011). Critical research on the governance of tourism and sustainability. *Journal of Sustainable Tourism* 19(4–5), 411–421, doi:10.1080/09669582.2011.580586.

Brown, J. and Bir, N. (2011). Bhutan's success in conservation: Valuing the contribution of the environment to Gross National Happiness. *Overseas Development Institute. ODI Publication, 111.*

Buckley, R. (2011). Tourism and environment. *Annual Review of Environment and Resources* 36(1), 397–416, doi:10.1146/annurev-environ-041210-132637.

Butler, R. W. (1980). The concept of the tourist area life-cycle of evolution: Implications for management of resources. *Canadian Geographer* 24(1), 5–12.

Byrd, E. T. (2007). Stakeholders in sustainable tourism development and their roles: Applying stakeholder theory to sustainable tourism development. *Tourism Review* 62(2), 6–13.

Choi, H. C. and Sirakaya, E. (2006). Sustainability indicators for managing community tourism. *Tourism Management* 27(6), 1274–1289, doi:http://dx.doi.org/10.1016/j.tourman.2005.05.018.

Clarke, J. (1997). A framework of approaches to sustainable tourism. *Journal of Sustainable Tourism* 5(3), 224–233, doi:10.1080/09669589708667287.

de Sausmarez, N. (2007). Crisis management, tourism and sustainability: The role of indicators. *Journal of Sustainable Tourism* 15(6), 700–714, doi:10.2167/jost653.0.

Department of Tourism Philippiness (2011). *DOT, The National Tourism Development Plan: Strengthening the Philippines Strategic Planning Process*. Retrieved on March 5, 2015. Available on: http://asiapacific.unwto.org/sites/all/files/pdf/philippiness_5.pdf

Department of Tourism Philippines (2014). *Tourism Industry of Performance 2014*. Retrieved on February 17, 2015. Available on: http://www.tourism.gov.ph/Pages/IndustryPerformance.aspx.

Department of Tourism Philippines (2014). *DOT, News Release DOT and DENR Bares Ecotourism Strategy and Action Plan*. Retrieved on March 5, 2015. Available on: http://www.tourism.gov.ph/Pages/DOTandDENRbareseco tourismstrategyandactionplan.aspx.

Department of Tourism Philippines (2015). The National Tourism Development Plan. *Strengthening the Philippines Strategic Planning Process*. Retrieved on February 25, 2015. Available on: http://asiapacific.unwto.org/sites/all/files/pdf/philippines_5.pdf.

Diaz, D. (2001). The viability and sustainability of international tourism in developing countries. *Paper presented at the Symposium on tourism services.*

Dorji, P. and Phuntsho, R. (2004). *Trends of Forestry Policy Concerning Local Participation in Bhutan from Policy Trend Report 2004*. Published by Institute for Global Environemental Strategies (IGES), Japan, Printed by Sato Printing Co. Ltd., Yokohama, Japan.

Dorji, T. (2001). Sustainability of tourism in Bhutan. *Journal of Bhutan studies* 3(1), 84–104.

Duval, D. T. (2012). Critical issues in air transport and tourism. *Tourism Geographies* 15(3), 494–510, doi:10.1080/14616688.2012.675581.

Ethirajan, A. (2013). Reality hits charming Bhutan. BBC News. By Anbarasan Ethirajan (2013). Available on: http://www.bbc.com/news/business-24726672.

European Commission, DG Enterprise and Industry (2013). *European tourism indicator system for sustainable destinations*. European Union, Brussels.

Food and Agriculture Organization of the United Nations (FAO) (1997). *Ecotourism And Other Services Derived From Forests in the Asia-Pacific Region: Outlook to 2010*. Available on: ftp://ftp.fao.org/docrep/fao/W7714E/W7714E00.pdf.

Forbes (2014). *The 10 Coolest Places to Visit in 2015*. Available on: http://www.forbes.com/sites/annabel/2014/11/25/the-10-coolest-places-to-visit-in-2015/.

Global Reporting Initiative (2013). *The Global Reporting Initiative (GRI) for Sustainable Organizations. G4*. Available on: https://www.globalreporting.org/standards/g4/Pages/default.aspx.

Global Sustainable Tourism Council (GSTC) (2004). *Sustainable Development of Tourism Conceptual Definition*. Available on: http://www.gstcouncil.org/sustainable-tourism-gstc-criteria/criteria-for-destinations.html.

Global Sustainable Tourism Council (GSTC) (2012). *Global Sustainable Tourism Council (GSTC) Criteria and Indicators Programme*. Available on: http://www.gstcouncil.org/en/gstc-criteria/sustainable-tourism-gstc-criteria.html.

Gössling, S., Peeters, P., Ceron, J.-P., Dubois, G., Patterson, T. and Richardson, R. B. (2005). The eco-efficiency of tourism. *Ecological Economics* 54(4), 417–434, doi:http://dx.doi.org/10.1016/j.ecolecon.2004.10.006.

Gössling, S. and Schumacher, K. P. (2009). Implementing carbon neutral destination policies: Issues from the Seychelles. *Journal of Sustainable Tourism* 18(3), 377–391, doi:10.1080/09669580903147944.

Gössling, S., Scott, D. and Hall, C. M. (2015). Inter-market variability in CO_2 emission-intensities in tourism: Implications for destination marketing and carbon management. *Tourism Management* 46(0), 203–212, doi:http://dx.doi.org/10.1016/j.tourman.2014.06.021.

Green Growth knowledge platform (2015). Tourism. Available on: http://www.greengrowthknowledge.org/sector/tourism.

Hall, C. M. and Page, S. J. (2014). *The Geography of Tourism and Recreation: Environment, Place and Space,* 4th ed. Routledge, New York.

Hamilton, J. M., Maddison, D. J. and Tol, R. S. (2005). Effects of climate change on international tourism. *Climate Research* 29(3), 245–254.

Hetter, K. (2013). Hotel towel dilemma replace or reuse? Available on: http://edition.cnn.com/2013/03/06/travel/sustainable-hotels/.

Hofstede, G. (1983). The cultural relativity of organizational practices and theories. *Journal of international business studies* 14, 75–89.

Hofstede, G. (2011). Dimensionalizing cultures: The Hofstede model in context. *Online Readings in Psychology and Culture* 2(1), 8.

Hummel, J., Gujadhur, T. and Ritsma, N. (2012). Evolution of tourism approaches for poverty reduction impact in SNV Asia: Cases from Lao PDR, Bhutan and Vietnam. *Asia Pacific Journal of Tourism Research* 18(4), 369–384, doi:10.1080/10941665.2012.658417.

International Labor Organization (2010). Developments and challenges in the hospitality and tourism sector. *Sectoral Activities Programme. Issues paper for discussion at the Global Dialogue Forum for the Hotels, Catering, Tourism Sector (23–24 November 2010).*

Imtiaz, M. (2008). Strengthening small and medium, sized enterprises in the Asia-pacific, travel & tourism industry. *Paper presented at the ITB ASIA, Singapore.* Available on: http://www.accessibletourism.org/resources/south-asia_sme_study_imtiaz_muqbil.pdf.

Inskeep, E. (1994). *National and Regional Tourism Planning: Methodologies and Case Studies.* Routledge, London, New York.

Jarvis, T. (2013). *Sustainable Tourism and Its Potential for Sri Lanka.* Retrieved on February 26, 2015. Available on: file:///C:/Users/Administrator/Downloads/TillyJarvisLiteraturereviewJuly2013PC.pdf.

Jauhari, V. and Manaktola, K. (2007). Exploring consumer attitude and behaviour towards green practices in the lodging industry in India. *International Journal of Contemporary Hospitality Management* 19(5), 364–377.

Kaiwa, E. (2014). Sustainable Tourism in Thailand: Current situation, trends and existing practices. *Paper presented at the The Third International Conference on Advancement of Development Administration* 2014 — *Social Sciences and Interdisciplinary Studies* (The 3rd ICADA 2014 — SSIS), Bangkok, Thailand.

Kamble, Z. and Bouchon, F. (2014). Tourism planning and a nation's vision: A review of the tourism policy of Sri Lanka. *Procedia — Social and Behavioral Sciences* 144(0), 229–236, doi:http://dx.doi.org/10.1016/j.sbspro.2014.07.291.

Karsten, M. (2013). *Why You Shouldn't Ride Elephants in Thailand.* Available on: http://expertvagabond.com/elephants-in-thailand/.

King, R. and Dinkoksung, S. (2013). Ban Pa-Ao, pro-poor tourism and uneven development. *Tourism Geographies* 16(4), 687–703, doi:10.1080/14616688.2013.865071.

Koldowski, J. and Kaiwa, E. (2013). *PATA Issue and Trend.* Volume 18,3&4 Quarter 2013, Bangkok.

Kontogeorgopoulos, N. (2005). Ecotourism and mass tourism in Southern Thailand: Spatial interdependence, structural connections, and staged authenticity. *GeoJournal* 61(1), 1–11, doi:10.1007/s10708-005-8631-6.

Lai, T.-W. (2002). Promoting sustainable tourism in Sri Lanka. *Linking green productivity to ecotourism: Experiences in the Asia-Pacific region*, pp. 208–214.

Lee, C., Pillutla, M. and Law, K. S. (2000). Power-Distance, Gender and Organizational Justice. *Journal of Management* 26(4), 685–704, doi:10.1177/014920630002600405.

Manning, T. (1999). Discussion: Indicators of tourism sustainability. *Tourism Management* 20(2), 179–181, doi:http://dx.doi.org/10.1016/S0261-5177(98)00084-3.

Meyer, D. (2007). Pro-poor tourism: From leakages to linkages. A conceptual framework for creating linkages between the accommodation sector and 'poor' neighbouring communities. *Current Issues in Tourism* 10(6), 558–583, doi:10.2167/cit313.0.

Ministry of Economic Development Sri Lanka (2011). *Sri Lanka Tourism Development Strategy*. Available on: http://www.sltda.lk/sites/default/files/English.pdf.

Ministry of Foreign Affairs of Japan (2014). *Kathomandu Declaration*. Available on: http://www.mofa.go.jp/mofaj/files/000061717.pdf.

Ministry Of Tourism & Sports (MOTS) (2012). Strategic Tourism Planning: National Tourism Development Plan (2012–2016) Thailand. Available on: http://asiapacific.unwto.org/sites/all/files/pdf/thailand_2.pdf.

Miura, A. (2012). *Daiyon no shouhi: Tsunagari wo umidasu shaykai he.* Asahi Shinbun Publications Inc, Tokyo.

Moore, W. R. (2010). The impact of climate change on Caribbean tourism demand. *Current Issues in Tourism* 13(5), 495–505, doi:10.1080/13683500903576045.

Munt, I. and Mowforth, M. (1998). *Tourism and Sustainability: New Tourism in the Third World.* Routledge, London and New York.

NaRanong, A. and NaRanong, V. (2011). The effects of medical tourism: Thailand's experience. *Bulletin of the World Health Organization* 89(5), 336–344, doi:10.2471/BLT.09.072249.

National Eco Tourism Steering Committee and Eco Tourism Working Group through the New Zealand Official Development Assistance (2002). *National Eco Tourism [NES] Strategy 2002*. Retrieved on March 3, 2015. Available on: file:///C:/Users/Administrator/Downloads/NES%20(1).pdf.

National Environment Commission. Royal Government of Bhutan (1998). *The Middle Path:National Environment Strategy for Bhutan*. Keen Publishing (Thailand) Co. Ltd., Thailand.

Niti, W. (2012). Policy on community development in Thailand. *Journal of Ritsumeikan Social Sciences and Humanities* 4(March), 13–26.

Nyaupane, G. P. and Timothy, D. J. (2010). Power, regionalism and tourism policy in Bhutan. *Annals of Tourism Research* 37(4), 969–988, doi:http://dx.doi.org/10.1016/j.annals.2010.03.006.

Okinawa Prefectural Government (2014). *Okinawa Kanko Toukei* (*Tourism Statistic Report 2013*). Retrieved on November 20, 2014. Available on: http://www.pref.okinawa.jp/site/bunka-sports/kankoseisaku/kikaku/report/tourism_statistic_report/h25_tourism-statistic-report.html.

Ong, L. T. J., Storey, D. and Minnery, J. (2011). Beyond the Beach: Balancing Environmental and Socio-cultural Sustainability in Boracay, the Philippines. *Tourism Geographies* 13(4), 549–569, doi:10.1080/14616688.2011.590517.

Pacific Asia Travel Association (PATA) (2014). *Asia Pacific Visitor Forecasts 2014–2018 Volume II.* Pacific Asia Travel Association, Bangkok.

PATAmPOWER (2014). *International Visitor Arrivals.* Retrieved March 15, 2014, from http://mpower.pata.org/.

Pearce, D. G. (1979). Towards a geography of tourism. *Annals of Tourism Research* 6(3), 245–272, doi:http://dx.doi.org/10.1016/0160-7383(79)90101-4.

Peeters, P. M. and Eijgelaar, E. (2014). Tourism's climate mitigation dilemma: Flying between rich and poor countries. *Tourism Management* 40(0), 15–26, doi:http://dx.doi.org/10.1016/j.tourman.2013.05.001.

People's Chinese National Tourism Administration (CNTA) (2015). *The number of Chinese outbound travel retrieved.* Retrieved on February 16, 2015. Available on: http://www.thepaper.cn/newsDetail_forward_1283008.

Richter, L. K. and Richter, W. L. (1985). Policy choices in South Asian tourism development. *Annals of Tourism Research* 12(2), 201–217, doi:http://dx.doi.org/10.1016/0160-7383(85)90057-X.

Rinzin, C. (2006). *On the Middle Path, The Social Basis for Sustainable Development in Bhutan*. In P. Glasbergen & W. J. V. Vermeulen (eds.).

Shah, K., Gupta, V., Boyd, C. and Concern, T. (2000). *Tourism, the Poor and other Stakeholders: Experience in Asia.* Overseas Development Institute, London.

Sharafat, A., Rashid, H. and Khan, M. A. (2014). The role of small and medium enterprises and poverty in Pakistan: An empirical analysis. *Theoretical and Applied Economics* 18, 67–80.

Sindecharak, T. (2013). *Creative tourism: Perception of Tourists, the Availability of Ownership and Possibility of Creative Tourism in Thailand.* Thammasat University, Bangkok.

Situationer, G. (2006). *Tourism as a Development Strategy.*

South Asia Association for Regional Cooperation (SAARC) (2014). *Tourism.* Retrieved on January 11, 2015. Available on: http://saarc-sec.org/areaofcooperation/cat-detail.php?cat_id=49.

Sri Lanka Tourism Promotion Bureau (2014). *Sri Lanka Tourism creates history by successfully achieving year 2014 arrivals target.* Retrieved on February 17, 2015. Available on: http://www.srilanka.travel/travel_news.

Stynes, D. J. (1997). *Economic impacts of tourism: A handbook for tourism professionals.* Urbana, IL, University of Illinois, Tourism Research Laboratory, pp. 1–32.

Thailand: A leader in sustainable tourism development in Asia (2013). *TIME,* pp. 3–4.

TAT News.org (2015a). *Chinese Investors aim for penetrating Thailand's Medical Tourism.* Retrieved on June 3, 2015. Available on: http://www.tatnews.org/chinese-investors-aim-for-penetrating-thailand%E2%80%99s-medical-tourism.

TAT News.org (2015b). *International arrival in 2014 Thailand.* Retrieved on February 24, 2015. Available on: http://www.tatnews.org/tat-will-highlight-%E2%80%9C2015-discover-thainess%E2%80%9D-asean-tourism-forum-2015-myanmar/.

The Bhutanese news (2012). *Undercutting on the Rise, "Clean" Tour Operators Losing Out, Sonam Choden.* Retrieved on March 3, 2015. Available on: http://www.bbc.com/news/business-24726672.

Theerapappisit, P. (2009). Pro-poor ethnic tourism in the Mekong: A study of three approaches in Northern Thailand. *Asia Pacific Journal of Tourism Research* 14(2), 201–221, doi:10.1080/10941660902847245.

The Hofstede Centre (2014). *Country Comparison.* Retrieved on January 3, 2015. Available on: http://geert-hofstede.com/.

The World Bank (2010). Countries and Economies. Retrieved on January 3, 2015, Available on: http://data.worldbank.org/country.

The World Bank (2013). Countries and Economies. Retrieved on January 3, 2015, Available on: http://data.worldbank.org/country.

The World Bank (2014). Countries and Economies. Retrieved on January 3, 2015. Available on: http://data.worldbank.org/country.

Tissera, M. (2014). *Janathakshan (Gte) Ltd and People In Need, Cz conduct, Sustainable Tourism Awareness Workshop on the EU SWITCH- Asia Initiative* [*Press release*]. Available on: http://www.switch-asia.eu/fileadmin/user_upload/Project_Downloads/Batch_5/Sustainable_Tourism_Awareness_Workshop_on_the_EU_SWITCH-_Asia_Initiative.pdf.

Tourism Council of Bhutan (TCB) (2014). *Bhutan Tourism Monitor Annual report 2013–2014.* Retrieved on March 3, 2015. Available on: http://www.abto.org.bt/wp-content/uploads/2014/06/BTM-2013.pdf.

Tourism Council of Bhutan (TCB) (2015a). *Minimum Daily Package.* Available on: http://www.tourism.gov.bt/plan/minimum-daily-package.

Tourism Council of Bhutan (TCB) (2015b). *Tourism Policy.* Available on: http://www.tourism.gov.bt/tourism-policy/tourism-policy.

Tourism Council of Bhutan (TCB) (2015c). *Visit Bhutan 2015.* Retrieved on June 6, 2015. Available on: http://www.visitbhutanyear.com/.

Tourism Development Department, Ministry of Information, Culture and Tourism, Lao PDR (2013). *Tourists Arrival in 2013.* Retrieved on Available on: http://www.nsc.gov.la/en/Tourism1.php.

United Nations Environment Program and World Tourism Organization (UNEP and WTO) (2005). *Making Tourism more Sustainable. A Guide for Policy Makers.* Retrieved from Paris & Madrid.

United Nations Environment Programme and World Tourism Organization (UNEP and WTO) (2012). *Tourism in the Green Economy — Background Report.* Retrieved from Madrid.

United Nations Sustainable Development Knowledge Platform (1999). *Economic Aspects of Sustainable Development in Thailand.* Retrieved on November 14, 2013. Available on: http://www.un.org/esa/agenda21/natlinfo/countr/thai/eco.htm.

United Nations Environment Programme (UNEP) (2014). *Negative Economic Impacts of Tourism.* Retrieved on January 12, 2015. Available on: http://www.unep.org/resourceefficiency/Business/SectoralActivities/Tourism/FactsandFiguresaboutTourism/ImpactsofTourism/EconomicImpactsofTourism/NegativeEconomicImpactsofTourism/tabid/78784/Default.aspx.

United Nations Environment Programme (UNEP) (2014). *UNEP news.* Retrieved on December 4, 2014. Available on: http://www.unep.org/newscentre/default.aspx?DocumentID=2812&ArticleID=11044.

UNEP. *Negative Economic Impacts of Tourism.* Retrieved on May 25, 2015. Available on: http://www.unep.org/resourceefficiency/Business/SectoralActivities/Tourism/FactsandFiguresaboutTourism/ImpactsofTourism/EconomicImpactsofTourism/NegativeEconomicImpactsofTourism/tabid/78784/Default.aspx.

United Nations World Tourism Organization (UNWTO) (2004). *Indicators of Sustainable Development for Tourism Destinations. A Guidebook.* World Tourism Organization, Madrid.

United Nations World Tourism Organization (UNWTO) (2005). *Sustainable Development of Tourism, Definition*. Retrieved on March 5, 2015. Available on: http://sdt.unwto.org/content/about-us-5.

United Nations World Tourism Organization (UNWTO) (2014). *UNWTO highlights 2014 edition.* Retrieved on December 4, 2014. Available on: http://dtxtq4w60xqpw.cloudfront.net/sites/all/files/pdf/unwto_highlights14_en.pdf.

Vainikka, V. (2013). Rethinking mass tourism. *Tourist Studies* 13(3), 268–286, doi:10.1177/1468797613498163.

Veal, A. J. (2006). *Research methods for leisure and tourism: A practical guide*. Pearson Education Prentice hall, New Jersey.

Wanhill, S. (1997). Peripheral area tourism: A European perspective. *Progress in Tourism and Hospitality Research* 3(1), 47–70, doi:10.1002/(SICI)1099-1603(199703)3:1<47::AID-PTH38>3.0.CO;2-F.

Wanhill, S. (2000). Small and medium tourism enterprises. *Annals of Tourism Research* 27(1), 132–147, doi:http://dx.doi.org/10.1016/S0160-7383(99)00072-9.

World Economic Forum (WEF) (2013). *Top 10 treads of 2014.* Retrieved on November 14, 2013. Available on: http://reports.weforum.org/outlook-14/view/top-ten-trends-category-page/ 8-the-expanding-middle-class-in-asia/.

World Travel & Tourism Council (WTTC) (2014). *Economic Impact 2014 Thailand.* Retrieved from London. Available on: http://www.wttc.org/-/media/files/reports/economic%20impact%20research/country%20reports/thailand2014.pdf.

Chapter 15

Sustainable Societies and Municipal Solid Waste Management in Southeast Asia

C. Curea

15.1 Introduction

Urbanisation is a mega trend in Southeast Asia and the urban population in the region has been growing at about 2.6% per year [UNESCAP, 2014]. Consequently, waste generation in Southeast Asian cities has increased rapidly over the last decade. The Waste in Asia report (2011) cites that the World Bank estimates waste generation in Asian urban areas to be around 450,000–760,000 tonnes/day; this is expected to reach about 1.8 million tonnes/day by 2025. With waste in Asia rising in tandem with the region's fast economic growth, cities are struggling to handle the growing amounts of household waste. The waste generated per capita is expected to increase in developing Asian countries while remaining constant or slightly decreasing in developed Asian countries (see Table 15.1).

The key Solid Waste Management (SWM) issues in the Asian Region can be summarised as follows:

1. Increase in the amount of Municipal Solid Waste (MSW) associated with accelerated urbanisation, population growth, economic growth, and changing lifestyles.

Table 15.1: Indicative comparison of waste generation across Asia and the Pacific countries

GDP USD/Capita, Year	**Low (<USD 5,000)**	**Medium (USD 5,000–15,000)**	**High (>USD 20,000)**
Municipal waste generated (kg/capita/year)	150–250	250–550	350–750
Collection rate	<70%	70–95%	>95%
Average composition of municipal waste (%):			
1. Food/organic matter	50–80	20–65	20–40
2. Paper & cardboard	4–15	15–40	15–50
3. Plastic	5–12	7–15	10–15
4. Metal	1–5	1–5	5–8
5. Glass	1–5	1–5	5–8
Waste regulations	None or poorly defined national environmental strategy, regulations are lacking, no statistics.	Presence of national environmental agency, strategy and legislations, limited statistics.	Presence of national environmental agency and strategy, strict regulations, comprehensive statistics.
Overview of waste management	Little organised collection, recycling by informal sector, open dumping or burning of mixed waste, high exposure to disease.	Moderate coverage of collection service, growing capacity for hazardous waste management, mixture of dumpsites, and semi-controlled landfill sites.	Increased emphasis on total waste reduction, resource recovery and prevention of hazardous waste; controlled landfill sites or incineration.
Waste recycling and disposal rates	Unauthorised disposal >50%; informal recycling 5–15%	Landfill >90%; start of selective collection; organised recycling 5%	Landfill and incineration at or close to 100%; organised recycling >20%

Source: Lacoste and Chalmin [2007].

2. Difficulty in securing land for intermediate treatment and final disposal (due to the NIMBY, or 'Not In My Back Yard' phenomenon), leading to serious public health risks.
3. High, but untapped, potential for 3R (Reduction, Reuse, and Recycling), and other alternative waste treatment solutions.

In most Southeast Asian developing countries, recycling is carried out under both formal and informal market mechanisms. The safety and health of informal waste pickers collecting valuable secondary materials from landfill sites, the air and water pollution from the recycling of e-waste and used lead acid batteries, water pollution from paper mills using waste paper, and the improper dumping of waste by recycling companies are all problems that affect society. Furthermore, recycled products sometimes do not meet product and safety standards, which could cause accidents or health problems. As household incomes increase from economic growth, the demand for low-quality products made from recyclable waste decreases. Improving the quality of recycled products to meet market preferences is therefore important for the recycling sector's economic sustainability.

Many Asian countries have policies in place to tackle the aforementioned problems. Nevertheless, such efforts are fragmented and not well coordinated. The primary focus is on the downstream solutions for which local governments allocate significant funds for waste collection and recycling/disposal, but without adequate consideration for resource-saving measures, economic returns, and inputs from secondary raw material use. Upstream process-integrated solutions would provide additional opportunities for resource reduction through increased resource efficiency, waste prevention, and eco-friendly design and products. This would require production processes based on principles of industrial symbiosis that the waste generated by a specific industry turns to be the required secondary raw material input for another industry. However, the current economic systems in Southeast Asian developing countries do not offer sufficient incentives for the conservation of resources and for potentially replacing primary inputs with distributed efficient waste inputs in the production processes. Currently, the dominant production and consumption patterns are not oriented towards resource efficiency, and, consequently, the amounts of waste generated are constantly increasing, ending up as a serious problem for final treatment and disposal. In this context, more sustainable consumption and production (SCP) patterns would help solve the waste issue from its root, in particular implementation of the 3R concept and sustainable product design to improve resource efficiency and reduce waste generation.

The remainder of this chapter will discuss and analyse the waste management of three countries: Cambodia, Lao PDR, and Vietnam.

15.2 Municipal Solid Waste Management (MSWM) in Cambodia

Solid waste has become an increasing concern for Cambodia, already facing various economic development issues, particularly in urban poor areas. There the population density is rapidly increasing, yet with extremely limited resources and safe alternatives for waste disposal. MSW in Cambodia (not including liquid and hazardous waste) contains many materials that can be recycled or "up-cycled" into products with a certain economic value, which should be separated before going to landfill or incineration for final disposal. This way, a recovery-based system (or a 3R strategy) not only contributes to the national economy through the production of valuable recovered materials (second raw materials), but it also alleviates the environmental stress by largely reducing the original volume of solid municipal waste, including the biodegradable fraction which is often the largest.

The lack of attention to sustainable urban waste management has resulted in large waste collection, transportation, and disposal facilities in major cities and towns in Cambodia. These are often operated by private small- and medium-sized enterprises (SMEs) that only fall under the weak supervision of local authorities and government-related technical agencies. In some cases, monopolies emerge, for instance, since 2003, the private-sector company CINTRI has held the 49-year monopoly contract for the capital Phnom Penh. Reliance on government officials to place the responsibility of waste management under the control of SMEs has raised the concern that the motivation to operate for a profit overwhelms the public's primary concern, which is a sustainable waste collection and disposal system to ensure efficient and safe disposal of waste.

15.2.1 *Legal framework for SWM in Cambodia*

The Cambodian sub-decree on Solid Waste Management was enacted in April 1999 and established the legal basis for solid waste management including MSW and hazardous waste. The main purpose of the sub-decree was to regulate SWM in order to protect human health and the conservation of biodiversity/environment. The sub-decree applies to all activities related to collection, storage, transportation, recycling and disposal of municipal waste, as well as to hazardous waste management.

The crucial roles and responsibilities defined in the sub-decree (Article 4) states that the Ministry of Environment shall establish guidelines on collection, transport, storage, recycling, minimising, and disposal of household waste in provinces and cities, in order to ensure safe management of household waste. Authorities within the provinces and cities shall establish a waste management plan for their provinces and cities.

Article 6 states that the Ministry of Environment shall also be responsible for monitoring the management of household waste, including collection, transport, storage, recycling, and disposal. The enforcement of the sub-decree is granted through Article 7, which states that waste disposal in public areas or any unauthorised site is prohibited. Articles 9 and 10 also provide guidance for the import and export of household/recyclable waste to and from Cambodia, given the fact that trans-boundary shipment of waste can harm human health and cause environmental impacts, particularly for developing countries.

Complementary legislative acts, which have been issued more recently, include the drafted National Strategy on Integrated Solid Waste Management (2011–2025), which also includes a 3R chapter. At the municipal level, the Annual Report of the Department of the Environment of Phnom Penh [2014] and the Decision of the Cambodian Council of Ministers on the improvement of liquid and SWM in Phnom Penh (February 2015) are the latest policy developments. So far, the practice of 3R, is active only in major urban areas, while in rural areas only the

Box 15.1 Classification of SWM in Cambodia

The Cambodian sub-decree on SWM defines the key terms of "solid waste" and "garbage" as follows:

1. "Solid waste" refers to hard objects, hard substances, products or refuse which are useless or disposed of, are intended to be disposed of, or required to be disposed of.
2. "Garbage" is that fraction of solid waste, which does not contain toxins or hazardous substances and is meant to be discarded from industry, services, public and private offices, households, and other economic sectors.

The MOE [2004], classifies solid waste into three categories:

1. Domestic/household waste.
2. Commercial waste (from businesses).
3. Industrial and hazardous waste, including healthcare waste.

concept of practical material reuse or recycling is implemented. In both rural and urban areas, it has been found that informal waste recycling is undertaken by private recyclers and some NGOs, but at a limited scale.

15.2.2 *Waste management system in Cambodian cities*

Cambodia's capital city, Phnom Penh, and 24 provinces (including 26 towns) under provincial supervision are all quickly developing their infrastructure and becoming more urbanised. Many of the cities within these provinces are extending their waste collection coverage to include the increasing population.

The Cambodian population in 2014 was approximately 15.4 million people [UNESCAP, 2014], generating an estimated 6,818,000 waste tonnes/year at the national level in 2008 [Sethy, Sothun, and Wildblood, 2014] which has since increased significantly. In the capital, the Environmental Department of Phnom Penh Municipality and the CINTRI sanitation company estimate that the current amount of waste has increased to approximately 500,000 tonnes/year [Sethy, Sothun, and Wildblood, 2014]. The Environmental

Department of the Phnom Penh Municipality's Annual Environmental Report [2015] informs that reported the amount of waste generated in 2014 was about 617,500 tonnes. According to Mongtoeun, Fujiwara, and Sethy [2014], based on data received directly from landfill sites, indicated that amounts of waste are quickly increasing from 1,027 tonnes per day in 2009 to 1,381 tonnes per day in 2013. Table 15.2 reconfirms the large variability in numbers indicating both a clear upward trend in waste generation for Phnom Penh, and insufficient capacity to account and manage the growing amounts of waste. This can be demonstrated throughout the country.

As shown in Table 15.3, JICA [2005] and MoE/DoEPC [2008] reported the average waste composition among the four largest cities of Cambodia are organic kitchen waste (63–81%), plastic (3–16%), and metal and glass (0.60–7.80%). Later in 2014, CINTRI refined its household waste compositions for Phnom Penh to cover organic kitchen waste (69.7%), plastic (14.5%), metal (0.5%), bottles/glass (1.8%), textiles (3.6%), paper (2.8%), grass/wood (1.5%), soil/stone (0.4%), and other (5.2%).

According to Sethy, Sothun, and Wildblood [2014], awareness of solid waste issues in Cambodia is poor and little attention is being paid to proper collection, transportation, and management of waste. Only a small number of towns (Phnom Penh, Preah Sihanouk, Siem Reap, and Battambang) have an official waste collection system, but without a related official

Table 15.2: Estimates of annual waste in Phnom Penh (in tonnes)

Year	Amount	Year	Amount
1994	14,500	2003	240,859
1995	14,548	2004	227,910[a]
1996	15,264	2005	266,781[a]
1997	15,203	2006	324,159[a]
1998	18,038	2007	343,657[a]
1999	20,440	2008	361,344[a]
2000	20,702	2009	393,045[a]
2001	21,050	2010	409,336[a]
2002	21,367	2011	438,000[a]

Source: MoE [2004]; [a] Environmental Department of Phnom Penh Municipality [2012].

Table 15.3: Estimates on household waste composition (in percentages)

Composition	Phnom Penh	Siem Reap[a]	Battambang[a]	Kampong Chhnang[a]
Kitchen waste	63.30	65.18	71.88	80.46
Textiles	2.50	4.34	2.88	1.26
Grass and wood	6.80	—	—	—
Metal	0.60	5.33	1.06	7.70
Ceramics and stone	1.50	—	—	—
Paper	6.40	0.88	2.72	2.10
Plastic	15.50	8.85	8.61	3.30
Rubber and leather	0.10	—	—	—
Glass	1.20	7.80	5.40	0.70
Other	2.10	—	—	—

Source: JICA [2005]; [a] MoE/DoEPC [2008].

reliable data collection system. Solid waste collection, transportation and disposal are properly administered only in the four population centres of Phnom Penh, Preah Sihanouk, Siem Reap, and Battambang.

New developments in the Cambodian waste management system, however, can be seen. In the past, CINTRI (the local sanitation company, part of CINTEC Canada) was the only contractor to provide the service of waste collection and transportation for Phnom Penh. However, in 2014, the Cambodian Government decided to put out to tender the opportunity to other sanitation companies, in order to reduce the monopoly on waste collection. In the same year, the Government of Cambodia requested three ministries (Ministry of Economy and Finance, Ministry of Environment, and Ministry of Industry, Mine and Energy) to survey and develop a plan for the taxation of waste collection services, separately from the electricity bill. The new taxation plan is, at the time of writing, still under development [Fondazione Acra CCS, 2015].

15.2.3. *Options for integration of a 3R strategy for Cambodia's SWM*

In 2009, the Cambodian Ministry of Environment, with support from the United Nation Environment Programme (UNEP), drafted a strategy on the

3Rs for sustainable SWM in Cambodia. The Cambodian national 3R strategy that was subsequently adopted aims to establish an efficient solid waste management system through an increased waste collection service, promotion of waste separation for recycling, enhancement of organic waste composting, and improvement of disposal sites. By end-2015, the government plans to compost 20% of organic waste from all sectors. By 2020, the government plans to increase composting of organic waste from households by 40% and from business centres by 50%. Because the 3R concept is new to Cambodian national and local officials, the Government of Cambodia plans to:

1. Establish the 3R policies and regulations for waste management at national and local levels, based on the existing environmental legal instruments and related statutes.
2. Organise capacity-building programmes for government officials.
3. Implement pilot projects in the selected urban areas.
4. Disseminate knowledge and implicate the 3R policies and regulations in both the public and private sectors, and
5. Integrate the 3R initiatives into national policy development.

It should be noted that only a few SMEs and NGOs have been involved in carrying out waste recycling in the country, while considerable amounts of valuable recyclable elements, such as plastics, have been exported to neighbouring countries, in particular Vietnam and Thailand.

15.2.4 *Improving the solid municipal waste management systems*

To improve the solid municipal waste management, a serious commitment to administer the existing regulations is required. The national government would need to develop practical guidelines for SWM suitable for different levels of implementation (cities, provinces) in the country. However, achieving real progress requires more synchronised efforts. Adequate budget allocations at both national and local government levels are required to ensure resources for proper SWM. Regulations directed at local governments should include increases in funding, which gives local governments the means to implement the regulations established by the national government. In some cities, the involvement of private sector and

SMEs in the waste collection creates business opportunities, as well as reducing costs and administrative workload at the local governmental level. However, local governments would need to monitor the contracted companies to ensure a correct and efficient waste collection service. Furthermore, public involvement through awareness raising and educational campaigns about waste reduction and proper disposal can support a more holistic approach towards sustainable consumption patterns (see a SWITCH-Asia case study in Box 15.2).

Box 15.2 SWITCH-Asia case study: Reducing plastic bag waste in some major cities of Cambodia: Less plastic, more opportunities

A project in Cambodia, under the EU-funded SWITCH-Asia Programme, is currently being implemented by ACRA-CCS Foundation (Italy), involving two local partners: the Department of Environment of Phnom Penh and the Royal University of Phnom Penh. The project objectives are to reduce the use and improper disposal of plastic bags in three main urban centres of Cambodia, which are the cities of Phnom Penh, Sihanoukville, and Siem Reap. Unlike in Europe, where plastic bags are mainly used for carrying packed dry goods, in Cambodia plastic bags serve as a low-cost substitute for widely different purposes (rice storage, gloves for food handling, containers for coffee, improvised measurement tools, etc.) without alternatives in place. It is estimated that around 3–3.5 million plastic bags/year — or about 16 tonnes — are disposed of in the municipality of Phnom Penh alone [Fondazione ACRA CCS expert interviews, in 2014].

Plastic bags are a rising national concern

In Cambodia, most of the used plastic bags are reused as waste liners and for further packaging. According to Fondazione ACRA-CCS's experts, the February 2012 Declaration by the Governor of Phnom Penh and the Clean City Contest (recently launched by the Cambodian Prime Minister) indicated that the issue of plastic bag disposal has received a higher level of political attention. The environmental impact caused by plastic bags has prompted some Asian countries to ban their use outright. However, instead of banning them, it is rather recommended that communication interventions, availability

(*Continued*)

Box 15.2 (*Continued*)

of substitutes, and incentives for the use of reusable bags to become part of the policy mix coupled with a behaviour change incentives for consumers.

The SWITCH-Asia project "Reducing plastic bag waste" aims at changing consumption patterns and consumer behaviour by working at three complementary levels:

- conducting a behavioural change communication (BCC) campaign that helps consumers in major Cambodian cities to adopt sustainable behaviour to use and dispose of used plastic bags correctly (level 1),
- providing eco-friendly alternatives to plastic bags (level 2),
- supplementing the efforts of the Ministry of Environment by setting an appropriate policy framework to minimise the impact of plastic bag disposal and on encouraging techniques for packaging replacements (level 3).

Through the project activities, local authorities and policy makers will gain knowledge on the **unrealised costs** associated with plastic bag usage to society, also skills and tools to reduce the environmental impact. There are an estimated 1,200 *commune* and district level officials who need to acquire internal expertise in order to effectively regulate, control, and monitor plastic bag waste in their communities. Other benefits are reduced numbers of plastic bags discarded outdoors. This will lead to an increased income generation for local SMEs and low-income artisans that produce viable and accessible alternatives to plastic bags. Tourists will benefit from cleaner cultural and recreational sites, which is a definite advantage to supporting and expanding Cambodia's tourism.

SMEs and low-income artisans are involved in the supply chain of alternative designs for plastic bags. The communication campaign is intended to change consumer behaviour and enhance the adoption of effective wrapping substitutes for a significant number of key actors: 1,000,000 women, 200,000 school children, 150,000 students, 12,000 vendors/SMEs, and 6,000 street stalls.

According to the ACRA-CCS Foundation experts, the inhabitants of Phnom Penh, Sihanoukville, and Siem Reap will benefit from a 50% decrease in plastic bag trade in target areas; a 60% decrease in the amount of

(*Continued*)

Box 15.2 (*Continued*)

plastic waste dumped in landfills in the three major cities; and an 80% reduction in the number of plastic bags improperly disposed. Additionally, they will benefit from improved knowledge on the costs of plastic bags to society and improved skills for 1,200 commune and district level officials who will acquire new expertise to regulate, control, and monitor plastic bag waste.

15.3 MSWM in Laos[1]

Most Laotians live a rural and subsistence-type of lifestyle. Household waste generation is small and mostly organic or bio-degradable. In the last decades, Laos has undergone a process of urbanisation that resulted in a growing urban population; between 1990 and 2014, the urban population increased from 15.4% to 37.6% [UNESCAP, 2014]. Along with urbanisation, Lao society experiences changing lifestyle and consumption patterns as urban residents consume more imported, processed, and manufactured products. Income levels are increasing through commercial and tourist activities. Laos' population and economic growth are concentrated in four main cities, the capital Vientiane, Savannakhet, Champasak (Pakse), and Luangprabang. Other cities, however, also experience economic growth, especially from tourism. Along with the economic growth that is partly caused by the flourishing tourism industry, Laos' new challenge is dealing with a growing amount of municipal solid waste. Between 40 and 70% of the waste, depending on the location, is being collected and disposed in designated open dumping sites, while the rest is being self-disposed by means of dumping or burning [Sang-Arun and Pasomsouk, 2012]. According to Ministry of Public Works and Transport and Ministry of Natural Resources and Environment [2013], in the city Kaysone Phomvihanh a recycling system exists, primarily based on

[1] The number of studies on municipal waste management in Laos is very limited, therefore this section about waste management in Laos mainly draws on the study by Sang-Arun and Pasomsouk [2012], prepared for the SCP Group of the Global Institute for Environmental Strategies (IGES).

informal collection in the city of the most valuable fractions, selling them to junkyards and dealers, and a private recycling contractor is operating a simple material recovery facility. The percentage of recycled materials is assumable low in the range of 5–10% of the total waste stream. The recycling patterns in other cities are likely very similar.

The capacity of local government to collect and appropriately dispose of waste is exacerbated by the lack of budget, e.g., to purchase sufficient new collecting trucks to replace the old, inefficient ones. The collected waste is mostly disposed in dumpsites, which are classified as uncontrolled, having no lining, leachate collection or treatment systems. Waste separation at source is not practised, except for those recyclable materials that can be sold by households (plastic, paper, glass) and food waste collection for animal feed that is practised by farmers. Finally, there currently exists no systematic urban organic waste use such as composting [Sang-Arun and Pasomsouk, 2012].

Laos also faces problems with waste management due to improper handling of waste. It is common for Laotians to burn or bury household waste in their backyards. However, rapid degradation of urban organic waste has made Laotians change their way of managing waste by starting to treat the organic waste in the household or at the disposal site. According to Sang-Arun and Pasomsouk [2012], a family with 2–3 members generated about 2–4 kg of organic and food waste/day. The majority of households are single rooms with a small space for gardening, which would allow for organic waste treatment by composting or anaerobic digestion.

15.3.1 *Lao legislation and policies related to SWM*

The framework and legislation for waste management in Laos have been in progress for a number of years. The Department of Housing and Urban Planning (DHUP) of the Lao Ministry of Public Work and Transport and the Ministry of Natural Resources and Environment (MoNRE) are both responsible for municipal solid waste management. While DHUP is responsible for urban planning and development, MoNRE deals with environmental issues related to SWM. Several Lao authorities have drafted relevant laws and national policies to improve MSWM. Under several legislative acts, the Urban Development and Administrative Agency (UDAA) is made responsible for solid waste collection and disposal in each city. More recent laws and regulations addressing waste issue include the Agreement of Waste Disposal Site Management of 2008 and the Agreement of the National Environmental Quality Standard issued in 2009. However, Laos still needs to establish a clear definition of waste, as categorised by main types of waste (municipal, household, industrial, healthcare, packaging waste, specific waste streams, etc.). Also, linking the policy and legal framework for SWM system with other established frameworks such as resource efficiency and SCP, would be an important next step to take. The government of Cambodia already in 2008 launched its Strategic Framework for the National Sustainable Development Strategy, which provides a conceptual framework to better integrate sustainable development principles into national and sectoral development planning.

Similarly, the National Environmental Strategy to 2020 and the Environment Action Plan 2006–2010 as well as the National Environment Strategy and Action Plan (NES-AP) aim at securing sustainable development and contribute to poverty eradication through proper environmental management and sustainable use of natural resources. So far, no specific SCP legislations or policies, which relate to waste management, have been issued.

15.3.2 *Classifying waste in Laos*

Laos still needs to develop a clear definition of waste based on the compositions to enable more efficient waste management. Establishing a reliable and harmonised national database based on clear definitions of waste compositions, statistical surveys for generation of data and indicators, and a national monitoring and control network for the SWM system is also required. So far a comprehensive national waste composition data in Laos are still lacking. However, research carried out in Laos' major cities by Sang-Arun and Pasomsouk [2012], who estimate waste composition at landfill sites of Vientiane, Luangprabang, Savannakhet, and Champasak.

Table 15.4: Waste composition in Lao four major cities

Waste Fraction	Vientiane %	Luangprabang %	Savannakhet %	Champasak %
Food & vegetables	30	51	54	62
Wood, grass, trees, leaves	19	23	16	21
Paper	6	8	9	4
Plastic	13	9	15	6
Glass	6	6	2	2
Metal	3	1	1	1
Textiles	2	1	1	1
Other	21	1	2	3
TOTAL	100	100	100	100

Source: Sang-Arun and Pasomsouk [2012].

It found the composition of waste from the four cities is largely the same: biodegradable waste (food and garden waste) is the largest waste composition in all cities, ranging from about 50% in Vientiane Capital to 70–80% in the other three cities, as shown in Table 15.4.

15.3.3 *Waste collection and transport*

Currently, the collection and disposal of municipal solid waste in Vientiane, Luangprabang, Savannakhet, and Champasak are much more organised than in other Lao cities. Waste collection service in urban areas is organised by the UDAA. However, some municipalities, such as that in Luangprabang, transfer waste collection attributions to private sector which in most cases are SMEs. Each city has a number of trucks that collect waste from households generally once or twice a week. The fee for the collection service is about USD 1.25–2.25 per month per household. Based on the UDAA records, the average amounts of waste collected and transported to landfill range from 40% to 70% of the total (Table 15.5). The coverage of this waste collection service is highly dependent on the number of waste collection trucks and the rate at which waste collection fees are received from the residents.

Table 15.5: Waste transported to landfill in 2010

	Vientiane	Luangprabang	Savannakhet	Champasak
Estimated waste generation in municipal areas (tonnes/day)	300	50	42	60
Collection and disposal in landfills (tonnes/day)	180	30	30	25
Coverage (%)	60	60	70	42

Source: Sang-Arun and Pasomsouk [2012].

15.3.4 *Recommendations to improve the MSWM in Laos*

Raising awareness of residents: According to Sang-Arun and Pasomsouk [2012], the main priority should be given to raise the awareness about waste management among consumers and urban residents. Due to a low level of awareness, many people still do not separate their waste, reuse it, or treat it properly. Changes in behaviour can contribute to improving the municipal solid waste selection for recycling and disposal by the simple practice of discarding the selected waste into specific waste bins, assuming that those waste bins are already in place. Local governments can increase public awareness not to dispose waste in public spaces, but to prioritise discarding waste in specific waste bins.

Implementing waste separation at source: Waste separation at source helps reducing the volume of waste transported and disposed of in final disposal sites, making transportation easier, increasing recovery rates of valuable waste, extending lifetimes of landfills, keeping the city clean, minimising the risk of sewerage clogging and overspills, and avoiding soil and water pollution. However, this practice is still to be established in Laos. Separation of recyclables or sellable waste can be encouraged through awareness raising campaigns. For this purpose, local governments could set up educational activities to promote city-wide recycling. Future SWITCH-Asia projects in Laos could also take up the waste issue and help raise the awareness to change the waste disposal behaviour of residents and enhance waste management capacities of local authorities and SMEs.

Improving organic waste management through composting: Taking into consideration the type of waste mostly produced by Lao households, that is organic waste, composting is a promising waste management method. The method has significant potential to reduce the waste disposed of in uncontrolled landfills, avoid methane emission during waste degradation, improve soil quality, and increase carbon sequestration into the soil. Laos has good opportunities to promote household composting and centralised small-scale composting facilities. Composting techniques can range from simple windrow composting to a complex in-vessel system that requires advanced equipment and automatic control. The windrow composting technique does not require high capital investment. This method can be put into practice from a small scale, at the household level with less than 1 kg waste input per day, to a large scale, such as at the municipal or sub-regional levels.

Household composting system is relatively simple and does not require large operating space. Households would only need to adjust the moisture/dryness ratio of waste composition in a composting bin. Centralised small-scale composting facilities can create new business opportunities for local SMEs and would be suitable to manage from one tonne to several tonnes per day of organic waste. The methods available are also based on simple composting techniques.

15.4 Waste Management in Vietnam

Currently Vietnam is experiencing a phase of rapid economic growth which tends to concentrate in big cities as business centres. As a result, the country is undergoing considerable urbanisation. According to statistics published by the Vietnam Housing and Population Census in 1999 and 2009, new consumption patterns have emerged due to higher living standards and increased average incomes per household [Central Population and Housing Census Steering Committee, 2010]. Economic reforms have transformed Vietnam, from one of the world's poorest countries 25 years ago to a lower middle-income country (MIC); the 2014 per capita income was about USD 1,890 [World Bank, 2015]. Consequently, solid waste generation increased to about 24 million tonnes per year in 2010 and several forecasts predict about 40 million tonnes for 2015 and 53 million tonnes for 2030, due to high rates of urbanisation, increasing household incomes, changing consumption habits, and population growth [Thai, Pariatamby, and Tanaka 2014].

15.4.1 *SWM in Vietnam*

Thanh and Matsui [2010] reported that the Urban Environment Company (URENCO) organised about 70–80% of the national waste collection, while the rest has been collected and managed by local small- and medium-sized sanitation companies. In this context, the partnership between government and SMEs is essential to ensure a well-organised solid waste management system in the country.

To have a more sustainable approach to waste management in the country, the 3R approach that minimises waste generation can play a key role. The recycling sector in Vietnam is already very active, thus providing a good basis for high reuse and recycling rates. The **informal recycling sector**, which includes waste-pickers and scavengers, also plays a significant role in waste management and recycling activities. Plastic recycling is a growing sector in Vietnam, which attracts large investments from private companies. For instance, the Vietnam-based Thanh Tai Gas Company installed a recycling plant in 2012, which has a capacity of up to 1.5 billion PET bottles per year [Waste Management World, 2011]. In addition to efficient recycling facilities, initiatives focusing on changing consumption patterns and waste generation of the growing urban consumer class are becoming increasingly important. An example of such an initiative is the SWITCH-Asia project "GetGreen Vietnam" (see Box 13.2, in Chapter 13).

15.4.2 *MSWM in Vietnam*

According to data reported by Vietnamese provinces in 2008 [Thai, 2014], the daily average waste generation volumes range from 0.8 to 1.2 kg per person per day in large cities and 0.35–0.50 kg per person per day in small towns. The generation volumes vary due to factors such as living conditions in urban areas, different categories of urban areas, topography, and socio-economic

Table 15.6: Variation of solid waste volumes in Vietnam (in tonnes per year)

Type of Solid Waste	2003	2008
Municipal solid waste	6,400,000	12,802,000
Industrial solid waste	2,638,400	4,786,000
Healthcare solid waste	21,500	179,000
Rural solid waste	6,400,000	9,078,000
Craft village solid waste	774,000	1,023,000

Source: Thai, Pariatamby, and Tanaka [2014].

development of each province, etc. The variation of solid waste generation in Vietnam is shown in Table 15.6.

Further, municipal solid waste among major cities in 2009 can be classified into:

- organic substances (accounted for a high rate of 50–66%),
- inert matters (13–28%),
- plastic (3–13%),
- paper and cardboard (3–10%).

Figures in Table 15.7 are based on the average composition of solids taken from selected samples from various city locations of Hanoi, Da Nang, Hue, and Pleiku (residential areas, markets, and landfill).

In most urban areas, MSW is not yet sorted at source. Few households separate their solid waste, selling bottles, jars, metal, and paper to scrap collectors. However, in recent years, a number of pilot projects promoting solid waste separation have been implemented in the large cities of Hanoi, Da Nang, and Ho Chi Minh. For several reasons, these efforts have not yet been very successful, partly due to the lack of community awareness and few processing facilities for the separated recyclables. In urban areas, household waste is mostly sorted by private waste collectors.

At the national level, the average rate of MSW collection is estimated to be about 72%. The collection rate in urban areas has increased from 80% in 2008 to 85% in 2010, but the percentage fell drastically to 45% in rural areas in 2010, while the reuse and recycling rate was estimated to range from 18 to 28% in the same year. In urban areas, SMEs and

Table 15.7: Average composition of solid waste (in % weight) in Vietnam's major cities in 2009

Composition	Hanoi[a]	Da Nang[b]	Hue[c]	Pleiku[d]
Organic	53.80	66.0	55.0	60.49
Plastic	3.42	4.0	5.2	12.77
Paper and cardboard	4.2	3.1	4.4	9.65
Metal	1.4	4.9	7.0	1.16
Glass	1.0	0.9	1.8	0.13
Inert matters	28.18	16.4	21.3	12.6
Rubber	4.9	1.6	1.5	2.8
Textile rags	1.7	2.3	3.0	0
Hazardous substances	1.4	0.8	0.8	0.4
Total	100	100	100	100
Moisture content (%)	43.04	51.2	50.0	50.5
Ashes (%)	13.70	16.0	15.5	13.9
Density in bulk (tonne/m^3)	0.41	0.40	0.40	0.38
Recyclable fractions (%)	16.62	16.80	22.90	26.51

Notes: a: city category special, b: city category I, c: city category II, d: city category III. *Classification in accordance with the 2009* Vietnam Governmental Decree No. 42/2009/ND-CP.
Source: Thai, Pariatamby, and Tanaka [2014].

cooperatives have a growing role in SWM. URENCO and other local sanitation cooperatives take care of the waste collection in most urban areas. In Lang Son, a city on the northern border of Vietnam, a small enterprise has recently replaced URENCO as the city's major waste collector. In Buon Ma Thuot, an SME collects municipal waste alongside URENCO [Thai, 2014].

Composting can contribute to a more efficient MSWM in Vietnamese cities, but is not yet implemented countrywide for a number of reasons, including: poor technical implementation that leads to low quality of compost, low input of feedstock, and low domestic market acceptance. For centralised composting facilities, organic waste is collected from households and businesses, also several neighbouring areas, to have sufficient quantities of waste. Centralised composting facilities, most of them operated in the north of Vietnam, are privately operated but governmental authorities undertake the required funding and technical assistance [Nguyen, n.d.].

Centralised composting facilities are currently operating in Vietnam without a pre-defined standard. The compost has low quality and often contains fragments of glass and metal, which makes the compost inappropriate for selling to direct consumers, commercial farmers, wholesalers, retailers, bagging operators, and brokers. Despite the potentials that the centralised composting facilities have, several factors still hamper their implementation where interventions could be made:

1. Improving the composting methods, where dry waste feedstock is manually applied with supervision to ensure a good, continuous distribution resulting in a stable, efficient loading capacity.
2. Switching the waste separation process from manual to automatic, which increases compost quality and reduces transportation and recovery costs.
3. Providing incentives for households or companies that support waste separation at source, and for farmers or businesses that use compost produced by the facilities. As the demand for good quality compost increases, there is, in turn, an incentive for composting facilities to increase their quality standards.

15.4.3 *Legal framework and 3R policies in Vietnam*

Vietnam has issued several policies and legal provisions on waste management. The Law on Environmental Protection [2005] provides incentives for the reuse, recycling, energy recovery, and other resource efficiency related activities. The National Strategy for Environmental Protection [MoNRE, 2012] sets targets for the recycling industry, including 30% of waste to be diverted for recycling. The National Green Growth Strategy [2011–2020] with a vision towards 2050 (as issued in 2012) includes directions along the whole chain of waste reduction and management processes. As recently as 2015, Vietnam issued new regulations concerning the imports of waste for recycling. With the new regulation, SMEs need to obtain permission to import plastic refuse as a production material, and are required to conform to certain conditions on waste imports and the materials allowed to be imported [Vietnamnet, 2015]. These policies provide sufficient targets and policy instruments for 3R implementation and a good waste management system. However, there is still a gap in their implementation. Concrete guidelines are, therefore, mandatory to enable all parties to understand the policies and regulations, assume their responsibilities and gain incentives.

The Government of Vietnam could also promote the 3R approach by issuing a directive on the reduction of material and energy use or on economic instruments for 3R implementation. Technologies for municipal waste recovery, recycling and disposal exist but they are underutilised. It should become a priority to make the existing technologies available, since the amounts of waste are constantly increasing. Low incentives for industry will not encourage waste recycling efficiency.

In general, NGOs are recognised as important in the implementation of 3R and SWM activities. Yet, sometimes the existing NGOs do not support such activities. Volunteer groups are present in Vietnam, but they lack organisation or coordination. There is also general lack of awareness in citizens regarding the importance of formal 3R.

15.4.4 *Improvement potentials in Vietnam's SWM system*

In relation to implementing a sustainable waste management system in the whole country, several proposals in close accordance to the Green Growth Strategy and the 2012 National Strategy on Environmental Protection to 2020, with Visions to 2030 can be made:

1. Developing a more-focused legal and policy framework for a solid waste management system. The framework would encourage increased coordination among authorities responsible for the waste management system.
2. Creating national and local plans towards an integrated SWM system.
3. Ensuring a reliable and harmonised national waste management database to help monitor and evaluate the entire network.
4. Promoting the 3R approach by means of technical assistance and potential funding as well as awareness raising campaigns on SCP and environmental education in schools from an early age.
5. Following the National Green Growth Strategy's objectives and tasks.

15.5 Conclusions and Recommendations

As discussed above, resource efficiency achieved through the 3R approach, is inherently part of the SCP agenda. It is clear that SCP and the 3R concept can contribute to effective municipal waste management in developing countries in Southeast Asia. Furthermore, it is essential to develop national SCP policy frameworks that regulate sound waste management for resource efficiency with clear targets, monitoring procedures, and benchmarks. Policies at national and local levels for integrated waste management, including the 3R approach, have been promoted in all three countries covered in this chapter.

Local initiatives are most effective when supported by national legislation or programmes, especially those which provide incentive mechanisms for local governments. Community-based organisations and NGOs can also play a role in local waste management programmes, especially in the areas of public awareness and education, and by working with the informal sector. Examples of such civil society initiatives are the EU-funded SWITCH-Asia project in Cambodia that aims to reduce the use of plastic bags by urban consumers, and the SWITCH-Asia "GetGreen Vietnam" project, which built the capacity of consumer groups to reduce waste as part of sustainable consumption practice. Meanwhile, international agencies, like EU DEVCO and other multilateral organisations, can further support countries by channelling financial and technical support at local level and by boosting collaboration to provide a common platform to share ideas, experience and knowledge on SCP and the 3R concept, and support local action for better SWM systems.

References

Central Population and Housing Census Steering Committee of the General Statistics Office of Vietnam (2010). *Report on Major findings of 2009 Vietnam Population and Housing Census for the United Nations Statistics Division (UNSD).*

Chin, J. (2011). Waste in Asia — Issues for responsible investors, pp. 16.

Decision of the Cambodian Council of Ministers (February 2015). *Improvement of liquid and solid waste management in Phnom Penh.*

Department of Environment of Phnom Penh (2014). *Annual Environmental Report.*

Fondazione ACRA CCS (2014–2017). *Less plastic, more opportunities*. Retrieved on September 10, 2015. Available on: http://www.acraccs.org/index.php?option=com_content&view=article&id=723&Itemid=900&lang=en

Japan International Cooperation Agency (JICA) (2005). *Study on Solid Waste Management in the Municipality of Phnom Penh: Final Report*. Kokusai Kogyo Co. Ltd.

Lacoste, E. and Chalmin, P. (2007). *From Waste to Resource, 2006 World Waste Survey, Indicative comparison of waste generation across countries in Asia and the Pacific table*.

Ministry of Construction and Ministry of Natural Resources and Environment (2012). *The National Strategy on Environment Protection to 2020, with Visions to 2030*. Approved by the Vietnamese Government by the Decision 1216/QĐ-TTg. Available on: http://www.hss.de/southeastasia/en/vietnam/news-events/2012/launching-of-vietnams-national-strategy-for-environmental-protection-until-2020-and-vision-toward-2030.html.

Ministry of Environment (MoE) (2004). *State of Environment Report*. Prepared by the Cambodian Ministry of Environment and the Danish International Development Agency.

Ministry of Environment (MoE) (2009). *The National Strategy on 3R for waste management in the Kingdom of Cambodia*.

Ministry of Planning and Investment and Ministry of Natural Resources and Environment (2012). *Vietnam National Green Growth Strategy for the period 2011–2020 with a vision to 2050*. The Law on the Environmental Protection of November 29, 2005 in Vietnam Approved by the Government of Vietnam, Decision No. 1393/QĐ-TTg. 25 September 2012, Hanoi, Vietnam.

Ministry of Public Works and Transport and Ministry of Natural Resources and Environment (2013). *Brief Country Analysis Paper Lao PDR*. Fourth Regional 3R Forum in Asia 18–20 March 2013, Ha Noi, Viet Nam.

MoE/DoEPC (2008). Department of Pollution Control, Ministry of Environment, Cambodia (2008). Report on solid waste management status in Cambodia.

Mongtoeun, Y., Fujiwara, T. and Sethy, S. (2014). A study of commercial solid waste generation and composition in Phnom Penh City, Cambodia. *Journal of Natural Sciences Research* 4(13), p. 49 — Special Issue.

Nguyen, T. (n.d.). *Solid Waste Management in Vietnam: An Industrial Ecology Study*. School of International and Public Affairs, Columbia University. Retrieved on November 15, 2015. Available on: *www.seas.columbia.edu/.../Nguyen_Vietnam_Waste_management.pdf*.

Sang-Arun, J. and Pasomsouk, K. (2012). Guide for improving municipal solid waste management and promoting the urban organic waste utilisation in Lao

PDR. *Working Paper for the Institute for Global Environmental Strategies*, IGES No. SCP-2012-01.

Sethy, S., Sothun, C. and Wildblood, R. (2014). *Municipal Solid Waste Management in Asia and the Pacific Islands*. Springer, Singapore.

Thai, N. T. K. (2006). *Annual monitoring report to the Ministry of Natural Resources and Environment*. The Center for Environmental Engineering of Towns and Industrial Areas, Vietnam.

Thai, Nguyen Thi Kim. (2014). Chapter: Municipal solid waste management in Vietnam, challenges and solutions. *In Municipal Solid Waste Management in Asia and the Pacific Islands*. Springer, Singapore Publisher, pp. 355–377.

Thanh, N. P. and Matsui, Y. (2010). Municipal solid waste management in Vietnam: Status and strategic actions. *International Journal of Environmental Research*. 5(2), 285–296.

United Nations Environment Programme. (2012). *Country Needs Assessment Analysis*. Available on: http://www.unep.org/gpwm/InformationPlatform/CountryNeedsAssessmentAnalysis/Laos/tabid/106530/Default.aspx.

UNESCAP (2014). *Statistical Yearbook for Asia and the Pacific 2014. United Nations Economic and Social Commission for Asia and the Pacific*. United Nations Publication, Bangkok.

Vietnam Governmental Decree No. 42/2009/ND-CP (2009). *Classification and Management of Urban Towns: Six Categories of Urban Towns.*

Vietnamnet (2015). Vietnamese regulations on the import of plastic waste. Retrieved on January 3, 2016. Available on: http://english.vietnamnet.vn/fms/business/131345/vietnamese-regulations-on-the-import-of-plastic-waste.html.

Waste Management World (2011). *Vietnam to Install 1.5 Billion Bottle PET Recycling Line*. Available on: http://waste-management-world.com/a/vietnam-to-install-1-5-billion-bottle-pet-recycling-line.

Workshop on waste recycling and environment, in cooperation with Taiwan Green Productivity Foundation. October 1, 2014, Ho Chi Minh City, Vietnam.

World Bank (2015). *Data Vietnam*. Retrieved on December 15, 2015. Available on: http://data.worldbank.org/country/vietnam.

Index